Dad Made
Dirty Movies

Dad Made Dirty Movies

The Erotic World of Stephen C. Apostolof

Jordan Todorov
and Joe Blevins

McFarland & Company, Inc., Publishers
Jefferson, North Carolina

LIBRARY OF CONGRESS CATALOGUING-IN-PUBLICATION DATA

Names: Todorov, Jordan, 1980– author. | Blevins, Joe, 1975– author.
Title: Dad made dirty movies : the erotic world of Stephen C. Apostolof / Jordan Todorov and Joe Blevins.
Description: Jefferson : McFarland & Company, Inc., Publishers, 2020 | Includes bibliographical references and index.
Identifiers: LCCN 2020032007 | ISBN 9781476668680 (paperback) ∞
ISBN 9781476638775 (ebook)
Subjects: LCSH: Apostolof, Stephen C., 1928–2005. | Motion picture producers and directors—United States—Biography.
Classification: LCC PN1998.3.A625 T67 2020 | DDC 791.4302/33092 [B]—dc21
LC record available at https://lccn.loc.gov/2020032007

BRITISH LIBRARY CATALOGUING DATA ARE AVAILABLE

ISBN (print) 978-1-4766-6868-0
ISBN (ebook) 978-1-4766-3877-5

© 2020 Jordan Todorov and Joe Blevins. All rights reserved

No part of this book may be reproduced or transmitted in any form or by any means, electronic or mechanical, including photocopying or recording, or by any information storage and retrieval system, without permission in writing from the publisher.

Front cover: Stephen C. Apostolof and his children (left to right) Polly, Maria, Steve, and Susie on set of *Lady Godiva Rides*, 1968 (Stephen C. Apostolof Estate)

Printed in the United States of America

*McFarland & Company, Inc., Publishers
Box 611, Jefferson, North Carolina 28640
www.mcfarlandpub.com*

"Filmmaker Stephen C. Apostolof's life is one of the great postwar American stories, a rollicking tale of rebellion, adventure and female breasts."[1]
—Tim Elliott, *The Age*

"The most amazing saga of modern Hollywood is probably that of Stephen Apostolof, young Bulgarian refugee, who escaped after three and one-half years of imprisonment and torture by the Reds from his native country in 1948, arrived at his ultimate destination here in 1952, and is now making major movies under the banner of his own independent production."[2]
—Walt Hackett, *Lansing State Journal*

"Los Angeles had its own bunch of sexploitation auteurs and distributors, men like David Friedman, Lee Frost, Don Davis, Pete Perry, Harry Novak and A.C. Stephen, aka Steve Apostolof, an Eastern European who talked of making 'smoot pictures.'"[3]
—Jimmy McDonough, *Big Bosoms and Square Jaws: The Biography of Russ Meyer, King of the Sex Film*

Table of Contents

Acknowledgments   ix
Prologue: On the Trail of Stephen C. Apostolof   1

Part One. Journey to Freedom (1928–1962)

1. The Burgas Years (1928–1948)   8
2. Passage to Istanbul (1948)   17
3. A Stranger in Paris (1948–1950)   21
4. Onward to Canada! (1950–1952)   30

Part Two. Adventures in La La Land (1952–1978)

5. The Man About Town (1952–1957)   38
6. The Propagandist (1957)   46
7. The Family Man (1958–1965)   65
8. The Director of the Dead (1965–1966)   72
   Orgy of the Dead (1965)   75
9. The Prince of Confidential (1966–1968)   102
   Suburbia Confidential (1966)   103
   Motel Confidential (1967)   118
   Bachelor's Dream (1967)   123
   College Girls (1968)   126
   Office Love-In, White Collar Style (1968)   135
10. The Executive Filmmaker (1969–1972)   144
    Lady Godiva Rides (1969)   144
    The Divorcee (1969)   153
11. The Master of Mayhem (1972–1978)   169
    The Snow Bunnies (1972)   172
    Drop-Out Wife (1972)   181
    The Class Reunion (1972)   187
    The Cocktail Hostesses (1973)   192
    Fugitive Girls (1974)   202
    The Beach Bunnies (1976)   215
    Hot Ice (1978)   225

Table of Contents

Part Three. The Last Mile to El Diablo (1979–2005)

12. In Exile (1979–1986) — 242
13. The Resurrection (1987–1997) — 250
14. State of Fear (1998–2005) — 264
    The Dying of the Light 268
    The End of the End 271

Appendix: The Immoral Artist (unused story outline) — 279
Timeline — 285
Filmography — 289
Chapter Notes — 293
Bibliography — 303
Index — 307

Acknowledgments

While working on this book, we came in contact with many wonderful people who knew and/or worked with Stephen C. Apostolof. To our deep regret, some of them have since passed away. Above all, we would like to thank Apostolof's family, and especially his children, without whom this book would not have been possible. We are particularly sorry that Apostolof's eldest son Steve did not live to read this book. His contribution to this project is beyond any measure. We would also like to thank Christopher Apostolof, the youngest son of Stephen Apostolof and the keeper of his archive, for generously granting us access to it and permission to use numerous photographs and documents. Without his continuing cooperation, this book could never have been written.

We would also like to thank Rudolph Grey, Ed Wood's biographer, for contacting some of Apostolof's friends and associates in the very beginning of this project. His written correspondence with Apostolof, spanning over two decades, provided details that would have otherwise been lost forever. Recognition must also go to the members of the *Ed Wood Jr.* Facebook group as well as to the staff of the Margaret Herrick Library in Beverly Hills, which helped us in the research of Apostolof's early Hollywood career.

Many thanks to all those who agreed to be interviewed (some of them numerous times over the years) for their valuable insights into the life and work of Stephen C. Apostolof: Alan Doshna, Arny Schorr, Barbara Higgins Graham, Boris Kutchukov, Brenda Fogarty, Chet Collom, Lt. Col. Christian Rascle, Christopher Apostolof, Conrado Puzon, Damon Wise, David Ward, Dessie Apostolova, Dino Dinev, Don McArt, Earl Kemp, Eve Brent, Forrest J Ackerman, Gary Kent, Ginette Kutchukov, Greg Goodsell, Guy Nicholas, Harvey Shain, Jacques Descent, Jane Giles, John Harrison, John Miller, Johnny Legend, Kina Apostolova, Larry Karaszewski, Margo Allsbrook, Maria Apostolof, Max Thayer, Michael DiRosa, Mike Mikhailof, Nadejda Dobrev, Polly Apostolof, Richard McCurdy, Rudolph Grey, Scott Alexander, Spas T. Raikin, Shelley Apostolof, Stavri Apostolov, Stefan Apostolov, Steve Apostolof, Susan Schmideler, Ted Newsom and Ted V. Mikels.

We are grateful to the following people for the permission to quote from private letters and various printed materials: Casey Scott, Dan Golden, Darrell Buxton, Frank Henenlotter, James Zink, Jimmy McDonough, Laura Schiff, Leisa Reinecke Flynn, Lisa Petrucci, Michael Faust, Michael J. Weldon, Mitch O'Connell, Raymond Young, Steven Puchalski, Todd Tranner, Vania Kutchukova, Yordanka Ingilizova and Zornitsa Keremidchieva.

Thanks, too, to Alan Shack, Prof. Alexander Grozev, Andrew J. Rausch, Andrew

Leavold, Anna Biller, Archimandrite Cyril, Archimandrite Damian, Aris Iliopulos, Arnold Ives, Ashley West, Bisser R. Stoyanov, Bob Blackburn, Boris Baykov, Prof. Bozhidar Manov, Dana Apostolof, David Del Valle, Dennis Phelps, Dimitrios Otis, Douglas North, Ed DePriest, Edwin Lee "Butch" Canfield, Ege Görgün, Georgina Spelvin, Giuliano Tosi, Greg Javer, Henry C. Parke, Howie Pyro, Jeff McKay, Joe Rubin, Leslie Morris, Michael Schlimgen, Mike Vraney, Mike White, Nancy Bartley, Dr. Nikola Altankov, Nikolay Penchev, Orlin Manolov, Radoslav Sharapanov, Raleigh Bronkowski, Robert G. Huffman, Robert Plante, Robin Bougie, Sky Brower, Prof. Stanislav Semerdzhiev, Steve Galindo, Svilen Dimitrov, Tim Lucas and Asst. Prof. Vasilka Tankova.

Prologue:
On the Trail
of Stephen C. Apostolof

"I believe in something. If I'm in the restaurant business, I'll give you good food and good drink. If I'm in the movie business, then I'll give you good girls with big bazookas. I call them 'ticket-sellers.'"—Stephen C. Apostolof[1]

Try to picture it. Top-heavy strippers gyrating in a plywood cemetery. Creaky sets seemingly held together with nothing sturdier than prayers. Stuffed ravens adding atmosphere from beyond the grave. Belching smoke machines to disguise the cheapness. The kind of stiff, self-conscious acting you'd see in a high school play. The Amazing Criswell, the self-proclaimed oracle whose alleged psychic powers are decidedly less than amazing, blathering about "ghouls" from the comfort of his cozy, satin-lined coffin. Bloodthirsty commies. Sex orgies. LSD. Transvestites. Hippies. Degenerates. The notorious Ed Wood himself on the sidelines, three sheets to the wind. Legendary erotic actress Marsha Jordan in her glory, nude atop a horse, her breasts pointed proudly toward the horizon, like twin beacons signaling a better, sleazier tomorrow. Exciting, right?

Welcome, my friends, to the wild world of Stephen C. Apostolof, master of low-budget erotic films from the 1960s and '70s and the most successful Bulgarian in Hollywood you've never heard of. It's a world you will soon know well.

Apostolof's unlikely biography reflects some of the most important political and cultural events of the 20th century. In a sense, then, his story is the world's story during a period of intense political, economic and social upheaval. As an ambitious young man, ravenously hungry for success, Steve escaped his Eastern European homeland just as it fell into the clutches of the hated Communists, and he migrated to the U.S. to make his dreams come true. He managed to do it *and*, like the song by one of his favorite singers says, he did it *his* way. Often working in tandem with Ed Wood, that eccentric filmmaker, cross-dresser and boozehound of cult movie infamy, Apostolof made over a dozen audacious, salacious and outrageous motion pictures on minuscule budgets that wouldn't cover the catering costs of a fancy studio-made epic. In the process, he became one of the true pioneers of adult entertainment in America just as that industry was coming into its own.

I first encountered the name Stephen C. Apostolof via a mysterious email from a fellow film buff in the summer of 2005. All it said was that I should check out the filmmaker who brought Ed Wood's erotic screenplays to life. Naturally I knew who Ed Wood was, having seen the quirky 1994 biopic of the same name, directed by Tim Burton and starring Johnny Depp. A quick internet search later, I was both amazed and frustrated by what I found regarding Stephen C. Apostolof.

Online information about Apostolof—who often went by the pseudonym A.C. Stephen professionally—was scarce. The few facts I could find were so contradictory that I started to feel like literature professor David Zimmer, the protagonist of Paul Auster's novel *The Book of Illusions* (2002). In that book, Zimmer sees a short silent film starring a long-forgotten comic named Hector Mann, who left his home one day in 1929, never to return. Zimmer becomes so intrigued by Mann's mysterious disappearance that he starts to investigate the actor's life with the intention of writing a book about him.

Stephen C. Apostolof triggered the same kind of curiosity within me. I wanted to know more (and more and more!) about this man. At the time, I thought I might get an article about Apostolof's life and unique career out of my investigations. Six years later, I made a feature-length documentary called *Dad Made Dirty Movies* about Apostolof, his films and his family. That's just how these things turn out sometimes.

Apostolof died two months before I tried to contact him, so I was never able to meet him in person, a fact that further piqued my interest. His career was so obscure, and the available information about him so confusing, that I had the strange feeling this was all one big snipe hunt. Was Apostolof in the French Foreign Legion in the 1940s or wasn't he? Did he study at the Sorbonne? Did he even exist at all? At one point, I felt that I was slowly going mad. I considered the possibility that Apostolof had been born out of my own imagination, and it was downright scary!

To preserve my sanity, I concentrated on the indisputable evidence at hand. What I knew for sure about Apostolof was that he had been, by turns, a political prisoner, an adventurer, a playboy, a tireless raconteur and a promising young Hollywood producer in the late 1950s. That much was corroborated by clippings from the trade papers of the era. But there was more to the man. He was a political activist in the 1940s and '50s in France, Canada and the U.S. He was one of the founders and a trustee for life of St. George's, the first Bulgarian Eastern Orthodox church in Los Angeles. He was a chairman of the Bulgarian-American Cultural Educational Society. He'd been married three times and was the father of five children. Truly adapting to life in America, he was a habitué of the golf course, like any self-respecting Hollywood big shot. But what did it all add up to?

Digging into the man's life a little further, I learned that after 1994's devastating Northridge, California, earthquake, Apostolof moved to Las Vegas, Nevada, with his family. They then migrated to other cities, eventually ending up in Mesa, Arizona. Over time, he seemed to fade away into nothingness. Some people thought he was dead. Others thought he'd never lived in the first place. Some even proposed the wild theory that he and Ed Wood were the same person and that "Stephen C. Apostolof" was just one of the many aliases Wood used in his career.

Rudolph Grey, author of *Nightmare of Ecstasy: The Life and Art of Edward D. Wood, Jr.* (1992), the definitive biography of Wood, summarized the situation:

In the world of low-budget exploitation filmmaking, producers were notorious for being literally "here today, gone tomorrow." Small corporations would vanish without a trace, and producers would often leave town, or even the country, posthaste. When these elusive individuals could be found, often they had kept no records of their own productions. No posters, no pressbooks, no stills. And quite frequently, no movies. Films listed as being in a company's vaults would, upon further research, have inexplicably disappeared. The most diligent detective work would lead to a dead end.[2]

Fortunately, that proved *not* to be the case with Apostolof. Information related to his films from the 1950s to the late '70s had been carefully collected by the director in several hefty, lovingly preserved scrapbooks. But despite the documentation Apostolof had left behind after his death in August 2005, I frequently reached impasses when searching for facts about his life and work. Due to the often disreputable nature of the films he shot, Apostolof was forced to lead a rather murky existence on the periphery of Hollywood. That presents a challenge to the would-be biographer, and also lends Apostolof's story an air of danger. One small but telling example is that, in press photographs from the '60s, the Bulgarian filmmaker has drawn dark sunglasses, a beard and a mustache on his face, all but concealing his features. He looks like he's on a mission from the CIA.

When I first started digging into Apostolof's life, one of the most frequent questions people asked me was simply this: "Why him?" The second question, always implied, but never spoken aloud: "What's so interesting about a filmmaker most people have never even heard of?" Through this book, I hope to answer both of those questions definitively. I must confess that when I graduated from the National Academy for Theatre and Film Arts in Sofia as a film critic, I was steeped in the works of Fellini, Tarkovsky and Bergman, to name but three of the cinematic masters. Little did I know that such a thing as sexploitation even existed, let alone that one day I would become a fan of the genre.

In November 2006, I was invited by the Apostolof family to explore his vast personal archive at his final home in Mesa. The opportunity to study hundreds of documents, letters, scripts and images was one that I accepted without hesitation. Some of the boxes had not been opened for more than half a century. Rifling through them was like traveling back in time. Once I started the research, I realized what a truly enormous task I had taken on. The scale of this endeavor was huge, much larger than I had anticipated. But this was a story that needed to be told. So I quit my day job as a journalist and plunged headfirst into the Apostolof project. Eventually I realized that I needed a co-author. That's why I teamed up with Joe Blevins, a Chicago-area writer and blogger whose articles about Ed Wood must surely qualify him as one of America's leading Woodologists. His knowledge and enthusiasm have given a major boost to this biography.

In the years since discovering Apostolof, I entered a strange parallel world of X-rated film stars, Communist spies, "insect porn" producers, FBI agents-turned-actors, ex–go-go dancers, and makers of low-budget horror movies. Generally, I was well accepted and found myself being wined and dined by some of Apostolof's friends, stars and associates. Others, however, were not as open. Remember *Citizen Kane* (1941, dir. Orson Welles), with poor, harried William Alland trying to wring the truth out of Dorothy Comingore? That's how I felt sometimes. Take Marsha Jordan, the reigning queen of sexploitation films during the Lyndon Johnson and Richard Nixon years. She was a major player in the Apostolof story, and I managed to locate her. But Marsha, who by then was a happily married woman in her 70s, did not want to remember the old times, nor did she care to talk about the films she was in half-a-lifetime ago. Another actress whom I cannot name threatened to sue me if I continued to call her. I took the hint. Then there was Fawn Silver, who memorably played the Black Ghoul in 1965's *Orgy of the Dead*. I managed to find her, too, but she shot down my hopes for an interview. Another one that got away.

But this story doesn't take place exclusively in the dark, smoky corners of Hollywood. Apostolof got his start in the film industry in the mid–1950s in the tabulating department of 20th Century–Fox. In 1956, he co-produced and co-wrote a semi-autobiographical Cold War melodrama called *Journey to Freedom*, whose cast included an unknown named Jacques Scott as well as Swedish wrestler Tor Johnson, the bald, hulking giant who was one of Ed Wood's close friends and repertory players. In the early 1960s, disillusioned by his experience with the big studios, Apostolof reinvented himself as an independent producer and took complete control over his films.

From that point on, "the Bombastic Bulgarian," as his friend David F. Friedman called him, also directed his own productions, cutting out the middleman. His first and most successful self-directed movie was *Orgy of the Dead*, a surreal, Ed Wood–scripted burlesque show featuring a bevy of topless dancers in a magnificently artificial cemetery. It's still the picture for which he's best known. Following that idiosyncratic triumph, Apostolof specialized in softcore erotic films, many of them comedic. His movies were shot on miserly budgets and were mostly confined to cramped interior sets, often with decorations borrowed from Apostolof's own home. Productivity was the name of the game. In a relatively brief career (just over 20 years), Apostolof managed to complete 15 feature films (plus one featurette), eight of which were written or co-written by Ed Wood. That's all the more impressive when you consider that working with the frequently soused Eddie was no easy trick.

Though sex was his stock in trade, Apostolof was never confined to any one particular genre. His filmography includes an erotic horror tale (*Orgy of the Dead*), a so-called "suburban exposé" (*Suburbia Confidential*, 1966), a Victorian costume drama with Western elements (*Lady Godiva Rides*, 1969), and even a diamond heist caper (*Hot Ice*, 1978). Until the filmmaker's luck ran out during the Jimmy Carter years, each one of Apostolof's films was just successful enough to finance the next one. That, essentially, was his business model. From the mid–1960s onward, Apostolof garnered a reputation as a director-producer capable of making fun, sexy movies with little or no money, invariably marked by a potent combination of campy humor, pulpy action and cheesecake erotica. Along the way, he had the opportunity to direct some legendary exploitation actors and actresses of the pre–*Boogie Nights* (1997, dir. Paul Thomas Anderson) era. Apostolof's stable of stars included Harvey Shain, Ric Lutze, Rene Bond and the aforementioned Marsha Jordan.

Apostolof's movies from the 1960s and '70s are too often dismissed as worthless, lowbrow trash due to their leering, sensationalistic treatment of such topics as adultery, homosexuality, sadomasochism and transvestism. Critics call his movies "banal" because of their predictable storylines and perceived lack of originality. Some may even label them as outright smut. But, even though Apostolof has been labeled a "patron saint of pornographers" at Steve Galindo's *Church of Ed Wood* website,[3] his films veer quite dramatically from widely accepted notions of pornography. For one thing, going against the tide, Apostolof never ventured even once into hardcore, though 1972's *Drop-Out Wife* was a close call. Certainly there was pressure within the industry to depict sexual intercourse graphically on the screen, especially after Gerard Damiano's *Deep Throat* shocked the world in 1972. But Apostolof stuck to his guns, regardless of the commercial consequences. Whatever it meant to his career, he refused to go into wildly profitable hardcore porn films because of his Christian values and his standards as a family man. Try finding that kind of integrity elsewhere in the adult industry.

The relationship between Apostolof and Ed Wood was, to say the least, complicated and fraught with tension. Apostolof hired and fired Wood many times during their tumultuous decade-plus association. The strange saga of Apostolof and Wood finally ended during the shooting of *Hot Ice*, a would-be James Bond–type flick with less nudity and more action than the average Apostolof production. By then in the late stages of chronic alcoholism, the unreliable Eddie was supposed to play a small role as a janitor who interrupts a jewel heist, but he's nowhere to be seen in the finished film. *Hot Ice* flopped, effectively ending Apostolof's career, and Ed died not long after its release. Sixteen years later, when the *Ed Wood* biopic was released, Apostolof was understandably jealous of Eddie's posthumous fame.

Today, more than a decade after Apostolof's passing, his films are remarkable not because of their artistic qualities but because they so aptly capture the spirit of 1960s and '70s America. In their crude way, they provide a portal into another time. Sexploitation films will never be mistaken for highbrow culture, but as researcher Randall Clark says in his study *At a Theater or Drive-In Near You: The History, Culture and Politics of the American Exploitation Film* (1995), they can be useful for sociopolitical analysis, because they have relatively few content restrictions compared to mainstream Hollywood films.[4]

In today's sex-saturated society, with all manner of pornography a mere click away, it is difficult to fathom the effect that Apostolof's relatively innocent movies had on audiences in the 1960s and '70s. His flicks might now seem naïve and even downright silly, but while working on this book, I gradually came to understand, appreciate and respect the world of sexploitation filmmaking. I should add that I find most of the attacks on Apostolof's films to be simply unfair and unjustified. While his movies are not masterpieces, they are no worse than the standard sexploitation fare of the time. Purely from a technical standpoint, they're a damn sight better than most. These movies deserve a modicum of respect, as does the man himself. Stephen C. Apostolof did his best and lived a life full of inspiration, courage and optimism. That's more than most people can say. Most important of all, once he got the filmmaking bug, he had the discipline and determination to follow through and actually make and distribute his own motion pictures.

Jordan Todorov
Berlin, 2020

PART ONE

Journey to Freedom (1928–1962)

Chapter 1

The Burgas Years (1928–1948)

Gonzales roared in rage and shame. Somebody was trying to smash the door in now. But Señor Zorro appeared to give it little thought. He sprang back and sent his blade into its scabbard like a flash. He swept the pistol before him and thus threatened all in the long room. He darted to a window, sprang upon a bench.

"Until a later time, señor!" he cried.

And then he went through the window as a mountain goat jumps from a cliff, taking its covering with him. In rushed the wind and rain, and the candles went out.

—Johnston McCulley, *The Mark of Zorro* (1919)[1]

Before delving into Stephen C. Apostolof's childhood, it's helpful to look at an incident that occurred when he was middle-aged, since it says a lot about his life and his values. This particular tale—a ghost story with shades of *Hamlet*—has since become a part of Apostolof family legend.

The legend goes that one winter night in late 1973, Apostolof awoke in his Los Feliz, Los Angeles, apartment with a strange craving for warm milk. Normally he never touched that stuff, but it was something he remembered that his father had loved back in his native Bulgaria. Shelley, Stephen's third wife, dozed soundly next to him. Unable to lull himself back to sleep, Apostolof had no choice but to shuffle down to the kitchen and heat up some milk. What happened then, at least according to him, was supernatural.

"He said his dad just walked through the windows and drapes, stood in front of him, looked right at him, and disappeared," remembers Christopher Apostolof, Stephen's youngest son.[2]

By this point in his life, long since settled in his adopted home of America, Stephen was in his mid-forties and an established producer-director of softcore erotic films. His life as an expatriate in California could scarcely be more removed from his childhood in Burgas, Bulgaria, the city of his birth. He had not even seen his father, Christo, in decades. Why should the old man appear to him now? But the devoutly religious Stephen was not the type to shrug off such an occurrence. Bulgarians often mix their Christianity with forms of mysticism. Christopher remembered his godmother consulting tarot cards. Christo's mysterious visit had to mean something.

The ghostly incident stayed with Apostolof, and he related it to Shelley the next morning. He didn't feel good about it. The spectral appearance of his father, who was still alive as far as he knew, seemed to be a bad omen. Nevertheless, Apostolof and Shelley went ahead with a planned vacation to Lake Tahoe. When they returned to their place in Los Feliz, Apostolof instinctively lunged for the mail that had accumulated in their absence. He soon found what he was both expecting and dreading: a letter from Bulgaria. It was a death notice. Christo had passed away at about the same time as Stephen's prophetic vision. Naturally, Apostolof couldn't attend the funeral back in Burgas. When he escaped from his homeland in 1948, the Communists had declared him persona non grata and threatened him with execution should he ever return. Even so, the death of his father was an opportunity for Apostolof to look back on his own life and ponder the incredibly unlikely path that had led him to Hollywood and the movies.

The saga of Stephen C. Apostolof began 6737 miles away from Los Angeles, on Bulgaria's humid, subtropical Black Sea Coast. He was born Stefko Christov Apostolov, the fourth and youngest child of Christo Nikolov Apostolov and Polyxena Popyaneva, on February 25, 1928, in Burgas, the Balkan nation's fourth largest city and the nexus of its still-vital fishing industry. Preceding him into this world were two sisters, Vesa (b. 1915) and Lila (b. 1919), and a brother, Stavri (b. 1920). On September 16, 1928, within the venerated walls of Saints Cyril and Methodius Orthodox Church, a structure built by the Italian architect Ricardo Toscani, the infant Apostolof was baptized by the priest Dimitar Nikolov, immersed in the baptismal font by his paternal grandmother, Elenka St. Apostolova, and given the name Stefko.

"Ah, Stefko! They used to call him Palyangata! He was a very sweet boy, a very popular boy in the neighborhood. When he was born, my mom took me to see him. He had a head that small!" says neighbor Violeta Todorova Paligorcheva, five years Apostolof's senior.[3]

Seen from above, Burgas looks like a narrow strip of land surrounded by three lakes: Vaya, Atanasovsko and Mandrensko. Some historians claim the city is as old as Troy, but don't you believe them. In truth, Burgas is a relative newcomer to the map. The city began in the late 19th century as a maze of grimy streets, slapdash dockside warehouses, and tumbledown buildings in a swampy, malaria-infested area fit for little save fishing. But Burgas developed faster than most of the other Bulgarian cities, including the country's then-new capital of Sofia, and soon it emerged as the country's most cosmopolitan hub. Burgas' multicultural population consisted of Bulgarians, Greeks, Turks, Armenians, Russians, Wallachians, Albanians, Italians, Czechs, Jews, etc. At least a dozen daily newspapers had been published there before Stephen's birth, and there were British, German, Italian, Swedish, Finnish, Norwegian, Belgian, Dutch, Greek, Hungarian, Romanian, Spanish and Turkish consulates in the city as well.

Burgas' debut on the world stage came on May 18, 1903, when 40 cannon shots heralded the opening of the city's modern port and the beginning of intensive trade with other ports throughout Europe and America. This new port significantly expanded Burgas' contact with the rest of the world. By the late 1920s, the Burgas harbor was notably larger than that of Varna (Bulgaria's third largest city), and its traffic accounted for a third of the Kingdom of Bulgaria's foreign trade.

Naturally, the booming metropolis attracted many people from the neighboring towns and villages. One pilgrim was Apostolof's father Christo, who originally hailed from Aytos, a small town about 18 miles from the coast. Another newcomer was Apostolof's maternal grandfather, real estate developer Christo Popyanev, who had migrated to Burgas from Istanbul and married a local girl, Elena Parvanova, with whom he had four children. There was a son, Socrates, and three daughters, Haida, Maria (who died in childhood) and Polyxena (who would become Apostolof's mother). Christo Popyanev built two of the most beautiful structures on Aleksandrovska Street; the oldest urban axis in Burgas, it leads to the port and connects the city with the sea. Both of Popyanev's buildings are now Bulgarian cultural monuments.

"They were modest people and good neighbors. My father built our house in 1927; theirs is older," recalls Paligorcheva.[4] The house in question is still there, at Oborishte 47, one of Burgas' central thoroughfares. It makes an appearance in what is probably the earliest surviving photo of Stephen C. Apostolof. This snapshot, taken in the early 1930s, shows the future filmmaker sitting on the large outer staircase leading to the second floor of the house. Apostolof is a chubby child with a lively face. He wears coarse woolen trousers and a hand-knitted bodice. Also pictured is Apostolof's mother Polyxena, described by Paligorcheva as an "sociable and open woman" who loved to sing.[5] According to Paligorcheva, "Stefko inherited her musicality. He played the accordion really well. He was a very nice guy, the leader of the gang in the neighborhood. Short, dark-skinned with curious brown eyes, artistic and probing. I wasn't surprised at all when I learned that he had his own film studio in America; it's the right job for him."[6]

A steely-eyed Stephen C. Apostolof (front) outside his childhood home in Burgas in the early 1930s. Standing left to right are his mother Polyxena, his maternal grandmother Elena, and his grandfather Christo with an unidentified child.

In his formative years, Apostolof busied himself with typical childhood antics. He and his mischievous pals would steal mulberries and quinces from the neighbors. Even then, Stephen was the undisputed ringleader. His friends, including the older ones, obeyed his orders without question. Long before he was in the motion picture business, play-acting was part of his regular routine.

"On the first of January, St. Basil's Day, we would carol from door to door. We would make one round and return. Then Stefko would make us wear some other clothes and go back again, as if we were different kids," remembers Dr. Mikhail Koldamov, a childhood friend of Apostolof.[7] Other Apostolof capers were riskier. Dr. Koldamov remembers how once, in the late 1930s while he and Stephen were in the attic of the Apostolof home, they saw a military car with two machine gun magazines in the back seat. Apostolof ordered his friend to steal them:

> I was about 12 years old, and I really went and took them. I hid them under my shirt and climbed the outer column to the attic, since Stephen's mother would not let us pass through the front entrance. Stefko took out the gunpowder from the shells, made a toy plane, filled it with the gunpowder, and lit a cigarette. He handed the toy plane to me and said I should light it with the cigarette. And what am I to do? I obeyed him. Then he quickly threw the plane, and it fell down with a bang.[8]

Stephen had ample opportunities to pursue his studies as a child, but classroom education was never his top priority. In 1938, he enrolled at the prestigious Deutsche Schule, where he reluctantly studied German. After that, he attended the equally renowned all-boys high school Georgi Sava Rakovski; he never completed his studies. His father later sent him to study to be a dental technician, but this didn't last long either.

In 1941, 13-year-old Stephen became a member of *Brannik* (the name means "defender"), a then-new Bulgarian youth league inspired by Germany's Hitler Youth (*Hitlerjugend*). The group was founded in 1940 by decree of the prime minister, Bogdan Filov, who sought to give order to the lives of his nation's youth. The structure of the organization was based on that of *Hitlerjugend*, but its ideology was neither Nazi nor Fascist. As Prof. Spas Raikin, a Bulgarian-American historian, émigré anti–Communist activist and an acquaintance of Apostolof, noted:

Apostolof as a member of the paramilitary organization *Brannik* in 1941.

> The Branniks were supplied with dark-green uniforms, smart ironed pants, Boy Scout type of jackets and a beret, leather belt with a stripe over the shoulder. Like the Legionnaires they saluted each other, raising a hand only from the elbow. One could say this was the Bulgarian version of *Hitlerjugend*. But unlike the Legionnaires,[9] they had no philosophy and no ideology whatsoever, except for their nationalism and their royalism.[10]

Apostolof was a member of *Brannik* until 1944, when the organization was disbanded. That same year, his mother Polyxena died of heart disease at age 45. The role of matriarch then passed to Stephen's older sister Vesa, then 29. Apostolof's father supported the family by working in the fish cannery Katsarovi Bros., as well as at the Chamber of Commerce of Burgas. Despite the setback of Polyxena's passing, the Apostolofs led a solid, lower-middle class life and wanted for nothing, including entertainment.

One of Stephen's favorite activities in the early 1940s was going to the local cinema. He loved *The Mark of Zorro* (1940, dir. Rouben Mamoulian) starring Tyrone Power, Linda Darnell and Basil Rathbone. Little Stephen was so absorbed by the black-and-white adventures of the masked hero that he once tried to jump through a window, cutting the left side of his chin deeply in the process. That scar stayed with him for life. (It was so prominent that it was cited as a distinguishing mark in his official documents.) Bitten by the movie bug at this early age, Stephen even organized improvised screenings in the basement of his family's house. Dr. Koldamov remembered, "We would hang a white sheet. I held a candle in front of it, and behind it Stephen would be making all kinds of movements with his hands. It was so cool-looking that we managed to interest the kids from other neighborhoods. However, we asked them to pay an entrance fee. You pay one penny and get in."[11]

The relative calm of Apostolof's early years was not to last; his homeland was too politically volatile for that. On September 5, 1944, the Soviet Union declared war on Bulgaria. Change came swiftly and decisively. Three days later, the Bulgarian government asked for an armistice but was overthrown by a military coup d'état organized by the anti–Axis Fatherland Front. The nation was soon occupied by Russian forces. On September 8, the Red Army, represented by the Third Ukrainian Front and the Black Sea Fleet, entered Bulgaria through the North and the Black Sea border with Ukraine without meeting any resistance from the Bulgarian army. The unopposed Soviet troops seized the cities of Ruse, Silistra and Dobrich.

By the evening of September 9, Soviet Army units occupied several key posts in Sofia, including the Ministry of War and the Ministry of the Interior, as well as the city's telegraph and radio stations. On the morning of September 9, the country's new prime minister, Kimon Georgiev, took to the radio airwaves to inform the public of the change. Georgiev was a practiced hand at this sort of thing by then. He'd taken part in coups in 1923 and 1934 and was known throughout Bulgaria as "The Old Coup-Maker." That same day, at dawn, the Soviet Black Sea Fleet landed at Varna. Meanwhile, Burgas suffered an air assault, followed 13 nervous hours later by a sea landing.

When the Communists came to power on September 9, 1944, Burgas was a flourishing European city with a bright-looking future. The coup quickly changed all that. Multiculturalism dwindled away to nothing under Soviet rule. Ninety percent of the city's Jews decamped for Israel. The Turks returned to Turkey; the Greeks to Greece. The Communists closed the local synagogue, and it soon fell into disrepair. The new government also seized the beautiful Italianate houses near the Maritime Garden, forcing the rightful residents to dwell with their families in single rooms. The inability of the Communists to manage the city led to shortages of food, clothing and fuel. Burgas suffocated in the chokehold of the new regime. The natural rhythm of daily life was interrupted, and political repression became commonplace. Many young people

Chapter 1. The Burgas Years (1928–1948)

from Burgas found themselves turned away from universities, while others were sent to Communist concentration camps.

In Burgas, the newly installed government nationalized more than 160 factories and private enterprises, including the city's mills, as well as its woodworking and metal factories. Also seized was Katsarovi Bros., the canning factory that had employed Apostolof's father Christo. The patriarch of the Apostolof clan was suddenly unemployed and unable to support himself and his children.

In early 1945, a teenaged Stefko Apostolof met Boris Kutchukov, who would remain one of his closest friends for more than six decades. Born in the neighboring city of Yambol, Kutchukov was a couple of months younger than Apostolof. In 1944, he'd been expelled from the military school in Sliven and then went to study in Burgas, where his father was a military commander. At the same time, Kutchukov became a member of an athletic club called Yunak (the name means "hero" in Bulgarian), where he served as a deputy leader. Yunak was founded in Sofia in 1895, and its main purpose was to strengthen its members both physically and morally. On one occasion, the group was asked to give a gymnastic performance on levers and parallel bars in the community center of the town of Pomorie. As leader of the group, Kutchukov had the responsibility of finding an accordionist who would play during the demonstration. The invitation was accepted by Apostolof. Kutchukov, who passed away in April 2017, recalled:

> Stephen had to play in front of a curtain for a couple of minutes until we changed the gymnastic equipment. However, he got distracted and started playing some boogie-woogie and songs by Glenn Miller. The hall went crazy and started jumping. Behind the scenes, waiting for me, was a comrade wearing a *kasket12* who told me to appear at the militia station after the show. Of course, we didn't obey his orders: After we finished with our performance, we just left and fled to the train station.[13]

Over the course of the next few months, Apostolof and Kutchukov became

Apostolof with his father Christo in the early 1940s.

inseparable companions. One day, full of youthful energy, they decided to make a day trip by boat to the Black Sea island of St. Anastasia, five miles from Burgas. They spent a lovely day there, but on their way back, a fearsome storm nearly capsized the boat. The two friends were saved by a fishing vessel that passed nearby; it towed their boat to Burgas.

Like many born in the kingdom of Bulgaria, Stephen C. Apostolof would idealize the world that collapsed around him when he was 16. With his father out of work, a naïve but impassioned Apostolof become involved in something that, for good or ill, would change his life forever. At the age of 17, he decided he would fight to overthrow the new Fatherland Front government.

"Then [in 1944] the Commies came in and they took everything and that was it," Apostolof remembered. "I was then involved in a conspiracy to overthrow the Commies. A punk!"[14]

Apostolof signed on with an underground organization that was conspiring to destroy the new Soviet-backed government. In March 1945, Apostolof's friend Krum Mollov, a 20-year-old who would later be described in an indictment as a "former legionnaire" and "an outspoken supporter of Hitlerism," decided to also fight against the Fatherland Front. In order to do this, he joined forces with a trio of other would-be revolutionaries: former legionnaire Dimitar Yordanov Kerelov; a former member of *Brannik* named Dimitar K. Katsarov; and a mysterious third person who would be identified in court documents only by his nickname, "The Fire."

In April 1945, these four young conspirators contacted Stefan Stefanov. He had been a member of the secret police before the coup, and was now leading his own organization to combat the despised Reds. Among Stefanov's recruits were Dimo Vassilev and a former Ratnik (far-right Bulgarian nationalist organization founded in 1936) member named Kiril Shivachev. Both organizations, Molotov's and Stefanov's, united under the name Homeland Legions. Dissatisfied with the Fatherland Front and eager for change, Stefanov became their leader.

At the group's first meeting, held in mid–1945, the conspirators decided to arm themselves and join up with the guerrillas who were then lurking in the mountains. They collected a small amount of money and sent "The Fire" to the town of Nova Zagora in Southeastern Bulgaria to establish a connection with the so-called *goryani*[15] in the mountains. Krum Mollov supported the organization, providing about 100 submachine gun cartridges and an egg-shaped bomb. He also bought a Beretta semi-automatic pistol with eight 9mm cartridges from one Peter Nedev. Apostolof procured another 16 rounds with money given to him by Stefan Stefanov. He also tried to buy a handgun from a Soviet soldier, but this gambit failed.

After another meeting, the newly formed organization dropped the idea of escaping to the mountains and decided instead to remain in the cities and fight the Communists through "organized sabotage and terrorist acts."[16] In early August 1945, Homeland Legions identified its first target: the strategically important Standard Petroleum factory on the outskirts of Burgas. It was built in 1921 by the American company Standard Oil by agreement with the Bulgarian government. The conspirators arranged to get some inside help from a couple of employees and planned to use a bomb and a bottle of gasoline to start a fire and burn it down. To delay the arrival of the fire brigade, the conspirators decided to blow up the two bridges leading to the factory. This plan never came to fruition.[17]

In mid–August 1945, acting on behalf of his fellow conspirators, Stefan Stefanov met up with a temporary resident named Georgi Koprinkov at a socialist youth club in Burgas. When the two later met on a bridge at the Burgas sea baths, Koprinkov proposed an ambitious idea for sabotaging the parliamentary elections, scheduled for August 26. He planned to do this by scattering leaflets denouncing the Fatherland Front on behalf of an organization called the Youth Democratic Bloc. Koprinkov also proposed sending telegrams describing some bogus arrests to foreign embassies in the capital city of Sofia. This would theoretically inspire interference from forces outside the country, thus allowing the conspirators to operate more freely. George Koprinkov, Stefan Stefanov and Krum Mollov prepared two leaflets calling for the removal of the Fatherland Front government and the expulsion of Soviet troops from Bulgaria, pointedly referring to the Russians as "occupiers." These leaflets were printed and distributed around Burgas by Stefanov, Mollov, Dimo Vassilev and Kiril Shivachev.

Later, his patriotic reserve apparently weakening in the face of legal consequences, Shivachev voluntarily went to the police and revealed the existence of the conspiratorial organization to which he belonged. That put a damper on all the group's future plans. On September 12, 1945, Apostolof and three conspirators were arrested. The police seized the following material evidence: "a rubber glove, 14 sheets of carbon paper, four boxes of white paper, a *Brannik* belt, and a bag in which the leaflets were carried around."[18] Ultimately, Apostolof and seven other plotters, the youngest only 17, were tried under a new law for the supposed protection of the people's power. On December 5, 1945, the Regional Court of Burgas convicted Apostolof and handed down a sentence of two years, two months and 20 days in solitary confinement for supplying an illegal organization with money and arms.

Ironically, this harsh sentence was pronounced "in the name of His Majesty Simeon II, Tsar of the Bulgarians," referring to the six-year-old Bulgarian boy king who had ascended to the throne upon his father Tsar Boris III's sudden death in 1943. Decades later, Apostolof remained a staunch royalist and one of the most ardent supporters of Tsar Simeon II among the Bulgarian community in Los Angeles. No less ironic is the fact that Krum Mollov, one of the leaders of the conspiracy, was sentenced to just a year in prison and a fine of 10,000 Bulgarian levs, the equivalent of a few thousand dollars in American money.

Apostolof entered the Burgas prison on March 8, 1946, two weeks after his 18th birthday. Behind bars, he continued to liaise with his friend Mollov. Apostolof's family felt his absence keenly; his older sister Vesa regularly visited the prison to bring him food. The time spent in custody was taken into account and in all, Apostolof served 508 of the 720 days to which he had been sentenced. He was released on January 14, 1948.

For a time, he adjusted to life on the outside again. After getting a job playing piano at the Marine casino in Burgas, however, he started plotting his escape from the country. He felt that Bulgaria was no place for him anymore; something better must lie beyond its borders. Violeta Paligorcheva, a neighbor of the Apostolofs in the 1940s, recalls the very day he did this. "It was damp and foggy. I remember exactly where I saw him, next to their house. He was unusually dressed in hiking boots and was oddly pensive. He didn't see me in the fog. As the time passed, I realized what he was plotting. He was an adventurer."[19]

Years later, Apostolof described his risky escape to his friend Boris Kutchukov:

> He was playing the piano the whole night for some Finnish sailors at the Marine casino, and they took a liking to him. He finally spilled the beans, telling them he wanted to escape, so they said, "Come on, buddy!" They gave him a coat, but since Stephen was a bit short, the garment dragged on the ground. On their way to the ship, a policeman stopped them and asked for their documents, but they just cursed him out in English and smuggled Stephen to the ship.[20]

Apostolof spent several days hidden in the cargo hold while it was being loaded with tobacco. The sailors who smuggled him aboard instructed him to keep quiet, and periodically brought him food. Finally the ship was loaded and left Bulgaria with Apostolof as a stowaway. The date: March 3, 1948, ironically the most significant national holiday in Bulgaria.

"The ship's captain learned about Stephen on the open sea," recalled Kutchukov. "The trembling Stephen told him, 'You had better throw me into the sea rather than return me to Bulgaria.'"[21] The captain calmed him down, saying he would not return him to Bulgaria, but he refused to take him further because of the trade relations between Finland, the Soviet Union and Bulgaria. Instead, as Apostolof family legend has it, the captain gave him $100 and left him in Istanbul, Turkey, where Apostolof turned himself in to the Turkish authorities.

Apostolof later molded these events and others into an inspirational narrative for his first movie. But according to Kina, wife of Apostolof's brother Stavri, the real reason for Stephen's escape from Bulgaria was very different, something quite trivial and totally unrelated to the Communist regime. "His father was a great tyrant," remembered Kina. "He used to lock up the food and not let him eat. Stefko was very distressed and decided to run away."[22]

This version of the story, an unhappy son escaping his tyrannical father, is indirectly confirmed by Christopher, Apostolof's youngest son. "My father told me that he liked to play the piano and he didn't do his homework. That's why my grandfather took two long nails and nailed the lid of the piano shut."[23]

CHAPTER 2

Passage to Istanbul
(1948)

When Stephen Apostolof escaped to Turkey, hidden in the cargo hold of a ship laden with tobacco, he realized something important. His life was turning out to be an adventure story. He was one of history's risk-takers. These were exploits he would retell for decades to come, as he actively curated his own personal mythology.

At first, though, Stephen's arrival in Istanbul merely meant more legal entanglements. According to one version of the story related by his nephew, Apostolof spent several months in an Istanbul prison as a suspected Bulgarian spy. In truth, he was released from custody almost immediately as a political refugee. Luckily, his interpreter at the police station was a Turk who had graduated from a high school in Burgas and coincidentally knew Stephen's father. Apostolof managed to phone his family in Bulgaria and assured them that he was safe.

Stepping out of the police station, now a young man at liberty in a large, excitingly unfamiliar locale, Apostolof breathed the Istanbul air deeply into his lungs. His nostrils were greeted by the smell of fried fish and freshly baked buns on trays balanced on the heads of street vendors. No longer under the thumb of Bulgaria's Communist government or his own father in this new place, Stephen could at last stretch his limbs a little. As he fell among the swarm of motorcycles on the streets of Istanbul, he saw the boats flocking to the quays of Eminönü and knew that he liked immediately this bright, noisy city.

Post–World War II Istanbul truly was a magical place. Due to the relative neutrality of Turkey during the war, the city on the Bosphorus flourished as a center of business and diplomacy. This was a city where an emancipated Apostolof could reinvent himself. He had nothing to his name, but possessions would only have tied him down at that point.

Apostolof spent the first couple of weeks sleeping on the benches of Istanbul. Ten years later, he would describe—albeit in dramatically embellished terms—this episode of his life in his first film, 1957's *Journey to Freedom*. He finally managed to find accommodations at Asmali Mescit 21 in Beyoğlu, in the European part of the city. Even though most of Beyoğlu's inhabitants were Armenians, Greeks and Jews, in the late 1940s, the area was known as the most bohemian neighborhood in Istanbul and a magnet for foreigners. In his 1933 book *Asmalimescit 74*, Turkish writer Fikret Adil described the street Apostolof lived on as being populated by "adventurers who left their countries, refugees, foreigners who travel the world on foot, and artists who work in bars."[1] Apos-

Apostolof clowning around with a donkey in Istanbul in July of 1948.

tolof quickly mixed with the colorful crowd and began playing piano in one of the Beyoğlu cabarets. The name of this establishment is lost forever in the mists of time, and today it is referred to by Apostolof's family as The Real American Bar.

Apostolof was getting paid in tips, which as he saw it was not bad at all. In fact, The Real American Bar was a brothel frequented mainly by American GIs who stayed in Turkey after the war. Years later, the still impressed Apostolof told the story of how the brothel's owner used to handle the money. He would collect the turnover at the end of the day and divide it into different envelopes: one for the girls who "worked" upstairs, one for the policeman at the corner, one for the bartender, and one for Apostolof.

The summer of 1948 was a carefree time for Apostolof. He walked to the Bosphorus and used it to take a day trip to the lush Prince Islands, an archipelago off the coast of Istanbul in the Sea of Marmara, featuring exotic palm trees, beautiful Ottoman-era mansions, and horse-drawn carts. He and his friends would try to beat the heat by swimming in the outdoor summer lido in the Ortaköy neighborhood. Located on the banks of the Bosphorus, this was considered the most famous and elegant beach in town.

But even this exotic locale did not entirely satisfy Apostolof's thirst for adventure. And so, in August 1948, the young man wrote to the city's U.S. military attaché with a rather naïve request to join the ranks of the United States Army. In his letter, he described his perilous escape from Bulgaria and his nigh-pathological hatred for the Communists. On August 21, Major Gilbert E. Bursley, who was in charge of the U.S. Military Attaché Office in Istanbul, wrote him back, thanking him for his letter but explaining that, in peacetime, only American citizens could enlist in the U.S. Army.

Chapter 2. Passage to Istanbul (1948)

Apostolof (top row, middle) with friends at the outdoor swimming pool in Istanbul's Ortaköy neighborhood in August of 1948.

"Your courage in risking escape because of your political convictions is that of a good soldier and I hope that some time we can serve in a common cause," wrote Bursley.[2] Little did either of them know how true these words would turn out to be less than a decade later.

Apostolof was not discouraged. On the contrary, after realizing he could not join the Army, he decided to try his luck with the French Foreign Legion. In the late 1940s, the Legion provided a haven for thousands of refugees from countries living under the Soviet boot. The Legion has always had a romantic reputation. It was a place for adventurers, men with mysterious pasts, those whose lives would later be dramatized on the big screen by stars like Gary Cooper and Richard Burton. In his book *The Bugle Sounds: Life in the Foreign Legion* (1927), Major Zinovi Pechkoff wrote,

> All civilizations have their sufferers. In every country in Europe, and without doubt in America also, live men for whom life is a penance. Some have been stricken down by misfortunes or by unforeseen happenings and the sight of the places where they have been unhappy has become unbearable for them. […] Others, citizens of countries which have been overthrown, cannot adapt themselves to new conditions; their only resource is to expatriate themselves. For all these beings, for all those whom Dostoevski calls "The Insulted and Injured," the Foreign Legion offers a refuge.[3]

In December 1948, Apostolof left Istanbul by train heading to Marseille, France. On December 12, he registered at the recruitment office of the French Foreign Legion in Aubagne, a town in Southern France, east of Marseille. Apostolof spent nearly a week there, passing all kinds of tests. But when the time came to enroll in the ranks of the Legion on December 21, he unexpectedly refused to do so. On Christmas Eve, he left the barracks.

Boris Kutchukov explained what happened next: "Luckily for him, a one-legged Bulgarian captain appeared and asked him, 'Boy, do you know where you're going? Are you crazy?!' He scolded him good, then took his papers and tore them to pieces. So Stephen, chased and unwanted and without any documents, appeared in Paris."[4]

Chapter 3

A Stranger in Paris
(1948–1950)

On February 1, 1949, his 21st birthday approaching, Apostolof rented a modest room at 4 Square de la Guyenne in Paris, at the easternmost edge of the city. When he relocated to the French capital, the restless Bulgarian could hardly have imagined that he would meet one of his closest friends there, over 1300 miles from his birthplace. Nevertheless, four eventful years after that memorable accordion performance in Pomorie, Bulgaria, Apostolof ran into his old friend Boris Kutchukov at a Paris Metro station. The chance encounter is described in Kutchukov's diary. At first, equally amazed by the unlikely coincidence, Kutchukov mistook his friend for a random lunatic:

March 15, 1949, Paris

> I was returning to the hotel, wondering how I was going to pay my rent and tired to death, when a screwball stopped me in front of the subway and asked me in French if I'm Bulgarian. "Vous n'est pas bulgare, monsieur?" I cursed him in my mind in the name of all Bulgarians. At first I was absent-minded and shifty-eyed, and then I answered, "Oui!" He cried, "Kutchuk! Brother! Is that you!? What are you doing here? Do you remember who I am?" I recognized the voice and his mannerisms, and I knew that this was one of my friends from Burgas, the one that played the accordion in an amateur orchestra composed of students.

Kutchukov had been in Paris just a few months himself and hadn't planned on meeting *any* of his old friends from Burgas. When the two met in front of the subway station, Apostolof was with one of his many lovers at the time. The two friends swapped stories about their trials and tribulations in getting to Paris. Their conversation was passionate but brief. Apostolof took down the address of the hotel where Kutchukov was staying and promised to visit him the next day between 10 and 11 to talk further. Apostolof also told Kutchukov that in Paris there was a committee of Bulgarian emigrants that could help him obtain the documents he needed to stay in the city.

Kutchukov arrived in Paris after a couple months in Prague, where he was studying architecture at the prestigious Academy of Fine Arts. He chose the French capital because his uncle, the famous painter George Papazov, was living there and was well-connected in the art world. Papazov arrived in Paris in 1924, joined the surrealist circle and in 1925 took part in two exhibitions with Jean Arp, Max Ernst, Paul Klee, André Masson, Joan Miró and others.

But the City of Lights was not as welcoming to Kutchukov in the 1940s as it had been to Papazov in the 1920s. Unemployment was one of Paris' biggest problems after World War II. Apostolof visited the immigration office every day to review the jobs

A dapper Apostolof in front of the Eiffel Tower, 1949.

offers there. In the meantime, he was making an occasional franc or two selling cigarettes in front of the Notre-Dame de Paris cathedral. Carrying on like Hope and Crosby in a *Road* movie, Apostolof and Kutchukov often sold their old suits at the flea market and used the money to go to dance and flirt in one of the many Parisian restaurants. Money was so scarce that, in most cases, Apostolof and Kutchukov could only afford

Chapter 3. A Stranger in Paris (1948–1950)

one drink for both of them in the evening. The two Bulgarians often shared their time with Ginette, a 20-year-old Parisian with a promising ballet career; she was dancing in the company of Maurice Béjart and Roland Petit. Ginette later married Kutchukov. She remembers:

> The boys were hungry all the time. My family always cooked well, so I often invited them for dinner. Once my family invited Stephen, and he brought flowers to my mother, although I'm sure he had not a single penny in his pocket. For starters, we had pretty *hors d'oeuvres*, and Stephen and Boris devoured them, without even realising there were other courses. At the end they were so full they could not even look at the main course.[1]

Boris Kutchukov also remembered the dinner in question in detail:

> Stephen said that in Bulgaria there are all kinds of fruits and vegetables. They smashed some artichokes in our plates, but since this was a virtually unknown vegetable back then in Bulgaria, we didn't know how to eat it. Ginette, who was my girlfriend back then, kicked me under the table and showed me how to eat it. You get each leaf and scrape the fleshy parts with your teeth. Then you cut and eat the core, dipping it in vinaigrette.[2]

Back then, Apostolof and his friend needed any food they could get. Kutchukov recalled,

> Man, those were hungry times. There were times when we had eaten bread and water only for 10, 15 days. In Paris, where there's everything! No one gave us a job. Once I saw some blood sausages called *boudin*, which were sold by the meter. I was thinking, "I'm gonna steal one!" But then I thought, "What if I get caught? They will put me in jail because of a loaf of bread like Jean Valjean." It was famine.[3]

But Kutchukov was lucky: In the winter of 1949–50, thanks to his uncle George Papazov, he was able to secure a modest job at the legendary cabaret Lapin Agile ("The Nimble Rabbit"). The place got its name in 1902, when famous French chanson singer Aristide Bruant bought it and ordered a mural in which a cunning rabbit pops out of a pan. In the late 1940s, Lapin Agile, also known as Cabaret des Assassins, was a meeting point of anarchists, eccentrics and all manner of kooks. Kutchukov remembered that his job "was to park visitors' cars. Also, if there was a fight, I had to throw out the culprits. I had a hat that I was ashamed to wear. Stefan used to come in the evenings to help me. He would put on the hat, and when he heard English speech, he would approach, saying, 'Don't forget the tip, please!'"[4] Sometimes the tips from Lapin Agile would be as little as half a dollar, but this was good money in postwar Paris. Apostolof collected the tips in his hat and at the end of the evening split them with Kutchukov.

"I had one broken bike," recalled Kutchukov. "Stephen would sit on the frame, and we both descended down from Montmartre, with no lights, no brakes, no nothing."[5]

The Parisian winter of 1949–50 was bitterly cold. In addition to parking cars at Lapin Agile during those frigid, merciless months, Kutchukov was also responsible for cleaning frost from their windshields. Despite the unkind weather, Apostolof was there to help his friend. The two Bulgarians would rub their hands, tap their feet and drink the hot grog with rum that the Lapin Agile waitresses brought them.

"I'm a little embarrassed to tell you this," confides Ginette Kutchukov, "but Stephen will forgive me. One day that winter, he went to help Boris. There was a lot of frost, and the windshields of the cars had to be cleaned. So Stephen climbed on the hood of one of the cars and started peeing on the windshield in order to defrost it."[6]

(Left to right, upper row) Stephen Apostolof and Boris Kutchukov and their friend Dimitri Yordanov (bottom left) in Paris in April 1949.

At Lapin Agile, Apostolof met yet another Bulgarian émigré: Dimitri Yordanov (1926–2001), a nephew of the famous Danchov brothers who had authored the first Bulgarian encyclopedia in 1936. "Bobo," as Dimitri was known among the Bulgarian emigrants, left Bulgaria in 1946 at age 20 and was a Lapin Agile regular. He would sit there for hours, sketching the patrons or singing chansons. Yordanov and Apostolof clicked right away and started hanging out together. They would often drop by the Chez Pomme, a cabaret on the corner of Lepic and Tholozé in Montmartre. It was frequented by stars such as Michel Simon, Jean Gabin and Fernandel. The owner, Madame Pomme (real name: Eugénie-Jeanne de Montfaucon), was a good friend of Kutchukov's uncle George Papazov, so Apostolof used this as an excuse to go there and eat and drink for free. In May 1950, Madame Pomme helped organize an exhibition of Yordanov's sketches of celebrities such as Simon, Gabin, Fernandel, Bernard Blier, Maurice Chevalier, Jean Marais, Gérard Philipe, Utrillo, etc. Kutchukov recalled,

> I remember Bobo had painted Jean Gabin, who had starred in Marcel Carné's *Port of Shadows* with a head like a lion with those wrinkles. But Bobo was in trouble. He was so hungry that his shirt clung to his back. He and Stephen walked in the parks around the Avenue des Champs-Élysées. Bobo would sketch a passerby, usually an American or other foreigner. Stephen would take the portrait and bring it to the "model," ask for some money, and make a franc or two.[7]

The Lapin Agile caper lasted only a couple of months. Finally, the French police figured out that Kutchukov and Apostolof were working illegally and threatened to haul them back to Bulgaria. Like Peter Rabbit, the ever-inventive Apostolof again found a way out of the situation. One day, he appeared before his friends wearing a white chef's hat and saying that he had found a job as a cook at the mansion of a famous millionaire in Southern France. The millionaire in question was Nicolas Fournier, owner of the famous company Vins Nicolas and one of the largest retailers of alcoholic beverages in postwar France. "Stephen probably sent [Fournier] a fake résumé. I wouldn't be surprised if that was the case. He used to boast that before coming to France, he was a chef in Istanbul," remembers Ginette Kutchukov.[8]

Vins Nicolas sent Stephen Apostolof a one-way ticket, and he left for Southern France. Once he got there, he saw that the huge mansion boasted an excellent kitchen. But according to Ginette, that wasn't what turned his head:

> The millionaire had two daughters who graduated from the famous culinary school Le Cordon Bleu. This suited Stephen well, because he couldn't boil an egg back then. So the girls did all the cooking, and he would just watch them and say, "Très bien, mademoiselle! Très bien!" But the father was not stupid, so he soon found out that Stephen was not a chef. He bought him a train ticket back to Paris and kicked him out of the mansion. So Stephen spent a three-day "vacation" in Southern France and then returned to Paris to tell us about his adventures.[9]

The establishment of a Communist regime in Bulgaria caused a wave of political emigration from the country. The scope of the exodus was massive. According to official statistics, over 100,000 people escaped Bulgaria between 1946 and 1950. Naturally, most of them ended up in neighboring Greece, Turkey and Yugoslavia, as well as in Western European countries such as Italy and France. But Bulgaria's political expatriates were too ideologically and politically divided among themselves to join forces and effectively oppose the Communist government.

After World War II, numerous Bulgarian émigrés like Stephen Apostolof went to Paris in search of a new home. In the late 1940s, some of them united around one man: Lt. Yordan Peyev, a former platoon commander of the Fourth Battery of the Sofia Artillery Regiment. Peyev arrived in Paris after spending years in Bulgaria's Communist prisons. He had been falsely convicted of human trafficking in his native country, and there were allegations that he had even facilitated the escape of the white Russian émigré Prince Dmitry Lobanov-Rostovsky,[10] who subsequently disappeared without a trace. After being released from prison with the help of an influential uncle, Peyev moved to Paris, where his energy and organizational skills helped him unite a large swath of the elite of the Bulgarian political emigration in France.

The Free Bulgarians organization was thus founded in Paris in 1949. Its members were former diplomats and intellectuals. Besides Lt. Peyev, its founders included Sava Kirov, a former foreign minister and ambassador of Bulgaria in France, the ex-consul general Christo Shishmanov, and journalist Stéphane Groueff (1922–2006). A good friend of Apostolof, Groueff later supplied him with stock footage for his first film *Journey to Freedom*. The objective of the Free Bulgarians was the liberation of Bulgaria from Communist rule and Soviet oppression.

The organization's first accomplishment was starting a monthly magazine called *Vazrazhdane* (Renaissance), which Peyev began publishing in January 1949 with Groueff and Dyanko Sotirov. Previous to his work on *Vazrazhdane*, Groueff had participated in another publication for émigrés called *Bulgarian Nation* (1947–48). In the 1950s and '60s, he would become a reporter for the magazine *Paris Match* and director of its New York office.

Foreshadowing? Apostolof fondles the breast of a statue on the terrace of the Palais de Chaillot, Paris, 1950.

Apostolof, who hadn't yet joined any political groups in Paris, established close ties with the *Vazrazhdane* circle, as described by Groueff in his memoirs *My Odyssey* (2003): "Students such as Matei Hroussanov and Dimitry Panev joined us, as did a cheerful, adventurous youth from the port city of Bourgas [*sic*], Steftcho Apostolov, recently escaped with his accordion, disguised as a sailor on a foreign ship."[11]

In addition to sharing similar political views, Apostolof and Groueff bonded over their shared love of music. Like Apostolof, Groueff was a fan of American jazz musicians Louis Armstrong, Rex Stewart and Sidney Bechet. Sometimes, according to his memoir, Groueff tried playing his clarinet, accompanied by Apostolof, "whose talent on the accordion and the piano matched his carefree, bohemian charm."[12] Boris Kutchukov remembered, "In addition to Apostolof, at *Vazrazhdane*, there were also such people as Yanko Dishliev, a pilot who had been fighting together with the flying ace Dimitar Spisarevski[13] against the Americans during World War II. Generally a group of nationalists who cared about Bulgaria."[14]

It was a tense, fractious and occasionally violent time. The *Vazrazhdane* circle consisted of avowed monarchists and defenders of Boris III. They didn't hide their sympathies for the ill-fated government of Konstantin Muraviev, who was overthrown by the Fatherland Front coup on September 9, 1944, after just seven days as prime minister. At the same time, they were also battling the supporters of the Pladne (Noon) faction of the Bulgarian Agrarian National Union, a major power in the Fatherland Front government. Apostolof and other immigrants at *Vazrazhdane* were in direct conflict with the supporters of the Pladne faction in Paris, a group known as the Farmers. According to Kutchukov,

> The Farmers were always fighting with us nationalists. One day they came to a meeting at the headquarters of *Vazrazhdane* in one of the Parisian schools. Stéphane Groueff told them to wait for their turn if they wished to speak. Instead of that, they jumped on one of our Bulgarian friends there, Dimitar Panitza, and started beating him. The meeting turned into a huge melee! I managed to hit two or three of the Farmers with a chair. The police came with the sirens on, but I had no documents, so I had no other choice but to go to the toilet and escape down the lightning rod from the third floor. Stephen somehow disappeared as well and we saved our asses.[15]

But Apostolof's troubles with the so-called Farmers continued. In 1949, Kutchukov was living in a rented room with his Czech cousin next to Temple de la Petite Étoile, a Protestant church on Rue Anatole France in Levallois-Perret, a commune in the Northwestern suburbs of Paris. One night in July, Apostolof appeared at Kutchukov's door with all of his worldly belongings, which at that time could fit into a military duffel bag. "He cried, 'Buddy, please help me! The Farmers are gonna kill me!' What am I to do? I sheltered him," remembered Kutchukov.[16]

These accommodations proved troublesome. "The room though had only two beds, one of which was occupied by the Czech cousin of Boris," remembers Ginette Kutchukov. "So Stephen had no place to sleep, and he decided to get rid of the cousin. He lay next to him and began hugging and pinching him. Finally, the cousin, who was worried Stephen might be gay, went to sleep on the floor while Stephen stayed in his bed."[17]

Initially, Bulgaria's Communist government didn't bother to deal with the emigration issue. But as more and more people escaped the troubled country, the Reds adopted a new Bulgarian citizenship law, which went into effect on March 6, 1948: All those who had escaped the country were henceforth deprived of their property and Bulgarian citizenship. What's more, Apostolof was tried in absentia for high treason and received a death sentence that would loom over his head for the next four decades. Naturally, contacting his family in Bulgaria was extremely difficult, if not impossible. "We would send ten letters of which only one might reach our families," remembered Kutchukov. "We avoided sending photos, which could help the Communists visually identify us. The authorities were trying to get us back to Bulgaria in any way possible, so that they could send us to a work camp. Had Stephen and I not escaped from Bulgaria, we would have been sent to one of the many work camps and exterminated no later than 1950."[18]

Bulgarian authorities used all kinds of tricks to entice the so-called *nevazvrashtentsi* ("non-returnees") back to the country. Sometimes the authorities would send secret agents to retrieve them, as was the case with the Bulgarian ambassador in Zagreb, Petar Karagyozov. In other instances, they just sent letters, as with Nikolay P. Nikolaev, a Bulgarian diplomat living in Stockholm: He was notified by post that he was sentenced to death by the People's Court and must return to Bulgaria to serve his sentence. Of course, Nikolaev didn't go back to Bulgaria and died in Stockholm in 1960. On April 13, 1949, Boris Kutchukov received a similar letter, summoning him to the city of Sliven in Eastern Bulgaria to serve in the labor forces of the Bulgarian Army. "They found out my address in Paris from my father," he remembered. "They sent me a subpoena in which they said I would be sued if I didn't go back to Bulgaria by a certain date. I sat down and wrote them literally the following: 'Gentlemen, I'm really sorry, but I will not be able to come back to Bulgaria. I'm busy with some important matters in Paris.' I was a cadet in a military school; they wanted me to join the labor forces."[19]

All the while, show business beckoned the young Bulgarians. In 1949, Kutchukov's girlfriend Ginette participated in the corps de ballet in German director Ludwig Berger's film *Ballerina* (also known as *Dream Ballerina,* released in 1950). Shot at Billancourt Studios in the suburbs of Paris, the film also featured 16-year-old Violette Verdy, who would become one of the rising stars of French ballet after the war. Apostolof and Kutchukov spent long hours behind the scenes at Billancourt watching the shooting of the film. At the end of the day, they would grab the exhausted Ginette and carry her to the nearest metro station.

"We ran through the streets, shouting and pounding on the doors in the middle of the night. We were young and reckless!" remembered Kutchukov.[20] He recalled that the shooting of *Ballerina* impressed Apostolof so much that he began dreaming about making films. This is very plausible, and is supported by a note found in Apostolof's archives written by Stafford B. Harrison, associate producer of Apostolof's first Hollywood movie *Journey to Freedom*. It reads: "Steve, may this serve to remind you of your plans for a picture in Paris and act as a spur towards gaining your goal…. The first step is a good *Escape to Freedom*."

The precise origins of Apostolof's filmmaking career are murky. Years later, when he was living in the U.S., Apostolof claimed that while in Paris he founded his own company, Apostolof Film Productions. He also boasted of producing a movie with the strange title *The Last Mile to El Diablo*, "released only in the European market."[21] No information about this alleged film could be found in Apostolof's diligently kept scrapbooks (or in any public archives, for that matter). This was apparently just one of the many legends Apostolof created about himself. He also claimed that while in Paris, he studied political science at the Sorbonne. This supposed autobiographical "fact" was later repeated in the directory *Who's Who in the West*,[22] as well as in the *Los Angeles Times*' announcement of his third marriage[23] and several of his professional résumés. Yet none of Apostolof's friends remembers him as a student at the Sorbonne.

What is clear and substantiated is that, in late 1949, Apostolof decided to emigrate

Chapter 3. A Stranger in Paris (1948–1950)

once again, this time to Canada. There were several reasons for this decision. After World War II, Canada needed workers. By the end of 1946, such manpower-intensive industries as agriculture, mining and lumbering began lobbying for new, more liberal immigration policies because of the labor shortage. In the spring of 1947, Canadian Prime Minister Mackenzie King informed Parliament about the government's decision to open Canada for emigrants.[24]

Apostolof's anti–Communist sentiments didn't hurt. As a neighbor of the U.S. during the Cold War, Canada was concerned about the threat of Communism. While in Paris, Stephen also learned a bit of French, one of Canada's two official languages. And so, at the end of January 1950, with the help of his friend Slavi Tashkov, who was already living in Canada, Apostolof began preparing the documents needed for his passage. On July 1, he got a transit visa from the British Embassy in Paris. Two days later, he left France aboard the RMS *Samaria*, a passenger ship operated by the Cunard–White Star line. It took him only as far as Dover in South East England. After a short stay there, Apostolof embarked upon a ten-day voyage across the Atlantic to a new life.

Chapter 4

Onward to Canada!
(1950–1952)

"It takes a wise man to handle a lie, a fool had better remain honest."
—Norman Douglas, *Alone* (1921)

On Monday, July 3, 1950, the 19,602-ton RMS *Samaria* left the Dover harbor bound for Canadian shores. Among its passengers was Apostolof, then 22 and eager to begin the next phase of his already eventful life. The *Samaria* had a storied past of its own. Built in 1920 as a transatlantic ocean liner for the Cunard line, it had served as a troop ship during World War II. After the war, it was given back to Cunard and again used to carry civilian passengers. Between 1948 and 1955, the *Samaria* was almost exclusively used on the Canadian route. Every two weeks, it would haul passengers across the ocean to places like Montreal, Quebec and Halifax.

Apostolof, dapper as ever, aboard the RMS *Samaria* on his way to Canada.

Chapter 4. Onward to Canada! (1950–1952)

The *Samaria* was slower than the ships built before World War I, so Apostolof's voyage across the Atlantic took ten days. The passage was rough, too, since the North Atlantic is a notoriously unfriendly body of water during the early summer. Apostolof spent most of his time sleeping in his cramped cabin, which lacked even a porthole. At least the ship had a cinema, so Apostolof could watch *The Three Musketeers* (1948, dir. George Sidney) starring Gene Kelly and Lana Turner. If he got really bored, he could participate in the various quiz games or wander over to the main lounge for some Keno or bingo.

Apostolof arrived in Montreal on July 14, 1950. It was one of the hottest days of the year with temperatures reaching 79°F. Apostolof only stayed in the city for a few hours before taking a night train to Toronto. There he bunked with a close friend, Slavi Tashkov, and through him met other Bulgarian political emigrants. Within this new circle of acquaintances, Apostolof found the support and consolation he needed in this new country.

It didn't take long for Apostolof's political leanings to resurface. In 1951, he joined the Bulgarian National Front, an anti–Communist political movement established in Munich in 1947 by Bulgarians living in exile under the leadership of Ivan Dochev. The Bulgarian National Front was part of the Anti-Bolshevik Bloc of Nations, a political union of immigrants from the USSR and other Eastern European countries under the Soviet boot, founded by Ukrainian nationalist Stepan Bandera in Munich immediately after the war.

April 13, 1952. Apostolof (far right) with the leader of the Bulgarian National Front Ivan Dochev (third from left) and other members of the organization at a meeting of the Anti-Bolshevik Bloc of Nations in Toronto.

On April 13, 1952, Apostolof participated in Toronto's largest anti-Communist rally, an event organized by the Anti-Bolshevik Bloc of Nations. Neither the heavy rain nor the fact that it was Easter Sunday stopped Apostolof and nearly 2000 others from demonstrating. A photo taken late in the day shows a determined Apostolof addressing the representatives of the Bulgarian National Front, including chairman Dochev and senior members Toncho Tanev and Ivan Paprikov.

Finding a job in Canada wasn't exactly easy. Although the Canadian economy as a whole grew during the 1950s, the rate of growth slowed as unemployment increased. So, even in this new country, Apostolof faced the same old problem of how to make a living without any education or special skills. "My dad heard they were looking for farmers," Apostolof's daughter Polly recalled, "so he said [to the immigration authorities] that he was a farmer and went to Canada. I guess the emigrants would say anything, just to board that ship and leave. I don't know what happened when the Canadians realized that they were tricked."[1]

In fact, Apostolof had identified himself in his emigration papers as a dentist. This was not entirely untrue, since he had actually studied to be a dental technician for a brief period in Bulgaria. And so, accidentally or not, in late 1950, Apostolof found a job at Toronto General Hospital where he met the first of his three future wives: Joan Mary Higgins, a 25-year-old nurse of French-Canadian descent. "They met in the hospital where they both worked. [Stephen] was a very pleasant man. He was one of the many displaced persons working there," says Barbara Higgins Graham, Joan's youngest sister.[2]

"The story we always heard is that [Dad] was an orderly at the hospital, which I find kind of funny to visualize," says Susan, the youngest daughter of Apostolof and Joan.[3]

Born on December 30, 1925, in Toronto, Joan Mary Higgins was Apostolof's senior by two years. An independent woman, she lived in her own place in Toronto. Joan grew up in a very conservative bourgeois family. Her father could trace his family's roots back to Miles Standish, an English military officer who was hired by the Pilgrims as military adviser for Plymouth Colony; he accompanied them on their journey on the *Mayflower* in 1620. Joan's mother was from Alsace in Eastern France. The family was quite traditional and on Sundays would have a formal dinner, complete with fine china and crystal tableware. Apostolof was often invited to these family gatherings even though Joan's parents didn't care for him. Apostolof was not to the taste of these blue bloods. According to Apostolof's oldest son Steve,

> My mother always said that my grandparents were very conservative. They were educated, professional and they had Dad come in. He was always very enthusiastic about life, very loud. He wasn't a professional. I don't think he was educated. And perhaps not maybe the best choice for your daughter to marry. If you are conservative, if you're professional, if you're educated, you want the same for your child. And that's probably why they weren't particularly happy with my mom's choice. And that's probably what Mom liked about him.[4]

Joan's sister Barbara sees it a little differently: "My parents were pleasant and very hospitable and treated everyone we brought home as an honored guest. They kept their opinions to themselves. But they must have thought enough of Steve, as they paid for their wedding, and it was a big one."[5]

One thing Joan's parents especially disliked about their new son-in-law was his vanity. In their eyes, Apostolof seemed to be overcompensating for his background as a

Chapter 4. Onward to Canada! (1950–1952)

poor European transient by making sure that his appearance and manners were always flawless. Susan, the youngest daughter of Apostolof and Joan, revealed, "Before Mom and Dad got married, my grandfather wrote a letter like the ones fathers usually write to their daughters. He wished them luck and wrote that he was happy for her. But he also noted that my father worried too much about his appearance."

"I think that in a lot of ways, Dad overcompensated for things," said Steve Apostolof. "He was bigger than life. I mean, he might not have a dime in his pocket but he sure had a nice suit. He would always have a nice haircut. And he was always whining about his haircut. For me, it was "Come on, Dad! At least you got hair." But he was always whining about his haircut because appearance was very important for him."[6]

In early 1951, Apostolof took a job with the Canadian National Railway. Around that time, several months before the couple's wedding, Joan found out she was pregnant. Today, this would be most exciting news, but in early 1950s Canada, pregnancy outside of marriage would cause mothers and their children to be virtually ostracized by society. Films and popular novels of the era reinforced the stereotype that unwed mothers were inexperienced, foolish and even criminally irresponsible. The fact that Joan came from a conservative family didn't help. Susan says, "My mother came from a very proper family. So for her to admit she was carrying an illegitimate child was pretty embarrassing. Not only for her but also for her parents and especially for Dad. He always had huge respect for her parents. Always tried to impress them, to make them feel proud of their daughter's choice."[7]

In early 1951, Apostolof took a job with the Canadian National Railway.

For Apostolof to recognize this illegitimate child would have been unthinkable at the time. And a shotgun wedding—a popular option for couples in this awkward situation—was out of the question. Especially when the wedding was already being planned. That left Joan with two unhappy options. She could have an abortion or carry the child to term and give it up for adoption.

"Mom never would have considered an abortion," says Polly Apostolof. "I honestly

Stephen Apostolof and Joan Higgins were married at Casa Loma, a Gothic Revival style residence in midtown Toronto, on November 4, 1951.

believe Mom wanted to marry first and then give birth to Maria and let the chips fall where they may. Mom always carried small, so Dad didn't know she was pregnant. The plan was for Maria to be delivered after the wedding, but she was born prematurely … a surprise to both of them."[8]

Maria Patricia Apostolof, the first of Apostolof's five children, was born in Toronto on October 14, 1951. Joan delivered the baby alone at home and placed her for adoption through a Catholic charity to the family of a Canadian diplomat living in Bogotá, Colombia.

On November 4, 1951, 20 days after Maria's clandestine birth, Apostolof and Joan were married. The wedding took place in midtown Toronto at Casa Loma, a lavish Gothic Revival style residence built in 1911–14 for financier Sir Henry Mill Pellatt. Joan's parents paid for the wedding. The newlyweds look happy enough in the surviving photos, with no hint of the family drama festering just below the surface.

Toronto is one of Canada's warmer cities but winters there are still severe, with snow on the ground most days between December and March. Perhaps because he wanted to escape from the cold (or simply from his icy relationship with Joan's parents), Apostolof decided to continue his journey westward and head to Hollywood. But this wasn't a decision made on a whim. "Steve wanted to go to California because he wanted to get into the movie business, and Joan said okay. I don't think she would have gone on her own," says Joan's sister Barbara.[9]

Then in late May 1952, one of Apostolof's ex-girlfriends arrived in Toronto from Paris. Steve, in true Apostolof fashion, went for a night out with her, brashly spending all the money he and Joan had saved for their journey. To say the least, Joan wasn't happy. Son Steve said of the story, "As far as I know Dad, I think it's true. I can imagine how uncomfortable my mother felt, when she had to call her parents and ask for money in order to go to America. Because they were not impressed by her selection of a husband to start with."[10]

Finally, on June 2, 1952, Apostolof and Joan left for Los Angeles by train—broke, unsure of how they would be able to support themselves, but full of optimism.

PART TWO

*Adventures in La La Land
(1952–1978)*

Chapter 5

The Man About Town
(1952–1957)

"I got into filmmaking like everything else in my life—by mistake. Many, many people come to Hollywood with the idea, 'Oh boy, I'm going to become a star or a director.' I came here because of the weather. If I was in Detroit, I would have to work with cars. If I was in Milwaukee, I'd have to work with cheese. So, I was in L.A.—why not make movies?"—Stephen C. Apostolof[1]

On June 2, 1952, after a five-hour journey from Toronto, Stephen and Joan arrived in Windsor, the southernmost city on the U.S.-Canada border. They then crossed the river by ferry and arrived in Detroit. From there, due to their difficult financial situation, they took an Amtrak train the rest of the way to Los Angeles. They traveled nearly 2000 miles, passing through Illinois, Iowa, Nebraska, Colorado, Utah and Nevada over vast plains and dusty deserts, and arrived in Los Angeles on June 4.

On June 20, the young couple rented an apartment in a small, multi-family dwelling at 1740 North Kingsley Drive in Los Feliz, a hillside neighborhood in northeast Hollywood. The building was just a year old then and already fitted with gas and air conditioning. The place was conveniently located near Griffith Park and only a few blocks from Hollywood Boulevard in a neighborhood immersed in lush greenery.

"Feliz" means "happy" in Spanish, and no name could have been more appropriate for the community that welcomed the Apostolofs to America. In the 1950s, Los Feliz was home to many directors, movie stars and musicians, as well as to countless newcomers determined to make it in Hollywood. Apostolof could have been easily confused for one of those people, but as he put it, the reason for his arrival in Los Angeles was far more prosaic. According to his son Christopher, Apostolof "really loved the sun, ocean, the palm trees, and the city somehow reminded him of his hometown of Burgas."[2]

But California's appeal wasn't just the climate. The Golden State was an exciting place to be in the 1950s. When the Apostolofs arrived there, California was experiencing immense postwar prosperity and undergoing huge sociological transformations. People were flooding into the San Fernando Valley in Los Angeles County like never before. By the end of 1945, the Valley was home to about 230,000 people. That number had more than doubled by 1950, and it would double again by 1960. During the peak growth years of the 1950s, the Valley was getting about 3650 additional people (or approximately 720 families) every month.[3]

What was attracting all these pilgrims? That eternal beacon, money. Just as it had

Chapter 5. The Man About Town (1952–1957)

been during the 1840s Gold Rush, California was once again seen as a land of opportunity during the middle decades of the 20th century. And not without reason. The entertainment, defense and electronics industries provided plenty of good paying jobs then, both white and blue collar. In the 1950s, 45 percent of families in the San Fernando Valley owned two cars, a classic milestone of American prosperity. Californians were buying plenty of backyard swimming pools back then, too. Anthony Brothers, then the largest manufacturer of pools in the world, installed 2000 of them in the Valley in 1956 alone, each one priced between $1500 and $10,000.[4] (That's $13,270 to $88,473 in today's money.)

Los Angeles had plenty of entertainment, too. In the early 1950s, the city was considered the epicenter of American night life west of Chicago. The City of Angels retained that title for many years despite fierce competition from upstart Las Vegas, which was just a few hours away by car. Back then, L.A. had many nightclubs and restaurants with such exotic-sounding names as Cocoanut Grove, Trocadero, Ciro's, the Mocambo, and Romanoff's. The hottest spots in town were the bars and restaurants along the glitzy mile-and-a-half stretch of Sunset Boulevard known as the Strip. Apostolof became a regular at Ciro's, a West Hollywood nightclub that was a favorite hangout for movie people in the 1940s and '50s. Being seen at Ciro's might lead to a mention in the Hollywood gossip columns of Hedda Hopper, Louella Parsons and Mike Connolly. Ciro's famous clientele included Marilyn Monroe, Humphrey Bogart and his wife Lauren Bacall, Frank Sinatra, Anita Ekberg, Cary Grant, James Stewart and, long before his days in politics, Ronald Reagan.

Another nightclub that Apostolof frequented was the Seven Seas, located at 6904 Hollywood Boulevard, just a stone's throw from the famous Grauman's Chinese Theatre. In the '50s, Los Angeles went gaga for primitivism and Polynesian culture. Fittingly, then, the interior of the Seven Seas was decorated in the so-called "tiki" style, which reflected America's infatuation with Hawaii and the South Pacific. The Seven Seas became famous for its roof that leaked during rainstorms, so owner Ray Haller installed sprinklers to replicate the effect every night. Apostolof frequented the Seven Seas because of its Hawaiian-themed show, led by entertainer Jennie "Na Pua" Wood (her nickname meant "Little Flower"), and he liked to occasionally dance in a conga line while draped in traditional Hawaiian garlands. Apostolof frequented the Seven Seas for years and he would find one of the dancers from *Orgy of the Dead* there, Mickey Jines, who was an exotic dancer.

Once settled in L.A., Apostolof reunited with Boris Kutchukov. Arriving in the city with his wife Ginette just a few months before the Apostolofs, Boris had found a job painting cars, a skill he'd picked up in Paris.

The two friends were soon up to their old tricks. One day, while cruising through L.A. in his brand new 1953 Chevrolet Bel Air convertible, Kutchukov almost crashed into something shiny that had been left in the middle of the road, and he got out of his car to inspect the object. He recalled, "It turned out to be a glossy, five-gallon tin can. I opened it, and what did I see? It was full of yolks! I said to myself, 'Gosh, what am I supposed to do with so many yolks?' So I called Steve and said, 'Steve, you love caviar, don't you? Grab your accordion and come to my place!'"[5]

A half hour later, Apostolof appeared on Kutchukov's doorstep. The two Bulgarians

Apostolof (far left) dancing the night away at the Seven Seas restaurant in Hollywood.

rolled their sleeves up and began mixing the yolks with olive oil and lemon juice to prepare *taramasalata*, a Greek spread made from salted and cured roe of the cod also called "the poor man's caviar."[6] Later that day, they decided to throw a "caviar party" for the other Bulgarians in the area, with Apostolof providing the music with his accordion.

Moments like these were important to Apostolof. In the 1950s, L.A.'s Bulgarian immigrant community was relatively small. Most Bulgarian expats preferred to move to big cities on the East Coast or in the Midwest. Chicago and New York were popular destinations, as were industrial towns like Detroit, Indianapolis and Cleveland. Not as many Bulgarians made it all the way to L.A. then, but the relatively few who did were close-knit.

In 1953, Apostolof, Kutchukov and some other transplants founded the Bulgarian-American Cultural Educational Society, known as the Bulgarian Club, whose main objective was the cultural enlightenment of L.A.'s Bulgarian diaspora. These enthusiasts raised money and bought a piece of land at 1530 North Vermont, near the corner of Sunset Boulevard. In 1954, they built a two-story clubhouse in which they held regular social meetings. "Looking back, it seems reminiscent of the Italian clubs you see in Mafia movies," remembered Apostolof's son Steve. "The white, green and red bunting. The 'regulars' that seemed to always be there and just looked like 'muscle.' The place just had a *Sopranos* kind of vibe."[7]

Apostolof, known among his fellow Bulgarians for his cheerful disposition, was often invited to play his accordion at the Bulgarian Club. Once, Kutchukov's wife Ginette, the French ballet dancer, gathered some of her friends and hosted a can-can–themed soirée at the club. It was quite successful, and the dancers were called out for an encore. "But instead of my girls, onstage appeared Stephen, Boris, and their friend Ivan Gugalov wearing petticoats and corsets," recalls Ginette. "At first the audience didn't recognize them, but when the boys began dancing and throwing their unshaven legs in the air, the audience started rolling on the floor laughing."[8]

In July 1953, Apostolof landed his first real job in California at Anderson, Clayton & Co., a company that *Fortune* magazine had named the world's biggest cotton trader in 1945. He only stayed with the firm until October, when he was lured away by something closer to his interests than cotton: the motion picture industry. Apostolof explained it this way: "A friend from Paris had a friend here, and I gave her a call when I came to L.A. and said I was looking for a job. And, contrary to the usual thing in Hollywood where everyone would give an arm and a leg to be in the industry, I got into it by just showing up. 'Here I am!'"[9]

In November 1953, Apostolof was assigned to the 20th Century–Fox tabulating department at 10201 West Pico Boulevard in West Hollywood. He may not have been working on a film set, but he was still one step closer to his dream of working in the movie industry. The experience Apostolof gained at Fox would prove extremely useful later when he ran his own film company as an independent producer. At Fox, Apostolof met and befriended Herbert F. Niccolls, a 34-year-old screenwriter who previously worked at the accounting department of MGM. Niccolls later wrote the script for Apostolof's first film *Journey to Freedom*.

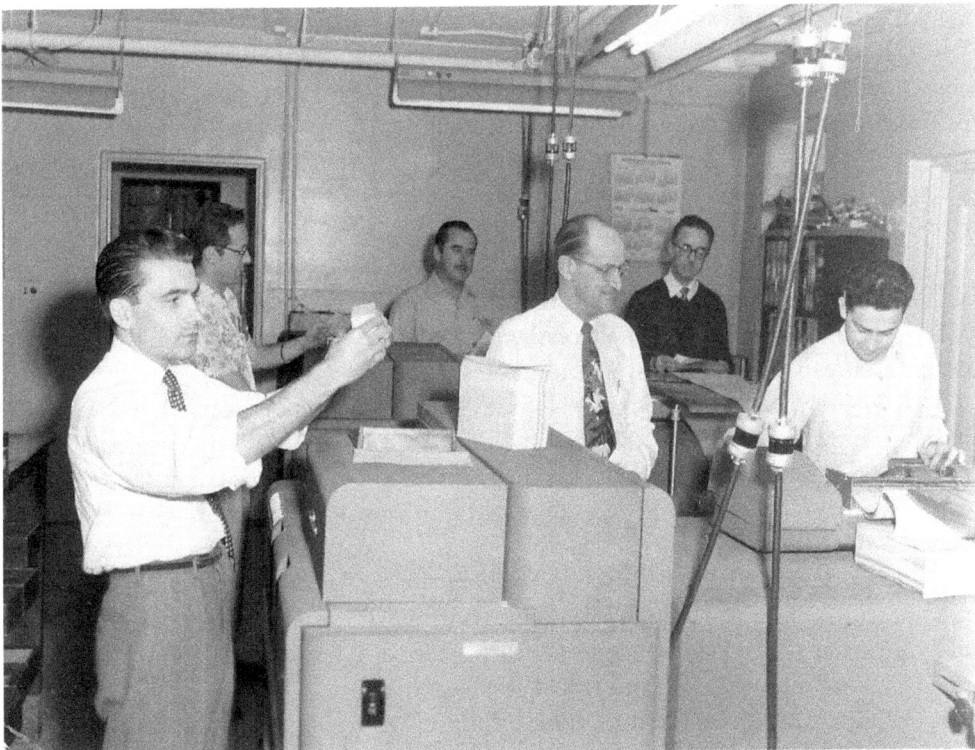

Apostolof (far left) and buddy Herbert F. Niccolls (second from left) at work in the 20th Century–Fox tabulating department in early 1954.

"Fox was mammoth. Huge! It had departments in departments in departments," Apostolof remembered. "And the only way to advance there was to wait for someone to die. I realized that to go through the majors was not my forte. So I said, 'I'm going to go on my own.'"[10]

Apostolof stayed at Fox for about six months, departing in April 1954, but he kept in contact with Niccolls after he left. A month earlier, Joan's younger sister Barbara started working as a traveling nurse at Kaiser Medical Center in Los Angeles, rooming with two of her co-workers. Joan herself worked at the same facility, and they would all go out for excursions in Apostolof's big Cadillac convertible, hitting up the local beaches and even venturing as far as Las Vegas and Tijuana. During one of those trips, Barbara started dating Herb Niccolls. She recalls, "They would have dinner parties, and that's where Steve brought some friends of his to meet us girls, and I dated Herb for a while. Nothing serious. Otherwise I wouldn't have gone back home, but I was a Canadian."[11]

Friends remember Niccolls as a good man who was loved by all who knew him. But buried deep in Niccolls' past was a dark secret, a shocking story that would only come to light after the publication of the 2013 book *The Boy Who Shot the Sheriff* by Nancy Bartley: In 1931, when he was just 12, Niccolls shot and killed John L. Wormell, the sheriff of Asotin, Washington, who caught him stealing candy and cigarettes from a local store. The incident shocked the nation, and an angry mob threatened to hang the "barefoot-boy murderer," as the juvenile criminal became known. Niccolls was sentenced to life imprisonment at Washington State Penitentiary in Walla Walla, becoming the youngest person on record in the state to receive such a harsh sentence.

While incarcerated, Niccolls developed an insatiable appetite for knowledge and even managed to graduate high school. In his early twenties, he was released from prison and went to work for MGM and then for 20th Century–Fox, which is where he met Apostolof. Niccolls encouraged Apostolof to make an autobiographical film about a young man escaping from Communist-run Bulgaria. He later wrote the sensationalized, romanticized screenplay for that film, *Journey to Freedom*.

"We were talking and [Niccolls] said, 'My God, Steve, you have such an interesting story,'" Apostolof recalled in an unpublished interview with Mike Vraney and James Elliot Singer. "I said, 'What's so interesting about it?' To me it was nothing. To me it was everyday. I realized later that it was an interesting story."[12]

So one day, Niccolls and Apostolof sat down over two bottles of wine and started hashing the whole thing out. By the time they finished the first bottle, Apostolof had managed to tell his story to Niccolls as the latter took notes. A week or so later, Niccolls came back with a story outline and together with Apostolof came up with the general concept of what the film was going to be.

"The original title for *Journey to Freedom* was *Escape to Freedom*," Apostolof remembered. "Before we knew it, we had a synopsis. Then I sat down and—on an old, old typewriter—typed the sequences of my escape the way I remembered it. When I finished, I put it on the shelf and forgot about it."[13]

Although Apostolof liked to think of himself as a potential producer or director, the moment didn't seem to be quite right for such a risky career move. Instead he pursued the kind of steady work that provided for his growing family. Or, at least, he tried to. Professional stability utterly eluded him. Jobs came and went, one after another.

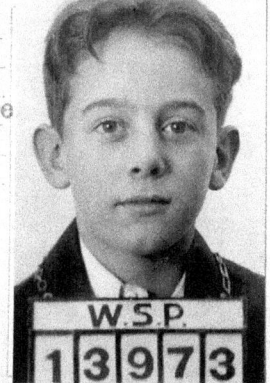

Washington State Penitentiary inmate record for Herbert F. Niccolls (courtesy Washington State Archives).

From May to September 1954, for instance, he was selling auto parts at Parts Wholesalers at 1717 South Figueroa. After that gig ended, he landed a job that was more seemingly suited to his personality. A well-known dandy who took conspicuous pride in his appearance, Apostolof started selling men's fashion accessories at Swank, Inc., located at 2530 South Broadway. But this assignment, too, proved short-lived, and by December 1954 he was working swing shifts (3 p.m. to 11 p.m.) in the accounting department of the ABC television network in their Los Angeles division at 4151 Prospect Avenue. He only lasted there until January 1955, however, and described the stint as a "disaster." "I did so much for ABC, and they threw me out like a dirty kitten," Apostolof later recalled with residual bitterness.

The reasons for Apostolof's dismissal from ABC are not known. What's important is that he lost his job at a crucial time in his life when Joan was pregnant with the couple's second child. But fate would smile on the lucky Bulgarian the day he vacated his desk at ABC. That afternoon, under rather amazing circumstances, he met a group of potential investors who were "very anxious" to finance a movie about his escape from Bulgaria. Negotiations advanced quickly. Apostolof got incorporated, and his backers soon put up the cash for what would become 1957's *Journey to Freedom*.

"Dad told me that his car broke down and some people stopped to help him," Apostolof's son Steve explained. "So he took them to a lunch in the restaurant nearby. He told them about his escape from Bulgaria, and his adventures in Istanbul, Paris and Canada. The strangers were very impressed and agreed to finance his first film, based on his life."[14]

This pivotal moment in Apostolof's career would coincide with another milestone in his life. "I got the financing on the day my daughter was born," remembered Apostolof. "We signed the contract, and I got a check for $24,000 [around $212,000 today]. I phoned my wife, my first wife, and she said, 'Well, I don't feel very good. I think the baby's going to come.' I said, 'I'm coming back to L.A.'"[15]

Apostolof dotes on his second child Polly on February 17, 1957.

Apostolof, who was out

of town at the time, immediately hopped in his car and headed for Los Angeles. When he reached Bakersfield, about two hours northwest of Los Angeles, he called home to check on Joan. No one picked up the phone and Apostolof assumed that Joan was already at the hospital. He said, "Now, I always bought big fast cars. I like Cadillacs. And after Bakersfield, I floored it. Put the pedal to the metal. And I saw a couple of police cars following me. I said, 'I'm not frightened,' and I continued to drive like a bat out of hell. And, believe it or not, they gave up. And I got to the hospital and even bought my daughter a little Easter present."[16]

Steve and Joan's second child, a daughter named Paula Christine Apostolof, was born on March 27, 1955, at Kaiser Hospital in Hollywood, where Joan worked. The girl was named after Polyxena, Apostolof's late mother. Polly, as she would become known, maintains that her father never failed to mention the fact that he got his first film financed on the day she was born.

Chapter 6

The Propagandist
(1957)

From the late 1940s to the mid–50s, Cold War tensions were steadily ratcheting up between the U.S. and the Soviet Union. The headlines were dominated by a series of nerve-wracking events: Soviet expansion in Eastern Europe, the blockade of Berlin (1948–49), the Chinese Civil War (1949) and, most dramatically, the Korean War (1950–53). It was, one might say, a golden age for fear and paranoia, giving birth to such propaganda films as *The Red Danube* (1949, dir. George Sidney), *The Woman on Pier 13* (1949, dir. Robert Stevenson), *I Was a Communist for the F.B.I.* (1951, dir. Gordon Douglas) and *Big Jim McLain* (1952, dir. Edward Ludwig). These films and others presented Communism as the single biggest threat to America's security. The situation could best be summarized by a popular catchphrase of the era: "Better dead than Red."

These were nervous times in Hollywood. In October 1947, the House Un-American Activities Committee served subpoenas to numerous writers, directors and others in the film industry, commanding them to testify about their alleged membership in or sympathy with the Communist Party of the United States of America. Among the first summoned were a group of screenwriters, producers and directors that became collectively known as the Hollywood Ten. Among their ranks were such legendary names as Dalton Trumbo and Ring Lardner, Jr. Their refusal to testify led to their *de facto* excommunication from Hollywood. In the coming years, more than 300 others in the entertainment industry lost their jobs because of suspected ties to the Communists.

Against the backdrop of these turbulent times, Apostolof keenly understood the tremendous potential of his own life story. This was not only his chance to break into Hollywood, but also the opportunity to condemn once again the Communist ideology he despised so passionately. A project like *Journey to Freedom* could do so much for him at once, both personally and professionally. The movie simply had to happen.

So in April 1955, Apostolof joined forces with show business lifer Harry A. Keatan (1896–1966) to form a company called Cosmopolitan Pictures Co., based at 5440 Hollywood Boulevard. Born Ark Keatan in Suwałki, Northeastern Poland, Harry was often confused for Buster Keaton's similarly named younger brother. Cosmopolitan Pictures Co. lasted until February 20, 1956, when Apostolof dropped out.

In August 1956, teaming up with pal Herb Niccolls, producer Edward Finney and longtime director Robert C. Dertano, 28-year-old Apostolof formed a new company called SCA Productions. With paternal pride, he gave this enterprise a name based on his own initials. The company's goal was simple: make a movie based on Apostolof's life.

Chapter 6. The Propagandist (1957)

Stephen Apostolof and partner Harry Keatan in mid-1955 in front of Geographic Films Inc., a film company owned by Keatan and located at 5440 Hollywood Blvd.

Apostolof served as SCA's main producer, with Finney as an associate producer, Niccolls a writer and Dertano a director. Finney, also a good friend of Apostolof, recruited a film crew for the upcoming production. The team would ultimately be joined by a true warhorse of the movie industry, cameraman William C. Thompson (1889–1963). A showbiz veteran with a résumé stretching back to the days of silent movies, Thompson spent most of his career working on low-budget exploitation and sexploitation flicks. Born in 1889 in Bound Brook, New Jersey, he began racking up film credits during the earliest days of Hollywood, working on such exotic-sounding fare as *Absinthe* (1914, dir. Herbert Brenon) and *The Demon* (1918, dir. George D. Baker). Interestingly enough, Thompson was colorblind—a biographical detail that found its way into the script of *Ed Wood* (1994, dir. Tim Burton)—but this didn't stop him from lensing more than 60 films over the course of 46 years, including such infamous titles as *Maniac* (1934, dir. Dwain Esper) and Ed Wood's *Glen or Glenda* (1953) and *Plan 9 from Outer Space* (1957).

(Right to left) Harry Keatan, his wife, Stephen Apostolof, an unidentified woman, and Apostolof's wife Joan at Ciro's nightclub in West Hollywood on May 26, 1955.

William C. Thompson snuggles with a lion during the shooting of *The Lion's Jaws* (1930) (courtesy James Zink).

Chapter 6. The Propagandist (1957)

Apostolof poses by a portrait of Lincoln on the set of *Journey to Freedom*.

Thompson was definitely a man with a past. Once, while working on *The Lion's Jaws* (1930, dir. Fred J. Balshofer), he even rode bareback on a wild lion and lived to tell about it. It seems that the hapless cinematographer stumbled over one of the lions and landed astride another; the beast carried him 18 feet before he fell off. "I have had narrow escapes in both cases," Thompson later joked, "but I would rather turn my camera on wild animals than wild women."[1]

With Thompson now on board, *Journey to Freedom* began filming on August 15, 1956, at Rockett Studios on Sunset and Gower. The film was shot in six days with a budget of $47,000 (about $370,000 in today's money) on a small soundstage that had once been a garage. The sets were designed by Lyle B. Reifsnider, who had previously been Oscar-nominated for his work on the Errol Flynn vehicle *Adventures of Don Juan* (1948, dir. Vincent Sherman).

An earnest, if exaggerated, political thriller, *Journey to Freedom* follows the adventures of Apostolof's semi-fictional alter ego, Stephan Raikin (played by relative newcomer Jacques Scott), a young man who escapes from a Bulgarian prison with the help of friends (Morgan Lane and Peter E. Besbas). The three fugitives then head to Istanbul, where Raikin makes a meager living playing piano at a bar. But the Communists are relentless in their pursuit of Raikin, and it's here where the story diverges from the historical timeline. The Commies kill Raikin's two friends, so our hero escapes again, this time to Paris. There he meets a lovely Frenchwoman named Nanette (Geneviève

Aumont credited as Geneviv Aumont) and starts working for Radio Free Europe. But Raikin's ultimate goal is to reach the U.S. "I can achieve so much more if I go to America," he insists.

Still pursued by the Reds, Raikin makes a hair's-breadth getaway from Paris and winds up in New York, where he weds a nurse named Mary (winsome Eve Brent, then in the early stages of a career that would span nearly 60 years). The lovebirds move to Los Angeles, where Raikin lands a radio job with Voice of America. But even there, some 6500 miles away from Bulgaria, he is not safe from the Commies. The villainous Reds try to frame poor Raikin for vehicular manslaughter, making it look like he killed a man while driving drunk. In the end, this plan is foiled, and an exonerated Raikin is allowed to enjoy a happy, free life in America with his wife and young daughter.

Even though the plot of *Journey to Freedom* veers pretty far away from the truth, the film was nevertheless close to Apostolof's heart. After all, he gave the main character his own first name. The uncommon surname came from one Spas Raikin (1922–2014), a fellow Bulgarian émigré and anti–Communist activist.

In some respects, Raikin's eventful biography vaguely parallels that of Apostolof. A theology student, he was teaching at the Sofia Seminary of St. John of Rila when religious persecution by the Communists forced him into a military labor camp. Raikin and some friends managed to escape, heading first to Southern Bulgaria before finally ending up in Greece. Raikin later continued his studies at various universities in London, Geneva and Basel, eventually coming to New York. There he got a political science degree from Columbia and was employed as a "case worker" for the Travelers Aid Society, a philanthropic service group that was under contract with the U.S. Department of Health, Education and Welfare to assist repatriation of American citizens. This is how Raikin met Lee Harvey Oswald in June 1962, less than a year and a half before the Kennedy assassination. Ex–Marine Oswald had defected to Russia in 1959 and then decided to return to his home country in 1962, bringing along his Russian-born wife Marina. When the Oswalds arrived at the Hoboken harbor, Raikin was there to meet them. The incident made it into the Warren Commission Report but wound up on the cutting room floor of *JFK* (1991, dir. Oliver Stone).

Director Robert C. Dertano lent his customary dark, minimalist vision to *Journey to Freedom*. It was a style he'd previously brought to such racy low-budget films as *Racket Girls* (1951) and *Paris After Midnight* (1951). Appropriately enough for a movie about a man being hounded by an oppressive government regime, *Journey* has a claustrophobic, almost suffocating feel. The only real relief comes from occasional exterior shots of Paris, Budapest and Istanbul. These were provided by Apostolof's old friend Stéphane Groueff and are amateurish in quality, betraying the movie's paltry budget.

Another indication of the movie's low budget was its cast, which consisted largely of unknowns. But this wasn't purely a financial decision on producer Apostolof's part. It also reflected what was happening in Hollywood at the time. Since 1948, movie attendance levels had been dropping precipitously, and movie companies were struggling to reverse that trend. But no one could agree on a strategy. Some thought the answer was to produce more low-budget films, thus giving the audience more variety. Others wanted to do just the opposite, i.e., churn out fewer films but make them of higher quality. For his part, 20th Century–Fox boss Darryl F. Zanuck thought the solution was

Chapter 6. The Propagandist (1957) 51

Jacques Scott and Eve Brent in *Journey to Freedom*. "Mr. Apostolof was a fascinating man and very good to me. Working for him was a great experience," said Brent.

to start cultivating the next generation of stars. "Hollywood is undergoing a period of transition," he wrote, "and in my opinion nothing is more important to meet the challenging conditions of thee future than the development of New Faces."[2]

In December 1956, *Motion Picture Herald* published an article about Apostolof, praising his decision to use unknown actors in *Journey to Freedom*. The magazine described the Bulgarian as a "'brave' young man with ideas" and stated that he had already tried the New Faces policy in Europe with "an independent feature entitled *The Last Mile to El Diablo*, with, of course, unknown actors."[3] Again, no solid information about this alleged movie has ever surfaced in the last half-century plus.

It's not necessary to have established box office names in your casts when you have an unusual story and a top-quality entertainment," Apostolof confidently stated in the article. "The public is mainly interested in sound entertainment—preferably something new and progressive in the way of subject matter—and the fans always welcome fresh faces in fine pictures." In another article, Apostolof made a rather bold prediction that, thanks to the ubiquity of television, the faces of some actors will "wear out" from use and this will lead to "the retirement of many of our long-established motion picture stars."[4]

True to his credo, Apostolof gave the lead male role in *Journey to Freedom* to the absolutely unknown Jacques Scott. After filming ended, Apostolof was surprised to find out that Scott was actually one Jacques Francis Scott-Quekett, son of the British ambassador in Nice, France, and entitled (at least in Scotland) to the title of "Sir." Such a gentleman was Scott, he even began a letter to Apostolof with the heading "Tuesday, after tea." Scott had arrived in Hollywood a few years earlier and, unable to crash the studio gates, he worked at such jobs as bartender, bank teller, dancing teacher, factory helper, machine operator, cook, painter and assistant restaurant manager. He had made something of a name for himself as a martial arts master, having won the California Judo Championships in 1952 and 1953. Scott was described in a newspaper write-up as "a male Bardot,"[5] whatever that means. Agent Wynn Rocamora, the man who discovered Dorothy Lamour and Diana Lynn, was touting Scott as Hollywood's next big star. This audacious prediction did not come true, but Scott did score a few more TV and film assignments. After starring in *Journey to Freedom*, he played June Allyson's fortune-seeking fiancé in *You Can't Run Away from It* (1956, dir. Dick Powell), a musical comedy whose cast also included Jack Lemmon. Appropriately enough, seeing as how Scott's parents were hotel owners in Nice, he snared the role of debonair hotel clerk Paul Monteney on the 1958 sitcom *The Ann Sothern Show*. Scott also worked "like a beaver on a petrified log to shed his accent,"[6] as one gossip columnist put it, merely to find himself pigeonholed. It seems Hollywood only wanted him to play Frenchmen.

The leading lady in *Journey to Freedom* was Eve Brent (1929–2011), a former Miss Texas who later enjoyed a successful career as a character actress in film and television. Brent was born Jean Ann Ewers in Texas in 1930 and began acting on the radio as a child. Apostolof recalled, "I saw her doing a small role in a film, *Gun Girl* [sic],[7] and I realized that she was the type of an actress I needed for my film. She is an excellent actress, has the potential, like Jacques Scott, to become a star."[8]

Brent would go down in Hollywood history as one of 12 actresses to play the role of Jane in the *Tarzan* film franchise. By her own account, she took this particular role to please her six-year-old son. Brent receives credit for rebooting Tarzan's love life in *Tarzan and the Trappers* (1958, dir. Charles F. Haas) and *Tarzan's Fight for Life* (1958, dir. H. Bruce Humberstone) but admits it was a "disastrous career move"[9] in the long run.

"I really couldn't get work as an actress because of Jane," Brent told a *Tarzan* fansite in 2007. "You get stereotyped, at least in the business at that time."

The other major female role in *Journey to Freedom*, that of temptress Nanette, was played by Geneviève Aumont, a French actress who, as Hollywood gossip columnist Mike Connolly once quipped, had "more lines than Maginot."[10] She would later play Cary Grant's girlfriend in *An Affair to Remember* (1957, dir. Leo McCarey) and got to enjoy some screen time with Grant before his character meets Deborah Kerr. Showbiz legend had it that Aumont was the daughter of the late Charles Aumont, who owned and operated the famous Paris cabaret Moulin Rouge between 1902 and 1935.

Perhaps the only actor from *Journey to Freedom* who is instantly recognizable to modern audiences is the Swedish-born wrestler Tor Johnson (1903–1971), a bald, hulking mountain of a man whose intimidating appearance earned him supporting and sometimes leading roles in low-budget horror and sci-fi movies for decades.

"I found Tor by looking through the Screen Actors Guild directory," Apostolof recalled. "I needed someone big and mean, and when I saw Tor's picture I said, 'That's him!'"[11] In *Journey to Freedom,* Johnson plays the Giant Turk, who brutalizes protago-

Chapter 6. The Propagandist (1957)

The Giant Turk (Tor Johnson) brutalizes *Journey to Freedom* protagonist Stephan Raikin (Jacques Scott).

nist Stephan Raikin in an Istanbul bar while shouting, "My grandfather was beaten to death by a Bulgarian!" As Tor's fans know, that's about all the dialogue he could handle.

Apostolof awarded himself a small role in *Journey to Freedom* as an anonymous Frenchman with a beret and mustache in a Parisian cabaret. This was just the first of a series of cameo appearances he would make in his own films. Like his favorite director, Alfred Hitchcock, Apostolof relished the opportunity to pass in front of the camera for a few seconds. He also cast his baby daughter Polly in the role of Stephan Raikin's child.

When Apostolof wrapped *Journey to Freedom* in the summer of 1956, he could not have been prouder of himself and his achievement. But his joy would be short-lived and would be tarnished by problems with the film's distribution. Initially, *Journey* was going to be distributed by Allied Pictures, but that never happened. Apostolof said, "Another friend of mine, Al Cushman, said to me, 'How can you make a film without distribution? What are you going to do with it now? Show it at the A&P?!' I was so concerned with making a film that I never thought about the distribution."[12]

Fortunately for Apostolof, the completion of *Journey to Freedom* coincided with the Hungarian Revolution of 1956. This uprising began on October 23 as a spontaneous student protest against the Soviet-mandated policies of the Hungarian People's Republic, i.e., the socialist state that controlled Hungary from 1949 to 1989. This leaderless protest grew into a nationwide revolt that was quickly crushed beneath the bootheel

Apostolof gave himself a cameo in *Journey to Freedom* as an anonymous Frenchman wearing a beret.

of the Soviet Red Army. Within the span of just a few weeks, the riots claimed the lives of 2500 citizens and 700 Soviet soldiers. As a result, over 200,000 Hungarians fled the country.

Naturally, these headline-grabbing events captured the attention of the West. Apostolof took this as an opportunity to secure distribution for *Journey to Freedom*. After all, he had a film ready to go that dealt with roughly the same subject matter. The timing was ideal. *Film Daily* noted that all the big companies, almost without exception, were registering titles and dusting off old stories for which they held the rights and were bidding on original screenplays related to the rise of Communism. The most sought-after book of 1956 was the nonfiction *Deliver Us from Evil: The Story of Vietnam's Flight to Freedom* by Thomas Anthony Dooley III, an American physician, humanitarian and staunch anti–Communist activist. In 1954, Dooley had been a key figure in Operation Passage to Freedom, which helped transport hundreds of thousands of Vietnamese citizens and soldiers from Communist-controlled North Vietnam into South Vietnam. Dooley sold the rights to his book to Universal, hoping to use the money to further the anti–Communist cause. But no movie of Dooley's story ever reached the screen.

In mid–December 1956, Apostolof traveled to Washington, D.C., to attend a world charity premiere of *Journey to Freedom*. Proceeds from the event went to the Hungarian Refugee Relief Fund, a charity established in Toronto by Hungarian expats to support refugees from the revolution in their homeland.¹³ In a gambit to attract more attention to his film, Apostolof met with U.N. officials in New York. This did garner some attention, with Radio Free Europe and the Bulgarian edition of Voice of America making brief announcements about the film. But this fleeting publicity was not enough to secure a distribution deal for *Journey to Freedom*. Apostolof had a serious problem: He'd made a movie but had no way of getting it into theaters. He said, "I wanted to submit the finished picture to 20th Century–Fox but they said, 'Who are the stars?' I said, 'What stars? What are you talking about? My budget was peanuts!' So I had a film but no distribution. Nothing!"¹⁴

Apostolof's salvation arrived in the form of his close friend Rudy Ralston, a producer at Republic Pictures.

In 1956, Apostolof bought a full-page ad in *Variety* announcing that he had wrapped *Journey to Freedom* and was preparing his next film, *7 Rue Pigale* [sic]. In early 1957, the entertainment press reported that Apostolof had cast actresses Yvonne Monlaur and Claudine Dupuis for the project.

That company's roots stretch back to the earliest days of Hollywood. It began as a motion picture processing lab in 1915. In 1935, under the leadership of president Herbert J. Yates, it became a full-fledged studio making movies of its own. Republic's maiden production was a revenge Western called *Westward Ho* (1935, dir. Robert N. Bradbury), starring John Wayne. The former Marion Morrison made dozens of cowboy pictures for Republic on his way to becoming one of Hollywood's all-time biggest stars.

The ultra-prolific Republic had its headquarters in Studio City in the San Fernando Valley. It made movies with the widest possible audience appeal, specializing in action films, Westerns, mysteries and melodramas. This type of entertainment earned Republic the nickname "The Thrill Factory." Though Republic did occasionally release high-profile pictures like *The Quiet Man* (1952, dir. John Ford) and *Macbeth* (1948, dir. Orson Welles), it was more closely associated with cheapies, the kind of films that might play at Saturday afternoon matinees. Besides Wayne, the studio's stable of stars included Roy Rogers and Gene Autry.

As it happens, Rudy Ralston's sister, actress Vera Ralston, was married to Republic's head honcho Yates. So Rudy arranged a screening of *Journey to Freedom* at the studio with brother-in-law Yates in attendance. After the screening, Yates approached Apostolof: "Ah, I think we can do something with it." The two men shook hands. Years later, Apostolof said of the fateful incident: "I'll never forget when I first met Yates. He said, 'You must be a very brave man!' I thought he was talking about my escape. But no. He said, 'Making a picture without distribution.'"[15] In Hollywood, that *was* a sign of true bravery!

Yates decided to distribute *Journey to Freedom*. This probably had less to do with the film's merits than with Yates' promise to shareholders that Republic would release 20 new films in 1957. Over the years, Republic gradually became a distributor of lower-quality films, producing fewer and fewer titles of its own. Republic had produced and released approximately 50 to 60 pictures annually in its best years but only managed 26 in 1957, 17 in 1958 and just five in 1959. Republic reported a loss of $1,362,420 in 1957, the year it adopted *Journey to Freedom*.[16] Meanwhile, the company had also cultivated a tradition of making and/or distributing Cold War–era propaganda titles like *The Red Menace* (1949, dir. R.G. Springsteen).

Journey to Freedom opened in American theaters on June 21, 1957. Reviews were both rare and unkind. According to *Motion Picture Exhibitor:*

> This is a strange picture. Everyone speaks English with an accent, including the off-screen narrator who connects many of the sequences. It has been given a very cheap production, and the acting seems pretty amateurish at times. There are okay scenic shots of Istanbul, Paris, American cities, and there is enough action, but for the most part this is below par filler for the lower half of the program in undiscriminating spots.[17]

The questionnaires Apostolof had circulated at a test screening of *Journey to Freedom* did not yield encouraging results either. The producer kept these disheartening surveys in his archives for years afterward. "You should have saved your money and spared us this film," wrote one disgruntled viewer. Despite its questionable reception, *Journey to Freedom* did achieve one thing for Apostolof: It put him on the map in Hollywood. In the months surrounding the film's release, he was mentioned in the pages of every major publication in Tinseltown.

In 1956, the American newspapers ran a syndicated article with the headline "Bulgarian Refugee Apostolof, 28, Making Big Stir as New Director." In it, the columnist Walt Hackett declared, "[T]he most amazing saga of modern Hollywood is probably that of Stephen Apostolof, a young Bulgarian refugee who escaped after three-and-a-half years of imprisonment and torture by the Reds in his native country in 1948, arrived at his ultimate destination here in 1952, and is now making major movies under the banner of his own independent production."[18]

When Republic started distributing *Journey to Freedom*, it marked the beginning of a lengthy collaboration between Apostolof and the studio. He became a fixture there, assisting in various capacities on numerous productions. His experience working for the low-budget studio helped him to eventually become a successful independent producer-director in his own right. He recalled, "Republic became like a family to me. I met lots of wonderful people there like John Wayne and Audie Murphy. I would spend all my time there, eating, drinking, having dinner and lunch there. And when I got

Chapter 6. The Propagandist (1957)

A color one sheet for *Journey to Freedom*.

Apostolof (seated in the front row, third from right) on the set of an unknown Republic Western in the late 1950s.

divorced [from Joan], I lived there."[19] A lot of the projects on which Apostolof worked in Republic in the late 1950s were Westerns filmed in the Los Angeles area.

Christopher Apostolof laughs when he thinks about his father's time at Republic. "My father was like one of those Italians who shot spaghetti Westerns. What the hell does a Bulgarian immigrant know about the Wild West?" He remembers his father telling him that he hated working with horses. "They were shooting another Western, so Steve was with the crew somewhere in the desert. The director yells 'Action!', and since the horses knew that word, they would suddenly lose it! After several unsuccessful attempts, the director finally found a solution and just said 'Go!'" says Christopher.[20]

In late 1956, shortly after the completion of *Journey to Freedom*, several brief items appeared in the press concerning Apostolof's upcoming projects. The *Los Angeles Times* reported that he was "negotiating through his European representatives" with French writer Françoise Sagan to write a screenplay based on the life of artist Amedeo Modigliani.[21] In 1954, at age 18, Sagan had published the bestseller *Bonjour Tristesse* (*Hello, Sadness*), a novel whose title came from a Paul Éluard poem. An instant hit, it became a film in 1958, directed by Otto Preminger. As for those "European representatives," this could be a reference to Apostolof's old friend Stéphane Groueff, who was well-connected in the French art and literary circles.

Apostolof wanted Sagan to write the script for a Modigliani biopic called *Jeanne*.

Chapter 6. The Propagandist (1957)   59

For this photograph, Apostolof, only five foot six, had to climb on a wooden box in order to look through the camera.

The film was named for Jeanne Hébuterne, lover and muse of the Italian artist. Hébuterne didn't live to see the age of 22, committing suicide the day after Modigliani's death in 1920. The ever-optimistic Apostolof said he was considering Leslie Caron for the title role. The French-born dancer Caron had been discovered several years earlier by MGM star Gene Kelly, when he needed a new leading lady to replace the pregnant Cyd Charisse in *An American in Paris* (1951, dir. Vincente Minnelli). That film made Caron a star, and by the late 1950s, she was committed to a seven-year MGM contract that didn't allow her to appear in outside productions. *Jeanne* would have been out of the question for her. It's possible that Apostolof wanted her for this thwarted project because she was a good friend of Ginette, the wife of his friend Boris Kutchukov. (In 1947, Ginette and Leslie had both been part of Roland Petit's company, Les Ballets des Champs-Élysées.)

Jeanne wasn't the only iron the ambitious Apostolof had in the fire. In late 1956, the press reported that he was also working on *From Out of the Darkness,* an American-French co-production with the German-born Hedi Duval in the lead. According to the *Los Angeles Times,* the movie, which Apostolof was slated to direct, would deal with "the conquest of mental illness under modern methods of mental hygiene."[22] On November 10, 1956, Apostolof and *Journey to Freedom* associate producer Stafford B. Harrison invited actors from the Little Theatre Group in San Francisco to a casting call for *From Out of the Darkness*.[23] Three days later, Apostolof signed a contract with successful Hollywood screenwriter Howard Estabrook, who had worked with such esteemed directors as George Cukor, Raoul Walsh, Frank Borzage and Victor Fleming and an Oscar winner for his work on *Cimarron* (1931, dir. Wesley Ruggles). Politically, Apostolof and Estabrook were definitely on the same wavelength. In the early '50s, Estabrook had cooperated with the House Un-American Activities Committee in its crusade against Communism.

As he had done with *Journey to Freedom*, Apostolof planned to use unknown actors in *From Out of the Darkness*, continuing to comply with Hollywood's New Faces policy. In November 1956, actor John Goddard tested for the role of an Irish policeman in the film. Another prospective cast member was *Journey to Freedom* veteran Jacques Scott. Despite all these preparations, *From Out of the Darkness* was never realized.

Another abandoned project from this era was *7 Rue Pigalle*. Apostolof said the title was inspired by an address where he had lived while in Paris in the late 1940s, following his escape from Bulgaria. In fact, 7 Rue Pigalle was the address of Rat Mort (The Dead Rat), a cabaret known for its *demimondaine* clientele. Apostolof described *Pigalle* to the press as a "mysterious melodrama" that he would direct himself. The script was originally to be penned by Houston Branch, working from an original story by Leslie Anton. But after some negotiations with Branch, Apostolof settled on his old friend Herb Niccolls. Again, Apostolof aimed high with this project, planning to shoot on location in Paris with a French cast. *7 Rue Pigalle* was another miscarriage, destined never to reach the screen.

Apostolof made some interesting show business contacts during his time at Republic. One example was prolific pulp writer Erle Stanley Gardner, creator of the fictional lawyer Perry Mason, whose courtroom heroics had been the subject of numerous novels since the 1930s. According to Apostolof, he was having dinner at a Studio City restaurant when he met Gardner. The Bulgarian proposed a TV series based on the Mason books, to be produced by Republic. Apostolof thought that Mason's cases were perfect for the small screen, and Gardner agreed on the condition that he receive one percent of the profits on each rerun of the series. A few days later, Apostolof approached Republic honcho Herb Yates with the idea for the series.

"Boss," said Apostolof, "I can bring Perry Mason to Republic!"[24]

But Yates was not enthusiastic about the project and was dead set against giving any percentage of the profits to a writer. So the Republic series was never to be. This proved to be a major miscalculation on Yates' part. Gardner's novels would later become the basis for an extremely successful 1957–66 CBS series with Raymond Burr in the title role. The show remains a staple of TV syndication to this day.

Apostolof later mused about Yates' miserly business practices: "At that time, actors had just started getting residuals. Every studio agreed to give them residuals except Republic. Yates said, 'No, I'm not paying them twice. They're not my partners. I paid them once already. That's it!'" Apparently, Yates wasn't keen on sharing the wealth with his writers either.[25]

Just how many films Apostolof worked on during his tenure at Republic is unclear. In some of his professional résumés, he claimed to have produced 12 films for the studio, including such titles as *Five Stations to Hell* and *Crazy Circle*. Some of these do resemble titles that were actually released by Republic. There was no *Crazy Circle,* but Republic did release a film called *The Crooked Circle* (1957, dir. Joseph Kane). Perhaps Apostolof was simply boasting. Or maybe he was really involved in producing these movies, but they were never distributed to cinemas. This is quite possible, since in the late 1950s Republic went through some big changes. In 1958, Yates told his shareholders that the studio would stop producing feature films. The distribution branch of the studio closed the next year. The whole Republic operation was defunct by 1967, but by that time, Apostolof was on his own.

"My father spent years at Republic, and one of his problems is that his films didn't see the light of the day," Christopher Apostolof says. "He produced films, but they didn't get screened, and he was frustrated more and more of his work in the studio system."[26] According to Christopher, this was the main reason why his father chose to become an independent producer-director.

Determined to keep his film career alive, Apostolof briefly considered making horror and sci-fi movies, possibly north of the border. In 1958, The *Toronto Daily Star* reported that "a Hollywood specialist in horror films hopes to make Toronto a base for filming up to 15 feature movies a year."[27] The newspaper also declared that Apostolof had completed negotiations to shoot two films in Canada. The first was called *Monster from the Grave* and was set to feature the legendary Lon Chaney, Jr., and Tor Johnson. (Apostolof had already worked with Tor on *Journey to Freedom*.) The second film was a sci-fi thriller titled *Man from the Moon*. Both films were to be scripted by Roger Garis, best known as the author of the *Outboard Boys* book series. According to the article, Apostolof chose Toronto because it was cheaper to film there than Hollywood, and there were plenty of English-speaking actors to play the supporting roles. And as the *Star* pointed out, it didn't hurt that Apostolof's own wife was "a Toronto girl."[28]

Ultimately, though, this proved to be more idle talk. When Apostolof began producing and directing his own films, he did so in California. Years later, he did set one of his films, *The Snow Bunnies* (1972), in Canada. But even this was filmed entirely in the Golden State.

If anything, living in the United States only strengthened Apostolof's anti–Communist leanings. In August 1956, America had a most unusual guest: Soviet Deputy Minister of Culture Vladimir Surin. He visited for two weeks, stopping in New York and Hollywood in an attempt to warm relations between the Soviet Union and the U.S. during an intense phase of the Cold War. Surin met with many cultural and entertainment ambassadors and stated that the Soviet Culture Ministry was open to any kind of "cultural exchange" between the two nations. When asked by American journalists if he'd give Marilyn Monroe a starring role in a Soviet-made film, Surin blithely answered, "We don't have anything against Miss Monroe or any other actress. Any one of them would be acceptable if they appeared in a film that was on a high artistic level."[29]

On August 18, Surin had a lunchtime meeting with producer Michael Todd, whose Oscar-winning *Around the World in 80 Days* (1956, dir. Michael Anderson) was due to be released two months later. That lavish, all-star film was just one of the epics

Apostolof as a Mexican on the set of an unknown Republic Western. His dark complexion would often make people think that he was Mexican. Apostolof's children even thought he was playing Ricky Ricardo in the 1950s TV show *I Love Lucy*.

Hollywood was producing in the mid–1950s in an attempt to lure audiences away from their TV screens and back into movie theaters. At the time, Todd was toying with the idea of adapting Leo Tolstoy's *War and Peace* for the screen. The dense Russian novel had every necessary ingredient for a blockbuster: epic battle scenes, historical intrigue and a love triangle. Best of all, it wasn't copyrighted. But two other major producers, David O. Selznick and Dino De Laurentiis, had similar plans for Tolstoy's book. Todd told Surin about his desire to adapt *War and Peace,* and the deputy minister assured the producer that Americans were welcome to film it in the USSR, where there was "complete freedom of speech."[30]

Apostolof, for one, wasn't buying it. He laughed out loud when he read about Todd's plans to shoot *War and Peace* in the Soviet Union. But when his amusement turned to anger, he decided to pen an open letter to Todd in the pages of *Daily Variety*, unleashing his anti–Communist sentiments and sarcastically mocking Todd's naiveté. Naturally, he did not miss the opportunity to work in a plug for himself along the way.

Identifying himself as "someone who has recently escaped from behind the Iron Curtain," Apostolof made the boldest of declarations (in all caps, no less): "FREEDOM DOES NOT EXIST IN RUSSIA." He elaborated: "Artistic freedom exists in one country without question and that is the United States of America." He offered his own film, *Journey to Freedom,* as an example: "Were I to attempt this picture abroad, it would not be made, and being made I probably would pay for it with my life." Apostolof insisted that for Todd or any American film producer to do business with the Russians would be like Judas betraying Christ. Apostolof begged Todd, "Don't sell your birthright or that of your American brothers for thirty pieces of silver." He signed the letter "Patriotically yours" and identified himself as the President of SCA Film Productions.[31]

Apostolof must have been happy to know that, in the end, Todd did not shoot *War and Peace* in Soviet Russia as planned. He never got the chance, since another producer had beaten him to the punch. Dino De Laurentiis knew that the only way to convince Paramount to greenlight the project was to supply them with a finished script. So he divided the novel into equal sections and assigned them to different Italian screenwriters. Three weeks later, he collected the pieces, hastily translated them into English, and sent Paramount a massive (506-page) script. The studio okayed the project, and *War and Peace* began filming in Italy with director King Vidor and a cast including Audrey Hepburn, Henry Fonda, Mel Ferrer and Vittorio Gassman.

"Dad passionately hated the Communists," remembered Apostolof's eldest son Steve. "Once, just joking about this topic at dinner, I said something about his 'Communist upbringing.' Just off the cuff, without thinking much. He didn't talk to me for months."[32] His brother Christopher cites an incident from the 1990s: His friend Scott visited the house wearing a then-fashionable "USSR" T-shirt with a hammer and sickle design. Apostolof was not amused.

Christopher tells what happened next: "Scott enters, Steve turns around, and his eyes stopped on Scott's shirt. And they stay there for 30 seconds ... dead silence! Finally he looks up and says, 'Scott, I love you like a son, so I will not kill you.' Scott just said, 'I will never wear this shirt again!'"[33] The incident says a lot about Apostolof's core beliefs.

"As you can call someone a Christian, a Muslim or a Jew, Dad was anti–Communist," says Christopher. "And if he knew that someone has leftist beliefs, he would never talk to him."[34]

In early 1957, Apostolof finished a course at the American Institute of Banking. In July of that year, he started working as a trust supervisor at Bank of America on 1130 South Figueroa in Central Los Angeles. On October 1, the filmmaker and his wife welcomed their first son, and Apostolof decided to name the child after himself, Stephen Christie Apostolof.

The pregnancy had not been without complications. "My dad was married to my mother when she contracted polio in 1957, maybe in Mexico, when she was pregnant with my dad's first son Stephen," remembers Apostolof's daughter Susan.[35] This proved to be a pivotal issue in the couple's marriage as well. According to Susan, Apostolof blamed Joan for not taking the proper medical precautions even though she was a nurse.

"He said, 'She gave the vaccine to others but never took it herself.' There was talk that maybe she contracted it in Mexico, but she had it while pregnant with Stevie, and he was born not at Kaiser, where my sister Polly and I were born, but at St. Joseph's Hospital because it could accommodate her condition. She was placed into an iron lung after the birth. Thankfully, she did not have any lasting effects from it, or none that we ever knew of. And Stevie has had no effects either."

Susan can sympathize with her mother's point of view, controversial as it was. "My mom was kind of a rebel and skeptical of many things, and the polio vaccine was one of them. I think it was a hard thing for my dad because when he told me about it, he was pretty mad about her not taking the vaccine."[36]

CHAPTER 7

The Family Man
(1958–1965)

"The nicest things in the world happen to me by mistake, by just happening. On this earth, I believe in the Big Power upstairs."—Stephen C. Apostolof

On November 26, 1959, Stephen and Joan Apostolof welcomed their fourth child into the world, a baby girl they named Susan Joanne. Meanwhile, as the patriarch of a growing household, Apostolof kept working. His job at Bank of America included operating an IBM 407, one of the first computers used by American banks after World War II. Debuting in 1949, the 407 wasn't exactly a computer *per se*, but rather a mechanical tabulating machine, closer in size and design to a lathe or a punch card machine than to today's desktop and laptop models. Apostolof's repetitive but necessary job was to sort the punched cards and load them into the machine that read them. Though hardly as exciting as making movies, the Bank of America job provided a steady source of income for the Apostolof family for years. On March 28, 1960, Apostolof was appointed "pro-assistant cashier" at the Bank of America data processing center. He worked there until April 1964, all while trying to make it in the film business.

Near the end of 1958, Apostolof applied for American citizenship for the first time. In the naturalization documents, he dutifully listed the major events in his life so far, but in the "family" column, he indicated only two children, not three. Intentionally or not, he had omitted his eldest daughter Maria, who'd been born out of wedlock. But Apostolof's past was about to catch up with him. In mid-1960, Maria's adopted family from Colombia called her grandparents in Toronto, who, in turn, called Joan. The woman who had adopted Maria eight years previously had died. Her widowed husband, moreover, had married another woman. They had started their own family, and the new wife didn't want an adopted child in it.

"Maria was very happy as a child," recalls Shelley, Apostolof's third and final wife. "But then her adoptive mother died, and her father met another woman. Maria reminded her of the previous woman, so the new wife wanted to get rid of her."[1]

Maria was sent back to Toronto where she lived for eight months with a temporary family. In November 1960, Joan flew to Toronto to reunite and bond with her daughter. Apostolof followed and soon after that the three of them traveled back to Los Angeles by flight via Chicago. Initially, Maria didn't speak any English, but she learned quickly and very soon got assimilated into the new family.

"Dad understood I needed a mother, always," says Maria Apostolof. "Dad loved

From 1957 to 1964, Apostolof worked as a clerk at Bank of America to support his family while trying to make it in the film industry.

all of his children and he always said 'We are family' despite his divorce with Mom. He taught us how to camp, ski and eat at restaurants and we were always grateful to him for his va-va-voom personality and love."[2]

Apostolof's woes did not end with his children. He had serious money problems as well. On February 25, 1961, he received a report from Republic stating that *Journey to Freedom* had earned a total of $26,069. Of this, $7105 was to be paid to him as the film's producer. But this wasn't enough to keep Apostolof afloat. On September 12, 1961, with only $4 left in his bank account, he declared bankruptcy. Apostolof lost control of *Journey to Freedom*, which was confiscated by his creditors. The court even took his favorite accordion, the one that had accompanied him from Bulgaria to America.

On December 8, 1960, Apostolof, together with Dr. Matthew Jeikoff (1908–1984) and a small group of Bulgarian emigrants, founded St. George, the first Bulgarian Eastern Orthodox Church in Los Angeles. The main sponsor and donor was Dr. Jeikoff,

In 1960, Maria (far right) shared her first Christmas with her siblings (left to right) Polly, Steve, and Susie. Says Polly, "Dad got mad no one noticed the TV he got us."

who bought a house on 150 South Alexandria Avenue in Hollywood's Little Armenia neighborhood. Apostolof later became a lifelong trustee of St. George. His portrait still hangs inside the church, and his name is listed on a memorial plaque on its facade.

"My father was very religious," says Apostolof's daughter Susan, "which is to a certain extent a contradiction. But Bulgarian church allows divorce, so why not adult films? But he was a very important person in the Bulgarian church, he was a well-respected man there."[3]

Eager to reconnect with their homeland, the Bulgarian diaspora in Los Angeles soon flocked to St. George. A staunch monarchist, Dr. Jeikoff maintained his connection with Simeon II, the exiled king of Bulgaria, and the church he had co-founded became a haven for the like-minded monarchists and anti–Communists in the city. But it was also a place where Bulgarian-Americans could gather socially and speak their native language.

A jubilant Apostolof shakes hands with Simeon II, the exiled King of Bulgaria, after a Bulgarian Orthodox divine liturgy at St. George church in 1993.

"There was a kitchen on the second floor where they were having parties every night," recalled Steve Apostolof, who visited the church regularly as a kid. "After the first-floor service was over, they would start drinking and eating Bulgarian food."[4] The children, not understanding a word of what was being said, simply sat off to the side and observed.

By the early 1960s, Apostolof's marriage to Joan was disintegrating. The filmmaker even accused his first wife of trying to poison him. According to documents that Apostolof's lawyer Harold A. Abeles (1926–2001) submitted to the court, "[I]n or about the month of March 1963, Cross-Defendant deliberately, wilfully and maliciously gave Cross-Complainant the wrong medicine with the intent to inflict upon Cross-Complainant grievous bodily injury and harm. Cross-Complainant was thus rendered sick, required extensive medical attention and was brought to the brink of death."

In other words, Joan supposedly gave Apostolof medicine that thickened his blood when he needed one that did just the opposite. Did this actually happen? Apostolof's third wife Shelley is convinced this is just one of her husband's many tall tales. Apostolof's eldest son was diplomatic on the subject:

> It depends on whom you ask. My father felt that she had done it. He used to tell me how she gave him the wrong medicine because she was a nurse and tried to kill him. My mother said that this was the

most ridiculous thing she ever heard. I cannot imagine her doing that, and I don't see a reason why she would. But then again, I don't know why my father would say that. It wasn't a nice divorce. It wasn't good for us kids at the time. He said a lot of things about her, but it's hard to know what's true and what's not.[5]

I think if my mother really wanted to get rid of Dad, she would have done it the right way. But I can't imagine it. In any divorce, things are sad. There are hurt feelings, a lot of anger. So it's not uncommon for people to invent things to be presented in a better light or, more importantly, to put the other party in the case in a bad light to take whatever they want from the court.[6]

Steve believed that the real cause of his father's divorce from Joan was infidelity. "Mom had known that Dad was not faithful for years and years. And it took its toll. Mom was unfaithful to Dad and when Dad found about it, that was it. There's a double standard here. It's okay for men to do it, but if a woman does it, you have to get rid of her. So they broke up."[7]

The divorce proceedings even complicated Apostolof's citizenship status. Or at least that's how he saw it. Joan became a U.S. citizen on June 17, 1960. Apostolof, however, tried for years to become a naturalized American citizen but faced numerous problems on this front following his divorce from Joan. The filmmaker believed his ex-wife had badmouthed him to immigration officials. Again, their son Steve put these events in perspective:

They came and said, "What can you tell us about Steve Apostolof?" You know, you don't really want to ask a divorced wife what she thinks of the guy. And she told the truth, that she wasn't happy with him, that she was having some problems with the child support. And Dad kind of blamed her for not getting his naturalization at that time.[8]

In December 1963, Apostolof and Joan officially ended their 12-year marriage. After the divorce, Joan left the family home at 3456 Rowena Avenue and moved to a new place at 1909½ Talmadge Street. Apostolof moved to 3710 Los Feliz Boulevard. Initially, the court granted Apostolof custody of his children, but in May 1964, the kids went to live with Joan. According to Shelley, Apostolof's third wife, this happened because Apostolof couldn't take proper care of them. He agreed to give up custody under the condition of being excused from paying alimony. Despite all this, the filmmaker helped his kids in any way he could.

Shelley still remembers how her husband supported his children. "He gave them money when they needed it," she says. "He might have $20 in his pocket and this could be his last money, but he would give it to the kids. Steve was very, very generous with them."[9]

Apostolof didn't see his kids as often after the court gave custody to Joan, but they would spend every other weekend at his place. As in many other American families touched by divorce, these bi-weekly sleepovers became routine. In the 1960s, most children of divorced parents lived with their mothers. Apostolof's kids were no exception. In 1965, they moved to a house in Canoga Park and stayed there a few years, and then in 1967 moved to Simi Valley, a town in Ventura Country. Sometimes Apostolof would take the kids to soccer games in Griffith Park. Other times, he would cook for them or take them to restaurants. Occasionally, he would take them skiing at Mammoth Mountain, a popular resort just west of the California-Nevada border. Mammoth became such a part of Apostolof's life that he even incorporated the resort into two of his later films. To this day, his children retain vivid memories of those ski trips. Susan says, "Dad would take us, the four kids, in his white Oldsmobile Cutlass, put the skis between the seats and drive us to the hotel of his Bulgarian friend Mike Mikhailof. On our way to the mountain, he would always stop at the street stalls and buy loads of fruit, more than we could ever eat."[10]

Apostolof, an avid skier himself, was extremely patient when teaching the sport to his children. He would descend the slopes with them, holding them by the shoulders, straddling them with his skis. He had affectionate nicknames for all his kids. Maria was Mechka (meaning "bear" in Bulgarian, although none of the kids remember Apostolof calling his daughter that), Polly was Banana, Steven was Stevie, and Susan was Zuzu—after Zuzu Bailey from the Christmas classic *It's a Wonderful Life* (1946, dir. Frank Capra). According to Steve Apostolof:

> Dad has always been a social animal. Whenever we went to see him on the weekends, there were a lot of friends. They were always drinking. The barbecue was always sizzling. Later on, in the 1970s when he bought the house in Studio City, he was having big parties once a year. He liked to be around people and loved to show off and spend money. For him, that was fun. The production was always big. Always expensive.[11]

Apostolof enjoyed his newfound bachelor lifestyle in the early 1960s and spent a lot of time entertaining his friends. With his magnetic personality, he was constantly surrounded by women. He treated his kids like grownups and regularly introduced them to his friends. Typically, at one of his lively get-togethers, Apostolof would sit quietly on the couch with his kids and watch TV as his house slowly filled with guests. While alcohol remains popular as a social lubricant today, that's nothing compared to its omnipresence in the early 1960s. And booze, his children still remember, was the fuel for those rather raucous parties.

"People would come around 10 or 11 in the morning and would start with Bloody Marys," recalled Steve Apostolof. "Then they would move to other cocktails and would end the evening with hard liquor. Meanwhile, they ate steaks, salad and so on, until late into the night."[12]

Those years made a strong impression on Polly Apostolof. "The apartment in Los Feliz was great. Today I imagine it like in the TV series *Melrose Place*, except that the action takes place in the '60s. Its location was fantastic: right next to Griffith Park, where there were a lot of hippies and couples. It was a crazy time living in Hollywood at the time."[13] Those much-remembered weekend sleepovers usually ended with Apostolof giving his kids some money and bringing them back to Joan.

Four of Apostolof's kids were born near the end of the year, so this was always a festive time for the family. Apostolof always threw elaborate birthday parties for them, organized like lavish Hollywood productions with large, ornate cakes and pristinely wrapped gifts. "Dad spent an awful lot of time packing every present. He had an eye for detail and everything looked wonderful," recalls Susan.[14] As she saw it, those birthday parties were the strongest evidence of her father's desire for total control over everything happening around him. Both on the set and at home, Stephen C. Apostolof was a consummate director. And, whatever the event, he always had a camera there to document it. "Dad would arrange us, take a picture and then would suddenly decide that the photo may not have turned out well and would say, 'Oh, no, no, no! Let's take another

(Left to right) Steve, Maria, Polly, and Susie Apostolof model their Halloween costumes in the early 1960s.

one.' Then he would make a few more photos until they were the way he wanted them to be," recalls Susan.[15]

Meanwhile, amid all this family togetherness, Apostolof's most famous film was looming on the horizon.

CHAPTER 8

The Director of the Dead
(1965–1966)

> *"Eddie's world was entirely different from yours and mine. I wake up in the morning, I look at the sun, I say, what a gorgeous day. He'd wake up in the morning and look at the sun and say, aha, the ghouls appeared in the dawn..."*—Stephen C. Apostolof about Edward D. Wood, Jr.[1]

By the late 1950s, Hollywood was in turmoil. The studio system that had defined the town's Golden Age was gasping for breath. Meanwhile, television was siphoning away viewers by the millions. Exhibitors were resorting to gimmicks to lure patrons away from their idiot boxes and back to movie theaters. America was undergoing demographic and cultural shifts that were affecting the nation's moviegoing habits. For one thing, Americans were fleeing the cities for the suburbs. This trend raised the cost of going to the movies, leading in turn to the construction of over 4000 suburban drive-ins across the country. In June 1956, for the first time ever, more Americans went to drive-ins than to traditional hard-top theaters.

Hollywood was also facing increased competition from foreign films, which at the time were more daring and outrageous than their domestic counterparts. Apostolof took notice of these trends and saw an opportunity for himself. "There were also those European films with lots of sex," he observed. "The arthouse films. I said that was one niche where I could compete."[2]

Indeed, by offering salacious stories and nudity under the semi-respectable banner of "art," foreign films like *The Twilight Girls* (1957, dir. André Hunebelle) and *Sexus* (1965, dir. José Bénazéraf) were doing brisk business in America. Both of these titles had been imported by Radley Metzger's Audubon Films, a distribution company targeting America's growing adult film market.

Naturally, American filmmakers didn't want to be left out of this action, and they started making more adventurous titles of their own. By 1960 or so, a new genre of motion pictures had come into existence and been labeled "sexploitation." Leading the charge was a macho, low-budget filmmaker named Russ Meyer, whose nudity-filled *The Immoral Mr. Teas* (1959) is most often cited as the movie that initiated the new era. Born in 1922 in San Leandro, California, Meyer had been an Army Signal Corps photographer during World War II, deployed at the Battle of the Bulge. After the war, he made industrial films and shot cheesecake photos, including some of the early *Playboy* centerfolds. He also served as a cameraman for producer Peter A. DeCenzie's *The*

French Peep Show (1949), essentially an hour-long filmed burlesque show. A decade later, DeCenzie produced *The Immoral Mr. Teas*, the first of the so-called "nudie-cuties." This 63-minute film was shot in four days on a budget of just $24,000 and earned more than $1,500,000 on the sexploitation circuit. Exploitation films had been around for decades, but Meyer brought cinematic sex to a whole new level of visibility, not to mention profitability.

When Apostolof saw *The Immoral Mr. Teas* in early 1961, it gave him ideas. "I started thinking about making more films," he later explained. "But I knew I had to have distribution. I also started thinking about what films were needed, what niche I could fill. Another friend of mine said, 'Steve, I just saw a film called *The Immoral Mr. Teas.*' So I went to see it. It was a cute premise, and I said, 'Well, I could do something like that.'"[3]

In April 1961, Apostolof wrote a synopsis and a treatment for a film called *The Immoral Artist*, which he then sealed in an envelope and mailed to himself. This strange practice, known as "the poor man's copyright," used postal registration to date intellectual property. Meyer's influence is obvious not only in Apostolof's title but also in the story itself. In *The Immoral Mr. Teas*, the goateed, middle-aged protagonist (played by and named after combat photographer Bill Teas) emerges from a dental appointment only to realize that the anesthetic has given him X-ray vision, enabling him to see through women's clothing. In Apostolof's *The Immoral Artist*, Peter, a young art student, decides to paint all women the way he sees them—naked. Very much like Meyer's film, *The Immoral Artist* consists of a series of vignettes, complete with a final nightmare episode in which the protagonist finally sheds his obsession. But this time he has another problem; He starts seeing women wearing too *much* clothing.

"I didn't want to follow in Russ Meyer's footsteps," Apostolof said of *The Immoral Artist*. "I just used *Mr. Teas* as a reference as to what can be shown on the screen. I knew with that kind of film that I could compete with the majors. And that's what I was looking for for years."[4]

The Immoral Artist never saw the light of the day but Apostolof was undaunted. Around 1960, at the height of the USSR-USA space race, he wrote a story entitled *The Plot to Destroy the Earth*, about a 17-ton Russian satellite that goes out of control and threatens to annihilate the planet with its gravitational pull. This story also never came to fruition.

As the 1960s wore on, Apostolof was still looking for a great screenplay, one that could possibly take his producing and directing career to the next level. What he found instead was a script by one of the most bizarre characters in B-movie history.

Edward Davis Wood, Jr., was a 39-year-old, cross-dressing alcoholic ex–Marine from Poughkeepsie, New York. In the 1950s, he had established himself as the Orson Welles of Poverty Row filmmaking and the patron saint of poor taste with a string of bizarre films. Though Apostolof couldn't have known it at the time, his partnership with this strange man would forever mark his life and career. Together, they formed an unusual and iconic creative symbiosis that would last over a decade.

According to Apostolof, the story begins with industry veteran William C. Thompson, who had served as cameraman on *Journey to Freedom* in 1956. One fateful day, Thompson offered to introduce Apostolof to one of his closest friends, a fellow he'd worked with on a number of film projects. Thompson thought his pal and Apostolof might make a good pair. And who knows? Maybe they could make a film of their own together.

"My friend is a cool guy; he's a writer and director," Thompson promised. "He's also a veteran of World War II, and he hates the Reds. His name is Eddie Wood, but don't forget to add Jr. at the end, because he's very particular about this."[5]

The fact that Wood hated the Communists was key for Apostolof, and he agreed to meet this man at an iconic Hollywood restaurant, the Brown Derby, in the Los Feliz neighborhood. In the late 1950s and early '60s, the hat-shaped eatery was frequented by such notables as Clark Gable, William Holden and Cecil B. DeMille. After his divorce from Joan, Apostolof moved to a place just a few blocks away from the restaurant. He'd often drop by the Derby for lunch or dinner in those days, and he got to know most of the waitstaff and several of the regular patrons by name. This was now Apostolof's home turf.

Apostolof's meeting with Thompson's friend was scheduled for five in the afternoon. Ever the professional, Apostolof arrived a little on the early side and told the waiter he was awaiting the arrival of "a gentleman" whom he didn't know, in case someone asked for him. The Bulgarian filmmaker then parked himself at the bar and ordered his usual, Chivas with ice.

What happened next is one of the most infamous episodes in the Apostolof-Wood saga, though whether it actually happened this way is dubious. In any event, it was a colorful anecdote that Apostolof told and retold for decades:

> So I'm sitting at the bar having a Scotch, and, a little while later, the maître d' comes over to me with a big smirk on his face like the cat that swallowed the canary. [He] said, "Mr. Apostolof" (he never called me Mr. Apostolof), "your date is here." I turned around and said, "Oh, shit!" There was Eddie dressed in drag: a red miniskirt, white boots, angora sweater with the phony tits, and a mustache and three-day beard. And when I saw him, I thought, "God, open up the earth and bury me quickly."[6]

"Nice to meet you! Ed Wood!" said the man in a disconcertingly deep voice as he sat next to Apostolof. He ordered a Bloody Mary, one made not with vodka but with bourbon. "And don't forget the ice," Wood shouted after the retreating waiter.

Apostolof's first impression was that this new acquaintance was an Errol Flynn look-alike. Wood described himself as a triple threat: a successful screenwriter-director-producer, well-connected in Hollywood. He bragged to Apostolof about such successful past movies as *Bride of the Monster* (1955) and *Plan 9 from Outer Space* (1957). Apostolof, however, was more impressed by his guest's outlandish appearance than by his filmography.

A couple of drinks helped Apostolof recover from the initial shock, and he decided to move to the business phase of the meeting. Apostolof suggested that he and Wood relocate to a table at the back of the restaurant, so as to avoid prying eyes. There, Apostolof asked Wood if he maybe had "something more sexy" among his cache of unfilmed scripts. Wood said he had just the thing, a little beauty he'd just finished writing called *Nudie Ghoulies*.

Years later, Apostolof admitted that he was flabbergasted by his first encounter with Ed Wood. That's why, as soon as he returned home after his big meeting at the Brown Derby, he looked up the word "transvestite" in the Merriam-Webster dictionary. Apostolof's memory was that "transvestite" was defined as "a man who loves women so much that he wears their clothes." This served only to confuse Apostolof further, but his early discomfort with Wood faded with each subsequent meeting. (Wood biographer Rudolph Grey does not believe that the story is true. On Vinegar Syndrome's 2017 Blu-ray edition of *Orgy of the Dead*, Grey points out that it would have been grossly unprofessional for Ed Wood to show up at such a meeting in women's clothes.)

"With Eddie, we clicked right away. He was a very nice guy," said Apostolof.[7] A few weeks after that memorable "first date," Apostolof bought the *Nudie Ghoulies* script from Wood for $400, paying him a hefty advance, and started working on perhaps the most ambitious film of his career. Ironically, considering its inauspicious origins, Apostolof's directing debut would ultimately emerge as his macabre magnum opus, a cult classic that remains his most popular film.

Orgy of the Dead (1965)

> **BOB:** Your puritan upbringing holds you back from my monsters, but it certainly doesn't hurt your art of kissing.
> **SHIRLEY:** That's life. My kisses are alive.
> **BOB (CHUCKLES):** Who's to say my monsters aren't alive?
> —William Bates and Pat Barrington in *Orgy of the Dead*

A funeral dirge plays as two muscle-bound slaves with leopard skin loincloths open the heavy, cobwebbed doors of an ancient mausoleum. Within, a beam of eerie red light shines through a circular window onto a stone sarcophagus. Working in unison, the slaves carefully lift the lid and then withdraw in respectful silence. Inside the sarcophagus is a white-haired gentleman, his arms folded across his chest. From a ledge, a bust of the Virgin Mary stares down upon him.

One dissolve later, we see that the white-haired man has raised himself to a sitting position. It is the famous TV psychic Criswell, looking both majestic and a little dazed. He is wrapped in a black cloak that once belonged to the legendary Bela Lugosi, who wore it in *Abbott and Costello Meet Frankenstein* (1948, dir. Charles Barton).[8] Sporting a pompadour and a drooping string tie, he looks like a cross between a vampire and a Southern colonel.

"I am Criswell," the oracle solemnly intones, his eyes seemingly fixed on another dimension. (He's actually reading his cue card.) "For years, I have told the almost unbelievable, related the unreal, and shown it to be more … than a fact. Now I tell a tale of the threshold people, so astounding that some of you may faint. This is a story of those in the twilight time … once human, now monsters, in a void between the living and the dead. Monsters to be pitied, monsters to be despised! A night with the ghouls! The ghouls reborn from the innermost depths of the world!"[9]

The film's opening titles are now superimposed over a still photo of a gilded nude female figure sitting atop the stone altar in the mausoleum. Then an incredible title flashes on the screen: *Orgy of the Dead*, four words that promise so much. The directorial debut of Stephen C. Apostolof is probably the first erotic horror-musical in the world and one of the most misbegotten films of its generation or any other. No wonder it remains a source of speculation and confusion to this day.

Contemporary viewers may wonder how this thing ever attracted a single paying customer when it opened in theaters across America back in 1966. Michael J. Weldon, publisher and editor of *Psychotronic Video*, the seminal cult movie magazine, calls it half-seriously "one of the greatest movies ever made"[10] and rightly points out that it looked pretty outdated even when it was brand new. Indeed, by 1966, the wave of so-called "nudie-cuties" that had crested in the 1950s had long ago crashed against the shore, and most of the genre's pioneers, including Russ Meyer, David F. Friedman and Doris Wishman, had moved on to films with more involved storylines. Nudity on its own was no longer enough to attract an audience.

Insofar as *Orgy of the Dead* has a plot, however, it is an exceedingly simple one. A staggeringly square horror writer, Bob (William Bates) and his shrill, flame-haired fiancée Shirley (Pat Barrington, aka Pat Barringer [1939–2014]), somehow manage to crash their car on a remote road and then seek help—or at least a telephone—in a fog-shrouded cemetery. In their aimless exploration of the boneyard, the bickering lovebirds are captured by a pair of "fiends," the Mummy (Louis Ojena) and the Wolfman (John Andrews), who tie them up. Helpless, Bob and Shirley must watch a series of awkward topless dances, all of which are being performed for the benefit of the Emperor of the Night (Criswell, naturally) and his sidekick, the Black Ghoul or Princess of Darkness (Fawn Silver). At the film's much-delayed conclusion, the Emperor attempts to

Fawn Silver and Criswell play the wicked Princess of Darkness and Emperor of the Night.

sacrifice Bob and Shirley to the dark forces, but their deliverance comes in the form of the first rays of dawn, which reduce the Emperor and the Princess to skeletons.

The shamelessly sleazy and yet somehow naïve *Orgy of the Dead* is quintessential Ed Wood. Here are all of his pet themes and motifs from his earlier films: obsession with death, eroticism, zombies, mummies, werewolves, etc. Even the heroine's name, Shirley, is one that pops up throughout Wood's career. It's the name that Ed himself used for the female character he often portrayed while in drag, and he named several characters Shirley in his films, novels and short stories.

Orgy of the Dead can also be seen as a modern-day interpretation of the *danse macabre*, the late-medieval allegory about the universality of Death. Typically, this is an artform peopled by kings, emperors, popes, peasants, ghosts and skeletons. Here, just as in the 15th century, the Dance of Death represents various social strata: the Prostitute, who attracts men, then robs and kills them; the Slave, a former princess, now tormented by those who once served her; the Bride, who kills her bridegroom and is doomed to live forever with his skeleton; the Indian Maiden, who cruelly casts her lovers into the fire and now must dance amid the flames for all time; the Native Girl, who uses deadly snakes to dispatch her paramours and is sentenced to live forever with reptiles; the Cat Lady, whose obsession with felines becomes both her identity and her destiny; and the Golden Girl, whose lust for the precious metal is sated when she is immersed in a bubbling cauldron of gold.

"Originally the script for *Orgy* was called *Ghoulies*," Apostolof recalled. "I liked it because of three things. First, it cost only $400. Second, there was no bodily contact, which at the time was very important, and third, the film could be shot almost entirely on a soundstage. So I said okay, why not give it a try?"[11] Apostolof admitted that the decision to make an adult movie, even one with no sex, was a difficult one for him, since he had no idea what he could and could not show on the screen. For a new director, this was virgin territory.

"I put up half the budget and had an investor who put up the other half," he revealed. "The total was less than petty cash on any film today, but I don't like to say how much; the standard answer is, 'under a million.' Of course that was when tickets cost $1.50, though *Orgy* was one of the first where tickets cost $3."[12]

Actually, the total production budget of *Orgy of the Dead* came to exactly $55,720.67. Peanuts indeed. Even with inflation, that's less than half a million. For comparison's sake, the average cost of a modern Hollywood movie is somewhere around $65 million.

Even with such limited funds, Apostolof was busy remaking himself in the image of a Hollywood mogul. In 1964, for instance, he became a member of the Independent Motion Picture Association. At the same time, he rented a small two-room office at KTTV Studios on Sunset Boulevard. His kids would often visit him there, and they even met some of their father's show business friends along the way.

One such pal was Forrest Tucker, a grizzled, raspy-voiced character actor perhaps best known today for his role as Sgt. O'Rourke on the classic TV sitcom *F Troop* (1965–67). Apostolof knew Tucker from his years at Republic, where the actor had been featured in some of the studio's trademark action and Western films. Another friend and frequent visitor to Apostolof's new KTTV office was Billy Barty, one of the most popular dwarf actors in history and a veteran of dozens of films and television shows over the

course of 70+ years. Unfortunately, neither Tucker nor Barty ever appeared in any of Apostolof's films.

According to Apostolof, Ed Wood was "in his glory" in the days leading up to *Orgy of the Dead* and even made himself a business card identifying himself as "Edward D. Wood, Jr., screenwriter." Apostolof said,

He loved to be around show business and was always in the office. He was very, very helpful, I have to admit. He even got the monster masks and Halloween costumes. He used to put them on and run around chasing people. He had a ball. He took the blonde wig that the Golden Girl [from *Orgy of the Dead*] wears, put it on his head, and ran into the commissary. It was a riot. Little Billy Barty was in there and started dancing with Eddie. I said, "Eddie, shut up, goddammit! This is a studio and we're not shooting here. We're going to get kicked out! Keep your mouth shut!"[13]

Still another eminent friend of Apostolof was the famously volatile superstar Mickey Rooney, whom Apostolof had known since his (Apostolof's) earliest days in Hollywood. "We were at the KTTV commissary, all sitting around a big table with my father, very proud to have his family there," remembers Susan. "Mickey Rooney came in and my father introduced everyone and he kissed Polly. Oh, that was a big deal! To be kissed by Mickey Rooney."[14]

Apostolof started gearing up to shoot *Orgy of the Dead* in August 1965, when he signed a contract with a company called Golden Land Properties to produce the film under the working title *The Ghoulies*. Apostolof invested about $25,000 of his own money and the other half came from his partner William Bates, a former FBI agent who dreamed of having a Hollywood film career. Bates gave up his rights to *Orgy of the Dead* in exchange for one of the main male roles, that of horror novelist Bob. Bates also received the title of associate producer. According to some sources, Ed Wood was an as-

Apostolof in his office at KTTV Studios in 1966, pointing at a map of all the states where his films were distributed. The walls are covered with pictures of his kids, behind the scenes photographs, posters from his movies, an autograph from Marilyn Monroe, and a phony diploma declaring Apostolof to be a "doctor of sexology."

Chapter 8. The Director of the Dead (1965–1966)

sistant director on *Orgy of the Dead*, but Apostolof denied this. Instead, he says, Wood served as a production assistant and casting director.

The majority of the action in *Orgy of the Dead* is set in a cemetery, so Apostolof began looking for a suitable studio in which to build the sets. He toured several soundstages in Hollywood and the surrounding areas and ended up in Glendale, a suburban community not far from Los Angeles, where producer-director-skinflint Roger Corman was shooting his latest low-budget production. "Corman was shooting something on a graveyard set, and I noticed a guy working his ass off," recalled Apostolof.[15] "I thought, 'That's the kind of guy I want on my set.'"

Stephen C. Apostolof on the set of *Orgy of the Dead* looking as swanky as can be. This was one of his favorite portraits.

The hard worker in question was Robert H. Caramico (1932–1997), a 32-year-old former combat cameraman who wound up working on a wide variety of film productions in his pursuit of one goal: to be accepted in the American Society of Cinematographers. Caramico was wounded in Korea and hospitalized for a year. He was also captured and imprisoned in a secret POW camp from which he managed to escape nine months later. In 1964, he came to the West Coast from New York and started working on features and TV shows. Apostolof hired him as a camera operator on *Orgy of the Dead*, but then promoted him to director of photography. Caramico's striking, lurid, almost comic book–like cinematography would be one of *Orgy*'s selling points in later years. After working with Apostolof, Caramico had a successful film-TV career, shooting such classic TV series as *Dallas, Falcon Crest* and *Lassie*. "[Caramico] was a nice guy, an ex–Marine, and I liked the way he worked. He asked if he could have a Chapman crane. I said, 'Go get it,'" remembered Apostolof.[16]

On that same film set in Glendale, Apostolof found one of his best-remembered performers: actress Fawn Silver (born in 1933), who would sexily play the role of the Black Ghoul. But Apostolof still needed a "real star," as he put it; a celebrity who could attract ticket buyers to the cinema and turn *Orgy of the Dead* in a box office hit. "So I came across the Amazing Criswell, a TV psychic, showman and the biggest charlatan I've ever met!" said Apostolof.[17]

With his jet-black cloak, his blond forelock rolled into a quizzical curl, and his pale face caked in heavy makeup, Criswell looked more like a displaced Ringling Bros. clown than the "Nostradamus of the 20th century," as he billed himself. And yet, with his piercing blue eyes and honeyed voice, there was something mysterious, compelling and even terrifying about the man. In his heyday, his far-fetched predictions ("I predict that another Black Plague will hit the Midwest with a shattering effect!"[18]) attracted the attention of millions of TV viewers, newspaper readers and book buyers. It was all in the presentation, he explained to friends. Criswell may not have known the future, but he did understand theatricality and showmanship.

Before he was the Amazing Criswell, he was simply Jeron Criswell King, born on August 18, 1907, in Princeton, Indiana. His family owned the largest chain of funeral homes in the South, an odd biographical quirk that led to his habit of sleeping in coffins as an adult. For Criswell, curling up in a casket was like returning to the womb. These days, the peculiar prognosticator is best known for his flowery monologues and narration from Ed Wood's infamous *Plan 9 from Outer Space,* for years the consensus choice among connoisseurs for the worst movie ever made. In the 1950s and '60s, however, Criswell was a genuine celebrity in his own right. He had his own show, *Criswell Predicts,* on KLAC Channel 13 (now KCOP-13) in Los Angeles, plus a syndicated weekly column that appeared in more than 300 newspapers across America at its peak, and even a radio show that reached 85 stations. These achievements made Criswell the "star" Apostolof needed to turn *Orgy of the Dead* into a box office contender. Or so the theory went. Apostolof said,

> I had never heard of [Criswell]. So Eddie introduced us and Criswell came up to me and said, "Hiiiiiiiiiiiiiiii." Cris never talks. Cris performs. And Cris never walks by himself. I've never seen Criswell alone. He's always surrounded by an entourage. I used to call these people "invisible means of support." Absolutely unknown to me people. He would come to me and introduce them: "Steve, meet the chief editor of the *Santa Monica Gazette,*" or the *Cucamonga Herald* or whatever.[19]

Cult film historian and *Screem* magazine contributor Greg Goodsell describes Criswell as "a cheerful rogue. His most famous line is: 'I can't look out the window and tell you what the weather is, and these people are paying me a lot of money to predict the future!'"[20] And yet Apostolof chose Criswell to play the Emperor of the Night, one of the main roles in *Orgy of the Dead*. Criswell was so enthusiastic about the project that he brought his own coffin to the set, which according to Apostolof "looked nice and photographically very beautiful."[21]

"[Criswell] also liked to sleep in [his coffin]," recalled Apostolof. "I remember, one afternoon, we needed Cris for a take and couldn't find him. Everybody looked around—it was a big, big set—and no one could find Criswell. Then somebody knocked on his coffin and Cris sat up and said, 'Yeeeeeesss?'"[22]

Criswell's imposing presence and hypnotic voice were not the only factors working in his favor. The fraudulent psychic was also a regular guest on NBC's *The Tonight Show* during the reigns of both Jack Paar and Johnny Carson (who would quantify his predictions as being "80 percent accurate, 20 percent of the time"). Criswell was perfectly willing to be an object of ridicule, so long as *The Tonight Show* brought him to millions of American television viewers coast to coast. Apostolof thought he could use his star's nationwide notoriety to publicize the film, and he was right. Criswell never missed a chance to promote himself or his latest project when he appeared on *The Tonight Show*. On October 2, 1965, as a guest on Carson's *Tonight Show*, Criswell plugged *Orgy* to a nation of millions of potential viewers. He also prognosticated that "the sleeper among the films will be *Orgy of the Dead*, a horrifier to end all horrifiers" in his syndicated column *Criswell Predicts*.[23]

Initially, the character played by Criswell had been conceived as the Skull, a creature draped in a black cloak with a skull for a head. That obviously changed when a familiar face became attached to the role. Criswell also wound up being the one who gave *Orgy of the Dead* its memorable name. The project had gone through a number of working titles, but none of them proved satisfactory until one day when Ed Wood excitedly called Apostolof: "Poppy, Criswell just came up with a killer title: *Orgy of the Dead*," said Wood.[24] Apostolof immediately liked the new name, but he talked to some of his friends, and they told him that films with words like "death" and "dead" in the title were box office poison. However, he decided to take the risk and used Criswell's striking title, even if the film bore little resemblance to a necrophile orgy. No wonder that when the film played on a double bill with *The Sex Cycle* (1967, dir. Joe Sarno) at Philadelphia's Studio Theatre in 1967, it was known as *Orgy of the Weirdos*. It was also advertised as *Revels of the Dead* (in Detroit) and *Party of the Dead* (in Newport News, Virginia), to appease publications uncomfortable with the word "orgy."

One might reasonably ask why, after hiring Criswell for the project, Apostolof didn't also hire some of the era's other camp horror icons, like Tor Johnson and Vampira, both of whom were part of the Ed Wood coterie. Apostolof had known Johnson when the latter played the Giant Turk in *Journey to Freedom*. The reason for Johnson's absence from *Orgy* was simple enough: Apostolof had no role suitable for the bald, massively proportioned Swedish wrestler. Apostolof also denied the rumors that the leading female role in *Orgy* was supposed to be played by Vampira, aka Maila Nurmi (1922–2008), an American actress of Finnish ancestry, best known as a late night TV horror hostess in Los Angeles as well as for her silent participation in Ed Wood's *Plan 9 from Outer Space*.

"Sometimes you can't see the forest for the trees," Apostolof said about his failure to cast Vampira in *Orgy of the Dead*.[25] The two eventually met in the 1980s, during a special screening of *Orgy* in Los Angeles organized by Ed Wood's biographer Rudolph Grey and attended by the New York punk-rock musician Tomata du Plenty. Grey remembers that screening well, since at its conclusion, Apostolof handed him a bill for $45.

Although classified as erotic horror, stylistically *Orgy of the Dead* is closer to burlesque and vaudeville, since it places more emphasis on topless dancing than it does on plot or atmosphere. It's advertised as a movie "starring Criswell and a bevy of beautiful girls," all of them filmed in "gorgeous Astravision and shocking Sexicolor." The "beautiful girls" in question were mostly strippers and dancers from various Los Angeles nightclubs. At the very least, this film gave them a few days of work in an interesting environment. And none of them had to participate in any sex acts, real or simulated. Apostolof said,

I would have absolutely no bodily contact [in my film] so I don't have to worry about the sheriff arresting me. Just T&A [tits and asses]. I figured I'd get the dancers from the strip clubs. I wanted them to look beautiful. I went to every agent in town that represented the clubs and got all new faces. I never said, "Come on, let's make a *Gone with the Wind*, because I have an epic story." No. Here, the show was primarily for a male audience to show them some tits and ass."[26]

On those counts, it delivered.

Apostolof chose some of the *Orgy* dancers from the files of CHN International, a talent agency on Santa Monica Boulevard and a common destination for all sexploitation producers looking for sexy girls for their movies. Agency owner Harold "Hal" Guthu (1923–2000) was quite a character himself, a genial veteran of the flesh trade with jet-black dyed hair, a near–Calvinist work ethic, a freshly pressed white shirt, and a talking parrot he kept on his desk.

Apostolof leafed through scores of photographs of erotic models from Guthu's catalogues and selected two dozen for an audition. Among these aspiring actresses was a petite, small-breasted but attractive young brunette. Hal explained that this girl was a performer at a popular Sunset Boulevard nightclub called the Whisky a Go Go, where she danced naked in a cage hanging from the ceiling while rock bands played on stage. Hal showed Apostolof an amateur 8mm film of the girl in which she was dancing half-naked on stage. He added that the girl's showbiz pseudonym was Nadejda and that she together with her father and younger sister had fled the Communist regime in Bulgaria. To say the least, Apostolof was intrigued.

This young woman, Nadejda Dobrev aka Nadejda Klein (born 1945) made her memorable screen debut as the tortured Slave Girl in *Orgy*, much to her family's horror. "My family, my dad, heard about me making this film and just basically disowned me," she says. "My sister wasn't allowed to see me."[27] Years later, when her relatives finally saw the tame movie, they wondered what all the fuss was about. "My sister saw *Orgy* and she said, 'This is *Orgy of the Dead*?! It's so innocent!'" Dobrev can laugh about her experience now.

From his first-ever day as a director, Apostolof began forging personal traditions he would follow for the rest of his career. He would always begin filming a new movie on a Wednesday, for instance. That way, if he needed more equipment, he had enough time to procure it by the end of the week. Apostolof was also quite superstitious and always wore a pair of white lace-ups when he started shooting a new movie. "I put on my lucky white shoes for the first time when I started shooting *Orgy of the Dead*. Ed Wood gave me a penny, and I put it in them, and it always stayed there. Today these shoes are full of holes. However, I always wear them when I expect a problem on the horizon."[28]

Apostolof would need those lucky shoes while filming *Orgy of the Dead*, because the production was plagued with headaches from the very beginning. A week before the shoot, for instance, Apostolof began working on his annotated screenplay only to realize, in horror, that the text Ed Wood had written was only 20 pages long. "I wish you could see the screenplay I had to work with! I had 20 pages of text to make a 90-minute film. And as we all know, the standard is one page per minute of screen time. That is why *Orgy of the Dead* has mostly dancing girls."[29] Years later, the producer-director would joke that *Orgy* was the first MTV movie, without him even realizing it at the time. With

Chapter 8. The Director of the Dead (1965-1966)

its abundance of music and almost total lack of plot, it does somewhat resemble the abstract music videos that the cable network played during the 1980s and '90s.

Apostolof originally hired a choreographer he thought was reputable, and the woman began rehearsals with the girls as expected, but the dancers soon started complaining that their taskmistress was extremely rude. "[The choreographer] was just nasty! She was directing like she was a Nazi commandant," recalled Apostolof. "Three days before I was to start shooting, I went to see a rehearsal. I hear her screaming and yelling and knew that wasn't right. There's only one person who screams on my films and that's me. I talked to her, she yelled at me, so I fired her."[30]

Apostolof now had a real problem. How could he replace the fired choreographer on such short notice? None of his friends was a good enough dancer to deal with a bunch of nightclub strippers. With shooting scheduled to begin in just three days, the situation was getting tense. Then, in one of his trademark moments of inspiration, Apostolof decided to hire his haberdasher, Mark Desmond. "I went to Mark and said, 'Here's your chance to become a big shot. I need a dance director. Here's the script.' And he said, 'Okay.' And he was great," recalled Apostolof.[31]

Desmond was no stranger to dancing. Born Alex Collebrusco in 1903 in Riverton, Illinois, he made a career as a tap dancer in the 1940s, using the pseudonym Alberto DaVinci and appearing in the Broadway musical *Earl Carroll's Vanities*. In 1943, while serving in the Army, Desmond was featured in *Ripley's Believe It or Not!* as "the dancer who could tap a thousand taps a minute." In the late 1950s and '60s, he got interested in acting and writing for television and film and eventually penned the script for Apostolof's 1967 *Motel Confidential*.

With Desmond now on board, the shooting of *Orgy of the Dead* began as scheduled on September 18, 1965, at Occidental Studios, a small but still-existent facility at 201 North Occidental Boulevard with four sound stages. Built by actor-filmmaker Hobart Bosworth in 1913, Occidental is one of Hollywood's oldest functioning studios. It's where screen legend Mary Pickford began her Hollywood career.

On the first day of shooting, Apostolof and cameraman Robert Caramico were sitting on a crane high above the set when Lorali Hart, billed under her stage name Texas Starr, began her cat-themed dance, dressed in a spotted catsuit with holes cut out for her breasts and buttocks. Apostolof looked down and noticed a uniformed sheriff observing the proceedings with great interest. Apostolof's heart was instantly seized with fear. And that's when the situation began spiraling out of control. "It was just as the Cat Girl started dancing and, being a stripper, she started peeling off everything and pretty soon she was dancing bare ass naked. And I'm screaming, 'Out! You're not supposed to do it that way!,'" remembered Apostolof. "And the goddamn sheriff was watching and my heart was beating like crazy. I'm thinking, 'That's it! My career's over!'"[32]

Apostolof descended from the crane and approached the man in uniform. Once they started talking, however, the relieved Apostolof realized that the "sheriff" was actually a subpoena marshal. It turns out that the choreographer that Apostolof fired a few days earlier had filed a wrongful termination lawsuit against him. This was comparatively good news.

With its heavy iron gates and crumbling tombstones straight out of an EC comic book, the elaborate *Orgy of the Dead* set was built especially for the film. The only thing

Crew of *Orgy of the Dead*. Middle row: Bill Davis, Ted V. Mikels, unidentified camera assistant, and Robert Maxwell. Robert Caramico is behind the camera. Bottom row: Edward D. Wood, Jr., Robert C. Dertano, Stephen C. Apostolof, and Mark Desmond. Man at far left is unidentified.

the crew used from the studio was the huge black curtain into the background, creating the impression that the action was taking place at night. Every other bit of set dressing was custom-made for Apostolof. The action of *Orgy* was largely confined to one locale, but at least that locale was evocative and memorable. "The set was really fantastic. I was so excited to light it in the best possible way to create the right atmosphere. I especially liked to illuminate scenes where there was fog," recalled Ted V. Mikels, a gaffer on *Orgy of the Dead*.[33] After working on this movie, Mikels became a low-budget filmmaker in his own right, directing such horror and sexploitation cult classics as *The Astro-Zombies* (1968), *Girl in Gold Boots* (1968) and *The Corpse Grinders* (1971).

Apostolof was proud of the set of *Orgy of the Dead* and claimed that even MGM could not have done a better job. However, the set still didn't have quite enough foliage to be convincing, so a couple of resourceful crew members chopped down some tree branches in nearby Griffith Park and added them to the set. Apostolof learned about this and became infuriated. "[The branches] looked good, so I kept my mouth shut," he recalled.[34] Apostolof also rented a real skeleton from UCLA for the film.

Apostolof's children visited him on the set of *Orgy of the Dead*. His eldest son Steve, who at the time was only seven, was really impressed by the fog machine: "You press a little button, and the machine starts spewing clouds of smoke. After a few min-

Chapter 8. The Director of the Dead (1965–1966)

Coleen O'Brien (The Streetwalker) gestures to the pelvis of a skeleton. Said Apostolof, "The skeleton was real, not a phony. I got that from UCLA and it scared me, it was so realistic."

utes, the entire film set is covered in fog."[35] He vividly recalled the day his father shot the opening scene in which the bleary-eyed psychic Criswell delivers his famous opening monologue, a demented keynote address of sorts: "Two muscular guys in loincloths lifted the coffin lid. Inside stood a big, bloated drunkard, Criswell, who began stuttering his lines, trying to do a speech. Dad was so furious that day! Cris was so drunk that he could barely sit upright in the coffin!"[36]

Apostolof directs Criswell on the ghoulish set of *Orgy of the Dead*.

Apostolof was beside himself. He was pacing around the set, swearing in perfect Bulgarian. The others present that day, as one might expect, couldn't understand a word he was saying. But they got the message nevertheless. Having vouched for Criswell, Ed Wood was justifiably worried and began circling around Apostolof and wringing his hands. Then Criswell tried to save the day with a brilliant idea. He said that when he was a guest on Johnny Carson's *Tonight Show*, he always used a teleprompter. Apostolof's answer was chilling: "Cris! I'm not Johnny Carson!"

"I was in trouble!" remembered Apostolof, "so I did the most humiliating thing for an actor. I wrote Criswell's lines in large letters on cardboard. Then I asked Eddie to hold them in front of him while we were shooting."[37] This didn't solve the problem; in fact, it made it even worse. Criswell was farsighted and couldn't see clearly from a short distance. He had forgotten his glasses and looked slightly cross-eyed while trying to read the cue cards. The smoke that surrounded the set further complicated the situation. Robert Caramico, enraged by Criswell's stutter, erupted, "Cris, watching you act is like watching paint dry!"[38]

Like his buddy Criswell, longtime alcoholic Ed Wood was frequently inebriated during the shooting of *Orgy of the Dead*. Robert C. Dertano, who directed *Journey to Freedom* and served as an assistant director on *Orgy*, warned Apostolof not to give Wood any money if he wanted to see him on the set again. Apostolof ignored this advice, a decision he later regretted bitterly:

> Eddie drank vodka on the set because it didn't smell. At first it was bourbon, and then he drank everything else he could get his hands on. Dertano warned me not to give him any money until we finished the movie. But one day Eddie came up with another crazy story that he had nothing to eat at home

Chapter 8. The Director of the Dead (1965–1966)

Apostolof discusses the screenplay of *Orgy of the Dead* with Robert Dertano while Ed Wood holds the cue cards for Criswell. Lou Ojena, who plays the Mummy, is behind Wood and Caramico at the camera.

and managed to claw some dough from me. The next day, he came in drunk as a skunk. I made a mistake that I didn't fire him right there."[39]

The production was riddled with such catastrophes until the very last day of shooting, when Apostolof filmed the infamous Golden Girl sequence. In this scene, the two giants grab actress Pat Barrington and submerge her in a cauldron of molten gold, from which she emerges as a golden statue. Apostolof acknowledged later that this sequence was directly inspired by *Goldfinger* (1964, dir. Guy Hamilton), a major box office hit just a year previously. In that classic movie, a Bond Girl (Shirley Eaton) is caught helping James Bond (Sean Connery) in a card game against the villainous Auric Goldfinger (Gert Fröbe). As a punishment, the poor lass is gilded from head to toe and dies of suffocation. Although she appears only for a few minutes in the film, Eaton became a star overnight and even posed (covered in gold paint) for the cover of *Life* magazine in November 1964.

Appearing as *Orgy of the Dead*'s own gilded damsel was a deliciously alluring 25-year-old exotic dancer, Pat Barrington. Born Patricia Annette Bray in Charlotte, North Carolina, on October 16, 1939, she became one of the first stars of sexploitation cinema with appearances in such fleshy favorites as *Mondo Topless* (1966, dir. Russ Meyer) and the Harry H. Novak productions *The Girl with the Hungry Eyes* (1968, dir. William Rotsler) and *Mantis in Lace* (1967, dir. Rotsler).[40] Barrington had a whirlwind romance with *Orgy of the Dead* cameraman Caramico and they even were briefly married. Besides the Golden Girl, Barrington played one more crucial role in *Orgy of the*

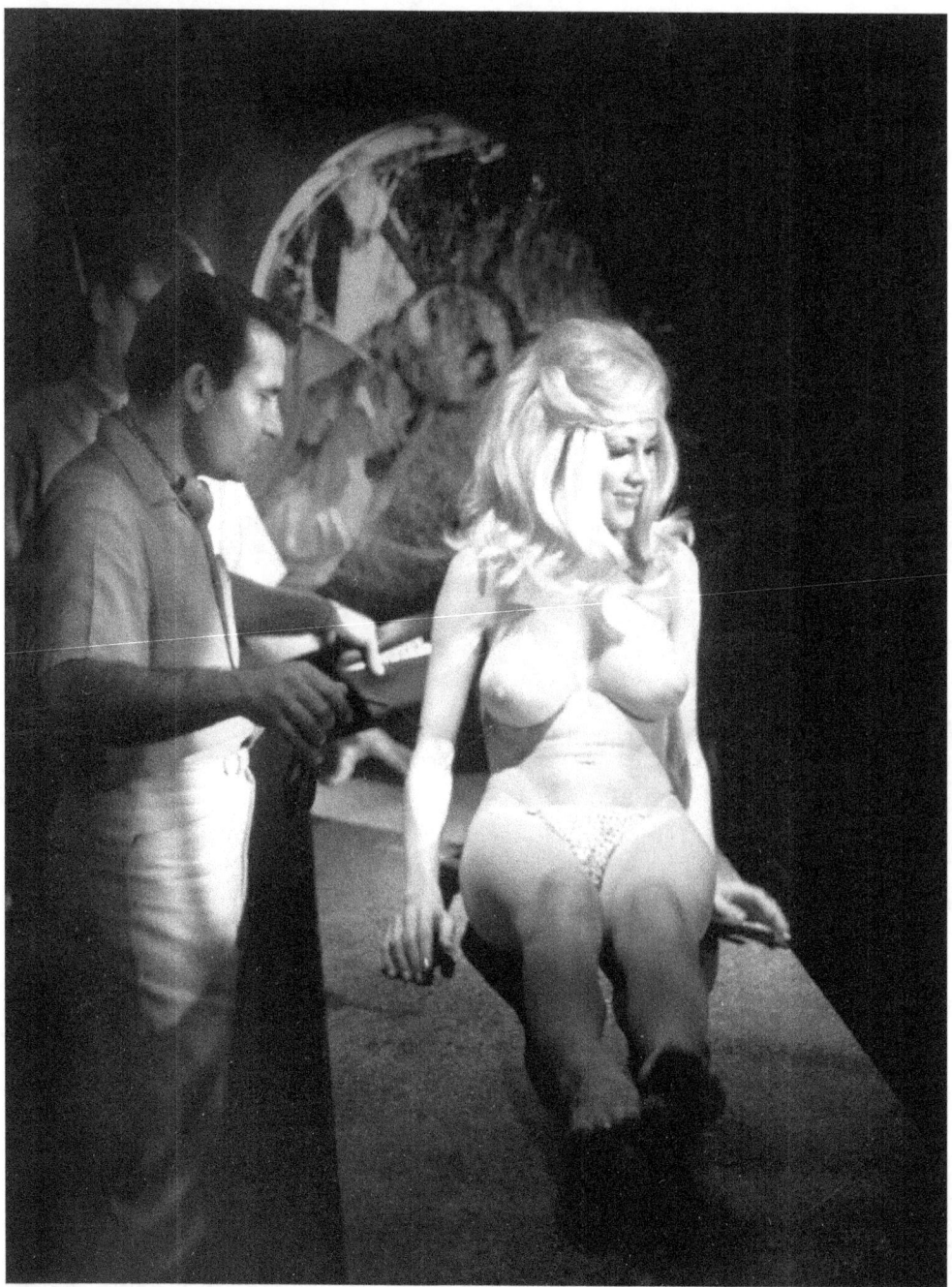

Apostolof gives Pat Barrington some direction on the mausoleum set of *Orgy of the Dead*.

Dead, that of Bob's carping fiancée Shirley. This double casting led to a bizarre moment in the movie in which Barrington watches herself dance.

"Someone, I cannot remember who that son of a bitch was, told Pat that if you paint someone in gold, he or she will suffocate and die because the skin can not breathe," Apostolof remembered.[41] Barrington started getting nervous because of such

Chapter 8. The Director of the Dead (1965–1966)

rumors. Trying to control the situation, Apostolof informed his leading lady that makeup artist Margaret Davies would be using a mixture of sunscreen lotion and gold paint and that Barrington would not suffocate or die. But "the snake pit," as Apostolof termed the makeup room, kept tensions high by telling Barrington that she would die if she allowed herself to be painted with gold and that she should consider getting special insurance. Barrington's agent called and insisted on having a medical team and an ambulance on set. Apostolof was furious.

"Yes, I want to kill her! I'll kill her! I'll shoot her while she's dead, and then you can sue me if you want!" responded the enraged Apostolof.[42] However, he dutifully provided an ambulance and medical team.

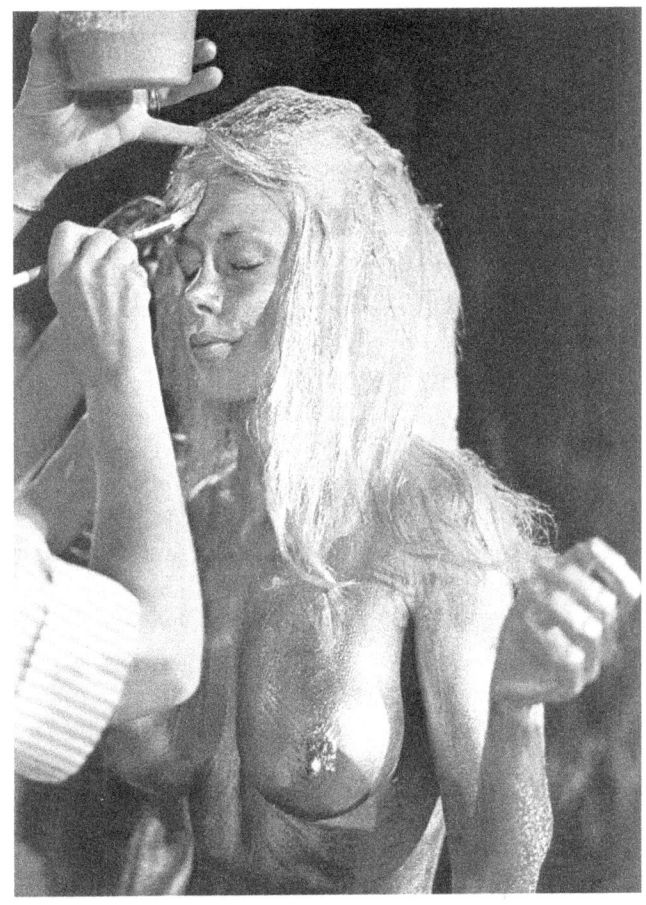

Pat Barrington being painted with a mixture of sunscreen lotion and gold paint for a scene inspired by *Goldfinger*, the third installment in the James Bond series.

Barrington was painted with gold paint as planned, and the whole scene was filmed in one take with three cameras. This was unusual because *Orgy of the Dead*, being a low-budget sexploitation movie, was typically shot with one camera and not in sequence.

"After we finished the scene, Pat took a shower, and everything was hunky-dory. But then another problem occurred. Pat could not scream," recalled Apostolof.[43] In one scene, Pat's character, Shirley, is tied to a cemetery post as the Black Ghoul (Fawn Silver) advances on her, clutching a long knife in her perfectly manicured hand. The screenplay called for Barrington to scream in horror. But what came out of her mouth resembled more of a hiccup. After another unsuccessful take, the frustrated Apostolof approached her. "What the hell was that? Can't you scream?" he asked.

"I feel it! I definitely feel it!" answered Barrington.

"You feel it, but I don't hear it!" Apostolof tersely replied.[44] He was forced to interrupt the shoot and send Barrington home to practice her screaming over the weekend. As extra insurance, Apostolof dispatched John Andrews and Lou Ojena, *Orgy*'s

Werewolf and Mummy respectively, to give the inexperienced actress some screaming instruction. The men had their work cut out for them. "On Monday, Pat returned to the set, screaming properly and everything was fine and dandy," Apostolof remembered. But his ingénue's education came at a price. "Later on, I learned that she was evicted from the apartment because of her screaming lessons over the weekend."[45]

Apostolof was known as a director who made his crew work around the clock, and he started earning that reputation from the beginning of his directing career. The shooting of *Orgy of the Dead* continued for eight days. In some cases, Apostolof's crew were working up to 16 hours a day. This was B-movie boot camp, and only the strong survived. But according to Apostolof, "Nobody complained. If my people were not so good, they would not work with me. When you work for Apostolof, you forget about short working days. Forget hours! When you work for me, you work all day and night! Why should I have a working time? I'm not a grocery store."[46]

On the last day of shooting, Ed Wood approached Apostolof to tell him that Criswell wanted to have a party to celebrate the wrapping of the film. "Eddie didn't say that he wants a party. Eddie said *Criswell* wants a party! I said okay and continued working," recalled Apostolof.[47]

At six in the evening on that last day, Apostolof was shooting the scene that opens *Orgy of the Dead*. In the film, skeptical Shirley (Barrington) and her impetuous fiancé Bob (Bates) are traveling by car in search of "an old cemetery" at night, but reckless driver Bob crashes the vehicle, leading the couple to seek help from the cemetery's caretaker. This relatively simple but crucial scene called for the actors to sit in a motionless car in front of a black backdrop. Closeups of the two lovebirds bickering in the '65 Chevrolet Corvair would later be clumsily mismatched to location footage of a car driving down a real California road. At one point during the filming of this sequence, Apostolof heard a noise similar to the hum of a beehive behind him. "I heard all this noise, turned around, and, my goodness, there were all these people I'd never seen before. People that Eddie and Criswell invited to the party."[48] Barrington stiffened in front of all those unexpected guests, and Apostolof started losing control of the situation. He called Ed Wood and told him to tell people to go away until the filming was over.

"Then came a delegation: 'Why don't you finish it tomorrow?' I said no. There's no party until I finished, goodbye." He then sent Wood, *Orgy*'s production manager, to buy food for the crew. Apostolof was then to receive a lesson in grocery shopping, Ed Wood–style: After about an hour, Wood returned to Occidental Studios with several boxes. Apostolof announced a dinner break and opened one of the boxes. It was full of vodka. He opened a second. Scotch. A third. Bourbon. Only the fourth, packed with potato chips and mini pretzels meant to serve as appetizers, contained anything like food. "I said, 'Eddie, where's the food?' To him, that *was* the food!"[49]

Appropriately enough, the shooting of *Orgy of the Dead* ended at midnight. But this time, it was far too quiet and peaceful around Apostolof. "I turned around and Eddie was nowhere to be found. My assistant director was nowhere to be found. My script girl, who was a man, was nowhere to be found. So I shook hands with [Caramico], gave him my congratulations, and went home."[50]

The next day, around nine in the morning, Ed Wood entered Apostolof's office fresh as a daisy. "I said, 'Where were you last night?' He said, 'I was tired.' I said, 'As long

Chapter 8. The Director of the Dead (1965-1966)

as I'm on the set, you're on the set.' Dertano walks in. I said, 'How can you leave the set? You're [the assistant director]! In case I collapse, you have to finish!' He said, 'Well, it was getting very late…' I said, 'Fine. From now on you can leave as early as you want to and come in as late as you want to. Forget it, it's finished, goodbye.'"[51]

This was the first of four times that Apostolof fired Ed Wood. Out of pique, Apostolof also fired his assistant director Robert C. Dertano, who was supposed to edit *Orgy of the Dead*. Now in need of an editor, Apostolof appointed Donald A. Davis (1932–1982), a close friend of Ed Wood's. At the time, Davis had just graduated from the film school of the University of California at Los Angeles and was eager to establish himself in the independent movie business. He met Apostolof on the set of *Orgy*, where he'd been summoned by Wood. Apostolof recalled:

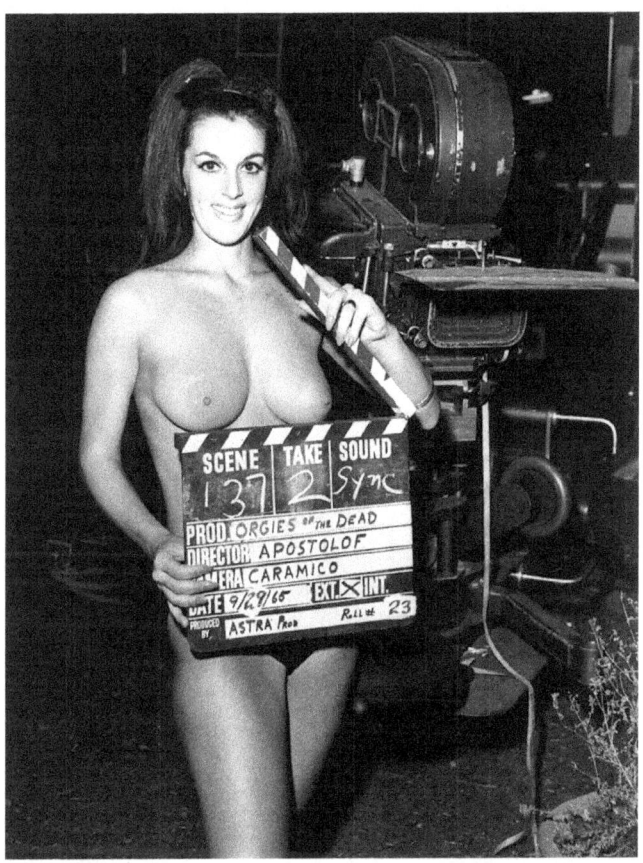

Sexy brunette Rene de Beau, who performs the so-called Fluff Dance in *Orgy of the Dead*, poses with the film's clapperboard.

> I liked Don, he was a funny guy, and I gave him a call, he came in, we made a deal, and he did [the post-production]. He edited the picture. And every week I'm knocking at the editing door. The agreement was, I show up with a couple of hundred bucks, then he'd sit on the little stool and start cutting. "Now I'm working for you! No money, I'm not working for you!"[52]

Apostolof took a liking to the good-natured Davis from the first time they met. Like Apostolof, Davis was recently divorced, so they had something to bond over. In addition to their professional partnership, the two soon became drinking buddies.

Stephen Apostolof was unusually ambitious while making *Orgy of the Dead*. He hired a composer by the name of Jaime Mendoza-Nava (1925–2005) to give it an original, eclectic score. A key figure in the Apostolof saga, Mendoza-Nava was a conductor of the Bolivian Symphony Orchestra and had written music for many Disney productions, including the TV series *The Mickey Mouse Club* (1955–1959) and *Zorro* (1957–1959). The composer was born in La Paz, Bolivia, on December 1, 1925, but studied his craft in Buenos Aires, at the Juilliard School in New York, and with renowned French composer Nadia Boulanger at the Madrid Royal Conservatory and the Sorbonne.

The *Orgy of the Dead* score reflected the composer's international background. His compositions were mostly inspired by the pentatonic music of the Andes. His melodies transported the listener to different exotic locations through unconventional sound effects and instruments. Mendoza-Nava's work was also influenced by mid–20th-century exotica composers and musicians such as Martin Denny, Les Baxter, Korla Pandit and others who sought to evoke the sounds of faraway lands.

Apostolof and Mendoza-Nava met circa late 1965 at a decidedly non-exotic location, a Hollywood hamburger stand. "Jaime was quite famous among the filmmakers of low-budget films in Hollywood. We met on Melrose Avenue in Los Angeles and ate hotdogs and hamburgers. The rest, as they say, is history," remembered Apostolof.[53]

After reaching an agreement with Apostolof, Mendoza-Nava wrote the *Orgy* score and hired a handful of musicians to record it. Apostolof also pitched in a few ideas of his own. "I am very musical," he explained, "so I participated in one of the pieces, and I sang along with Jaime an Indian song. We were about four, five people there, but Ed [Wood] was not present. He couldn't sing."[54]

In 1995, Strangelove Records, an obscure soundtrack label started by eccentric New York musician Kramer, released an *Orgy of the Dead* soundtrack, with audio taken directly from the film. The album combined Mendoza-Nava's music with Ed Wood's florid dialogue and sound effects. Steve and Jaime's ersatz Indian chanting ("Hey-a-ho! Hey-a-ho! Wa-ho! Wa-ho!") was thus preserved for the ages. Strangelove got Apostolof's permission to release the album, even giving him a small stipend, and he was generally pleased with the finished product. But he was greatly irritated to see that his name was misprinted as "A.S. Stephen" on the cover.

Orgy of the Dead's troubles didn't end when it wrapped. One day during post-production, Apostolof received a subpoena to appear in court. The film's script supervisor, Bill Davis, was also suing him. Davis claimed to have hurt his back after being asked to remove the giant cauldron in which the two giants submerged Pat Barrington. The charge didn't hold up. Apostolof appeared in court along with Ed Wood, who was a witness for the defense, and won the case. "I told Bill, 'You're a liar! The cauldron weighs 700 pounds! It took four people and special rails to load it on the truck when we finished filming!'" remembered Apostolof.[55]

Once *Orgy* was edited and ready to go, Apostolof organized a sneak preview for friends at West Hollywood's Monica Theatre, a future Pussycat cinema at 7734 Santa Monica Boulevard. (It is still in business, now as a gay porn theater called Studs.) Like the prodigal son of yore, the disowned Ed Wood returned for the event, as did Criswell and his eccentric entourage. After the screening, everyone gathered for drinks in the theater lobby. The feedback, as might be expected, was extremely positive, but Criswell was strangely silent. "Well, will there be no prophecies?" asked Apostolof. Criswell grabbed his hand and started crying: "Oh, Poppy, you made me look so regal!" Apostolof said, "Yeah, sure. Next time learn your lines!"[56]

Fawn Silver, who played the Black Ghoul, also organized a lavish party to celebrate the film's completion. The fete was held in the prestigious Franklin Hills community

Chapter 8. The Director of the Dead (1965-1966)

Actors William Bates (Bob) and Pat Barrington (Shirley) on the cover of a special 1967 issue of *Torrid Film Reviews* magazine.

at her wealthy father's house, designed in 1935 by the famous Los Angeles modernist architect Milton Black. As Apostolof strode through the party, a Scotch in his hand, he saw a familiar face. It turned out to be Fawn Silver's father, Victor. Apostolof knew him from somewhere, but he couldn't place him. Finally, he realized that this man was Victor Carter, who in 1959 had acquired a controlling stake in Republic, the studio where

Fawn Silver (billed here as Fawn Silverton) as shot by Tom Kelley, best known for his iconic 1949 red velvet nude photograph of Marilyn Monroe. This photograph was published in the Heiress of the Month section of the May 1966 issue of *Millionaire* magazine. According to the accompanying article Fawn Silver studied at Chadwick's Finishing School for Young Ladies in Palos Verdes, California, and graduated from Miami University and the University of California.

Apostolof started his filmmaking career. In fact, Carter became president and chairman of the board of the film company. "Afterwards, I said to Fawn, 'What the hell do you need me for? Your father can make ten pictures for you!' She said, 'Because I want to do it on my own,'" recalled Apostolof.[57]

Fawn Silver was never more than a dilettante in the film world. In spite of its late-blooming cult status, *Orgy of the Dead* failed to turn her into a Hollywood star, let alone a household name, though she did land minor roles in a handful of now-forgotten films, like *Mother Goose à Go-Go* (1966, dir. Jack H. Harris) with Tommy Kirk and Henny Youngman. Like co-star Pat Barrington, Silver dropped out of sight after the 1960s. Today, the actress, whose real name is Fanya Carter, lives in Los Angeles, where she has a successful practice as a psychologist and deflects any and all inquiries about her semi-scandalous past. All of our attempts to talk to her proved unsuccessful. Like many former sexploitation stars, Fanya has no desire to dig up her past. Best to leave it buried in Stephen C. Apostolof's phony cemetery.

Orgy of the Dead hit American cinemas in February 1966. At first, the film was mostly shipped out to theaters in Southern California, where exhibitors were starved for new titles at the time. In the mid–1960s, the major American studios (Fox, Columbia, Paramount) wouldn't provide prints of their latest offerings if exhibitors couldn't guarantee a few thousand dollars in ticket sales per week. So, in order to survive, some struggling theaters were willing to show just about anything they thought could turn

Chapter 8. The Director of the Dead (1965–1966)

A color one sheet for *Orgy of the Dead*.

a quick profit, even a no-star flick called *Orgy of the Dead* featuring a gaggle of topless strippers in a graveyard. Something was better than nothing.

In those early days, Apostolof was at the mercy of others when it came to distributing his movies. The distribution rights for *Orgy* were initially purchased by a man named Fred O. Gebhardt from F.O.G. Distributors. Gebhardt produced a poster in two colors, brown and black, which jokingly advertised the film as using nonexistent formats and processes such as "gorgeous Astravision" (a nod to the name of Apostolof's company, Astra Productions) and "shocking Sexicolor." This kind of ballyhoo was typical at the time. For example, the classic sexploitation film *The Adventures of Lucky Pierre* (1961, dir. Herschell Gordon Lewis) was advertised as being filmed in "Fleshtone color" and "Skinamaskope," while *The Lustful Turk* (1968, dir. Byron Mabe) was promoted as "a movie in the tradition of *Lawrence of Arabia* ... but with girls" and "filmed in 1001 colors."

Orgy's poster looked quite cheap, something even Apostolof had to admit. But its pressbook was something completely different. It was so colorful and attractive that many distributors "forgot" to return it to Apostolof, so he had to print a second, cheaper black-and-white batch. Apostolof revealed that Gebhardt "gave me three checks for $5000 each. Advance. And what do I do when I have the money? I make a picture!"[58]

Flush with cash, Apostolof started planning a new film about the adventures of a transvestite detective in Paris.[59] The screenplay, as the topic itself suggests, was written by Ed Wood, and Apostolof bought it before Wood became persona non grata. There still exists a complete, undated screenplay entitled *7 Rue Pigalle*, carrying the credit "Original Story and Screenplay by Edward D. Wood, Jr." and denoted as the "property" of Apostolof's Astra Productions.[60] Wood recycled this material for a novel called *Parisian Passions*, originally published in September 1966 by Sundown/Corinth. The novel was also known as *69 Rue Pigalle*.[61]

"[Ed Wood] had all kinds of screenplays sitting on the shelves," remembered Apostolof. "Eddie loved to write. Of course, he didn't know anything about directing. I used to joke and tell him, 'Eddie, you couldn't direct traffic in a parking lot.'"[62] Apostolof also had to admit that Wood was a skilled typist. "He was the fastest typist I've ever seen in my life. His spelling was atrocious [Apostolof claimed Wood used to spell 'cat' with 'k'], but who cares? Kathy, his wife, used to write the final scripts for him. But Eddie was fast. I said I was getting two in one. I got a secretary and I got a writer."[63]

"Ed was a very poor speller and also he frequently, amusingly misunderstood the meaning of words and would use them in an awkward fashion," said Wood's "*illiterary* agent" (as he called himself) Forrest J Ackerman.[64]

Apostolof described *7 Rue Pigalle* as "a murder story like [Edgar Allan Poe's] *Murders in the Rue Morgue*,"[65] comparing it to the world's first detective story, originally published in 1867. The shooting was scheduled for April 1966. "I cast the picture and built the sets—beautiful sets—at the same place I shot *Orgy*," remembered Apostolof. "So the day before we start shooting, my art director tells me, 'Boss, the checks are bouncing! The checks are no good!' Then I went bananas. I went to the bank and the checks were no good, so I should have known: F.O.G. distributors."[66]

Apostolof abandoned *7 Rue Pigalle* and learned a valuable lesson: Never trust others too much, especially when it comes to money. In later years, when he was more established in the sexploitation business, he distributed his films himself under the banner of his own company, SCA Distributors, and at one point he even opened his own cinema. He did all of this to cut out the middleman and keep as much of the profits for himself as he possibly could.

But in the meantime, Apostolof still needed a home for his debut feature. Ultimately, the distribution of *Orgy of the Dead* was handled by producer Alfred N. Sack through Sack Amusement Enterprises, a company based in Dallas, Texas. Subsequently, "Papa Sack," as he was known among the producers of exploitation films, would become the main distributor of Apostolof's films in the '60s. Papa Sack owned Coronet Theatre in Dallas, a foreign and art film house with 470 leather and blue mohair upholstered seats as well as some extra wide "love seats." In his autobiography *A Youth in Babylon: Confessions of a Trash-Film King*, legendary producer-director David F. Friedman described Sack as "a Southern gentleman. He belonged to an exclusive Dallas club. He lived in a beautiful home in one of the city's best sections. He was a neighbor of Stanley Marcus, the Texas department store magnate. And he possessed one of the largest privately owned collections of costly Steuben glassware, all bought from the rentals of movies none of his neighbors or fellow club members even knew existed."[67]

But Papa Sack was, at heart, a paranoid businessman who was extremely suspicious that his partners would team up against him and screw him out of the money he was owed. And so he developed the nasty habit of keeping his producers on a short leash. Apostolof was no exception. He recalled, "Jerry Purcell represented the 13 Western states for Sack through his company Crest Distributors. What was so infuriating was that I lived five minutes from Jerry but I couldn't talk to Jerry unless I spoke to Alfred first. Everything had to be okayed by Alfred. Sometimes Jerry would call me because Alfred told him to call me. It was ridiculous."[68] In the end, despite such headaches, *Orgy* did receive both foreign and domestic distribution, sometimes under very strange circumstances.

It's interesting to note that *Orgy* was one of only two new films that played in Paris during the Social Revolution of May 1968, those heady days when the radio was playing songs by the Equals, Demis Roussos, Sam & Dave, Françoise Hardy and Sylvie Vartan, interrupted from time to time by news of the latest clashes between the police and protesting students. Film distribution in the city was all but paralyzed by the uprising; virtually no new titles were reaching theaters. One movie that did break through was *Orgy of the Dead*, which ran at La Scarlet on Clichy Boulevard and the now-defunct Midi-Minuit. After playing for a week, *Orgy* was replaced by *The Rape of the Vampire* (1968), directed by European low-budget horror master Jean Rollin.[69]

Orgy of the Dead proved to be extremely successful for Apostolof, financially if not critically. While it is difficult to ascertain the film's exact box office total, it is safe to say that, in the long run, the film's revenue far exceeded Apostolof's initial investment. This was characteristic of the director's other movies as well. "All my films [turned a profit] in the long run," Apostolof liked to boast.[70]

Today, *Orgy of the Dead* is best remembered as the first collaboration between Apostolof and Ed Wood. Theirs is one of the most bizarre partnerships in the history of B-movies.

Wood was born into a comfortable middle-class home on October 10, 1924, and came of age during the Great Depression before serving as a Marine in World War II. Wood was heavily influenced by the films he saw at the local movie house in his native Poughkeepsie, New York. He grew up on a steady diet of primitive cowboy pictures—he idolized Buck Jones—and Universal horror classics, particularly *Dracula* (1931, dir. Tod Browning) with Bela Lugosi. After moving to Los Angeles in 1947, he worked in the theater for several years before migrating to the film and television world. He managed to parlay his enthusiasm and an opportunistic friendship with the waning Lugosi into a uniquely bizarre moviemaking career of his own.

Starting with the autobiographical *Glen or Glenda* (1953), which dealt with themes of transvestism, Wood wrote and directed a series of odd low-budget exploitation films for the thrill-hungry moviegoing market. The idiosyncratic but sincere movies he made during that era of his life, including *Bride of the Monster* (1955), *Plan 9 from Outer Space* (1957) and *Night of the Ghouls* (1959), have given him a widespread but unfair reputation as the worst director of all time. His infamy was promoted by horror fan magazines like *Famous Monsters of Filmland* during the 1960s and '70s before Harry and Michael Medved's book, *The Golden Turkey Awards*, officially coronated him as the all-time worst director in 1980, two years after his death.

What few people know, however, is that in addition to being a screenwriter, producer, director and actor, Wood was one of the most prolific American authors of the 20th century. Between 1963 and 1978, he wrote hundreds of short stories and more than 75 novels, not to mention a slew of non-fiction articles and books on a variety of topics, including the occult. Most of Wood's literary output was cheap pulp fiction, generally erotic or pornographic in nature, often with a horror twist. He wrote of girl gangs, vampires, killer transvestites and more. With an imagination as fast as his typing fingers, Wood could turn out a complete manuscript in days. He signed his work under any number of pseudonyms, including Dick Trent, but he used his own name whenever possible.

Orgy of the Dead turned out to be a watershed film in Wood's career. The project reflected both his past and his future. The screenplay combines horror and eroticism in a way that demonstrates the influence of the Universal and Monogram horror movies of his youth as well as the radio shows like *I Love a Mystery* and *Chandu the Magician* that he grew up with in the 1930s. With its abundance of female flesh, on the other hand, *Orgy of the Dead* also showed where Wood was heading in the 1960s and '70s. For the rest of his tragic, alcohol-soaked life, Wood was forced to write and shoot pornographic films, both hardcore and softcore, to make ends meet.

The opening credits of *Orgy* declare: "Screenplay by Edward D. Wood, Jr. From his novel *Orgy of the Dead*." This was probably done to lend the film an air of prestige. In fact, the novel was published a month *after* the premiere of the film and has little direct connection to it, apart from a cover illustration by Robert Bonfils (1922–2018) that depicts Bob, Shirley, the Wolfman, a topless dancer and a giant skull. The so-called "novel" is actually a 160-page collection of short stories, all written by Wood, published in March 1966 by Greenleaf Classics. At the time, the San Diego company was the world's largest adult publishing house. The manuscript for *Orgy* came to Greenleaf through *Famous Monsters* founder Forrest J Ackerman, who was Wood's literary agent in the 1960s. Other Ackerman clients included Ray Bradbury and Isaac Asimov.

Chapter 8. The Director of the Dead (1965–1966)

Paperback version of *Orgy of the Dead* written by Ed Wood and published by Greenleaf Classics in 1966. Today the book sells for hundreds of dollars on eBay. "Too bad I didn't have psychic powers enough to get Ed Wood to autograph a hundred copies or so for posterity and my retirement," joked the publisher Earl Kemp.

"I sold a pornographic paperback for [Ed Wood] called *Orgy of the Dead*," said Ackerman. "He had scripted a story of the same name and I believe the way he turned it into a novel was simply to take the shooting script and then add a number of adjectives, adverbs and extra little bits of action that didn't appear in the film."[71]

"*Orgy of the Dead* came in as a submission from a legitimate literary agent," remembers Greenleaf's editorial director Earl Kemp. "It was a full package, including the still photos from the film. And it was part of a two-part sale, the other being [Charles Nuetzel's] *Queen of Blood*. The book was quite successful, mostly because of the cover painting by Robert Bonfils that sold for a high price. The film was about as successful as anything Ed Wood touched, which was not very much." Kemp doesn't remember seeing the film but admits that he might have done so. "The book and the film varied away from each other considerably, and I seem to be familiar with both versions."[72] But he certainly remembers his first meeting with Wood and Criswell in 1966:

> They were fantastic together, moving like a well-oiled machine, empathetically communicating with each other, each finishing the other's sentences, etc. I didn't know if I should be scared or amused most of the time. Fortunately, amused won out, and rightly so. Had I not accepted them, I would have missed out on one of life's really rare moments … sharing in fleeting touches of greatness. When I handed [Wood] that check, time froze. He looked at it in disbelief, then lit up like a Christmas tree, broke into a big grin, and did an involuntary quick two-step dance in excitement, all in double-time. I guessed that $500 check represented the largest amount of money Ed Wood had seen all at once in a long time.[73]

A limited reprint of 250 copies of *Orgy of the Dead* published in 2015 by Centipede Press as part of their Vintage Horrors series. Each hardcover copy was signed by artist Ben Baldwin who did the new artwork for the book.

Chapter 8. The Director of the Dead (1965–1966)

That check from Greenleaf would be worth $3,674.88 in today's money. Unfortunately, the *Orgy of the Dead* book also caused a serious rift between Apostolof and Wood. Decades later, Apostolof lamented in an interview with Wood's biographer Rudolph Grey,

> I am still very angry at Eddie, and because of him I have so little pictures from *Orgy of the Dead* today. I had all the pictures arranged in folders. One day Eddie comes and brings me six copies of his book *Orgy of the Dead*. I asked him, "So where did you get these photos?" It turns out he took them from the shelf in my office and gave them to Greenleaf. The publisher told him he would return them. I forgot, he forgot, and the rest is history.

Apostolof couldn't replace the photos because they were made by a hired photographer, and he had no negatives.

And thus ended the first, but far from the last, of Apostolof's absurd adventures with Ed Wood. These two men, who formed sort of a cinematic comedy team for the ages, would not work with each other again for six years. Perhaps they both needed time to recover from *Orgy of the Dead*.

CHAPTER 9

The Prince of Confidential (1966–1968)

By 1966, when *Orgy of the Dead* was released, the so-called nudie-cuties had already shown everything allowable on the female body in every possible way. What was left to do? It was time to start getting more creative.

A year before, Russ Meyer, the breast-worshipping, he-man director who inspired Apostolof to make erotic films, unleashed what many consider his masterpiece: *Faster, Pussycat! Kill! Kill!*, an explosive drama about three manic, sex-crazed go-go dancers who embark on a spree of kidnappings and murders against a stark desert setting. Still potent today, the film grabs the viewer by the throat with its opening shots, in which the three hormonal young ladies gyrate wildly for the benefit of their lecherous male admirers before hopping into their three individual sports cars in search of cheap thrills. Meyer's film is not only fast-paced and satisfyingly violent, but it also boasts energetic music (including an indelible theme song by the Bostweeds) and "dialogue to shame Raymond Chandler," as author Dean J. DeFino puts it.[1]

When Apostolof saw *Faster, Pussycat! Kill! Kill!*, he understood one thing: He needed more than just tits and asses to get viewers to the theater. He needed a story. Or better yet, several stories, one to suit every taste. So, between 1966 and 1969, Apostolof produced and directed three movies that contained the word "confidential" in their titles. Together, these films formed a loose trilogy. They claimed to offer insight into modern life in three seemingly banal locations—suburbia, motels and colleges, respectively.

In the 1950s and '60s, American cinema was overwhelmed by movies with the tempting word *Confidential* in their titles. Producers must have thought that adjective had some irresistible charm to it. In 1968 alone, the same year Apostolof's *College Girls* was released, there were at least three films on the market containing the same magic word: *Campus Confidential* (dir. unknown), *Free Love Confidential* (dir. Gordon Heller) and *Mail Order Confidential* (dir. unknown).

Harry H. Novak (1928–2014), a veteran exploitation producer and a friend of Apostolof, explained the phenomenon in Ray Greene's 2001 documentary feature *Schlock! The Secret History of American Movies*: "Everybody wants to know whose wife is doing what with whom. You give it that sort of secret element to it. Like *Free Love Confidential*, *Motel Confidential*.... It gives a connotation that something is going on behind the doors, under the sheets. People wanna see what took place and that's what brings them in."

Suburbia Confidential (1966)

One day in late 1965, Apostolof leafed through an issue of *Confidential*, a notorious gossip rag described by *Newsweek* as "sin and sex with a seasoning of right wing politics."[2] There he found an article about the sex life of the suburban American housewife. After reading it, he decided that this salacious topic would make a good subject for his next film.

Besides the *Confidential* article, Apostolof was also inspired by the Kinsey Reports published by the controversial American sexologist Dr. Alfred Kinsey in the years following World War II. Upon their initial release, Kinsey's *Sexual Behavior in the Human Male* (1948) and *Sexual Behavior in the Human Female* (1953) were greeted with a mixture of shock, disgust and fascination by an American public not accustomed to this degree of candor in print. Kinsey's books, drawing from thousands of personal interviews, not only questioned some long-held public beliefs about sex but also covered numerous topics considered taboo at the time, including infidelity. Kinsey found, for instance, that approximately 50 percent of all married men had had extramarital affairs at some point in their marriages, while 26 percent of women over 40 years of age had had sex outside marriage.

The opportunistic Apostolof, always keeping his finger on the pulse of society, decided to dramatize the sex lives of American housewives in a film with the working title *Neglected Wives*. He envisioned the action taking place in one of the many newly built American suburban neighborhoods that sprouted like toadstools in the 1940s and '50s. The stereotypical suburban American home, with its white picket fence, perfect mowed lawn and backyard swimming pool, had already become iconic by the mid-1960s. But the suburbs also had a dark side. So Apostolof changed the name of the prospective film to *Suburbia Confidential*.

Despite their popularity and ubiquity, the postwar suburbs were already attracting their share of criticism by the time Apostolof decided to make a movie about them. In 1961, for instance, American sociologist Lewis Mumford unkindly described them as "a multitude of uniform, unidentifiable houses, lined up inflexibly, at uniform distances, on uniform roads, in a treeless communal waste, inhabited by people of the same class, the same income, the same age group, witnessing the same television performances, eating the same tasteless pre-fabricated foods, from the same freezers, conforming in every outward and inward respect to a mold, manufactured in the central metropolis."[3]

In 1963, using plainer language than Mumford but communicating the same basic message, folk singer and political activist Malvina Reynolds recorded the definitive anti-suburbia anthem, "Little Boxes," a sly political satire aimed at those who "all play on the golf course and drink their martinis dry." Apostolof, an avid golfer and no stranger to alcohol, fit that description pretty well. Meanwhile, British architect Peter Blake made no secret of his feelings about suburbia when he sardonically titled his 1964 book on the subject *God's Own Junkyard*.

While squeaky-clean family sitcoms set in suburbia were the norm on television in the 1950s and '60s, epitomized by *The Adventures of Ozzie and Harriet* (1952–66) and *Father Knows Best* (1954–60), movies could afford to be a bit more critical in their depiction of the 'burbs. During the Eisenhower years, Gregory Peck struggled with the pressures of being a family man and a nine-to-fiver in *The Man in the Gray Flannel Suit* (1956, dir. Nunnally Johnson). A decade later, the world was ready for *The Graduate* (1967, dir. Mike Nichols), in which horny, boozy suburban matriarch Mrs. Robinson (Anne Bancroft) all but throws herself at befuddled young Benjamin Braddock (Dustin Hoffman).

And that was just what was happening in mainstream films. Exploitation films went even further. *Suburban Roulette* (1968, dir. Herschell Gordon Lewis) unabashedly focused on wife-swapping. In the trailer, the director declared: "Here is the picture that strips the suburbs bare and shows scenes you've never before seen on any screen!" He describes the film's suburban-dwelling characters as "desperate" and "frustrated." Essentially, they're so bored living outside the city that they have to resort to infidelity just to make it through another endless day.

Meanwhile, Apostolof was encountering some serious difficulties with the financing of his second movie, despite the attractive subject matter. "Distributors who had seen *Orgy of the Dead* criticized me that there weren't enough close-ups of the girls in which one can see better their 'ticket-sellers.' But what could I do? When I was shooting the movie, I had no zoom lens, and this is the reason why the film consists mostly of wide shots."[4]

Fate was kind to the Bulgarian when it came time to direct his second feature. One day in June 1966, while playing golf in Palm Springs, Apostolof bumped onto Donald Francis Nagel (1926–1996), an old friend from Republic, and told him about his idea to make his proposed film. Nagel had a successful restaurant in the Golf Capital of the World and agreed to invest $10,000 in it. That was enough to hire a cast and crew, so Apostolof and his pal shook hands on the back nine, and *Suburbia Confidential* was on its way.

A few days later, Apostolof started the casting process. Roughly 300 to 400 people showed up for the open call, all competing for the 20 or so roles Apostolof had to offer. The task of narrowing down the candidates was not terribly daunting, since many of the hopefuls had no clue about acting. Apostolof: "Most of those who showed up had never been in front of the camera in their life. They had no technique, not to mention style. Which was a challenge for me as a director, because I could mold them the way I wanted," said Apostolof.[5]

Apostolof said that *Suburbia Confidential* "was my version of the Kinsey Report. If you'll notice, there is not one single exterior shot. It's all shot indoors. I got spoiled shooting in a studio."[6] Indeed, the finished film has an almost claustrophobic feel, with a series of extramarital trysts occurring in cramped interior spaces. The film's horny, lonely housewives are both literally and figuratively trapped by their stultifying lifestyles.

Suburbia Confidential was ghostwritten by veteran screenwriter Michael Kraike (1908–2006), known as the producer of Robert Siodmak's exemplary 1949 film noir *Criss Cross*. Kraike also co-wrote *The Wild Scene* (1970, dir. William Rowland), a sexploitation film in which psychiatrist Dr. Virginia Grant is writing a book about young patients and their troubles. As in *Suburbia Confidential*, each chapter of Grant's book is a vignette in the movie.

Like a surprising number of sex films from the era, *Suburbia Confidential* takes the form of a pseudo-documentary, complete with a stern authority figure to act as a narrator and guide. In this case, it's humorless psychiatrist Dr. Legrand (George Cooper), who sits behind a desk in a drab office and addresses the camera directly. The good doctor tells us that many American housewives feel neglected and unappreciated by their husbands, so much so that they seek solace in extramarital affairs. He then illustrates this theory with a series of vignettes in which various housewives relieve their daily tedium by having sex with strangers, including TV repairmen and bellhops. Basically these women pounce on any man who enters their lives. And they don't really seem that conflicted by it either, since most of them are perfectly willing to strip for action after a minute or two. But these women must have felt pangs of guilt afterward, since they're all currently seeking treatment with Dr. Legrand. The film is admirably sympathetic to the women, explaining that they were driven to infidelity by their cloddish, inattentive husbands.

Ironically, just as he was about to film his scandalous exposé of American suburbia, Apostolof made his own second attempt at domestic bliss. This time his bride was 20-year-old Patricia Jeanne Rudl (nicknamed Pat), whom he married in September, 1966, three months after *Suburbia Confidential* went into production. Rudl served as Apostolof's secretary during the making of that movie. By then, Apostolof had his office at the old Raleigh Studios founded by Charlie Chaplin, Douglas Fairbanks and Mary Pickford. Funnily enough, this was where *The Mark of Zorro*, one of Apostolof's favorite films from his childhood, was partially shot.

Apostolof and Pat tied the knot on September 4, 1966, in a small ceremony held at Las Vegas' infamous Silver Bells Chapel. For the Orthodox Christian Apostolof, this was purely a lark, a spontaneous gesture, so the wedding required no special preparations. A photo from that day shows a very suave-looking Apostolof kissing the hand of his much taller brunette bride as a ring glistens on her finger. After the wedding, the couple took up residence at 3710 Los Feliz Boulevard in Los Angeles.

Production on *Suburbia Confidential* began in mid–July 1966 at Larry Smith Studios, a tiny Hollywood soundstage on

Apostolof kisses Pat Rudl's hand on the day of their wedding.

Melrose Avenue, where many exploitation filmmakers had their offices. Apostolof also shot several of his later films at this humble facility. "The studio was so dilapidated that we spent the whole first day in a futile attempt to run the lights on the set," he recalled.[7]

Filming took a mere two weeks. Don Nagel, who put up $10,000 and received an associate producer credit, was a near-constant presence on the set, much to Apostolof's annoyance. Nagel may simply have been protecting his investment, since he had risked the modern-day equivalent of $74,000. According to Apostolof, "Donnie thought he was the only producer on set and all others were rogues. He also had one huge flaw: He used to start drinking vodka with water at six in the morning, and he was constantly around the actresses, bothering them. I think he was in love with all of them."[8]

But Nagel had even more flaws, beyond his drinking. A film actor himself, with credits including Ed Wood's *Jail Bait* (1954) and *Bride of the Monster* (1955), he fancied himself an expert on moviemaking. On the second day of shooting, while Apostolof was filming one of Dr. Legrand's somber monologues, actor George Cooper flubbed a line. Apostolof naturally interrupted him but then heard Nagel, who was standing behind him, say, "It seems okay to me. Keep going!" Like any professional director, Apostolof was irked that someone was interfering. Cinematographer Robert Caramico, also peeved, told Nagel to shut up. This led to an argument between Nagel and Caramico. Apostolof had to pull Nagel aside and tell him, "Listen, Don, you're embarrassing me and making my job difficult. Who should the actors listen to, me or the voice behind me?" Nagel took the hint, but the film's greatest problems were still ahead.

The next morning, Caramico approached Apostolof and told him he wanted to be paid in advance, just to rub Nagel's nose in it. Caramico added that he would shoot the film only because he'd previously worked with Apostolof on *Orgy of the Dead*. This blunt approach, however, did not appeal to Apostolof. The director decided to lay down the law: "I said to Bob, 'Wait a second, pal! I don't work like that! Donnie is an associate producer. He's my partner. I talked with him and he assured me everything will be fine from now on.'" Caramico dug his heels in and said he didn't want Nagel on set. Apostolof reminded Caramico that the latter was just a cameraman and could not decide who should and shouldn't be on set.

Gary Kent, one of the actors in *Suburbia Confidential*, recalls what happened next: "Caramico got angry and left, and no one could find him. It was a big mystery what happened to him. It turned out Caramico was working back to back on another movie and hadn't slept much. He was very tired, and Steve found him sleeping in a room in the studio. Then [Apostolof] dragged him behind the camera and ordered him a coffee. And they *did* bring him coffee! A whole bucket of it, enough to wake up a dead man!"[9] Ultimately, though, Caramico wouldn't back down, and he and Apostolof were forced to part ways.

The director didn't regret this difficult decision. "I had to look for a new cameraman for three days, but at least I showed them who's boss," he recalled with some pride.[10] In the end, he replaced Caramico with Robert Charleton Wilson, a production photographer who had worked on *Orgy of the Dead*, and who had been a U.S. Army cameraman during the Korean War. Robert Maxwell, who had been serving as Caramico's assistant and who'd previously worked on *Orgy*, wanted to continue working on

Suburbia Confidential, but Nagel wouldn't let him on set. Maxwell, he felt, was from the enemy camp.

While filming *Suburbia Confidential*, Apostolof constantly made script changes and even added a whole new episode at the last moment. In the so-called "Korean War Bride" segment, a veteran visits a former comrade and meets his exotic wife May Lang, brought back from Korea. Nagel suggested this scene because he happened to know an Asian actress named Lolita Williams who was suitable for the role. Williams' good looks combined both Eastern and Western features, and Apostolof agreed to include her in the cast. Then he sat down and wrote the episode with her on a paper napkin in a restaurant over lunch.

Williams' screen partner was the aforementioned Gary Kent, then 33. He might not be a household name today, but if you've seen at least three exploitation movies from the 1960s, chances are he's in one of them. With his muscular physique and husky voice, the Walla Walla, Washington, native Kent was equally at home playing heroes and villains. Factor in his extensive work as a stuntman, stunt coordinator and production manager, and his filmography reads like a directory of exploitation cinema. Besides Apostolof, he worked with such iconic directors as Al Adamson, Monte Hellman, Ted V. Mikels, Brian De Palma, Peter Bogdanovich and Ray Dennis Steckler, to name but a few. Over the course of several decades, Kent made a name for himself as one of the best stuntmen in TV and film, with credits ranging from *The Man from U.N.C.L.E.* (1964–68) to *Color of Night* (1994, dir. Richard Rush).

Initially, Kent was employed on *Suburbia Confidential* as an electrician. He got the gig through his friend Donald M. Jones, a jack of all trades who went on to be a director in his own right, helming two sexploitation features in the 1970s before transitioning successfully to horror. According to Kent, "Don, who plays a servant in *Suburbia Confidential* and who previously had worked as an electrician on a variety of films, called and asked me if I'd like to work as an electrician. So I met with Stephen Apostolof, and he asked me if I'd play one of the roles. He said, 'You're good-looking! You should be in the movie!'"[11]

Gary gladly agreed and snared the role of Pat Harrington in the "Korean War Bride" segment. Wanting his actors to be comfortable during filming, Apostolof introduced Kent to his screen partner Lolita Williams on the set. The two clicked immediately. "At that time, the big thing was to show the girls' tits," Kent remembers. "Men in most cases were standing there with their clothes on, because nobody was interested in them. Everyone was looking at the girls. And we were forbidden to touch their breasts. We had to pretend to touch them, but had to bypass them. We were shooting a sex scene with Lolita Williams and I became so excited that I instinctively reached for her breasts. The next thing I hear was Steve yelling, 'Stop! Stop! Stop! Gary, you know that you should not touch the ticket-sellers, don't you?!'"[12] Apostolof had to do a second take, and this time everything went according to plan. Kent says,

> Apostolof's mood was elevated. You know, people become irritated when there are so many hot spotlights and when things go wrong. But Steve didn't let things get out of control. He joked a lot and managed to reduce tension on the set. Telling people what to do, but not teaching them. He was just great![13]
>
> Steve paid me $100 for one day's acting work and another $50 per day for my work as an electrician, which wasn't bad money in those years. He also gave me a chance to make love with a beautiful girl in

Gary Kent and Lolita Williams in the rarely seen "Korean War Bride" sequence in *Suburbia Confidential*.

front of the camera and behind it. I must admit that the evening after we finished filming, I took Lolita to my place and continued the sex scene but this time for real. She had great breasts and was a great lover albeit a bit shy, so I can't complain."[14]

"Making movies should be fun. If it's not, we'd better go home," Apostolof liked to say. And so, while filming *Suburbia Confidential*, he was constantly pranking his crew members. This spirit of mischief was apparently infectious. In one early scene, for example, housewife Helena Fox (Helena Clayton) decides to seduce amorous TV repairman Ralph Harris (John Bealey, who'd played a detective in *Orgy of the Dead*). The script called for the actress to make drinks for herself and her lover from a living room bar, then pour hers over her bare chest and exclaim, "Ahhh! There's nothing like a nice, cold shower!"

The TV repairman was then to do likewise, drizzling alcohol directly onto his bald head. The ice cubes in these drinks were supposed to be plastic, but some joker (Apostolof later blamed "the crew") used real ones instead. Bealey was suitably shocked, and the crew erupted in laughter. Apostolof was so hysterical he couldn't even manage to say *cut*. Then, according to Apostolof,

> The real fun came afterwards, when Budd Costello, who was the art director, came to me worried and said, "Boss, we don't have another pair of pants!" John's underwear was all wet and stained, and that was pretty evident in the frame. Then we decided to throw his pants on one of the lights and let them dry there. However, the lights were ten kilowatts and the pants started smelling. They were soon going to catch fire. Finally I got tired of all that, and I told Budd to wet the whole pants, so that they're all one color.[15]

Unsuspecting John Bealey pours a glass of ice-cold water over his head while Helena Clayton watches.

In the end, the director did several takes of the icy "shower" scene, but every time John Bealey was about to say, "Ahhh! There's nothing like a nice, cold shower!" the crew burst into laughter. Even Apostolof couldn't stop himself from cackling.

"We had to make more than 20 takes until I finally shot the scene," Apostolof recalled. "I was gripping my nose in order not to laugh and not to fuck the scene up. Finally, I told the crew, 'Brace yourself! I'm not MGM; we can't roll the camera indefinitely!'"[16]

Suburbia Confidential provided some employment for Apostolof's old cronies. Lou Ojena, who had played the Mummy in *Orgy of the Dead*, was cast as a lingerie salesman with a fetish for women's shoes. According to Apostolof he "had a big beard and looked like Mephistopheles."[17]

Meanwhile, Jaime Mendoza-Nava, composer of *Orgy*'s kitschy score, also wrote the languid, lounge-lizard music for *Suburbia Confidential*, this time using the absurd pseudonym Igor O'Gigagusky, which sounds like a cross between a leprechaun and Igor Stravinsky. Apostolof and Mendoza-Nava continued their professional relationship on several subsequent films, with the composer working under various, vaguely Eastern European–sounding pseudonyms, including J. Mendozof.

Like the Kinsey Reports that inspired it, *Suburbia Confidential* attempts to cover a wide spectrum of sexual activities and desires, both traditional and non-traditional. Among the topics broached here: lesbianism, transvestism, bondage and nymphomania. The movie even attempts to pass itself off as a pseudo-scientific study presented by the eminent (fictional) psychiatrist Dr. Henri Legrand. The stoic, upright doctor serves the movie as both its narrator and its unwavering moral compass. *Suburbia Confidential* is an example of what is known in American exploitation cinema as a "white coater," i.e., a sexually explicit film that pretends to be educational or instructive rather than lewd. The name derives from the fact that these films are often narrated by alleged doctors, many of whom wear white coats. In the 1940s and '50s, this kind of cinematic subterfuge was meant to ward off possible prosecution. Sexploitation filmmakers carried on the tradition for decades, well into the 1970s.

Over the course of the film, Dr. Legrand presents six different examples of marital infidelity, ostensibly to show the men in the audience what could happen if they keep neglecting their wives. The first vignette concerns frustrated hausfrau Helena Fox, who seeks retribution against her absentee husband by seducing a TV repairman

Lou Ojena plays a lingerie salesman with a fetish for women's shoes in *Suburbia Confidential*. Note the tattoo on his forearm.

and then, three weeks later, a milkman. Then Patsi Palmer (Hidie Shnee) falls for a transvestite who becomes a passionate lover slipping on some jewelry and lacy underwear. Sally Dane (Janice Kelly) woos a shy carpet dealer who ties her to the bed and starts tickling her.

Naïve Mona Carter (Brandy) is seduced by a lesbian cosmetics saleswoman and then by an underwear salesman (Lou Ojena) with a fetish for women's shoes. Korean bride May Lang (Lolita Williams) cheats on her husband with one of his army buddies (Gary Kent). Finally there is the case of Joy Graham (Jade Green), a nymphomaniac. Left alone by her husband in a motel, she tries to seduce a bellboy (Mark Crowe), only to find out he's gay. The frustrated Joy then all but pounces on a hapless room service guy (Don Jones) who barely manages to escape after a vigorous lovemaking session. Dr. Legrand describes these episodes in cold, clinical language and assures us that all of these women are now receiving proper psychiatric treatment. This, apparently, makes it acceptable for the audience to peep in on their indiscretions.

Apostolof had originally planned *Suburbia Confidential* to be in color, like his previous *Orgy of the Dead*, but the minuscule budget would not allow it. So the film was shot in black and white, which not only saved money but also added to the movie's documentary feel and suited the director's aesthetic tastes as well: "I love black and white, because it's more artistic. I always insisted on low-key light in all of my pictures, and that is one of the most difficult things to shoot. Most films are what I call television lighting—they bounce light off the back and everything is lit, it kills the double shadows. I created special shadows for black and white that you could see better than in color, the tones and halftones that are so important."[18]

Though wholly fictional, *Suburbia Confidential* purports to be based on the case files of a psychiatric professional. The fact that one of the stories deals with cross-dressing might lead some to believe that Apostolof was influenced by Ed Wood, who was a transvestite in real life and frequently incorporated that theme into his work. But Apostolof was adamant that Wood had no involvement in the creation of *Suburbia Confidential*. "It was just after *Orgy of the Dead*, and I wasn't even talking to Eddie," Apostolof averred. "I wrote the script of *Suburbia Confidential* in half an hour. I sat down and dramatized the life of the housewives from the suburbs, their sexual perversions, etc. I used the alias Jason Underwood, the brand of my typewriter. I just didn't want the film to begin with [a credit reading] 'Produced, Directed, Written and Conceived by...' So I decided to use Jason Underwood instead of my name."[19]

But the historical record suggests this is a fabrication on Apostolof's part. The true author of *Suburbia Confidential* was one Michael Kraike, as corroborated by a contract dated July 13, 1966. On subsequent films, Apostolof hired unknown screenwriters but then claimed writing credit for himself. He did this, in all likelihood, not only to flatter his own ego but to ensure that he held the rights to all of his movies. This was a canny move that paid off years later when he was making a living by distributing his old films.

Some of the confusion about Ed Wood being connected to *Suburbia Confidential* comes from the fact that in October 1967, Triumph published a 160-page paperback novel with that same title. The book was credited to Emil Moreau, one of dozens of aliases that the hyper-prolific Wood used as a writer in the 1960s and '70s. On its back cover, the book promised readers that its "macabre wife swapping escapades will make

[them] vomit." Although the salacious novel covered the same subject matter as Apostolof's film and had a similar vignette structure, Apostolof maintained there was no connection between the book and the movie.

"Eddie just used the title of my film," Apostolof said. "I told him, 'Eddie, you had to at least stick to the storyline in the movie.' But no, he was always desperate for money."[20]

This was not the only time an Ed Wood novel borrowed something from Apostolof's film. In 1967, Wood also published a paperback called *Death of a Transvestite*, a sequel to his 1963 book *Killer in Drag*, continuing the saga of a cross-dressing hitman. The first edition of the book used a photo of actor Hugh Hooker (1919–1987), who had played a transvestite in *Suburbia Confidential*. Although the actor's eyes were cancelled out with a discreet black bar, Hooker was still mortified to have his image used this way. At that time, he was working as a stand-in for Richard Basehart on the ABC prime time series *Voyage to the Bottom of the Sea* (1964–68). Some of his friends recognized him from the cover of *Death of a Transvestite* and ridiculed him for wearing women's clothes. "Hugh called me and was pretty damned angry," Apostolof recalled. "He asked me how his picture got into the hands of the publisher. I told him I don't know what he's talking about. And I really didn't! Hugh just could not believe that someone else besides me had access to his photos in women's clothing from *Suburbia Confidential*."[21]

In the mid–1960s, psychiatrists were common figures in both mainstream and exploitation movies. Producers felt that the presence of a medical professional could add legitimacy and even social relevance to what might otherwise be dismissed as a "dirty movie" with little to offer but a string of sex scenes. Before the introduction of the MPAA rating system in 1968, audiences were subjected to such offerings as *3 Nuts in Search of a Bolt* (1964, dir. Tommy Noonan), *The Twisted Sex* (1966, dir. Sande N. Johnsen) and *Ragina's Secrets* (1969, dir. Fletcher Hand), all of which portray psychiatrists in a highly implausible light. Meanwhile, the big Hollywood studios created serious films that dealt with psychiatrists and their patients in a more realistic manner. In *Splendor in the Grass* (1961, dir. Elia Kazan), the audience understands that Dean (Natalie Wood) has suffered a nervous breakdown when she emerges, dripping wet and naked, from her bath and reveals much of her bare back to the camera. The scene was praised by critics as a depiction of the character's mental instability.

Beside the influence of the Kinsey Reports, *Suburbia Confidential* drew its episodic structure from George Cukor's 1962 film *The Chapman Report*, which Apostolof saw at the Pantages Theatre on Hollywood Boulevard, and which was based on a controversial Irving Wallace novel. Wallace, too, had taken a cue from the research of Dr. Alfred Kinsey. In the Cukor film, Andrew Duggan plays psychiatrist Dr. George C. Chapman, a fictional version of Kinsey. Along with his assistant, Paul Radford, Jr. (played by Efrem Zimbalist, Jr.), he interviews four women about their sex lives. Not surprisingly, *The Chapman Report* met with fierce criticism from the National Legion of Decency, forcing Warner Brothers to recut it. The studio added a new epilogue explaining that these four women were exceptions and that most American wives had very normal sex lives. Apostolof's film ends with a similarly solemn coda.

After relating the tale of a nymphomaniac, Dr. Legrand addresses the camera directly:

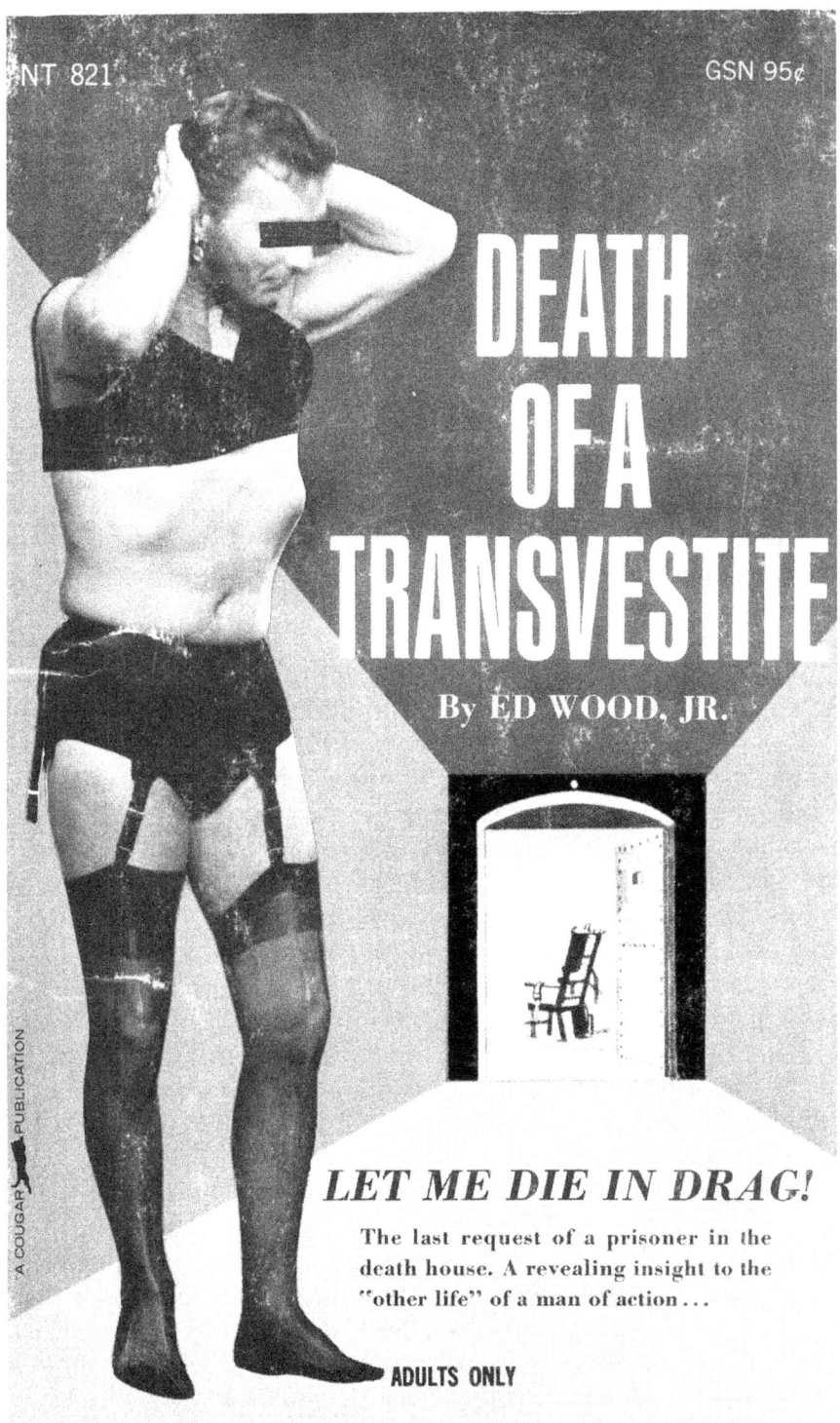

Hugh Hooker wears women's underwear in a scene from *Suburbia Confidential*. Unbeknownst to Hugh, Ed Wood took a similar photograph of the actor and used it for the cover of his novel *Death of a Transvestite*.

These cases are typical of dozens in my files and thousands in the files of other psychiatrists. They point out the problem of the suburban neglected wife. Authorities claim that, out of every 100 neglected wives who are badly neglected, at least 20 of them will resort to extramarital activities. The other 80 presumably supplement their emotions in various activities. For economic and other reasons, many wives do not wish to dissolve their marriages, yet they yearn for regular sexual satisfaction. We have just seen how these subjects have tried to solve their problems. Are they justified in what they did? Society frowns upon their behavior. What do you say?

In a way, especially by the standards of SCA's often chauvinist output, this speech is remarkably open-minded, even progressive. Apostolof's film stops short of condemning the women for their wanton ways and instead admonishes their neglectful husbands.

Suburbia Confidential premiered on November 16, 1966, at two Baltimore cinemas, the Rex and the Lord Baltimore. It reached the Midwest on December 1 with a premiere at the Aster Theatre in Minneapolis, one of the most popular adult cinemas of the 1960s and '70s. The film was distributed by Apostolof's own SCA Distributors as well as Sack Entertainment Enterprises, the company that had previously handled *Orgy of the Dead*. The *Suburbia Confidential* posters lured viewers with promises like "The Kinsey Report shocked readers, *Suburbia Confidential* ... will shock you!" and "It starts where the Kinsey Report left off." The pressbook claimed the film was "so startling the lab refused to process [the negative]."

In 1967, *Suburbia Confidential* played the Rialto in downtown Los Angeles together with *Bed of Fire* (1964, dir. Antonio Santean) under the ad line "Come See What Happens in a Quiet Neighborhood." Funnily enough, that put *Suburbia Confidential* in direct competition with *Who's Afraid of Virginia Woolf?* (1966, dir. Mike Nichols), another film about marital troubles that was playing in the Tower cinema nearby.

On October 20, 1967, *Time* magazine published an article called "The Trade: Nude Wave" about New York City's infamous 42nd Street, then a hotbed of adult theaters. The story included a photo of a theater window plastered with posters for *Suburbia Confidential*. The film's salacious title wasn't mentioned in the article, but this was the closest Apostolof would ever get to coverage in a respectable publication, at least for one of his sex films. He was so proud that his film found its way into the pages of *Time* that he bought several copies and kept them in his archives. After that article, *Suburbia Confidential* played on 42nd Street for years. During a climactic car chase in the black comedy *No Way to Treat a Lady* (1968, dir. Jack Smythe), we see a theater marquee and the titles *Suburbia Confidential* and *Pink Pussy: Where Sin Lives* (1964, dir. Albert Dubois), a Venezuelan sexploitation film.

The film was booked at other prominent movie houses. In February 1968, for instance, it played at the Lamar Theatre in Memphis on a double bill with *Confessions of a Bad Girl* (1965, dir. Barry Mahon). This same cinema later achieved notoriety when it played the pioneering hardcore feature *Deep Throat* (1972, dir. Gerard Damiano), resulting in a Memphis pornography trial for bringing the film across the Tennessee state line. In April 1968, *Suburbia Confidential* was advertised in the *Los Angeles Times* and played at the Monica Theatre at 7734 Santa Monica Boulevard in West Hollywood, a location that would later be turned into the infamous Pussycat Theatre.

In 1969, *New York* magazine published "Bumping the Grinds," an article in which film critic Judith Crist called *Suburbia Confidential* "one of the all-time grind greats, an anthology of the dire experiences that had driven a sexology of suburban housewives

A two color one sheet for *Suburbia Confidential*.

into the hands of a psychiatrist." But this seemingly laudatory appraisal is followed by harsh criticism: Crist ridiculed *Suburbia Confidential* and other exploitation movies for "sub–Warhol cheap production" and "technical and artistic ineptitude." She also noted that these films were on a "perpetual search for a moral overtone or conclusion after the depths of depravity (like transvestiterism [sic]) had been lovingly probed."[22]

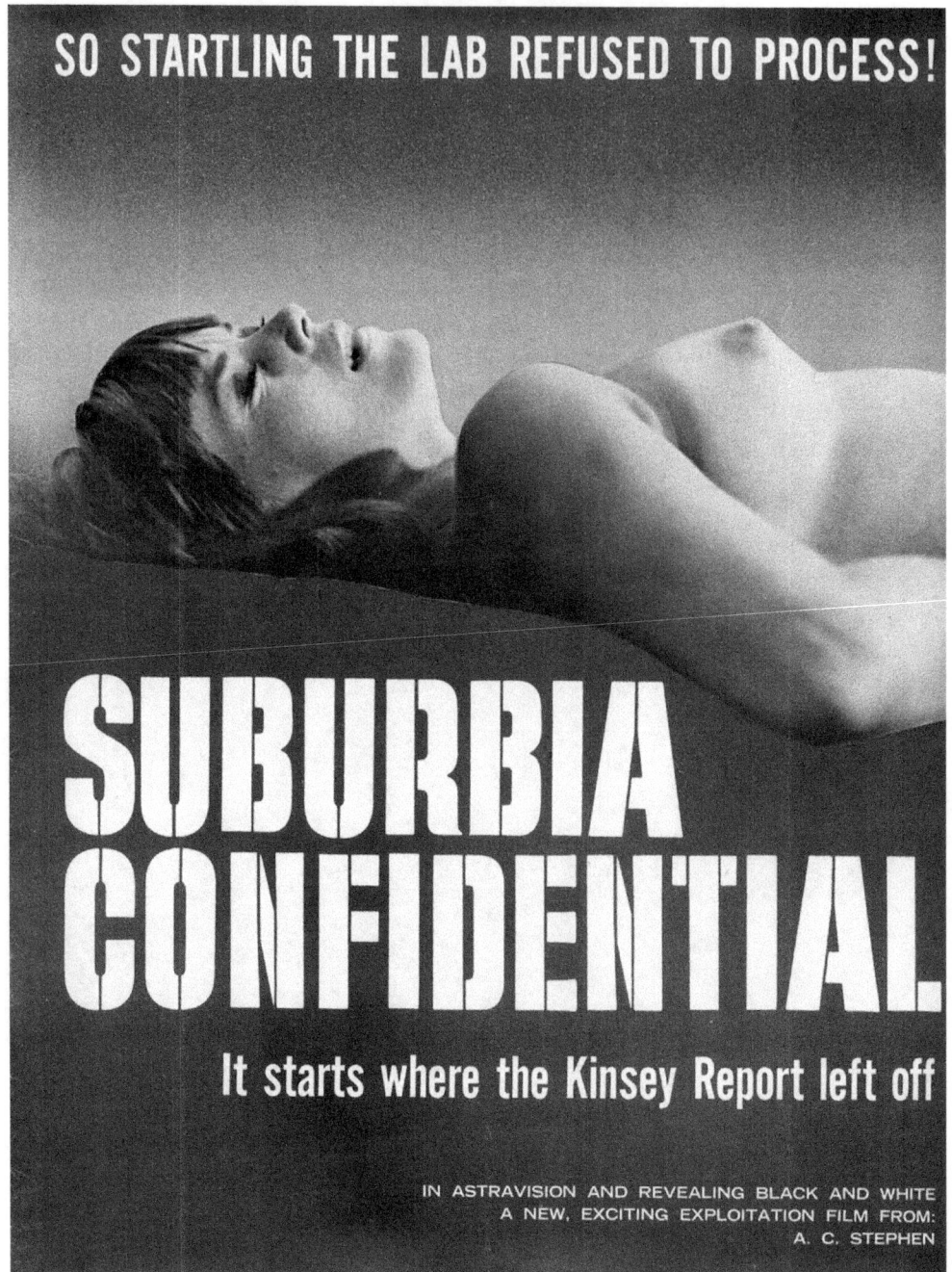

A monochrome press book cover for *Suburbia Confidential*.

Suburbia Confidential turned out to be one of Apostolof's most profitable movies. Years later, the director still boasted of its financial success. "The whole film together with copies and advertising cost me exactly $30,002. And do you know how much I made from it? About $700,000!"[23] Apostolof was so proud of the movie that once, while he was in New York, he decided to take a fellow producer and friend to watch it with

Chapter 9. The Prince of Confidential (1966–1968)

In 1967 *Suburbia Confidential* played at the Rialto in downtown Los Angeles, competing with *Who's Afraid of Virginia Woolf?* at the Tower next door.

him at a 42nd Street grindhouse. "But first we went to the Greek restaurant Mykonos in the West Village. We had a dinner, a couple of glasses of ouzo, and I felt very good. The cinema was full. I had seen the movie a hundred times, and I began telling my friend what will happen next. Someone from the audience shushed to me two or three times. A few minutes later, a guy with a flashlight came and said, 'You two, out!' They kicked me out of my own movie, can you imagine that?!"[24]

In December 1966, Apostolof gave his new spouse Patricia Rudl a generous Christmas gift: ten shares of stock from his company. He ordered his lawyer Harold A. Abeles to give one share to accountant Geoffrey Lidman and another to Don Nagel. Apostolof kept 88 shares for himself. Little did he know that his second marriage, a hasty, unplanned affair, would prove ill-considered in the long run. "Steve mentioned he married Pat in Las Vegas after a drunken weekend, and it was a bad idea," reports Christopher Apostolof. "He said more than once that his lawyer Harold Abeles saved him on that one. Harold represented him for both his divorces, and Pat ended up with nothing from the divorce somehow."[25]

To put it mildly, this union was not built to last. On February 24, 1967, the eve of Apostolof's 39th birthday, Pat left him. Harvey Shain, a longtime friend of Apostolof, recalled,

> All of a sudden, I hear that she ran away with a young actor. Young, good-looking actor. They had driven a truck up to the house when Steve was out of town. He might have been shooting, I don't know, and they just cleaned it out, all the furniture, a lot of things.[26]

Steve took this very hard, and he couldn't stop drinking. He basically hit the skids. One night I got a call they were looking for him. They thought he was maybe with me. And they found him drunk in the street, up near the post office here, in Hollywood, near Wilcox Avenue.[27]

In all, the marriage between Apostolof and Rudl lasted a little more than a year and was officially dissolved on August 25, 1967. Polly Apostolof maintains that the marriage failed because her father had tricked Patricia into thinking he was rich. When she learned the truth, she felt deceived and "ran for her life."[28]

"The year after Pat left was the year when we didn't see Dad a lot," remembered Apostolof's oldest son Steve. "I think she crushed him for a while. The visits that we went to see Dad every other week, they dwindled dramatically after that. Eventually, things got back together, but you know, when you lose love, you do change."[29]

Motel Confidential (1967)

> *"A raw, hard-hitting story from A.C. Stephen, who brought you* Suburbia Confidential, Motel Confidential *is made up of the type of pure action that sells tickets. Beautiful girls? Yes. Production quality? Yes. But most important of all? Blunt, down-to-earth scenes that set new levels for other producers to shoot for. Scenes that will leave the customers gasping ... and coming back for more."*—from the *Motel Confidential* pressbook

Suburbia Confidential was a smash hit for Apostolof, and others were soon to follow. In a pattern he would follow for the rest of his moviemaking career, the ambitious producer-director invested the profits from his previous production into his next one. Unsurprisingly, Apostolof stuck with his winning formula when it came time to make a follow-up. "*Suburbia Confidential* was particularly successful," he said, "and every distributor was trying to get their hands on it. At the same time, the price of movie tickets increased from $2 to $3, so I said to myself, 'Why not make another movie from the series *Confidential*'? Thus *Motel Confidential* was conceived."[30]

On January 19, 1967, Apostolof bought a film script called *Quickie* by *Orgy of the Dead* choreographer Mark Desmond (aka Mark Del Monde or Marc Da Vinci), supposedly based on his novel of the same name. The action in *Quickie* takes place at a pleasant but slightly seedy establishment appropriately called the Quickie Motel, managed by a squabbling Italian-American family. Naïve, old-fashioned Campobello (played by Apostolof's regular Vincent Barbi) and his shiftless, lascivious nephew Chi-Chi (Timothy Paola) aren't too worried what the Michelin guide will say about their establishment, nor are they terribly concerned with long-term bookings. Instead, their business comes from short-term clients (most of whom check in under the name "Jones") seeking only a discreet, inexpensive place to have quick but fulfilling sexual trysts.

Apostolof summed up the film's plot thusly: "The father's name was Saverio Campobello, but he insisted on people calling him Campbell. He runs a seedy motel, but thinks it's the Hilton. Chi-Chi is his nephew who knows everything that's happening in the motel and who's banging all the guests."[31]

With a brisk running time of 85 minutes, *Motel Confidential* was hyped as "an

Monochrome one sheet for *Motel Confidential*.

exposé of the hot sheets industry." The structure of the film, like that of *Suburbia Confidential*, is episodic. It consists of several comedic vignettes about various couples enjoying the motel. Business tycoon Stanley Buddington III (Mark Shannon), for instance, manages to seduce his beautiful secretary Ann Pepper (Desiree D'Andre) after a few drinks. Donald (Hugh Johnson) and Susan Harrison (Pat Niece), whose argumentative marriage is falling apart, spend a second honeymoon in the motel on the advice of their psychiatrist. Newlyweds Harry (John Patino) and Daisy Ferguson (Sharon Patino) are just about to have sex for the first time, only to realize at the last moment that they have no condoms. Poor Harry, who looks like a Wayne Newton impersonator, has to cross the whole city to avoid "firing up the population explosion" as he puts it, and when he finally manages to buy condoms, he forgets his way back to the motel. Along the way, he meets Apostolof buddy and fellow adult filmmaker Don Davis, typecast as a drunk. Davis' character manages to spill both perfume and booze on hapless Harry, making for an awkward scene when the groom finally returns to his bride.

Spinster Phyllis Doogoodie (Helena Clayton) orders room service and winds up in bed with the bellhop Chi-Chi, who catches her doing topless calisthenics. While cruising for chicks at a nearby bar, self-styled macho man Romeo Rampart (Vic Lance) picks up a Monroe-type blonde (Michael DiRosa) who turns out to be a transvestite. Milquetoast Casper Murk (John Bealey) brings his companion, petite brunette Sadie Jones (Paula Allison), to the motel, where Sadie's angry husband Masher (Robert Dodson) catches them in bed together. Casper manages to get away by giving his money to the cuckolded spouse, but it turns out the Joneses are scammers who have pulled this same con on other victims. Once Casper victim has fled, the con artists stick around and have sex. Why not? The room is already paid for.

In the humorous finale, sailor Willy King (Harvey Shain), starved for physical affection after nine long months at sea, is unable to keep up with nymphomaniac Helen Gibbins (Diana Denning), whose appetite for sex proves insatiable. Much like the beleaguered hotel employee in *Suburbia Confidential,* Willy is barely able to escape the clutches of his lustful paramour. Luckily for Helen, the ever-amorous Chi-Chi gladly takes Willy's place in bed.

Three of the actresses in *Motel Confidential*—Barbara Nordin, Bunny Glaser and Coleen O'Brien—had previously appeared as dancing ghouls in *Orgy of the Dead*. That's no coincidence. A key element of Apostolof's success as a sexploitation filmmaker in the 1960s was that he worked with the same reliable people on multiple productions. He explained:

> It was like a repertory theater. My position was this: If someone was good—and they better be good, otherwise I'll kick his ass out. I don't have time to teach. I'm not UCLA. And they knew it. I work very, very hard. I was known for late hours, no nonsense. But the end result was good, everybody knew that. So if you work on a picture for me, you know the picture's going to be good. And that's important to an actor. The second thing was, the people I worked with were good, and if they were good why should I take a chance working with someone else?[32]

Motel Confidential is a pivotal entry in Apostolof's filmography because it marks the first in a decade-long series of collaborations between the producer-director and New York-born Harvey Shain (born in 1937). Sometimes billed as Forman Shain or Forman Shane among other aliases, Harvey went on to appear in nearly every subse-

Chapter 9. The Prince of Confidential (1966–1968)

Harvey Shain pretends to be a toreador in Apostolof's *Hot Ice* as actress Teresa Parker looks on in amusement.

quent Apostolof film, often taking leading roles. The affable, curly-haired Shain brought his innate likability and easygoing charm to a number of parts both serious and comic for Apostolof, becoming the director's go-to male star. In SCA productions spanning a decade, he played everything from a dashing hero (*Lady Godiva Rides*) to a bumbling fool (*Hot Ice*) with aplomb. Though he lacked the lantern jaw or muscle-bound physique of a stereotypical leading man, he was still believable as the kind of guy women might find cute. In *Motel Confidential*, he was perfect for the role of Willy, the sailor who meets his match in maneater Helen Gibbins.

One of Shain's most useful talents was his ability to make even the most stilted and contrived dialogue sound natural. He was, in short, a quickie screenwriter's best friend. And since SCA was in the business of making sexploitation films for an adult audience, Shain also participated in the down-and-dirty bedroom scenes with no apparent embarrassment. Apostolof quickly recognized Shain's value, even if the actor's work ethic wasn't always up to Apostolof's high standards. Apostolof reminisced,

Harvey is so talented, but he's so lazy. He's shy about promoting himself, which is very unusual for an actor. My editor is Italian, Tony Mora.[33] He was watching Harvey on the Moviola, and praising him: "Aha, look at how he knows how to make love, that's an Italian boy!" I said, "Tony, shaddup, Harvey's Jewish!" I'll never forget the look on his face. I'm going to surprise [Harvey]. He doesn't have all the pictures he's in, so I'm going to send him the whole package. That's for his grandchildren! I'm just joking.[34]

Lazy or not, Shain became a key figure at SCA throughout the late 1960s and '70s, serving as an actor and as Apostolof's right-hand man behind the scenes. Future Apostolof films would occasionally credit him as assistant director, casting director or dialogue director. Shain also became a personal friend of Apostolof's and, as such, was well known to the director's family. Polly Apostolof recalls, "For us he was just Uncle Harvey. We did not know exactly what his roles were. We only knew him as an actor. Only later did we realize that he was in every single one of Dad's movies."[35]

Apostolof's children, however, did not always guess the exact nature of Harvey Shain's participation in their father's films. "I was really quite shocked when I found that he was involved in so many sex scenes in my father's movies," remembers Susan.[36]

"Harvey Shain is a really nice guy," son Steve Apostolof said. "He was a good friend of Dad. Kind of hammy, but he is an actor. You can expect that. But a real good guy. I like Harvey."[37]

Shain's memories of Apostolof and the SCA films have faded with time, but some moments still stand out. Now retired and living in a modest one-bedroom apartment in Van Nuys, California, he says,

> I don't remember how I appeared at an audition for *Motel Confidential*. Most likely, Steve had placed an ad in one of the trade papers of the film industry. I remember the pay was very low. I think this is one of Steve's best films, because once I went to see it with him and his girlfriend, who then became my first wife. The theater was full, and everyone was laughing because the film has a lot of comedy.[38]

Apostolof considered the *Motel Confidential* script hysterically funny since it contained numerous examples of wordplay and other verbal comedy. In one scene, for instance, the hotel manager says to his lazy nephew, "Chi-Chi, take the bag." He then points to a frumpy female customer, who takes offense before realizing that the manager is referring to her luggage. In another scene, a guest asks the manager for "quarters," meaning lodging, but the manager thinks he's looking for 25-cent coins. And the entire sequence between Don Davis and John Patino plays like a vaudeville routine, with the two men talking at cross purposes like Abbott and Costello.

Motel Confidential reunited Apostolof with his pal Robert Caramico, the hardworking cinematographer of *Orgy of the Dead*. Under the pseudonym Robert Ruben, Caramico became Apostolof's go-to cameraman for many of his sexploitation classics of the 1960s and '70s. Over the course of these films, Caramico became very familiar with Apostolof's working style. Typically, a scene in an SCA movie would be filmed in one long master shot and then covered with a series of close-ups. Well aware of his budget limitations, Apostolof rarely did retakes. "If you made a mistake," Shain recalls, "Steve would simply cut the shot from the film."[39]

As careful as he tried to be, Apostolof still had some trouble on the *Motel Confidential* set. In one scene, for instance, the director decided to play some background music while shooting the scene in which a transvestite dances in his underwear in order to seduce the man who picked him up in a hotel bar. And so Sam "The Man" Kopetzky (1937–2003), who worked on *Orgy of the Dead*, and served as the sound recorder on this and numerous other sexploitation films (plus a few Ed Wood titles), dragged a couple of huge speakers to the set. Kopetzky was a successful sound man in B-movies for years, but this time he might have misjudged the situation. According to Apostolof,

> When Sam turned the speakers on, it was like we were at Dodger Stadium. But during the dance scene, the whole thing went "poof," and the set fell into silence. And because the scene had turned out really well so far, I began to sing: *"Sam-Ko-Pet-zky-what-have-you-done? Sam-Ko-Pet-zky-I-am-gonna-kill-you! 1, 2, 3! Listen-to-my-voice! Don't-listen-to-anything-else! Keep-dancing!"* So I saved the shot, because it was really great. When I said *cut*, the whole crew began applauding me.[40]

Motel Confidential premiered on November 10, 1967, at the Monica Theatre, at 7734 Santa Monica Boulevard. Alfred Sack, who had distributed *Orgy of the Dead* and *Suburbia Confidential*, acquired the rights to distribute *Motel Confidential* nationally, with the exception of the West Coast and New York. These territories were instead given over to Jerome "Jerry" Balsam (1923–1999), a veteran distributor who would later become one of Apostolof's closest friends and partners. Balsam's company J.E.R. Pictures, Inc., was one of the largest distributors of exploitation movies on the East Coast and handled the films of such directors as Doris Wishman and Andy Milligan. Balsam, together with producers and distributors like Stanley Borden, William Mishkin, Barry Mahon, Chelly Wilson and Joseph Brenner, had secure positions on 42nd Street in New York. His films played at such theaters as the Cameo, Lyric, Avon, Globe, World and Malibu.

Bachelor's Dream (1967)

> *"I never screwed around with my cast. That way I stayed the boss and they respected me. In fact, whenever I auditioned them, I always had another person with me. Preferably a woman. I wanted them to feel comfortable. I didn't want them to think they were putting on a show for some pervert. It was all very professional."*—Stephen C. Apostolof[41]

In 1967, when Apostolof was working on *Motel Confidential*, he also produced and directed a little-known film called *Bachelor's Dream*. "Making a film was never a problem," he explained. "That, to me, was like a well-oiled machine. I used practically the same key people. I used practically the same leads. The moment I announced I would make a film, Sack was already lining up bookings."[42]

So Apostolof had no problem completing a movie and getting it distributed. But, he felt, he did have a problem with theater owners stealing from him. In those days, it was customary for theaters to book a supporting feature film along with the main feature, and these lesser films were entitled to a substantial cut of the box office proceeds. That obviously didn't sit well with Apostolof. "I was getting sick and tired of getting theater reports and seeing what was being deducted for the second feature. It's very difficult to make money with just one film on the bill. I figured I needed the whole program to be mine so they couldn't steal as much."[43]

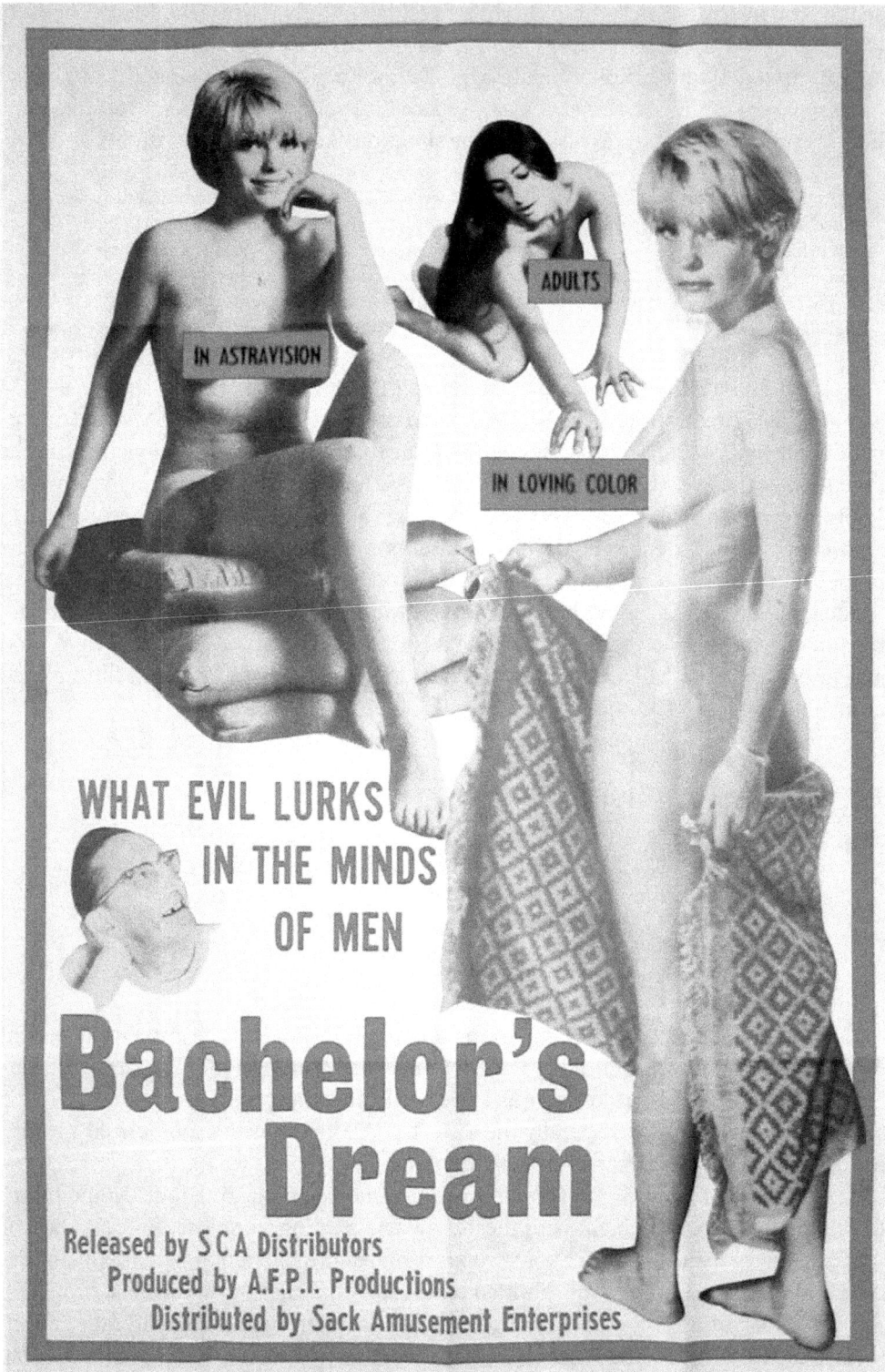

A color one sheet for *Bachelor's Dream*.

Chapter 9. The Prince of Confidential (1966-1968)

The resourceful filmmaker had a solution. He remembered he had some footage shot by cameraman Bob Wilson during *Orgy of the Dead* with a couple of lights and a little handheld camera. It was just some tests of a couple of the girls doing their dances. Nothing earth-shattering. At first Apostolof didn't think he could use the footage, so he didn't even get it developed. It was just sitting in film cans. "But when I got the idea to make a second feature, I hired two new girls just for one day to shoot the color scenes with the character—what was his name?—Abner Bidle. He was just lying around dreaming of beautiful girls."[44]

The old *Orgy of the Dead* test footage was repurposed as a sepia-tinted daydream sequence in *Bachelor's Dream*. What's more interesting about this movie is that it's a short (or featurette) lasting only 33 minutes, but its advertising campaign made it sound like a feature. And, like *Orgy of the Dead* before it, it was said to have been shot in "loving color" and "Astravision.""

The thin plot of *Bachelor's Dream* revolves around a protagonist (Abner Bidle) who fantasizes that he is in a dark theater watching scantily clad girls dancing on stage. It bears a passing resemblance to *Not Tonight Henry* (1960, dir. W. Merle Connell), in which a frustrated husband fantasizes about having sex with such historical figures as Cleopatra, Delilah, Pocahontas and Lucrezia Borgia. But the clearest cinematic ancestor of *Bachelor's Dream* is the pioneering nudie-cutie *The Immoral Mr. Teas* (1959, dir. Russ Meyer), in which the sex-obsessed title character can't help but mentally undress every attractive woman he encounters.

Here, as in *Orgy of the Dead,* Apostolof decided to play it safe: There's no bodily contact or simulated sex to offend the censors. The film's "action" takes place in Bidle's overstimulated mind. Each day, as he returns from the office, the shy, meek Bidle retires to the solitary paradise of his girlie books, bringing the models to life with his lively imagination. In his reverie, he watches Anita dance sensuously and feasts his eyes on Angie as she plays with her collection of stuffed animals. In his dreams, women undress until the finale, when he finally asks a stunning blonde out on a date.

In 1969 *Bachelor's Dream* played on a double bill with Apostolof's *Lady Godiva Rides* at the Pussycat Theatre in Torrance, California, while members of the local Christian community protested it in front of the building. This is the same cinema where the 16-year-old Quentin Tarantino worked as an usher in 1979. The cinema was also featured in Tim Burton's *Ed Wood* as the place of Wood's *Bride of the Monster* premiere.

College Girls (1968)

Educated women are a threat to the reproduction of the human race. Or so wrote Harvard professor Edward H. Clarke (1820–1877) in his bestselling 1875 book *Sex in Education: Or, a Fair Chance for the Girls*. Clarke suggested that women who engaged in vigorous mental activity risked atrophy of the uterus and ovaries, masculinization, sterility, insanity, even death. He likened educated women to the "sexless class of termites"[45] whose only task is to feed the colony.

Decades after having been compared unfavorably to a subterranean insect, the college girl developed into an icon of 20th century American sexuality. In her study *College Girls: Bluestockings, Sex Kittens, and Co-eds, Then and Now* (2006), Lynn Peril makes the case that 20th century women striving for better education were often associated with sexual emancipation. The liberated, fun-seeking college girl has long been a staple character not only in men's magazines, but in many sexploitation and mainstream movies, stirring up carnal thoughts in the male audience. Apostolof, always on the lookout for another big hit, decided to set his next film behind the ivy-covered walls of an unnamed American college where the students *and* faculty members are obsessed with getting their "kicks."

The surprisingly dramatic *College Girls* (aka *College Girls Confidential*), the third in Apostolof's *Confidential* series, marks a significant departure from the other two. For one thing, it abandons the episodic structure of *Suburbia Confidential* and *Motel Confidential*. More significantly, unlike virtually every other film in the Apostolof canon, *College Girls* focuses on the lives of young people. Generally, the SCA films tend to be about full-fledged adults, often with stressful jobs and troubled marriages.

At heart, this is a typical nudie-cutie in the grand tradition of low-budget films like Albert Zugsmith's *Sex Kittens Go to College* (1960) and *College Confidential* (1960). One troubling subplot, however, is more typical of Apostolof's other films. It involves a biology teacher who fools around with his female students because he isn't getting enough (or any) sex from his "cold, passionless" harridan of a wife. In the film's darkest sequence, he physically forces himself on her as she audibly protests. Later, the teacher's wife makes love to a sobbing coed who has just been sexually assaulted at a frat party by a male guest. "All men are such beasts," she insists.

Perhaps most importantly, *College Girls* is the first Apostolof film to feature Marsha Jordan, a statuesque actress who became known as the Queen of Softcore Cinema for her work with numerous adult film directors in the 1960s and '70s. Busty and blonde and unashamed about showing off her physique, Jordan may have been a few years older than most of her co-stars, but she made up for it with a commanding, strikingly erotic screen presence. Like Harvey Shain, Jordan also had a knack for delivering dialogue clearly and with proper emphasis. Her performances often stand out for this reason, especially when her co-stars are reciting their lines in a flat manner. Jordan excelled at playing take-charge women who would not be easily dominated by men, yet her characters are often hedonistic and adventurous behind closed doors. She was a natural for the SCA movies, and Apostolof cast her again and again.

The other female roles in *College Girls* are performed by "decorative actresses,"[46] as film historian Tom Lisanti termed the various *Playboy* models, beauty pageant contestants and Las Vegas showgirls who flocked to Hollywood in the 1960s hoping to become TV and film stars. Many of these young ladies spent their careers being photographed for men's magazines while scantily clad or without clothes. And a handful found a curious form of immortality by landing bit roles in exploitation movies, including those made by Apostolof.

In 1967, Apostolof began working with William A. Cushman of the consulting firm Williams & Associates to find backers for his next movie. Quite often during this era of exploitation filmmaking, a movie's so-called backers had nothing to do with the movies themselves and saw films as merely another way to make quick money in a relatively risk-free way. In most cases, their names didn't even appear in the credits. A prime example is R.G.F. Byington, a middle-aged real estate developer from Lahaina, West Maui, Hawaii, who became one of the backers of *Motel Confidential* in December 1967.

On January 12, 1968, Apostolof signed a contract with his old friend Herb Niccolls, who sold him the rights to a story tentatively named "College Kicks." The planned budget was $35,000 but it quickly rose to $46,525. Apostolof's payment as a director and producer of the movie was $6000 (about $44,500 today)—not a bad amount of money for a couple of months of work.

As with the previous two entries in the series, Apostolof shot *College Girls* in black and white, again giving the film a gritty, almost documentary look. According to Harvey Shain, the script was "long and involved" and covered a wide range of subjects. And indeed, the film includes references to oral sex, S&M, lesbianism, homosexuality and group sex, while its characters use a number of drugs, including marijuana, LSD and "goofballs" (presumably barbiturates). But the film also includes moments when characters break the fourth wall and speak to the viewer directly, as when a gay man surveys the showers in a men's locker room and declares, "Wow! Smorgasbord!" Apostolof also makes some rudimentary attempts at creating psychedelic visuals in order to represent the mindset of the film's chemically altered characters.

The characters in *College Girls* are students and teachers who indulge unabashedly in sex and drugs, seemingly without regard for the moral or physical consequences. Silver-haired Prof. Bryce (Sean O'Hara), for instance, teaches biology by day but does most of his experimenting in bed with willing coeds rather than in a lab. Knowing this, one of his students, Fluff (Gee Gentell), a willowy blonde in danger of flunking, seduces the professor in exchange for a passing grade. Rosie (Marsha Jordan) and her roommate (Capri) help initiate their fellow student Wistfull (Randy Lee) into a fraternity cheekily named Lambda Sigma Delta (or LSD). At the party after the ceremony, the male and female guests take a lot of drugs and lose their inhibitions, as well as their clothes. Prof. Bryce attends, with his wife (Michelle Rodan) in tow, but mostly stays parked on a couch.

Meanwhile, in an upstairs bedroom, campus football hero Harry (Moose Howard) rapes Jane (Dianna Rosano). The sobbing young lady then finds solace in the arms of Prof. Bryce's unhappy wife, who turns out to be a lesbian. In the film's final moments, *College Girls* becomes an anti-drug scare film. Good-natured Charlie (Harvey Shain credited here as Forman Shane), president of Lambda Sigma Delta, takes acid and decides he can fly. He jumps from a second-story balcony, lands with a sickening thud on

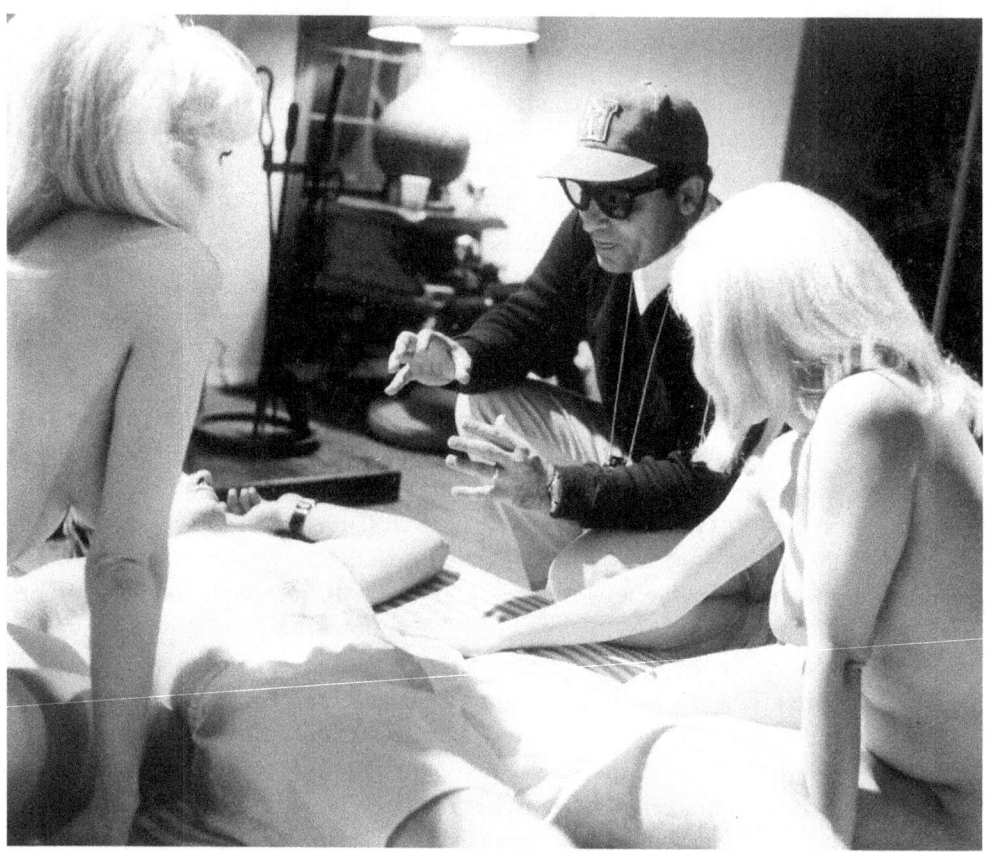

Apostolof directs actors Marsha Jordan (left), Randy Lee (middle) and Capri (right) in the initiation sex scene in *College Girls*.

the floor, and ends up in a hospital, where a stern lecture from a doctor convinces him never to touch drugs again.

College Girls was conceived at the height of the Summer of Love, when drug use was a very hot topic in America. In 1967, Gerald Priestland, the BBC's chief American correspondent, reported that four tons of marijuana and half a million LSD tablets were consumed each month in San Francisco, epicenter of the hippie movement. Priestland also reported that some stoned hippies "jumped out of the windows, convinced that they can fly."[47] This wasn't an isolated incident, and the phenomenon definitely made an impression on Apostolof, who was apparently so fascinated by it that he carefully collected newspaper clippings describing such accidents.

College Girls' protagonist Charlie is the film's poster child for the ill effects of LSD. Under the effects of the wicked drug, he becomes so delusional he takes a swan dive from the second floor of the frat house and nearly winds up as a paraplegic acid casualty. For a moment, he looks dead. In the next scene, we see him strapped to a hospital bed, suffering horrible hallucinations but having only minor injuries. Nevertheless, the anti–LSD message is clear. "You are a very fortunate young man," says the white-coated doctor, who grimly notes that the drug may have damaged his nervous system permanently. Shain recalls with a laugh,

Chapter 9. The Prince of Confidential (1966-1968)   129

Steve knew nothing about drugs. When I was in college, alcohol was more popular than drugs. In the so-called college fraternities, we were drinking. Then in the '60s came the hallucinogenic drugs—LSD, mushrooms and marijuana. But I did not grow up with the drug culture, so I was never a hippie. I was too old to be a hippie. However, in the film I play a college student who sleeps with all the girls. What else could I play?[48]

Apostolof's youngest son confirms his father's naiveté. "My father never understood drugs. He thought that young people just drink a lot," says Christopher.[49] The politically conservative Apostolof was totally alienated from rock music and the youth-driven counterculture it spawned. The director's own musical tastes were forged in the 1940s and '50s, during the heyday of the big bands, and remained basically unchanged for the rest of his life. When he made *College Girls,* Apostolof was on entirely unfamiliar terrain. "Steve did not know much about the parties and the way the young people had fun in the '60s," Shain explains. "He had put a table on the set with several bowls on it. On one he wrote 'LSD,' on another 'Cocaine,' on a third 'Marijuana.' I told him, 'Steve, people don't get high like that. They secretly give each other drugs.'"[50]

Shain's greatest aggravation came during the scene in which he was supposed to chew on some allegedly illicit drugs that were actually aspirin tablets. He suggested to Apostolof that they use M&Ms or some other candy instead, but the proposal fell on deaf ears. "So we had to chew on his aspirins! It drove us crazy!" remembers Harvey.[51]

While shooting *College Girls,* Apostolof employed some rather unusual directing methods to get the most from his actors, especially when directing Shain in the infamous and potentially dangerous balcony scene. According to Shain, "Steve said, 'I'd never want anything from my cast, which I wouldn't do myself.' So he climbed the balcony and jumped down, head first. He was supposed to land on a mattress, which several people were holding for him."[52] So far, so good. Unfortunately, the people holding the mattress dropped it when Apostolof hit. Apostolof confirmed the incident:

Harvey Shain watches dubiously as Apostolof jumps from the balcony during the shooting of *College Girls.*

I almost killed myself on *College Girls*. Harvey Shain is supposed to pop pills and jump from a two-story balcony. Well, for that scene I had a couple of big guys holding a mattress, but looking down he didn't like it. I said, "Harvey, goddammit, it's easy." So I jumped out, and—holy Toledo!—the guys didn't have a good grip on the mattress. I broke my watch. I flew off one side. I said, "See, Harvey, it's nothing!" So I got the guys to put a rope around the mattress, and Harvey jumped.[53]

But Shain had other objections to the scene, including the dialogue he was required to perform. He said, "I still remember the line I had to say right before jumping from the balcony myself. 'I'm the king of kicks! I'm the king of kicks!' The dialogue was so outdated, so I told Steve, 'Young people today don't speak like that!' But he wouldn't listen."[54]

The actor also warned Apostolof that Marsha Jordan was too old to play a college student. "I told Steve, 'Look, Marsha is great, but let her play a teacher, not a student.' But Steve said, 'No, no, no. She needs the money, I know. She has troubles at the moment.' I argued with him and told him that she wouldn't look good on the screen. And guess what? Marsha didn't really look good in the movie. She was too old to play a student."[55]

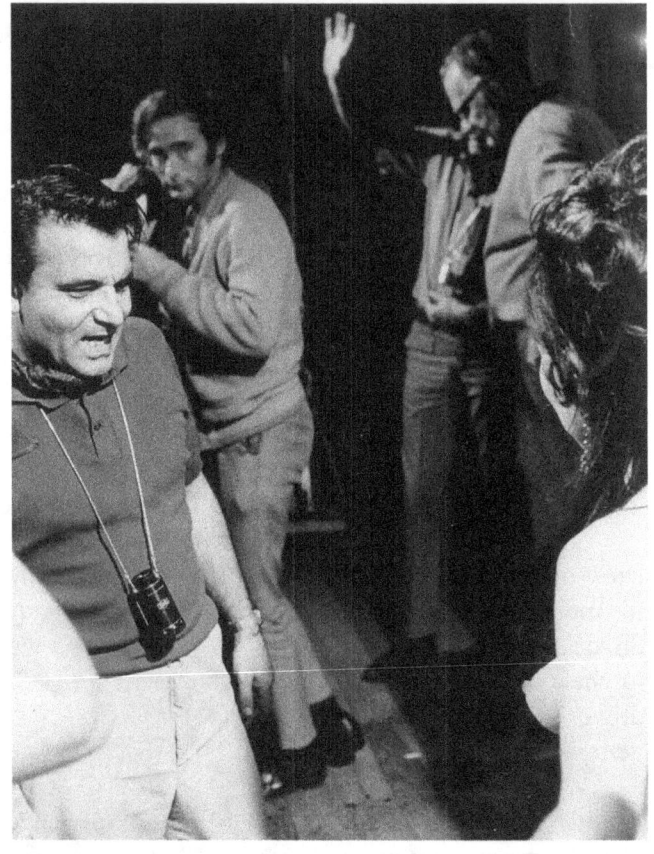

Apostolof inspects an actress' breasts during the making of *College Girls*. Behind him, looking in the same direction, is Titus Moede (aka Titus Moody), an actor who became a pioneer in the adult film industry. Moede worked as set photographer on numerous sexploitation films in the 1960s and sold photographs to the adult magazines at the time.

Even the actress herself had misgivings about the unlikely role. "Marsha thought [the actresses] might've been a little too old to be a college girl," Apostolof later recalled, "but I told her, 'If I say you're a college girl, you're a college girl.' From then on, I started using Marsha and practically the same people over and over."[56]

Shain has his own special memories of the starlets hired by Apostolof:

> Many of the girls that Steve used in movies were something like hippies. Several of them were very beautiful. The 1960s were the first time I saw girls with tattoos. They looked quite interesting. I remember one of them had tattoos across her breast. I had to do a love scene with this girl and the tattoo was quite distracting. Watching this tit with the drawing on it was like looking at the Sistine Chapel.[57]

Chapter 9. The Prince of Confidential (1966–1968)

(Left to right) Gee Gentell, Harvey Shain, Marsha Jordan, and Stephen Apostolof on the set of *College Girls*.

College Girls hit theaters in May, just before the turbulent summer of 1968. On August 14, 1968, it reached New York's notorious 42nd Street. Due to its skimpy 65-minute length, it was often shown as part of a double bill with other pictures. Unlike Apostolof's previous films, the youth-oriented *College Girls* was not a financial success. The movie's budget was $46,525, but it had earned Apostolof and his investors a mere $14,237 by the end of the year. Apostolof lost money on his collegiate sex romp, possibly because he had tried to capitalize on a market he didn't know or understand.

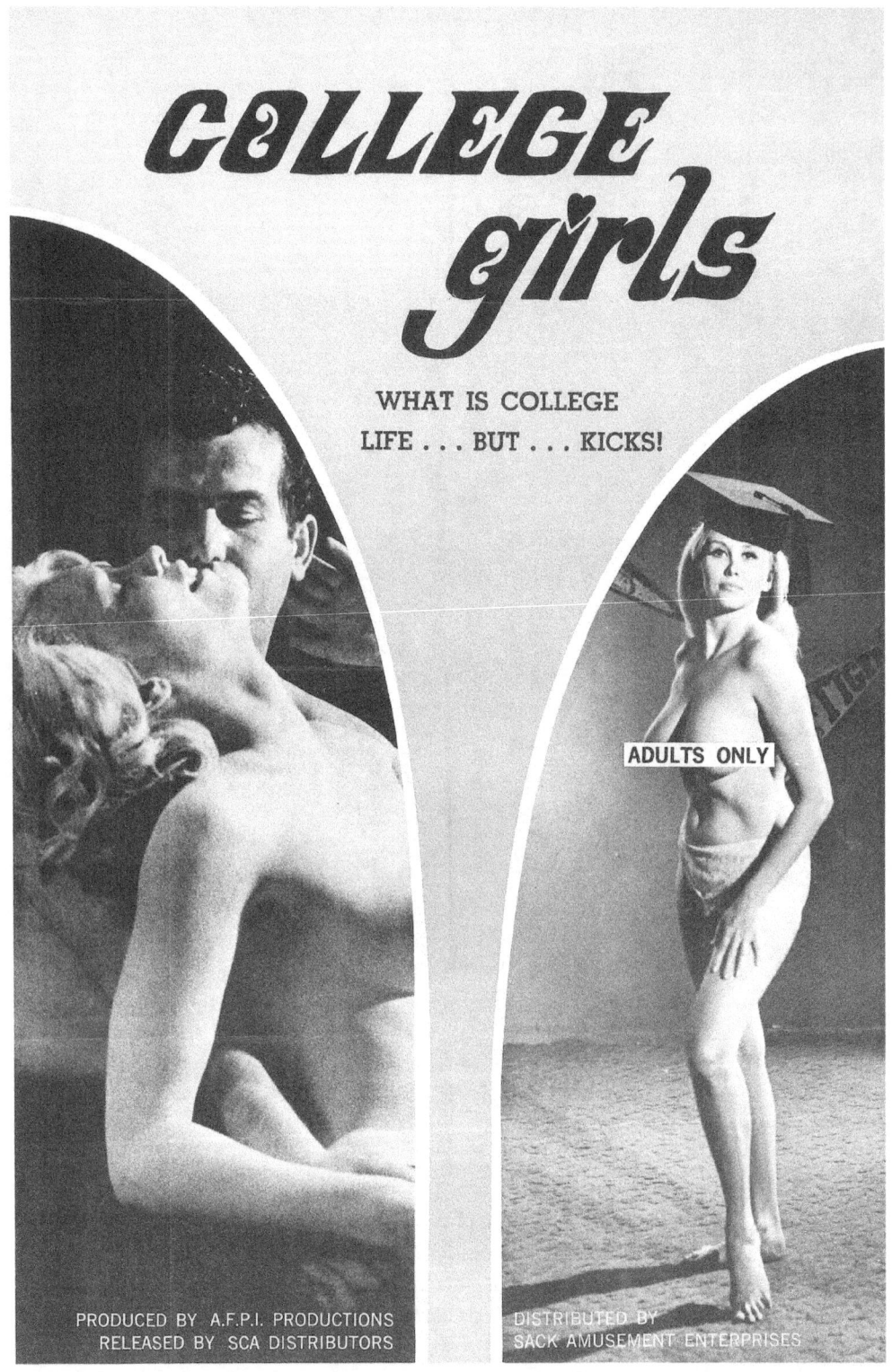

A color one sheet for *College Girls*.

Chapter 9. The Prince of Confidential (1966–1968)

In retrospect, the most significant aspect of *College Girls* was the fact that it introduced Marsha Jordan into the Apostolof fold. The golden-tressed, top-heavy actress provided a degree of star power that SCA's productions otherwise would have lacked. "I think the only difference between exploitation movies and films of major studios was that [the majors] had a lot of money and used stars," said Ted V. Mikels, a veteran exploitation filmmaker and Apostolof buddy who had served as a gaffer on *Orgy of the Dead*. "We had little or no money and no stars, so we had to find the right people and turn them into stars."[58]

Legendary B-movie producer David F. Friedman once claimed that Jordan was "probably the one female star that has been developed in the exploitation business."[59] And he should know, since he worked with the actress numerous times himself: on *The Head Mistress* (1968, dir. Byron Mabe), *Nude Jango* (1968, dir. Byron Mabe) and *The Ramrodder* (1969, dir. Ed Forsyth).

Even though Marsha's name and face were familiar to a generation of exploitation filmgoers, the actress herself was always something of an enigma, since the details of her life were not widely reported. She was born Carolyn Marcel Jordan in Gadsden, Alabama, on February 10, 1936. The granddaughter of a preacher, she grew up in a Catholic convent. In 1960, she started working as a Delta Airlines flight attendant. That same year, she entered the world of sexploitation filmmaking, a world she would make her home for the next decade and a half.

"I got into exploitation films more or less by accident. But I really had fun," Jordan told Kenneth Turan and Stephen F. Zito, who interviewed her in the early '70s for their book *Sinema: American Pornographic Films and the People Who Make Them* (1974).[60] That book remains one of the best sources of information on the late actress. In the years following her humble debut, Jordan participated in more than 20 adult films, appearing in both starring and supporting roles. She even had the honor of having one film, *Marsha: The Erotic Housewife* (1970, dir. Don Davis), named after her. Thanks to these appearances, Marsha became the biggest softcore actress on the West Coast. Arguably Apostolof's biggest star, she scored prominent roles in five of his films. Understandably proud of her physique, Marsha had no qualms about showing off her body on camera. What did concern her, though, was the prospect of people thinking a nice body was all she had to offer. She wanted viewers to appreciate her acting talents, too. "Marsha is a person that you cannot decipher. She's a very talented actress," said Apostolof, who often insisted that Jordan's acting talent was more important than her willingness to disrobe on screen.[61] "I liked to put Marsha Jordan into as many pictures as possible," Apostolof said. "Here again, Marsha was a very, very good actress. She knew her lines, at least. And she delivers them good. Especially in the picture called *The Divorcee* where she was in every scene. We were good friends."[62]

Although a legend in sexploitation circles, one big enough to have genuine marquee value, Marsha never achieved mainstream celebrity status. Turan claimed that she became a star on a person-to-person basis, lending a touch of humanity to the films she was in. Specifically, she conquered the hearts of ticket buyers in a highly unusual way: She traveled from theater to theater, personally promoting several of the films she was in. She even did a promotional tour for one of Apostolof's films, *The Divorcee,* in 1969.

"And that killed me. That killed me," said Apostolof of the tour. He continued:

A behind the scenes photograph of Marsha Jordan from Stephen C. Apostolof's *The Divorcee*. The caption falsely claims that she's 25 years old. She's actually in her early thirties.

I remember being at some theater in Joplin, Missouri, a university town. The theater was a big old palace with an orchestra and balcony. Tickets were $2.50. Marsha was signing autographs for university kids in the lobby. I went to look inside the theater and saw that it was packed. Upstairs was packed, downstairs was packed. I went back to the lobby and the theater manager told me that business was bad. I said, "What are you talking about?! The theater is packed! Any more and we'll have to put them on the ceiling!" He said, "No one's buying tickets." I said, "Come on, I'll show you." So we went into the theater and, sure enough, the place was packed and the guy was shocked. And as we stood there, boom! Someone opened the back door and another 300 people ran into the theater!⁶³

Over the years, Marsha's travels took her through the South and Midwest, with stops in Grand Rapids, Denver, Minneapolis, Memphis, New Orleans, Tampa, Jacksonville, Savannah, Nashville, Chattanooga and even Canada. Her visits followed the same basic pattern every time. First, there would be a small press conference, followed by some newspaper and TV ads informing the public that Marsha would be autographing 8x10 photos at the local movie theater. Finally, the organizers would set up a small table with flowers in the lobby of the cinema, and customers would start pouring in.

But Marsha's celebrity status wasn't the reason Apostolof kept hiring her. In fact, he claimed to be ignorant of her fan following. "I did not make films because I thought the audience would like to see this personality or that one," the filmmaker explained. "I cast them because they worked well with me, Rene [Bond] had a good body, but I never thought that she or Marsha had a following. That came afterwards."⁶⁴

One of Marsha's most vivid memories was the day she managed to outshine even U.S. Vice-President Spiro Agnew during one of his visits to Indianapolis. The actress recalled, "This guy got on TV, and he said, 'With our vice-president coming to the airport, where do you think 23 newspaper reporters and umpteen number of TV reporters that were supposed to be at the airport interviewing him were? They were at the Art Theater interviewing Marsha Jordan, sexploitation queen.' It was funny."⁶⁵

Marsha and Apostolof were introduced back in 1965, when she showed up on the *Orgy of the Dead* set to see if he needed more girls to round out the cast. In later years, Apostolof admitted that he did not remember that first meeting. Working well into her 30s, Marsha was rather an exception in the world of sexploitation, a genre dominated by younger actresses. But Marsha possessed the voluptuous body of a mature woman, complete with jumbo-sized "ticket-sellers" that would put most other actresses' assets to shame. Those, along with Marsha's golden tresses and false eyelashes, won her the affections of adult movie patrons everywhere.

She won over her co-workers, like Harvey Shain:

> Marsha had a good figure, very voluptuous, very buxom. And of top of it all, she remembered her lines. I remember Marsha being very professional, unlike some of the other kids that Steve used to cast. And I became good friends with her. She actually became good friends with me and Steve. We were buddies. And Steve tried to use her in just about every picture. She was a professional. All the way.⁶⁶

Office Love-In, White Collar Style (1968)

After his sex-laden exposés of suburbs, motels and colleges, Apostolof decided to make his next film about the surprisingly steamy love lives of office workers. The ludicrously titled *Office Love-In, White Collar Style* (1968) involves nine-to-fivers—lustful, martini-swilling businessmen and their nubile, ever-available secretaries. None of these people manages to get much actual work accomplished; they're all too busy hopping into bed with each other at every opportunity. This, apparently, was Apostolof's vision of industrial America in the 1960s. To him, the modern workplace was a veritable Sodom and Gomorrah.

Apostolof broke with tradition by not calling the film *Office Confidential*, even though it was very much in line with his three previous movies. The title *Office Love-In* was the director's attempt to capitalize on a popular hippie buzzword of the era.

"It was made at the time when there was a so-called love-in for this and a love-in for that. I said, 'Well, let's do it in an office building,'" explained Apostolof.[67] Never mind the fact that no self-respecting hippie would be seen anywhere near an office building. Real love-ins were supposedly about expanding consciousness through physical affection. Apostolof breezily skipped past that high-minded stuff and got right to the sex.

Like Apostolof's previous films, *Office Love-In* reflected what was happening in American society at the time. In the mid–1960s, decades before modern dating sites like OkCupid and match.com, America became obsessed with relatively primitive computer dating services, which used machines to match single men and women with compatible partners. Customers sent in their vital statistics and preferences to one of many computer dating services, typically by mail, and then wait for weeks or even months as the companies processed their submissions and found their ideal matches. The hapless title character in Tom Wilson's comic strip *Ziggy* frequently used a computer dating service, as did Jonathan Warden in the satirical anti-war film *Greetings* (1968, dir. Brian De Palma).

Apostolof, who had a flair for keeping up with social trends, zeroed in on this fad and used it as the basis for *Office Love-In,* which is set at the fictional Date-A-Mate Corp. Along with Apostolof's desire to stay current and topical, this intriguing choice of setting might also have been influenced by the director's experience as a Bank of America punch card operator in the late 1950s and early '60s and his fascination with computers in general.

The lead role in *Office Love-In* went to actress Kathy Williams, probably best known to exploitation film junkies for the cult women-in-prison/Nazi flick *Love Camp 7* (1969, dir. Lee Frost). In *Office Love-In,* Williams plays Stephanie Morris, a squeaky-voiced secretary who sleeps with her much older boss, Winthrop A. Albertson, Sr. (Hugh Thelman). In the meantime, computer department employee Mae Flowers (Felicia Phark) succeeds in seducing her cloddish boss Lionel Smythe (Clete Bennett, looking like an especially sleazy Nicolas Cage) in her apartment, and this results in a hilarious bathtub scene. Obviously gay personnel officer Vincent Sowash (Michael DiRosa) is smitten with job applicant Jane Leary (Lynn Harris), who agrees to help him rediscover his manhood. This leads to Vincent wearing Jane's clothing, and the two become lovers.

A few days later, the boss' son, Winthrop A. Albertson, Jr. (Ray Cyr), also seduces Stephanie. When he learns that she has already slept with his father, he abandons her outside of town. While hitchhiking back to the city, the unfortunate Stephanie is picked up by Ann (Marsha Jordan), an attractive, middle-aged lesbian who takes her back to her house and seduces her. The next day, Stephanie meets charming bank clerk Tom Brandon (Harvey Shain), who invites her along with his colleague and friend Cosmo Thrank (Apostolof's old friend John Bealey, who uses the pseudonym Nemo Nomus here) and Marie Corbin (Sheri Jackson, credited here as Colleen Murphy) to his apartment. There Stephanie watches a sex loop (actually excerpts from Apostolof's *Motel Confidential*) and the two couples repeat what they just saw on the screen. The next day, Stephanie is promoted at work, but her joy is short-lived when she realizes that

Chapter 9. The Prince of Confidential (1966–1968)

Apostolof directs actor Michael DiRosa in *Office Love-In, White Collar Style*.

all the people she has had sex with in the last days, are, in fact, members of the same family. Her lesbian lover Ann is her boss' wife, Tom Brandon's sister, and Winthrop A. Albertson, Jr.'s mother.

Office Love-In was filmed in early April 1968 at Raleigh Studios on Melrose Avenue. It was shot by Apostolof's frequent collaborator Robert Caramico, using the pseudonym Robert Ruben. The surprisingly convoluted screenplay was written by Taggart Casey, a good friend of Apostolof who was in Alfred Hitchcock's *North by Northwest* (1959). Casey is credited here as J.T. Casey; he'd previously served as a production manager on *College Girls*. *Office Love-In* was reportedly based on Casey's novel *Sex in the Office*, though no such book seems to have ever existed. Casey's script is full of double entendres ("Is that the brush or are you happy to be here?") and groan-inducing puns (as when Vincent and Jane listen to a radio station identified as "M.U.F.F. Diver, Colorado").

As in *Motel Confidential*, there is also a scene involving cross-dressing. The young gay Vincent Sowash confesses to Jane Leary that he's not attracted to women, to which she replies, "Haven't you ever tried to be normal and healthy?" Then she decides to "help" Vincent with his problem. While preparing to get into bed with Jane, Vince tries on her lingerie. She watches him while deep-throating a banana.

In the movie's most eccentric twist, Vince and Jane's actions during the love scene are timed to sync up with a cowboy show that's playing on the radio in the background.

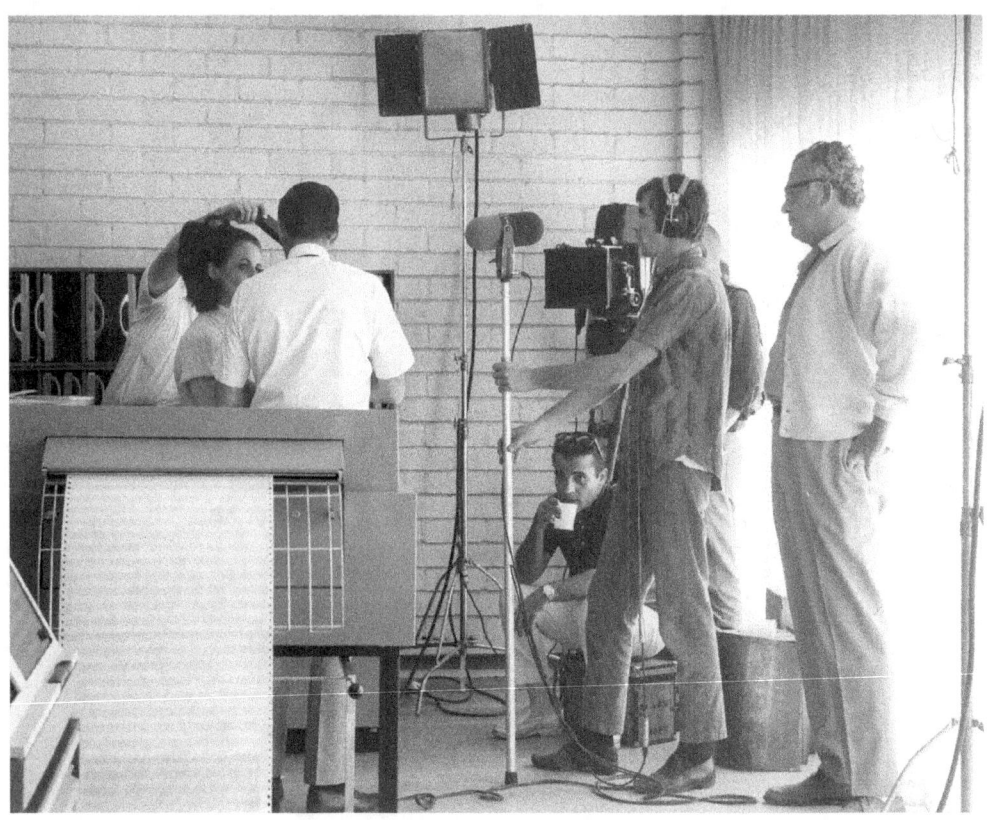

Apostolof (seated) calmly sips coffee on the set of *Office Love-In, White Collar Style*, between two takes with actors Clete Bennett and Felicia Phark.

Apostolof confers with cameraman Robert Caramico on the set of *Office Love-In, White Collar Style*.

Everything they do onscreen corresponds with something they hear on the radio, even the station breaks and ads. Hands down, it's the single most bizarre, inexplicable element of the entire movie.

"The radio show was dubbed in when the film was edited," remembers Michael DiRosa, who played Vincent Sowash. "Never had any music during the shoot. Stephen did tell me to undress slowly, so I think they had plans to add some different sound for the actual film."[68]

While shooting *Office Love-In,* Apostolof almost electrocuted two of his actors. In one of the scenes, actor Clete Bennett is sitting on the edge of the bathtub scrubbing the back of Kathy Williams with a long brush. According to the screenplay, Bennett had to slip and fall accidentally in the water with his clothes on. According to Apostolof, "Budd Costello ... forgot to secure the electricity cable and when Clete fell into the bathtub the water started flowing out, crawling slowly towards the cable. But the scene was turning out so well that I decided to continue shooting."[69] As the water neared the cable, one of Apostolof's assistants kept his hand on the electric switch, ready to turn it off as soon as Apostolof shouted *cut.*

Apostolof's film reflected a societal change that had been occurring in postwar

In this photograph published in *Cinema Keyhole* magazine in 1968, Apostolof demonstrates the proper body-brushing technique for the benefit of actor Clete Bennett. Note the fake beard, mustache and sunglasses drawn on Apostolof's face before the photograph was published. "Apostolof wanted to keep it hush-hush that he was making 'dirty movies' and asked his pictures never to be published," says the publisher of *Cinema Keyhole* who wishes to remain anonymous.

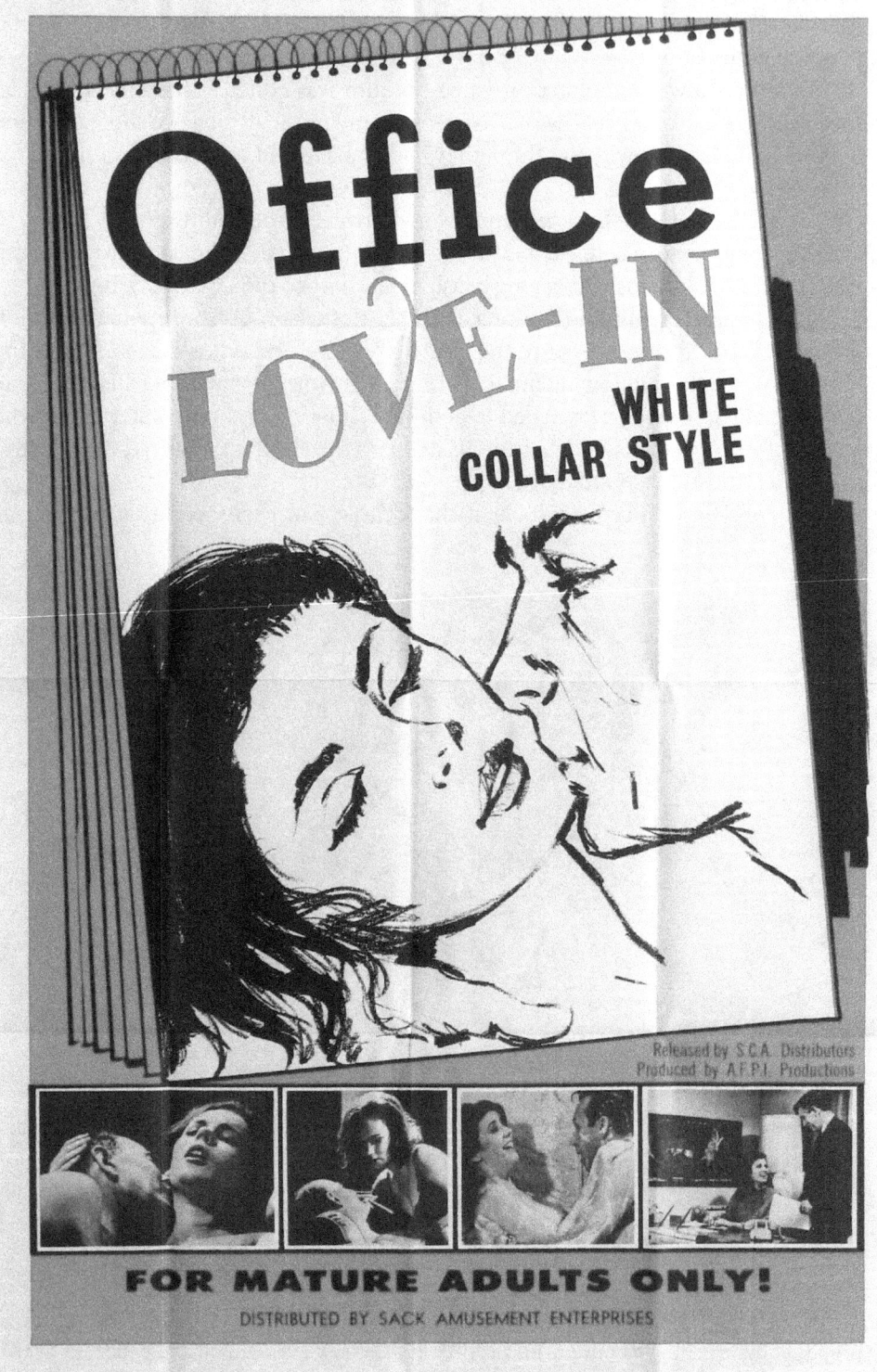

A color one sheet for *Office Love-In, White Collar Style*.

Chapter 9. The Prince of Confidential (1966–1968)

America for decades. In the late 1940s, American anthropologist and sociologist Charles Wright Mills (1916–1962) conducted an extensive survey of office workers, eventually publishing his findings in his 1951 book *White Collar: The American Middle Classes*. In it, he described not only a new breed of American professionals but also the alienation of a modern industrial society dominated by "salesmanship mentality." Mills argued that white-collar employees "sell not only their time and energy but their personalities as well. They sell by the week or month their smiles and their kindly gestures, and they must practice the prompt repression of resentment and aggression."[70] This idea is reflected in Apostolof's *Office Love-In*, when the boss' son tells his father's secretary, "Part of your job is to give me that big reception desk smile. You know, job description GS-40, paragraph 15, clause 69."

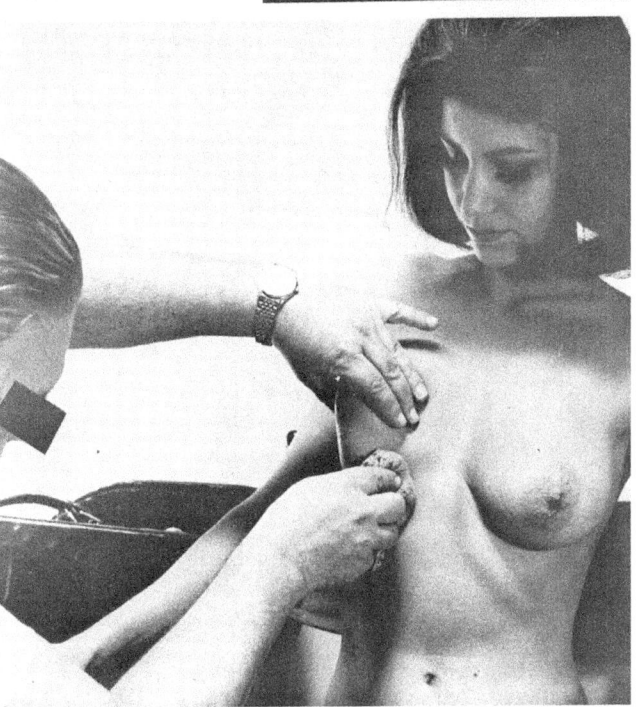

A makeup man touches up actress Kathy Williams' breast during the making of *Office Love-In, White Collar Style*.

Office Love-In was released domestically in August 1968. Its initial title was *The Swinging Secretary*, but Apostolof later changed it to *Office Love-In, White Collar Style*. At that point, he received a phone call from Whit Boyd, producer of the softcore film *The Office Party* (1968, dir. Ron Scott). "Whit called me once and said there was a problem. He said we had a similarity of titles. He had *Office Party*, I had *Office Love-In*. I said to him, 'Yeah, but mine's a good picture, yours is a piece of crap!'" joked the ever-confident Apostolof.[71]

Releasing a film under multiple titles, as Apostolof often did, was a common ploy in exploitation cinema. Back then, the rights to low-budget films were routinely passed from one distributor to another. If a film was being exhibited in another territory, a company might change its title (depending on the laws of the respective state), so as to maximize viewership and possibly avoid prosecution. In 1966, the Supreme Court ruled in *Ginzberg v. United States* that some sexually explicit material was only legally obscene when promoted through so-called "pandering." As a result of this decision,

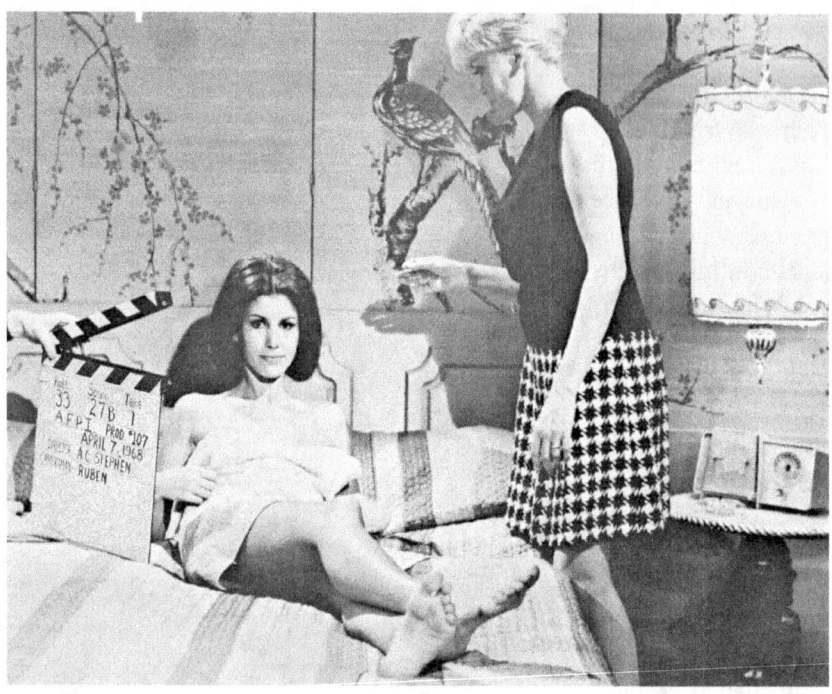

Kathy Williams and Marsha Jordan between takes on *Office Love-In, White Collar Style*.

Apostolof directs Ray Cyr and Kathy Williams in one of the few exterior scenes from *Office Love-In, White Collar Style*. Cameraman Robert Caramico is in the middle, looking down. Note the assistant handing equipment to the sound recordist, sitting on a branch above the car.

Chapter 9. The Prince of Confidential (1966–1968)

most exploitation producers started creating multiple ad campaigns for their films. For example, in certain states, the David F. Friedman–produced *Thar She Blows!* (1968, dir. Richard Kanter), marketed as "a story of men and women who GO DOWN to the sea in ships," had a second, less risqué title for more conservative territories, *Thar She Goes!* Friedman employed similar strategies for films like *Trader Hornee* (1970, dir. Jonathan Lucas) and *The Big Snatch* (1971, dir. Byron Mabe and Dan Martin). "We had ads for *Trader Hornee* with two *e*'s and ads with one *e*," the producer explained in a 2003 interview with exploitation film historian Eric Schaefer. "*The Big Snatch* became *The Big Catch*. We just printed extra c's that the exhibitor could substitute in the ads."[72]

In an interview with Mike Vraney and James Elliot Singer, Apostolof admitted that he got spoiled shooting in a studio while working on the *Confidential* films. *Office Love-In* continues this tradition. With the exception of a couple of scenes shot on location, the camera barely leaves the drab, flimsy studio interiors. The majority of the action takes place in four sets that are basically indistinguishable from one another. To make things even more confusing, Apostolof continually recycled furnishing and props from other films, some of which he brought from home.

The signature look of Apostolof's films was guided by his set designer, Budd Costello, who worked with him for a decade. "He was very good," Apostolof remembered. "He knew my furniture in the house and the office. He used to take it out and put a sign on the door: 'No, we have not been repossessed, we're shooting a picture!' We'd just use my furniture from the house. I never mixed the business with my house."[73] Funnily enough, one can see a set of pictures of Bulgarian folk costumes on the wall during *Office Love-In*.

Vincent Barbi (1912–1998), a regular in Apostolof's movies, had a small role here as a bartender. Barbi made a career as a bit player in such classics as *Sweet Sweetback's Baadasssss Song* (1971, dir. Melvin Van Peebles), *A Woman Under the Influence* (1974, dir. John Cassavetes), *The Killing of a Chinese Bookie* (1976, dir. John Cassavetes) and *Raging Bull* (1980, dir. Martin Scorsese).

As the 1960s drew to a close, Apostolof was in a rut with his films. He was telling the same basic types of stories over and over, just in different locations. It was time for a change. The ever-inventive Bulgarian was about to enter the next phase of his career.

Chapter 10

The Executive Filmmaker (1969–1972)

"In Hollywood, to be a producer, all you need is a screenplay, a Cadillac and a cigar."—Stephen C. Apostolof

By the late 1960s, Apostolof was comfortably established as one of the major players in the softcore sexploitation industry. Distributors, exhibitors and ticket-buyers alike knew exactly what was expected from SCA: flesh-filled films showing what supposedly "average" Americans were doing with each other behind closed doors. Apostolof specialized in movies about ordinary American life and just how naughty it could be. He had already shown his audiences the seamy side of suburbia, motels, colleges and offices. What was left to do in this vein? Not much. That's perhaps why his next project was his wildest offering since *Orgy of the Dead*.

Lady Godiva Rides (1969)

"One of the independent producers who has taken much of the MUT out of SMUT is a modern-day producer named Steve Apostolof. His films include: ORGY OF THE DEAD (in full color and I incidentally wrote it), SUBURBAN CONFIDENTIAL, MOTEL CONFIDENTIAL and LADY GODIVA RIDES (a real color spectacle of the old west combined with overtones of the English countryside)."—Ed Wood, A Study in the Motivation of Censorship, Sex & the Movies, Book 2 (1973)

In September 1968, Apostolof embarked upon his most expensive and extravagant film to date. Instead of being a behind-closed-doors exposé of American life, *Lady Godiva Rides* is a historical costume drama with an abnormally high budget for an Apostolof film. The director's ambition is evident in the costumes, the sets and the larger-than-normal cast, as well as the use of camera dollies and cranes in certain sequences. The film's trailer is bombastic, proudly proclaiming that *Lady Godiva Rides* was made in "the entertainment capital of the world—Hollywood." The film even has an epic length for a sexploitation film, 105 minutes. Possibly to lend the film an air of respectability, the opening credits declare that it features "an original screenplay by A.C. Stephen from his novel *Lady Godiva and Tom Jones*." Unsurprisingly, no such novel exists.

Lady Godiva Rides is a very loose interpretation of the well-known legend of 11th-century British noblewoman Godiva, Countess of Mercia. In the classic version of the (mostly fictional) story, she sympathized with the residents of Coventry, who were being excessively taxed by her husband. Lady Godiva asked her spouse to have mercy on his people, but he steadfastly refused to lower their taxes. Finally, weary of discussing the issue, the nobleman said he would fulfill his wife's wishes if she would ride naked through the streets of the city. Agreeing to this odd demand, Lady Godiva asked the townspeople to go home and close their shutters while she passed on horseback through their streets covered only by her long hair. Only one person in the city, a tailor who would subsequently become known as Peeping Tom, failed to comply with that request. He drilled a hole in his shutter in order to see Lady Godiva naked, and he was blinded because of his curiosity (and "Peeping Tom" forever became a synonym for voyeur). Ultimately, Godiva's husband kept his word and lowered the taxes.

Italian one sheet for *Lady Godiva Rides*.

In *Lady Godiva Rides*, Apostolof teamed a descendant of the eponymous English noblewoman with an equally famous character from British literature, Tom Jones from Henry Fielding's picaresque 1749 novel *The History of Tom Jones, a Foundling*. The result, a cinematic mashup between Victorian drama and classic Western, was advertised as a tale of "love and lust on two continents."

In Apostolof's version of the legend, which updates the action to the late 1800s, Lady Godiva Betherli (Marsha Jordan) is a shameless adulteress who takes after her notorious ancestor. At the outset of the film, Godiva is caught with her dashing lover Tom Jones (Harvey Shain) by her husband Lord Betherli (Mark Desmond, again billed as Mark Del Monde), who draws a gun on the two. Tom knocks the firearm out of Lord Betherli's hand, and then Lady Godiva grabs the weapon and shoots her cuckolded husband in the shoulder.

Apostolof, wearing his lucky white shoes, poses with his son Steve on the set of *Lady Godiva Rides.*"

The noblewoman is promptly sentenced to death by hanging for adultery and attempted murder. She manages to escape from prison after seducing a guard and travels to America via ship, Tom Jones having arranged her passage. On board, after dyeing her blonde hair brown and adopting the alias Edie Tipton, Lady Godiva meets a group of women who naively believe they are going to America to marry rich miners and farmers. They're accompanied by Dora Williams (Meri McDonald), a treacherous lesbian madam from a London brothel. Miss Williams has secretly selected some of her girls, including Edie-Godiva, to accompany her to a saloon in Goldstone, a prosperous Wild West town. There, the ladies will be expected to provide "entertainment, companionship and anything your heart desires" to the lonely, love-starved male clientele. Two of Dora's girls, Fifi (Mary Bauer) and Blanche (Elizabeth Knowles), are already experienced prostitutes, but Lady Godiva and her friend Liz (Deborah Downey) don't suspect what awaits them in America. Along the way, Lady Godiva develops a rivalry with Blanche, who knows our heroine's true identity and blabs it to Dora. When the ship crosses the equator, the sailors engage in the famous line-crossing ceremony, which soon turns into a wild orgy.

The ship arrives in San Francisco, and Lady Godiva and the other girls board the stagecoach to Goldstone. There, hotel owner Dan Kirby (James E. Myers) informs them they'll pay for their trip to America by becoming prostitutes. After "a couple of years,"

Chapter 10. The Executive Filmmaker (1969–1972)

Dan Kirby (James E. Myers) forcing himself on Lady Godiva (Marsha Jordan).

he says, they'll have enough money to buy their own places. Lady Godiva and her friend refuse to submit to this glad-handing, mustachioed pimp. At first, their only strategy is to price themselves so high that the men of Goldstone can't afford them. But Kirby commands, "From now on, a ten spot is plenty!"

Liz quickly finds true love with one of her customers, virginal homesteader Davie (Bob Kendal), and runs off with him. Godiva pays her friend's debt to Kirby with a diamond necklace. But things start to go downhill when Blanche again blurts out Godiva's identity, this time to Kirby. A down-and-dirty catfight ensues. Their topless brawl starts in the barroom and spills out into the street, allowing Apostolof to work in some mud wrestling.

Some time later, Tom Jones is shown traveling to Goldstone to rescue his love—but he may be too late. Kirby plans to capitalize on Godiva's notoriety, selling her body for $100 a pop. Wanting to be her first customer, the pimp attempts to force himself on her. Tom arrives by stagecoach at that exact moment and punches Kirby in the gut. It all comes down to a classic Western-style duel between Tom and Kirby, both of whom consider themselves expert marksmen. Kirby shoots first and wings Tom. Just when all hope seems lost, Lady Godiva finally imitates her ancestor by riding, totally nude, through the streets. When Kirby is distracted, Tom shoots him in the belly, killing him. Lady Godiva and Tom (who wasn't really injured after all) make plans to leave Goldstone on the next stagecoach, and the film ends happily with the lovers reunited.

Despite having a relatively generous budget for a sexploitation filmmaker, Apostolof remained true to his working methods from his earlier films, such as using one

Lady Godiva makes her historic nude ride through the streets of Goldstone during the gunfight between Tom Jones and Dan Kirby. This unusual sight diverts Kirby's attention, thus giving Tom Jones a split-second chance to fire the fatal shot that kills his foe.

master shot from start to finish taken from an angle that keeps all the players in view, then shooting close-ups and details. "This was a fast and secure mode of operation imposed by budget constraints," he explained.[1] His budget-conscious ways can also be seen in the shots of the ship that transports Lady Godiva to America. It's clearly a model and actually resembles a child's toy. Apostolof wisely didn't linger on it.

Shooting of *Lady Godiva Rides* began on the Warner Brothers studio lot in Burbank in September 1968. The set of the film was immense, and Apostolof rounded up more than 50 background extras to fill it, including some of his Bulgarian friends. The main cast consisted of 30 actors, and the director himself made a cameo appearance as a character called "Deadeye Apostolof." Shooting continued for 15 days and the crew worked literally around the clock. "One of the actresses got angry at Steve. He didn't have time to argue with her, so he just fired her," remembers Harvey Shain, who used to spend the time between shots sleeping somewhere in the dark corners of the huge soundstage.[2] Shain added, "I drank a little bit more vodka one night, so I fell asleep on the set. Steve had to wake me up and put me in front of the camera. But I had no problem with that; I was always very professional. I was walking around the set, fooling with the people when I suddenly hear: 'Be ready, Harvey! Bubelah!' And I would just jump in front of the camera, ready to shoot."[3] In addition to playing the male lead, he also served as a dialogue director.

Shain was paid $400 to play Tom Jones. "The girls were better paid," he recalls, "but for a male actor, $400 was a big salary. Guys were just used to further the script, sexually. The girls were always the central attraction, so to speak. Or, as Steve would say, they were the ticket-sellers."[4]

The film was memorable for the director's kids. Apostolof's son Steve, 11 at the time, remembered, "The whole family got to go on the set of *Lady Godiva Rides*. And it had probably, as the production value goes, the nicest sets. They made a ship and a bar and actually had a real horse and a monkey. The film was shot on a big movie studio lot that had a whole Western town in it. The whole family got to go there and pose for pictures with Dad."[5] (The Western town in question was Warner Brothers' outdoor set Laramie Street, where the likes of Errol Flynn, Randolph Scott, James Garner and Clint Walker played cowboys, lawmen, outlaws and cavalry through the years.) Steve continued:

> I also remember going to Pioneer Chicken [restaurant] with Budd Costello. They were running late on the shoot, and he was sent to get food for the crew. We stand in line, everybody placing relatively normal-sized orders, then we step up. Budd starts reeling off what he wants and with each item the kid's jaw just keeps dropping lower and lower. The total comes to like $300 [around $2000 today]. This had to be the biggest chicken order the kid had ever taken![6]

"Steve always served chicken for lunch," says Harvey Shain. "It was the cheapest! And this fat lady who weighed at least 300, 400 pounds opened her purse and started cramming chicken legs and wings in it. And Steve started yelling at her, 'Stop it! There are other people who want to eat too!'"[7] The woman in question was Tootsie O'Hara, a middle-aged, overweight actress who performed lewd songs with a deep male voice, somewhat like the drag performer Divine. She appears as a cabaret-style performer in the movie.

A few years previously, in 1963, British director Tony Richardson had enjoyed

Tootsie O'Hara entertains the menfolk in a saloon scene from *Lady Godiva Rides*.

critical and commercial success with his own adaptation of Fielding's *Tom Jones* with Albert Finney in the title role. It was an Oscar-winning hit, despite (or because of) its risqué-for-the-time nature, including a suggestive dinner scene between Finney and actress Joyce Redman. Determined to repeat the success of Richardson's film, Apostolof instructed Shain to play the part of Tom Jones just as Finney had. Harvey, who'd started his career on the Off-Broadway stage in New York, saw this movie as a chance to shine as an actor. Apostolof gave him and his leading lady Marsha Jordan almost exactly the same food used in Richardson's original, including chicken, pears, oysters and bananas. Shain recalls filming the infamous scene: "So, Marsha Jordan sits at one end of the table, I sit on the other and we eat chicken. But we eat it very lasciviously. I push a chicken leg inside my mouth, because I want Marsha to give me, you know…. Marsha herself is sucking on a banana." The actor thought everything was going well, until he heard his director's angry voice booming behind him.

"Cut!" yelled Apostolof. "What's this? What are you doing?"

"Steve, this was in *Tom Jones*!" Harvey said.

"Oh, okay. I'm sorry, I haven't seen the movie," admitted Apostolof.[8]

Lady Godiva Rides' pseudo–Victorian score was provided by Jaime Mendoza-Nava, using the pseudonym Igor O'Gigagusky. Some additional songs were credited to Sons of the Keystone Kops, a 1960s Southern California band, described as a "psychedelic bubblegum outfit."[9] *Lady Godiva Rides* was shot by Apostolof's favorite cameraman Robert Caramico, working under the *nom de guerre* R.C. Ruben this time.

The role of pimp Dan Kirby was played by James E. Myers (1919–2001), a songwriter and occasional actor who achieved fame early in his career as one of the composers of the smash 1952 rock 'n' roll hit "Rock Around the Clock," using the pseudonym Jimmy DeKnight. Myers, a good friend of Apostolof, participated in one more SCA film, 1969's *The Divorcee*. The cast of *Lady Godiva Rides* also includes two of Apostolof's usual suspects, Vincent Barbi and Lou Ojena. Apostolof: "Lou was a funny guy. He was lucky they didn't shoot him. Or shall I say, I was lucky I didn't get shot by him."[10]

Ojena previously played the Mummy in *Orgy of the Dead* and had small roles in *Suburbia Confidential*, *Motel Confidential* and *College Girls*. This time the ever-loyal Apostolof didn't have a speaking role for Ojena, so he made him an extra during the Goldstone scenes. On the last day of the shoot, around three in the morning, Apostolof got an urgent call, telling him to go to his office at KTTV in Los Angeles.

"Lou went there and wanted to be paid," Apostolof remembered in an interview with Ed Wood biographer Rudolph Grey. "He was high as a kite. My partner, who was dealing with the money, told him that instead of $100, he would pay him only $50 as an extra.[11] Lou said, 'I'm not a fucking extra and I don't need your money, because I'm a star.'"

Apostolof tried to calm Ojena down. "Lou, that man has no power to change anything. Why don't you talk to me?" Ojena got even angrier and threatened to return to the set and destroy the lighting. The director recalled, "He was still in his cowboy costume and carried two guns on his gun belt. I did not know that, but later on Vincent Barbi told me they were loaded with real bullets."

After a while, the weary Apostolof started getting fed up with Ojena's antics. The situation was getting more tense, and Lou seemed to be in an altered state of conscious-

Chapter 10. The Executive Filmmaker (1969–1972)

A color one sheet for *Lady Godiva Rides*.

ness. Barbi, who had been a professional boxer in his native Italy, approached Apostolof with a quizzical expression when he saw what was going on.

"Boss, do you need help?" Barbi asked.

"No, Vince," Apostolof assured him. "Everything is okay."

Later, Apostolof admitted he had never seen a stoned person before. According to his eldest son Steve, he was absolutely oblivious to the rampant drug use of the 1960s.[12] "I did not know what he had taken," Apostolof said, "whether marijuana or something stronger, but he was high as hell. He wasn't drunk for sure because he didn't smell. Lou was determined to make it in Hollywood, thinking, 'If anyone can do it, why can't I?'" This was the last time Ojena worked for Apostolof, but they encountered each other in the early 1980s on Hollywood Boulevard. By that time, Ojena had become a New Ager and was wearing an Egyptian ankh symbol—fitting for an ex-mummy! "Lou had turned into a bum. Do you think it's easy being a bum?" Apostolof asked rhetorically. "It's not!"

Lady Godiva Rides opened on January 29, 1969, in Detroit in "uncut, uncensored color." The eventual Los Angeles premiere (August 25, 1969) was spectacular. Marsha Jordan rode a horse in front of the Movie, a theater from the Pussycat chain in Long Beach, California, dressed in her Victorian costume from the film. Marsha made a couple of other appearances that week, in Anaheim, Torrance and Hollywood, among other places, to promote the film.

By the late 1960s, the sexploitation industry was so well-established that the makers of adult films decided to create their own organization, like any other group of respected professionals. In November 1968, Sam Chernoff from the Dallas-based distribution company Astro-Jemco sent letters to all the major sexploitation producers and directors, asking them to unite. On January 13 and 14, 1969, about 120 people representing nearly 300 different production companies, distributors and theaters met in "a third-rate hotel in Kansas City, Missouri"[13] to establish the Adult Film Association of America (AFAA). Apostolof attended that inaugural meeting and subsequently became one of the organization's most active members. The AFAA was essentially a lobbying group to protect the interests of sexploitation moviemakers. One of its first tasks was to create a set of legal principles to protect the adult film business. "That's when the law really started to get tough," Apostolof remembered. "It got nasty. The police would come and arrest the projectionist! And the ticket seller! […] I said, 'Okay, since there's a White House, let's build 'em a Smut House.' We had a ball."[14]

Apostolof claims he came up with the name of the group. Actually, the Adult Film Association of America had been preceded by another similar organization, the Adult Film Producers Association formed in February 1968. "The Adult Film Producers Association was the brainchild of myself and Don Davis," remembered Apostolof. He continued:

> [Davis] was its first president. Basically, we were sick and tired of getting ripped off by the theater owners and we hoped this would give us some leverage in getting paid. At the first meeting was Don Davis, myself, Bob Cresse and Dave Friedman. And Bob started getting grandiose. He said, "We're going to have $25,000 initiation fees!" It started to deteriorate from there. Anyway, the organization needed a seal. So Dave said he'd bring the seal. At the next meeting, Cresse's $25,000 was forgotten about, but Dave reached into his pocket and said, "Here, I brought the seal." And, son of a bitch, that's what it was. A picture of a seal! [*laughs*] That was the great thing about the people in L.A. They were very

strong characters, real individuals. If you were a producer, you had to be an egomaniac in the good sense of the word. And we respected each other and we helped each other out.[15]

The AFAA's first lawyer was New York's Stanley Fleishman. Born in 1920 to a family of Russian-Jewish immigrants, Fleishman graduated from Columbia Law School and built a spectacular career as a First Amendment advocate and civil liberties lawyer. He was admitted to the New York bar in 1945 and specialized in protecting the rights of authors, publishers and film distributors. Fleishman was one of the first attorneys to argue an obscenity case before the U.S. Supreme Court in the late 1950s. A dozen of his free speech cases subsequently reached the Supreme Court, including his defense of porn kingpin Reuben Sturman, who had been sentenced to 25 years hard labor for distributing an all-text dirty booklet called *Sex Life of a Cop* (first published in 1959).

Fleishman's other high-profile First Amendment cases included: *Roth v. United States* (1957), a key Supreme Court ruling on freedom of sexual expression; *Smith v. California* (1963) in which he successfully defended Los Angeles bookstore owner Bradley Smith, charged with obscenity for selling Henry Miller's *Tropic of Cancer*; and the groundbreaking *Miller v. California* (1973), in which the Supreme Court redefined obscenity as "utterly without socially redeeming value." These cases and others solidified his reputation as America's leading pornography lawyer.

The headstrong Fleishman had also represented Greenleaf, the publishing house that released the *Orgy of the Dead* paperback in 1966. Fleishman, physically handicapped from a childhood bout with polio, was later involved in constitutional law and civil rights for the disabled.

In addition to the authorities, the AFAA members had to fight with the producers and distributors of crudely pornographic 16mm films that, in their opinion, gave a bad name to the sexploitation industry and were harming the business. Most of these dirty movies came from the notoriously liberal San Francisco Bay area and seriously threatened the status quo of Apostolof and the other producers' movies.

The Divorcee (1969)

> "Bare bodies on the Silver screen have become so commonplace in the last year or so that movie producers have been getting frantic. Nudity is no longer knocking up box office sales the way it used to. How do you cope with something that had become commonplace? Marsha Jordan had the answer. Nudity might be commonplace, but Marsha isn't. And the exceptional gifts that she displays in even the barest of story plots are what has been putting the boom back in the box office where it counts."—Publicity for *The Divorcee* in *Adam Film Quarterly* magazine (1969)

Apostolof was getting more and more involved in the distribution of his own films through his company SCA Distributors. He unleashed *Lady Godiva Rides* in late January 1969, and by April of that year he already had another film out, *The Divorcee*. Like *Godiva*, it was conceived as a star vehicle for busty blonde Marsha Jordan. But this time, the script was closer to the director's own life. Apostolof chose a subject in which he was well-versed. With two failed marriages under his belt, he knew all about divorce.

The late 1960s were a watershed time for the U.S. film industry. In May 1966, Jack Valenti, a former advertising man and adviser to President Lyndon Johnson, became president of the Motion Picture Association of America (MPAA). Valenti proclaimed the Motion Picture Production Code, in place since 1930 and rigorously enforced since 1934, to be outdated. On November 1, 1968, the MPAA introduced a new film ratings system that told audiences what kind of content was in a specific movie. In March 1969, the controversial, sexually frank Swedish film *I Am Curious (Yellow)* (1967, dir. Vilgot Sjöman) finally came to America and truly opened the market up for more explicit fare.

But contrary to expectations, the change didn't happen overnight. In the year following the adoption of the new film ratings system, the Code and Rating Administration of the MPAA reviewed 418 films. Of these, 137 (32.6 percent) were rated G, suitable for general audiences; 162 (38.7 percent) M, suggested for mature audiences; 98 (23.5 percent) R, unsuitable for persons under 16 unless accompanied by a parent or adult guardian; and only 22 (5.2 percent) as X.[16]

The new permissiveness in general-release movies was hard on sexploitation producers. Russ Meyer, who made *Vixen!* in 1968, asked, "Why should the guy in the street shell out for a Russ Meyer flick, when he can see lesbianism and masturbation in *The Fox* (1967, dir. Mark Rydell), blood and guts in *Bonnie and Clyde* (1967, dir. Arthur Penn), and nudity in everything else?"[17]

In the late 1960s, sexploitation movies started to attract a wider range of viewers, including couples. Movies like *Vixen!* and *I, a Woman* (1965, dir. Mac Ahlberg) paved the way for other flicks capitalizing on this potentially lucrative niche. For instance, the producers of *Bunny and Clod* (1970, dir. Robert A. Poore), a sexploitation parody of the Warren Beatty-Faye Dunaway hit *Bonnie and Clyde*, wanted distributors to know that their film was to be marketed toward both sexes. "Think couples," advised the pressbook. "They are the key to the future of our business." Adult films were suddenly out of the art houses and in the mainstream, and couples were lining up around the block to see them. That's how *The Stewardesses* (1969, dir. Allan Silliphant), a softcore theatrical 3D film, became a big hit.

Apostolof was paying attention to the trend. In particular, the influence of *I, a Woman* on Apostolof's *The Divorcee* is clear not just from the latter's similar plot but also from its working title: *I, a Divorced Woman*. He claimed he never thought in terms of couples or singles when it came to shooting his next film. Still, his point of view was noticeably changing. "I just knew that my audience was predominantly male. And that's who I catered to," he explained. "However, when I realized that women also liked [my films], I made *The Divorcee*. Everything in that film was from a woman's point of view. And [the women] loved it."[18]

Apostolof's timing was ideal. In the late 1960s, the so-called "second wave" of feminism spread across the U.S. By 1969, the women's liberation movement had received extensive media attention, and feminists were working for change in education, employment, reproductive rights, etc. In 1969, California became the first state to adopt a no-fault divorce law, allowing couples to divorce by mutual consent. Apostolof maintained that he was just following his instincts when he chose divorce as the topic for his next film. "I didn't do a study or anything. I didn't examine grosses. I just had a feeling," he said.[19]

With her voluptuous figure and towering hairdo, Marsha Jordan was at the peak of her career that year, appearing in no less than nine films for producers like Carlos Tobalina and Don Davis. Despite her busy schedule, Apostolof never had to wait for the actress to finish a film before starting one of his. "She was always ready," he recalled.[20]

In those days, the pace of low-budget shoots was often back-breaking. "Sam Kopetzky wanted me and Marsha Jordan for one of his movies called *2069 A.D.*," recalls Harvey Shain. "That was the entire cast. The film took place on a Civil War battlefield where I played a Union soldier dreaming about his wife. I have these sex scenes in my dream, and that was the whole movie. Kopetzky shot the entire 54-minute film in one day—24 hours non-stop! I got $50 from that, and I think the whole budget was two, three thousand dollars."[21]

Jordan complained about being taken advantage of. A so-called friend once called her and wanted her to play a small role for three days at $100 per day. "And then they cram it in one 18-hour day and hand you a check for $100," Marsha revealed. "Or people asked me, would I do a little vignette, a little cameo thing in the film they were doing, as a favor to them, and I said okay. Well, I worked like a half-day or whatever for $100, and then when you get the calendar section of the *Los Angeles Times* and see a double-page ad saying 'Starring Marsha Jordan,' you feel a little bit abused and a little bit upset."[22]

Production of *The Divorcee* began in November 1968. It was shot by Robert Caramico using the pseudonym R.C. Ruben. Bud Costello designed the set and Mark Desmond, the choreographer of *Orgy of the Dead* (credited as Mark Delmonde), played a crucial acting role.

The Divorcee was likely influenced by the identically named 1930 classic (dir. Robert Z. Leonard) in which Norma Shearer plays a sexually liberated woman, a role that brought her an Oscar and set the tone for the next 20 years of her career. Today, Shearer is considered a pioneer of silver screen feminism and the first American movie star who made it chic and acceptable to be a sexually experienced, unmarried woman on-screen.

In Apostolof's surprisingly grim *The Divorcee*, protagonist Betty Brent (Jordan) catches her worthless, ill-tempered husband Hank (Marland Proctor, his name misspelled "Marlan" on-screen) cheating on her with a brunette floozy. After reluctantly divorcing the lout, Betty rejoins the singles scene and discovers the unpleasant truth that most available men see her only as a sex object. Her sleazy lawyer, Mr. Munson (Lloyd Nelson, billed as Lloyd Bilson), takes an advantage of her post-divorce vulnerability to have sex with her against her will. Upset by the direction her life is taking, Betty descends further into alcoholism to forget her problems.

Things spiral downward from there. Betty accepts a dinner invitation from her best friend Sally (Liza Renay, not to be confused with actress and gun moll Liz Renay), only to have Sally's horndog husband Bill (Mark Desmond) try to seduce her. The aggrieved wife is so jealous that she kicks her pal Betty out. The desperate divorcee then embarks upon a string of short-term romantic and sexual relationships. Along the way, she manages to attract but then lose a nice insurance salesman, Bruce Travis (Robert Wielie), who might have been her salvation. Attempting to numb her senses with booze and sex, Betty engages in some wild carnal escapades, including a tryst with the sadistic Dr. Carlton Wright (James E. Myers), who beats her with birch branches in a sauna. Poor Betty goes insane, realizing too late that her divorce has not brought her freedom.

Apostolof consults his script while making *The Divorcee* in November of 1968.

"Marsha was perfect," said Apostolof. "She was a trouper. Marsha was like a sister to me. In *The Divorcee*, I showed her the production board. I said, 'You see these scenes? You're in every one of them. If you want to go pee, I have to stop shooting.' Which was the truth. And she understood."[23] *The Divorcee* gives Jordan one of the most memorable and emotional roles of her career. Like *Lady Godiva Rides*, this was a vehicle for the actress, with the entire movie hinging on her performance.

"People who saw *The Divorcee* would also say, 'Gee, I never knew Marsha was such a good actress.' I got a letter from a woman who said she was glad I understood how women felt," recalled Apostolof.[24]

The Divorcee was markedly different from all of Apostolof's previous movies. Here, for the first time, he tried to give his audience a more complex storyline and a more fully developed main character. For obvious reasons, women were always central to Apostolof's films, but never before had he treated them with such sympathy and compassion, depicting them as victims of an unscrupulous world dominated by men.

Chapter 10. The Executive Filmmaker (1969–1972) 157

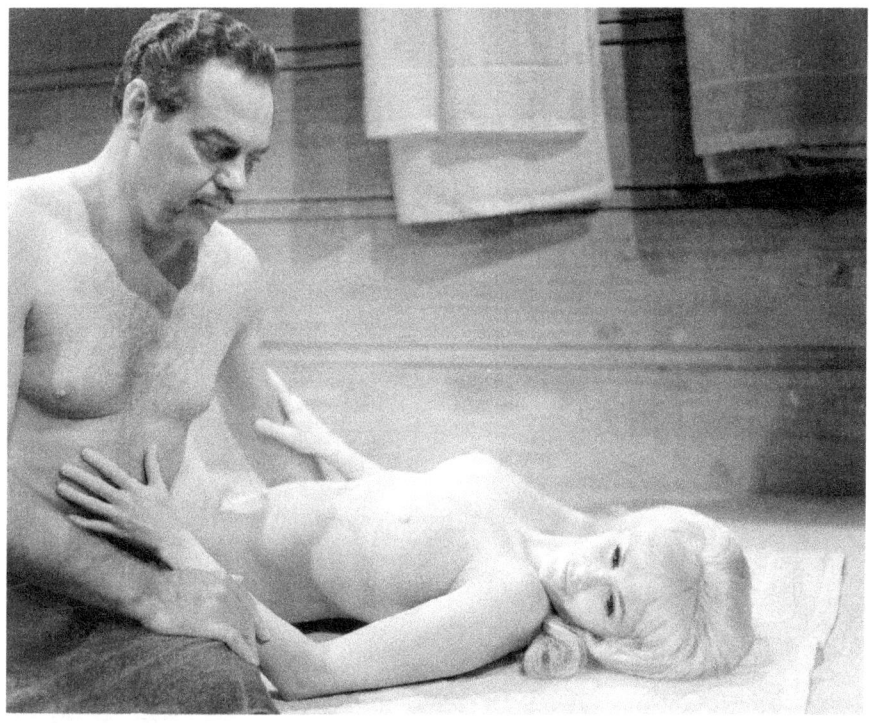

James E. Myers eyes Marsha Jordan in the sauna scene in *The Divorcee*.

Apostolof plays piano between takes on *The Divorcee*, accompanied by members of the Red Garter band.

Marsha Jordan with her confidante, a plastic doll, in a scene from *The Divorcee*.

The Divorcee's finale is especially noteworthy. Throughout the film, the title character's life has been rapidly deteriorating, as one relationship after another has failed. Alcohol and sex are no longer able to numb her pain as they once did. By the end, she is alone and afraid, so despondent that she even attempts to call her ex-husband to beg for a reconciliation. The last scene shows Betty delivering a tearful monologue to "Little Orphan Annie," a doll that serves as her confidant throughout the film. (The doll was also at the premiere. It was later given to Apostolof's daughter Susan.) Betty is depicted from above, emphasizing how isolated and helpless she is at this moment. "Help me!" she cries to an empty room.

Apostolof knew that this scene was crucial to the film. "When I was shooting the end of *The Divorcee*, I knew that I was doing something special," he remembered. "I did it on purpose. I wanted to show that now this woman is nothing. The only thing I regret is that I did not have a Chapman crane to do it smoothly, because now there are jumps, I had to do with jump cuts."[25]

Making a movie like *The Divorcee* might be enough to put anyone off matrimony.

But Apostolof, a two-time loser in love, got hitched a third time in 1971. This was the union that lasted the rest of his life.

The filmmaker's third wife, Shelley Apostolof, was born Barbara Rachelle Cooper in Coral Gables, Florida, on March 21, 1947, to Madeleine Gramling and Dr. David Cooper. She attended Monterey Peninsula College in Monterey, California, then went to Pacific Airlines School in Santa Barbara to become a flight attendant.

"I was coming from Cambria, a seaside village in San Luis Obispo County, California," remembers Shelley. "I spent some time in Santa Barbara and my friend told me I should go to Los Angeles. She said there's work and it's fun."[26] In 1970, she moved to her friend's place and started paying half of the rent. She recalls how she met Apostolof:

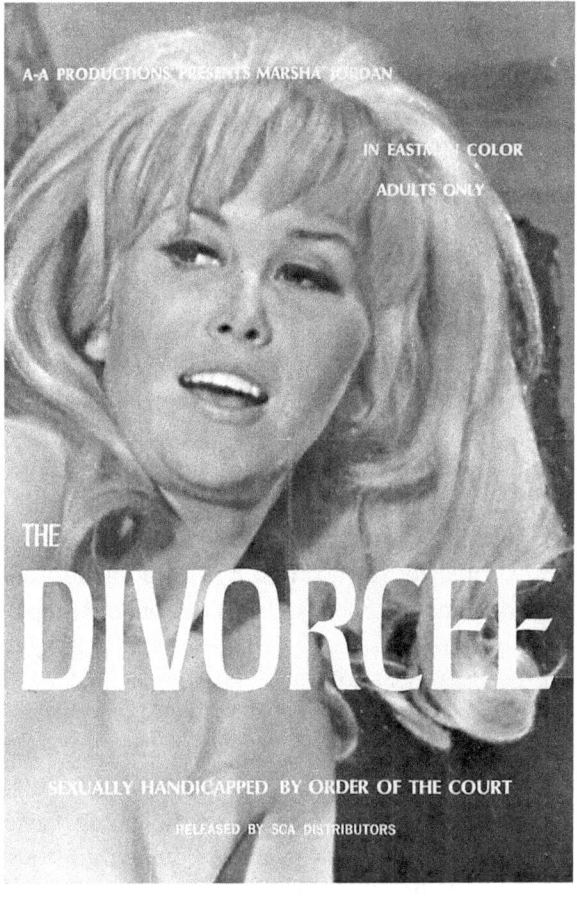

A color one sheet for *The Divorcee*.

> My friend Brenda used to go often to an Italian restaurant called Panza's Lazy Susan whose owner she was dating. Steve was a friend of the owner and used to go there often. Jane told me she was introduced to a film producer and suggested meeting him. I told her, "Are you crazy? I'm not going anywhere with some film producer." I thought he would secretly take photos of us when we go to the bathroom or something.[27]

Shelley agreed to go out with her girlfriend and Apostolof under one condition: The meeting had to be in a restaurant. But Apostolof called and invited the ladies to his house instead. "We went there just out of courtesy to tell him that we have to see each other [in a public place]," says Shelley. "But he had bags of steaks and potatoes, and we hadn't eaten normal food for a long time. He said he'd make french fries, salad and steak. He was so polite and jovial that we couldn't refuse his invitation."[28]

While cooking, Apostolof talked about all kind of things. He told the girls about his turbulent past. He also told them he had four kids. Shelley (who came from a large family: five children) didn't buy it, because he seemed very young to be a father of so many children. "I told him I didn't believe him and made him prove it. So the next weekend he took me to Mammoth Mountain, and his son Steve was with us and he confirmed that he had three sisters," remembers Shelley.[29]

From that point on, Shelley spent almost every weekend with Apostolof's kids.

Initially Apostolof was worried about the way they would react to this new woman. At 23, Shelley was only four years older than Maria, Apostolof's eldest daughter. "Initially I did not like Steve," Shelley admits. "I thought that he had a very big ego and was very conceited. I did not fall in love with him at first sight, as he claimed it happened with him. It took time because he was so sociable and friendly. Eventually, he got me. Seduced me."[30]

Shelley's parents were less than thrilled with the idea of their daughter marrying a man 19 years her senior—and the director of erotic films. Shelley came from a conservative family that expected men to have normal, respectable jobs. Her father had been a dental director for the U.S. Public Health Service, for instance. And Shelley still remembers when, just before marrying her, he showed her parents his most recent film, *The Divorcee*, in a rented theater. "My mom and dad came out of the cinema in shock," laughs Shelley.[31]

Despite his future in-laws' misgivings, Apostolof considered *The Divorcee* his finest film, the one in which he took the most pride. Maybe that's why, when his brother Stavri visited him in the U.S. in 1988, that was the film Apostolof showed him.

Ultimately, the fact that Apostolof made adult movies was not a huge factor in his relationship with Shelley's parents. Son Christopher explains:

> For one, my grandfather David died pretty early on. I was three when he passed away. He had some heart condition. I don't think my grandmother Madeleine really cared. It was never something that was brought up. It didn't come up in that kind of conversation. When business was good and something was sold, it was, "Hey, great! Fantastic! Making money!" That kind of thing.

On February 14, 1971, St. Valentine's Day, the 42-year-old Apostolof and 23-year-old Shelley married at St. George, the Bulgarian Eastern Orthodox church in Los Angeles founded by Father Antim Enev, a Bulgarian priest who had arrived in America just a few years earlier. Apostolof's best man was Bill Storey, an old friend who also provided insurance for some of his films. The ceremony was attended by all of Apostolof's children. Eldest son Steve, 13, remembered the wedding as a stunning event: "Dad had costumes, traditional costumes brought from Bulgaria. At least they looked traditional. They had crowns on their heads. I didn't even recognize Shelley, I was so touched. But the costumes were pretty crazy! At a wedding, you usually wear a tuxedo or suit. You don't wear traditional Bulgarian costumes from the 17th century! It was a great event. Lots of fun."[32]

"We had no rehearsal," Shelley remembers. "They pushed me and said, 'Say "I do!"' That's what happened."[33]

The wedding, though spectacular, had a few hitches. When the guests moved to the second floor of the church after the ceremony to celebrate with *rakia* (Bulgarian fruit brandy) and *kebapcheta* (a Bulgarian traditional sausage), someone stole the traditional Bulgarian costumes, as well as Shelley's purse with about $900 inside. Meanwhile, in true Bulgarian fashion, Apostolof got drunk at the ceremony before clambering into his Cadillac to go on an impromptu honeymoon with his new wife.

"I wanted to go to the Beverly Hills Hotel, but he said he would drive to Las Vegas," remembers Shelley. "I told him that he probably would not be able to drive, but he said he was okay. I was right, so we ended up in a bedbug-riddled motel in the middle of the Mojave Desert where we spent our wedding night. I was furious."[34]

Chapter 10. The Executive Filmmaker (1969–1972)

Although in keeping with Bulgarian tradition, Stephen and Shelley Apostolof's costumes at their wedding came not from Apostolof's hometown of Burgas but rather from the capital city of Sofia.

"When Dad married Shelley, he told her that he had a PhD," remembered his son Steve.[35] This "fact" was also included in the *Los Angeles Times* wedding announcement, which also claimed that Apostolof had "graduated from the Sorbonne and was a director at 20th Century–Fox."[36] Information about Apostolof attending the Sorbonne has never turned up, not even in his own files, so this was apparently another of the director's tall tales.

After the wedding, Apostolof and Shelley became inseparable. It seemed Apostolof had finally found the woman he wanted to spend the rest of his life with. He taught her how to cook traditional Bulgarian dishes. He also taught her how to belly dance and had her perform in front of him to the music of George Abdo and his *Flames of Araby* orchestra. According to Apostolof's friends, the years with Shelley were some of the happiest in his life. The newlyweds initially lived in an apartment on 3710 Los Feliz Boulevard with a balcony and a lot of geraniums. After a couple of months there, they moved to 4055 Tujunga Avenue in North Hollywood.

In 1971, Apostolof bought a spacious home in Studio City, an upscale L.A. neighborhood. This district was named for a film studio that producer-director Mack Sennett began building in 1927. (The facility was later renamed CBS Studio Center and is still in use.) With so many residents working in film, TV and music, Studio City was perfect for Apostolof. Constructed in 1939, his single family residence at 12024 Sarah Street consisted of a four-bedroom main house, plus a guest house that doubled as

On March 18, 1976, Christopher got a kite for his third birthday from Apostolof's set decorator Budd Costello.

Apostolof's office. Budd Costello, Apostolof's set decorator, furnished the house in the French provincial style with Louis XIV furniture. The property had a huge swimming pool and was surrounded by dense tropical vegetation, requiring the services of a gardener. Apostolof also had a maid who took care of his son Christopher. Christopher recalls, "In the backyard, there was a golf course with eight holes. When I was a kid, I used to play golf. Furthermore, my bedroom had its own bathroom. None of the other kids at school had this. I thought this was the order of things—every child had a bedroom with an in-suite bathroom."[37]

The new digs suited Apostolof. "I love working from home," he said. "I've had offices in different parts of Hollywood, but I prefer to work from home because my office was there and nobody bothered me. My phone was nearby, and I could call whoever I want."[38]

Apostolof invited Ed Wood over to show the place off. Wood walked around the homestead, and when he arrived at the built-in BBQ he began to cry. "Eddie was a

Chapter 10. The Executive Filmmaker (1969–1972) 163

In this photograph from July 1973, Apostolof and Shelley pose with their newborn son Christopher outside the family's house on Sarah Street.

very emotional person, but many people don't realize this about him," said Apostolof. "He just told me, 'Boss, I'm so happy! I wish Kathy could see it!'"[39] According to Apostolof, Wood was delighted because his (Apostolof's) prosperity was good for him, too: It meant more work.

Ed never seemed to be able to maintain a residence for long. He and his wife lived a chaotic existence. "Eddie and Kathy probably changed five, six apartments," Steve said.[40] "They moved constantly. And they were drinking heavily. It was a way of life for them. In the last two, three years, Eddie seemed to be losing his mind because of the drinking. I used to buy him clothes because he wouldn't do it himself. I had to give him rides because he had no car which in L.A. is hell. But in his last years, his whole world was ten blocks away."

Apostolof often invited friends to stay for the weekend. Sometimes his lawyer Harold Abeles would come in Friday and leave on Sunday. A Southern gentleman, he was a noted Beverly Hills entertainment attorney who represented celebrities including

In a snapshot dated May 6, 1975, Stephen Apostolof and his friend Mike Mikhailof chill out near the swimming pool at the Apostolofs' Sarah Street home.

Mickey Rooney, George Hamilton, Ernest Borgnine and Steve McQueen. Apostolof and Abeles would stay in the guest house up until five or six in the morning, drinking and talking. Then they would sleep for a couple of hours, get up in the early afternoon for lunch and start all over again.

"Harold was an amazing man," says Christopher Apostolof. "Always tried to be there for Steve. He was one of those people Steve could call and have a conversation with any time. He always took time to chat, or meet for coffee. Harold also was the way Steve was able to get a home loan when we bought in Westlake."[41]

Steve and Shelley often went to Lake Tahoe for skiing and stayed at Mike Mikhailof's Continental Ski Lodge. Before escaping Los Angeles with Shelley, Apostolof would leave a blank check for his secretary to pay the rent and the bills. But instead of that, she bought herself a convertible Chevrolet Corvette. Needless to say, this did not go over well with her employer ("Steve was very angry," recalls Shelley[42]). It turned out that the thieving secretary was a professional con artist, and the police had been searching for

Chapter 10. The Executive Filmmaker (1969–1972)

A rather informally dressed Apostolof camps with his son Christopher at Lake Tahoe in October 1977. Says Christopher, "The man owned one pair of jeans for camping and ironed them."

her for a long time. So Shelley began working in the office, at Apostolof's insistence. In the beginning, she helped him distribute his movies, calling theaters to make sure they received the prints. Shelley later took on the role of associate producer for several of Apostolof's films.

In 1970, the adult film industry received some support from a highly unlikely place: the President's Commission on Obscenity and Pornography, funded by the Congress. Originally created by President Lyndon B. Johnson to study pornography's social effects, the commission eventually prepared a detailed multi-volume evaluation called *Report of the Commission on Obscenity and Pornography*, which it delivered to Johnson's successor, staunch right-wing Republican Richard Nixon. It concluded that pornography is not inherently harmful and that no further restrictions should be placed on entertainment intended for adults. Outraged by this apparent disregard for traditional values, Nixon rejected the commission and its report. "I have evaluated that report and categorically reject its morally bankrupt conclusions and major recommendations," declared an incensed Nixon. "So long as I am in the White House, there will be no relaxation of the national effort to control and eliminate smut from our national life."[43]

Interestingly, the report called Apostolof Film Productions "[one of] the most important producer-distributors or distributors in the exploitation industry" as of the spring of 1970. Other Los Angeles–based companies mentioned by name included Harry H. Novak's Box Office International Films, Russ Meyer's Eve Productions and Donald A. Davis, Inc.[44]

Strange as it may seem, some sexploitation filmmakers, including Apostolof, were not pleased with the commission's liberal recommendations. Even Russ Meyer, hailed as "The King of the Nudies," thought that outright pornography was anti-erotic. To the end of his career, Meyer's movies were strictly softcore, meaning that the sex acts depicted on-screen were simulated.

Prolific producer David F. Friedman also railed against hardcore movies in those days. As it turned out, Friedman's objections were influenced by financial considerations. When the industry changed, he became one of the first sexploitation producers to start shooting hardcore porn in the late '70s. Friedman explained that early hardcore filmmakers couldn't legally distribute their movies the way softcore producers could.

Cult film historian Greg Goodsell further explains the woes of the 1970s porn industry, again differentiating between hardcore and softcore:

> Hardcore filmmakers had a lot of ties to organized crime. They were not very nice with their actors. The actors they got, they would get them for $50, use them for a day, and they would never see a cent again. Whereas the softcore people worked with a select group of actors, they were faithful. Apostolof always made sure there were roles for Marsha Jordan. He had his favorites and his stable of actors. And Russ Meyer had his stable of actors. While the hardcore people, with little exceptions, would hire prostitutes off the street. They would use people. They would stab their partners in the back.[45]

Despite the commission's recommendations, American authorities showed no mercy on producers and distributors of hardcore pornography. In November 1970, New York City police, with the support of the city council, began raiding porn theaters. The Paree and the Capri on 7th Avenue and the Avon 7 on 8th Avenue had their loudspeakers destroyed and projectors and film reels confiscated.

Sexploitation distributors were afraid they'd be the next targets of the anti-smut crackdown, and even though they always fought for greater creative freedom, they also acted as *de facto* censors themselves by trying to run hardcore producers out of business. Operating in the shadows of Hollywood, rather like the *Arabian Nights*' Forty Thieves, sexploitation producers had been rebels and outcasts during the classical period of exploitation cinema (1920–1958). But by the 1970s, it seems they had become complacent businessmen.

Apostolof's strictly softcore films often ran afoul of the authorities, but the producer himself managed to remain unscathed. It was always the distributors, the theater owners and the technical staff who got dragged into the mire.

On May 7, 1966, for instance, the police arrested Jack Caldwell, manager of the Autodrome Drive-in Theatre near Radford, Virginia, during the showing of two films: a sleazy Greek thriller called *The Rape* (1965, dir. Dinos Dimopoulos) and Apostolof's

Orgy of the Dead. Caldwell, who resigned after his arrest, was fined $50 by Judge Alan D. Groseclose from Pulaski County Court. Caldwell's arrest climaxed a year of controversy between some area residents and the owners of the drive-in theater over the films shown. The court moved into a Pulaski movie house where the films were viewed by the principals in the trial. At the June 7 hearing, Groseclose ruled that *The Rape* was not obscene, but regarding *Orgy of the Dead*, which he called "absurd," he said: "The motion picture in its entirety is obviously designed to arouse sexual desires of a male viewer through the exotic gyration of the dancers. It nearly falls within the definition of obscenity contained in Virginia law."[46]

On February 17, 1970, Pasadena, Texas, police raided the Red Bluff Drive-In, a theater that opened in 1953 as a family-oriented venue but later started booking "art films for adults." They confiscated prints of three films and charged the manager R.J. Barlow and the projectionist William Russell Jones with possession and display of obscene material. The films were *The Defilers* (1965, dir. Lee Frost and David F. Friedman), *Suburban Pagans* (1968, dir. William Rotsler) and *Orgy of the Dead*. Bail was set at $2500 for each of them. The problem was that the huge outdoor screen was clearly visible from afar. The police raided the Red Bluff again the following night and arrested the assistant manager and projectionist on the same charges. That night the theater was showing *Hot Skin and Cold Cash* (1965, dir. Barry Mahon). This time the bond was set at $400.[47] According to Pasadena Mayor Clyde Doyle, the films had no redeeming value and in addition they were traffic hazards. "It's kind of disconcerting to be driving along the road and see a naked woman up there and try to cope with the traffic," said Doyle. "That fence they put up doesn't hide it."[48]

Apostolof's first and only direct encounter with the law took place in July 1972 in Memphis, dubbed "the buckle of the Bible Belt" by porn star Harry Reems.[49] This was the same city where, in 1976, after a series of federal cases, over 60 individuals and companies connected to the all-time porn classic *Deep Throat* (1972, dir. Gerard Damiano) were indicted for conspiracy to distribute obscene material across state lines. Prosecutors hoped that a conservative Southern jury would get them the convictions they so desperately wanted. But this was not the first major porn-related case to be tried in Memphis. Four years earlier, Apostolof *et al.* were roped into the obscenity trial of his friend and *Orgy of the Dead* editor Donald A. Davis. Among those asked to appear in court was sexploitation mogul David F. Friedman.

Davis got into producing and directing 16mm adult films early on, and used Memphis as a distribution point. But he chose his business partners unwisely and was nabbed for interstate transport. The other defendant was a Memphis man named Carl R. Carter, proprietor of Academy Films Corp. Apostolof was subpoenaed to appear as a witness for the prosecution, summoned by the court to testify against Davis: "Which surprised the hell out of Don," Apostolof said. "They subpoenaed everybody. And I got subpoenaed to show up in Memphis along with everybody else, the whole caboodle, including people who just knew him. But I had no business with Don. So I told the prosecutor that it was all art. Picasso painted naked women. You go in the Louvre and see naked women. You go to the movies and see naked women, blah, blah, blah."[50]

Davis is an intriguing figure in sexploitation history. He was born in Florida on June 7, 1932, and served as a production assistant on Ed Wood's *Plan 9 from Outer*

Space (1957) where he also played a small role as a staggering drunk. He became a director and producer in his own right and made a couple of sexploitation films, the most famous being *Marsha: The Erotic Housewife* (1970), in which Apostolof's superstar Marsha Jordan played the title role.

Apostolof thought the case against Davis and Carter was a "witch hunt,"[51] but the court had a different opinion. U.S. District Judge Bailey Brown set up an 8×10-foot screen at the back of the courtroom and made sure it was out of sight for hallway passersby, even covering the glass panels on the door with cardboard. A sign outside read: "No admission while movie is being shown." Brown asked anyone under 18, the legal age in Tennessee, to leave voluntarily.

"This place is just like an adult film house, the way people come in and go out all the time," observed one spectator, as others came in and out between the showing of *One Into Three* (year and director unknown) and *Bride's Delight* (1971, dir. unknown), two of the 36 movies Davis and Carter were accused of illegally shipping across state lines. (*Delight* featured future Apostolof starlet Terri Johnson.[52])

These courtroom screenings were arranged by 32-year-old Larry Parrish, a highly ambitious assistant U.S. district attorney from Memphis, who in the early 1970s was on a crusade to topple the adult film industry. It was Parrish who, in June 1975, prosecuted *Deep Throat* and indicted its star Harry Reems on federal charges of conspiracy to distribute obscene material across state lines. "Parrish's efforts were so exhaustive ... that Hollywood worried the aftershocks of the prosecution would rock the entire film industry," wrote journalist Jacqueline Marino.[53]

The jury found Davis and Carter guilty on 27 individual counts, each of which carried a five-year prison sentence. That totaled a staggering 135 years behind bars apiece! These convictions were reversed on appeal. This was Apostolof's only serious skirmish with the law. After the trial, he returned to California, seemingly not humbled by the experience in the least. According to his wife Shelley, he came back boasting that the court paid all of his travel expenses.

Chapter 11

The Master of Mayhem (1972–1978)

"[E]verything starts with an idea. You are what you think you are. If you think you are beaten, you are beaten. If you think you can, you can. I believe in the words, 'I can.' And yes, I can. I can move mountains, so to speak."[1]—Stephen C. Apostolof

Sexploitation directors and producers weren't just fighting America's legal authorities in the early 1970s. They were also fighting against thieving theater owners, the exhibitors who were siphoning off the filmmakers' hard-earned profits. This realization led Apostolof to one of his boldest gambits yet—a movie house of his own. In those days, numerous adult filmmakers were opening their own theaters in order to intercept those crucial box office dollars. It was their way of cutting out the middlemen.

"You're making a movie and somehow it manages to 'grow legs' and get away from you," said filmmaker Ted V. Mikels. "People take it for distribution and automatically think they own it and keep all the money that it brought. Ha ha! It wasn't easy! It wasn't easy at all!"[2]

People in the adult film industry opened theaters where they played their own films. David F. Friedman and Dan Sonney, for instance, founded the Pussycat theater chain in 1966. Bob Cresse and Carlos Tobalina owned the Star Theatre in La Puente, California, the Mayan Theatre in downtown Los Angeles, and the Theatre on Hollywood Boulevard. Apostolof decided that he, too, needed to expand his horizons and become a theater owner. His eldest son Steve said,

> Dad had always said that within the distribution arm of the business, everybody stole. The movie theaters would under-report their sales because everybody was working for a percentage. It wasn't like, "I'll give you ten dollars and I will show your movie." It was more like, "I'll give you ten percent of each seat that I sell." And the movie theater would lie to the distributors. The distributors would lie to the producer. So Dad came up with the idea of having his own theater. He found about technology where it didn't need to have a projectionist.[3]

Apostolof chose a modest 40,000-square-foot space at 2838 Wilshire Boulevard on the corner of Wilshire and Yale Street in Santa Monica. The theater was at an intersection with traffic lights and had excellent visibility. Behind it, there was a huge parking lot, accessible from both Wilshire and Yale. Everything about the place was perfect.

Apostolof named his new enterprise the SCA Mini Art Theatre. The so-called "mini theaters," also known as "pocket cinemas," were similar to nickelodeons, the small, primitive cinemas that thrived in America at the beginning of the 20th century.

The SCA Mini Art Theatre on its opening day.

Typically set up in converted storefronts, these miniature theaters could only accommodate about 200 viewers at a time, though the seating capacity could be as low as 40. On the upside, they required far fewer resources to maintain than the hard-tops and drive-ins where movies generally played in those days. The advertising budget, for instance, could be slashed if the theater was in a good location where pedestrians could just stumble onto it.

Apostolof was also one of the first exhibitors in L.A. whose theater came equipped with special technology that didn't require a specialized employee to load and run the projector. He revealed, "Since the biggest expense for the average theater was the operating expense, I got someone to design a fully automated theater for me. It had a rear screen projector. You'd press a button and the curtain would open or close and the music would play, the lights would dim down and the picture would start."[4]

Apostolof used an automatic projection system known as a platter, which became commonplace in the 1970s. It allowed an entire film to be spliced onto one huge reel and played at once. The technology slowly pushed projectionists into extinction.

"But mine was so primitive, the guy who invented the thing used to kick it here and kick it there, which used to tear the film to pieces," remembered Apostolof.[5]

The SCA Mini Art Theatre opened on July 22, 1970, with a screening of *The Divorcee*. Apostolof wanted the night to be special, so in true Hollywood fashion, he brought a huge spotlight to illuminate the cinema's facade. *Divorcee* star Marsha Jordan attended, along with other "usual suspects." Ed Wood was there, as was Criswell. Shelley was also in attendance, naturally.

The night of the opening, Criswell predicted that the SCA Mini Art Theatre would be a great success. Like so many of his other predictions, this one didn't come true. A few months after the opening, Apostolof started losing money and was forced to close the place. Today there's a vitamin store and a sushi place on that spot.

All that remained from the unsuccessful enterprise was the theater's emblem, made of acrylic glass: a profile of a Roman centurion. Apostolof had also used the centurion in the logo of his company SCA Distributors, and the character appears at the beginning of most of his movies. His youngest son Christopher maintains that the character was inspired by the USC Trojans. Another memento from the ill-fated adventure was a framed dollar coin, the first and probably the only one the theater ever earned. Steve Apostolof recalled,

Stephen Apostolof, Marsha Jordan, and Mark Desmond at the opening of the SCA Mini Art Theatre.

> The theater was a management of a day-to-day business. And the best thing about motion pictures for Dad was that if you want to take a week off, you can take a week off. Except when you're in production, your time is kind of your own. Even with the distribution, yes, he had to get prints to the people, he had deadlines to meet. But it wasn't this kind of business where you had to have employees showing up to work every day to open the door of the business and actually run it. And I think ultimately that's why the business didn't make it. Because Dad wasn't there every day. Dad *didn't want*

Apostolof used the profile of a Roman centurion for the logo of his company SCA Distributors.

to be there every day. And if he had a manager, well, you're right back in the same problem where you have people and they are handling cash. And now you get your own people stealing from you.[6]

Besides, Apostolof had movies of his own to make, and that meant joining forces with an unlikely collaborator from his past. Even Criswell himself probably could not have prognosticated a professional reunion between Ed Wood and Apostolof, considering how calamitous their working relationship was in 1965. And yet that is what happened in the early 1970s. They joined forces for a half-dozen new softcore features.

The 1960s had not been kind to Ed Wood. His film career largely atrophied in those years. After his anti-smut crime thriller *The Sinister Urge* (1960), he didn't even direct another feature until the early '70s. During that hiatus, some of his scripts were filmed by other directors, including Don Davis, Boris Petroff, Ed DePriest, Joe Robertson and, yes, Stephen C. Apostolof. In retrospect, *Orgy of the Dead* is probably the most significant addition to the Wood filmography in the 1960s, and Wood himself wasn't even in the director's chair for it. Meanwhile, Eddie's two perennial problems—a lack of money and an addiction to alcohol—only worsened. He could barely cover his rent. How was he going to get a movie off the ground? Without help, he couldn't.

As his film work dried up, Wood increasingly turned to prose writing to earn his meager living. Even in the depths of his alcoholism, he still possessed a feverish imagination and formidable typing skills. These useful gifts allowed him to churn out lurid paperback novels at a staggering pace, starting with *Killer in Drag* in 1963. By the end of the decade, he'd landed a steady gig at Pendulum Publishing, one of the era's leading producers of adult books and magazines. Pendulum's head honcho, Bernie Bloom, had Ed writing everything from short stories to pseudo-scientific guides to sex and the occult. It wasn't glamorous work, but it provided Ed with steady income. His long-suffering wife Kathy was grateful.

But Wood's true home was in the movies, and he saw Apostolof as the man who could lead him back there. Sure, Wood was writing and directing X-rated features (*Necromania*, *The Young Marrieds*) and loops (including titles for the *Swedish Erotica* series) during the Nixon years, but these projects did not have the relative glamour and production value of the SCA films. Interestingly, Apostolof and Wood had not lost contact with each other in the intervening years. Apostolof even owned a copy of Ed's paperback novel *It Takes One to Know One* (1967), complete with a personal dedication from the author. "To Steve," it said. "I guess there's always another one around the corner." And it was signed "Edw. D. Wood Jr., 10/10/67." The dedication proved prophetic.

The Snow Bunnies (1972)

What project could possibly reunite Ed Wood and Stephen Apostolof? At this point in their careers, the type of film they would make together was not in question. By 1972, the only genre that would still have Wood was pornography. At least Apostolof was on the classier softcore end of the spectrum, compared to the hardcore features and loops Wood was making during this era as a sidelight to his writing career.

But this was a pivotal time for screen sex, the era of so-called "porno chic," ushered in by the groundbreaking hardcore feature *Deep Throat*. At the time, it was acceptable in American society for husbands and wives to attend screenings of this notoriously raunchy sex comedy starring Linda Lovelace and Harry Reems. For a flickering moment, it looked like explicit sex was finally going to seep into the mainstream. This was also the era of the controversial and widely discussed *Last Tango in Paris* (1972, dir. Bernardo Bertolucci), a non-porn film whose uninhibited sex scenes were still believable enough to warrant an X rating. Would more stars follow Marlon Brando's lead by appearing in films of this nature? No one knew.

Just as hardcore pornography was having its moment in the national spotlight, Apostolof and Wood created *The Snow Bunnies,* a nudity-filled but otherwise relatively quaint bedroom farce set at a ski lodge. A far cry from *Deep Throat* and *Last Tango*, this was a film with almost no aspirations to topical or social relevance, making it just about the least hip career move either of these men could have made.

There was at least some historical precedent for *The Snow Bunnies*. American International Pictures basically created the template with *Ski Party* (1965, dir. Alan Rafkin), a spinoff from the company's popular *Beach Party* series. Despite appearances by James Brown and Lesley Gore, this wholesome, lighthearted film underperformed at the box office, which may explain why ski movies were never as popular or as ubiquitous as beach movies in the decades to come. But the strange subgenre did eventually amass its own canon of sorts, mostly raunchy, low-budget affairs like *Hot Dog ... The Movie* (1984, dir. Peter Markle), *Ski Patrol* (1990, dir. Rich Correll) and *Ski School* (1991, dir. Damian Lee).

The Snow Bunnies was Apostolof's predictably skewed attempt at a ski-and-sex farce. Typical of his 1970s output, it takes place in the bleary-eyed, booze-soaked world of jaded, neurotic adults. Normally, ski comedies feature happy-go-lucky high schoolers and college kids. That wasn't quite Apostolof's style, however, and it definitely wasn't Wood's. Eddie would have been in his late 40s when he penned this script, and his middle-aged desperation is all over it. In several important ways, *The Snow Bunnies* presages *The Class Reunion*, a Apostolof-Wood collaboration filmed back to back and released the same year. The two films have nearly identical casts, including headliner Marsha Jordan, and were both shot by Allen Stone, but more important is what they have in common thematically: restless, dissatisfied twenty- and thirty-somethings who try to drink and screw their problems away, if only for a few days.

Like *Reunion, The Snow Bunnies* contrasts the beautiful, unblemished natural world with the dank, ugly man-made world. The film has an abundance of cheerful outdoor footage, complete with lens flares, shot at a real ski resort. It's almost like a travelogue. Apostolof shows happy skiers slaloming their way down the mountain, riding the chairlift and relaxing at the cozy chalet. The director even makes a cameo, alongside his third wife Shelley. But then there is the sleazy indoor footage, shot on dreary-looking soundstages in Los Angeles. This is a world of tacky bars, depressing lounges and grotesque hotel rooms. These places are where the horny characters go to flirt and fornicate when they're done skiing. In some cases, Apostolof barely attempts to cover up the gray acoustic panels on the wall.

Shooting of *The Snow Bunnies* began in February 1972, but Apostolof didn't finish the picture until December of the same year. Although it is ostensibly set somewhere in Canada, the location footage was actually shot at California's picturesque Mammoth

Apostolof hoists his 8mm Bolex film camera in December 1972 while finishing *The Snow Bunnies*, which he'd started shooting earlier that year.

Mountain, about a five-hour drive east from Los Angeles. Seeing California's distinctive state flag featuring Monarch the grizzly bear among the Flags of All Nations at the hotel's entrance is the viewer's first hint that Apostolof didn't really take a film crew across the Canadian border to make this thing. Moviegoers who had already been to Mammoth would also recognize the Yodler Haus, a real-life restaurant and biergarten that figures prominently in the film. Mammoth was a favorite destination for Apostolof family vacations and also hosted numerous movie crews over the years, including *Indiana Jones and the Temple of Doom* (1984, dir. Steven Spielberg) and *The Golden Child* (1986, dir. Michael Ritchie). Apostolof had a friend, a Bulgarian émigré named Mike Mikhailof, who owned a hotel at Mammoth Mountain.

Harvey Shain still has fond memories of this production. "We filmed *Snow Bunnies* up in the mountains. In Big Bear Lake. I remember my mother, she had crocheted hats for everybody on the set. Wool hats! Because it was freezing up there. It was cold. Everybody wore my mother's hats and you can see them in the film. It was the first time I ever rode a jet-ski snowmobile. Professional cast and everybody did their jobs. A lot of laughs, I remember."[7]

Thematically and aesthetically, *The Snow Bunnies* is as dense and baffling as any SCA film. Plotwise, however, it is stock simple. Four attractive young ladies in need of a break from their personal and work routines spontaneously decide to take a road trip to a Canadian ski resort. There, instead of spending quality time on the slopes, their real goal is to meet and bed some attractive, available strangers. Having accomplished this goal, the women reunite and drive back home. Although the real Mammoth Mountain is a family resort, the unnamed mountaintop hotel in this film seems to attract a lot of lecherous swingers. What's surprising here is the tone. One might guess that a film called *The Snow Bunnies* would be lightweight, slightly naughty fare. But Apostolof and Wood went in a darker, more troubling direction.

Apostolof makes his intentions clear with the film's opening shots: It begins with Marsha Jordan nude in the shower, languorously lathering her impressive breasts. She is wearing lipstick and eyeshadow at the time. Her character, overworked nurse Joan Bradford, is enjoying a staycation when she receives an unwanted call from the hospital. A co-worker, Miss Pastor (Apostolof's wife Shelley, who used the pseudonym S.B. Cooper "because Steve didn't want to pay an actress"[8]), tells Joan she needs to come back to work as soon as possible.

Joan refuses in no uncertain terms, making liberal use of profanity to drive the point home before hanging up. This pricelessly funny scene proves to be the catalyst for the plot. Joan picks up a convenient Air Canada brochure from a nearby coffee table and decides on the spot to take a skiing vacation with her (noticeably younger) friends

February 13, 1972. Apostolof's wife Shelley plays Miss Pastor in *The Snow Bunnies*. Note the closet doors behind her.

Harvey Shain and Terri Johnson in a cozy love scene from *The Snow Bunnies*.

Brenda, Tammy and Carol. All of these women will be paired up with temporary romantic partners at the ski lodge.

Brenda (played by Terri Johnson, whom Apostolof called "a natural" and "a very good actress [with] very good diction"[9]) is a willowy blonde teacher whose status as an intellectual is denoted by her horn-rimmed glasses. Though she has term papers to grade, she decides to go with Joan because, in her words, "maybe an old maid schoolteacher might get male-connected!" Brenda's designated sex partner for the film is overaged, vest-loving college student James Eldridge (Harvey Shain, here billed as Forman Shane), who's paying his way through school by working at the pro shop. Between lovemaking sessions, they engage in some semi-incoherent political debates. But James wants Brenda to know that he's not into the whole commitment scene. Towards the end of the film, for no reason whatsoever, Brenda dances nude in front of a bunch of tourists at a cocktail lounge. This is apparently to illustrate that the once-stern schoolmarm has really loosened up on this vacation. What would her students say?

Tammy (Sandy Carey) is a promiscuous, fun-loving model who gives up a cover shoot for *Teen Magazine* to go on the trip. At the lodge, she'll be the only one to spend any time on the slopes, trying and failing to ski. She's paired with fair-haired boy Chris (Chris Geoffries), who at first seems like an ideal lover, even if he can't keep up with her in bed. Later, Chris reveals that he has some dark ulterior motives for getting involved with Tammy. Basically, he wants to become a gigolo for rich women, with Tammy acting as his pimp. She is not too thrilled with this idea. So that's the end of their relationship.

Carrol (Starline Comb) is a troubled single woman who's been drowning her sorrows in martinis since being dumped by her married boyfriend, Herbie. Carrol is the film's token depressed alcoholic character. Even though she's eager to engage with mindless, sweaty sex with strangers, she is not taking this trip lightly. "I came here to get a man, and that's what I'm gonna do," she says with a total lack of humor. Her plan doesn't work out so well, though. Her temporary boyfriend is a curly-haired lothario named Fred (the overly tan Ron Darby), who seduces her by surreptitiously getting her drunk, and then tries to make their relationship "a permanent thing." Carrol wisely says no to this offer. Even though she doesn't get a man out of this vacation, that's probably for the best.

Once again, Apostolof opted for an episodic format. After a leisurely driving sequence, the amorous ladies spend virtually the entire movie apart in their own individual storylines. Most of the screen time is devoted to drawn-out sex scenes featuring them with their male partners.

Jordan's character disappears for a long stretch in the middle of the movie, but she makes a dramatic reappearance in the final third, when her story intersects with that of the film's fifth major female character: Madie (Rene Bond) is a scantily clad Yodler Haus waitress. Her disagreeable boss Cappy (*Orgy of the Dead* choreographer Mark Desmond) says he'll fire her from this high-paying position if he catches her hitting on any of the male clientele. But she does so anyway, aggressively coming on to well-dressed young skier Paul (Ric Lutze, Rene's soon-to-be-ex-husband), who at first insists that he's not interested. But she gives him a hand job under the table, which changes his mind. They go back to his room and attempt to make love. But he just can't maintain an erection, which causes Madie to accuse him of being gay. This obviously trips an alarm in his brain, and he smacks her. Later, perhaps having been beaten more severely, the waitress awakens to find herself alone, traumatized and injured. She staggers around the hotel, soon running into Nurse Joan, who tends to her injuries, then seduces her in the movie's most staggeringly inappropriate scene.

Apart from one underwhelming sauna scene between Chris Geoffries and Sandy Carey, the sexual couplings in this movie are mostly filmed in the characters' cheaply furnished, tacky hotel rooms. Art director Mike McCloskey, an industry veteran who worked on such cult classics as *Please Don't Eat My Mother!* (1973, dir. Carl Monson), *Loose Shoes* (1978, dir. Ira Miller) and *The Undertaker and His Pals* (1966, dir. T.L.P. Swicegood), attempts to establish atmosphere by plastering the walls with ski equipment posters and travel ads. Apostolof does not skimp on the downhill action, including plenty of skiing footage along the way. Jaime Mendoza-Nava is back, his music giving the outdoor scenes the feel of a jaunty, upbeat documentary. Modern-day viewers will notice how many long-haired ex-hippies were going skiing back then. Apparently the Woodstock Generation had infiltrated the ski set. There are even some VWs in the Mammoth Mountain parking lot.

But neither Apostolof nor Wood had any affinity for the counterculture, a fact demonstrated by the ridiculous dialogue between Brenda, a conservative teacher, and James, a pacifist college student. These two lovebirds meet in the pro shop, where they flirt and philosophize. James' motto: "Life's very short. We should take advantage of every minute." He then branches out to other timely topics: "Who's got time for wars, drafts, dictates of the establishment?" For Brenda, that kind of talk brands James as "one of those kind."

Incidentally, by this stage in his career, Apostolof was having his actresses get fully undressed and show pubic hair during their love scenes. For some reason, these young women wear panties but never bras. That's very consistent from scene to scene and movie to movie during this phase of Apostolof's career.

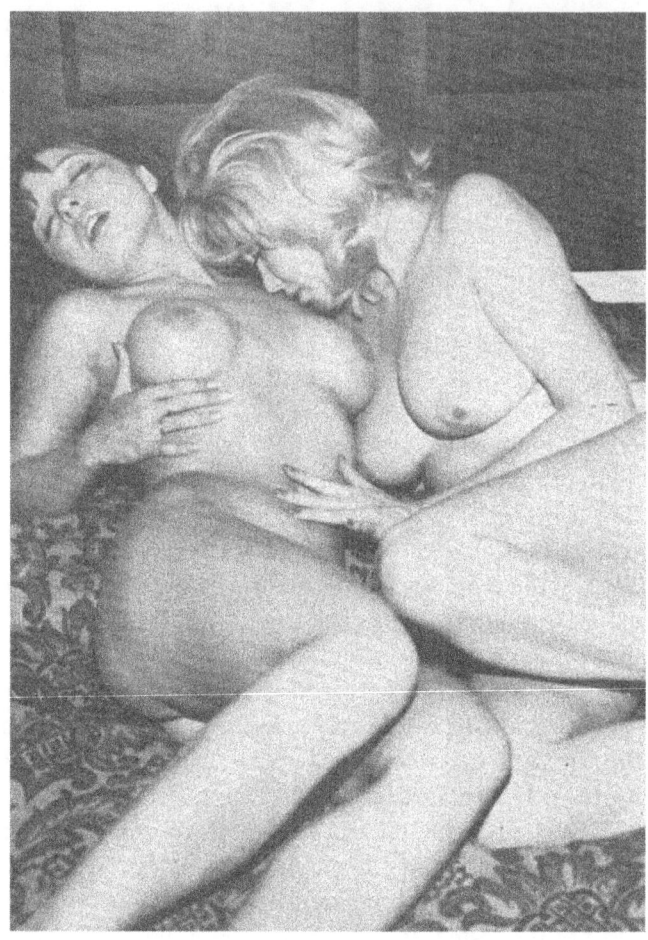

Nurse Joan (Marsha Jordan) seduces Madie (Rene Bond) near the end of *The Snow Bunnies*.

Beyond marking Apostolof's reconciliation with Wood, *The Snow Bunnies* was also the first of the SCA films to feature actress-stripper Rene Bond, one of the best known and most prolific performers in adult films and loops during the 1970s. Under a variety of screen names, this cult-favorite starlet appeared in dozens of hardcore and softcore productions. It was only natural that her path should cross Apostolof's at some point.

"Everybody liked Rene Bond," says film critic and historian Greg Goodsell.[10] And why shouldn't they? With her toothy smile, apple cheeks, chestnut hair, button nose and wide brown eyes, she was an accessible and appealing screen presence, the kind of sweet-natured girl you might have had a crush on in high school. Here was your typical girl next door, cheerfully disrobing and performing sex acts both real and simulated in motion pictures and on stage—not sexually aggressive in a threatening way (you'd never cast her as a horny Nazi commandant, for instance) but sexually assertive and willing to take the lead in the bedroom. According to Bond's biographer John Harrison,

Chapter 11. The Master of Mayhem (1972–1978)

A color one sheet for *The Snow Bunnies*.

When the hardcore scene started to explode in the early 1970s, Rene had such a youthful and innocent look about her that it helped her stand out amongst the sea of more mature and hardened faces that were starting to find work within the industry. Rene combined this innocence with an obvious enthusiasm for what she did. She rarely looked like she was doing it just for the money. Her sweet, cheeky smile and big doe eyes just leaped off the screen and commanded your attention, both in her hard and softcore work.[11]

Born to a middle-class family in San Diego on October 11, 1950, Rene left home when she was 19. After a succession of odd jobs as a seamstress, an airplane knob painter and a directory assistance operator (she got fired because she told someone how to cook a meatloaf), she moved in with her boyfriend Ric Lutze (1944–2011). He later became the first of her three husbands. "We got to know the owners of a Swinger's Club in Encino, and we eventually joined," Rene said. "My husband was like a kid with candy; being in contact with all those beautiful girls. I was inhibited. It was a bizarre experience. Then the owners told us that they were making $100 a day as stag film actors. My husband had quit his job, grown his hair long and got into the swinger role. But, since we were not working, we were starving, so I took a job as an actress."[12]

Rene eventually got used to making a lot of money. She had clothes, cars and other comforts. She was represented by talent agent and cinematographer Hal Guthu, who remained a friend for the rest of her life. "We used to shoot films called 'one-day wonders,'" she said. "I always played the virgin. There were three basic roles for women in those films, the virgin who was taken advantage of, the bored or neurotic housewife, and the prostitute type. We usually worked at least 12 hours a day."[13]

Among Rene's earliest employers was legendary sexploitation producer Harry H. Novak, who gave her a leading role in one of his beloved "hicksploitation" features, *Country Cuzzins* (1970, dir. Bethel Buckalew). The next year, Rene's career trajectory intersected with that of Ed Wood, who directed the vivacious starlet in his lovably ludicrous, self-penned spooky sex epic *Necromania* (1971). And from there came a string of films with Apostolof. In fact, she is second only to Marsha Jordan in the pantheon of SCA leading ladies. While Marsha's ample bust was all natural, Rene's was the result of plastic surgery. Apostolof also occasionally worked with Bond's frequent co-star and boyfriend-turned-husband Lutze. It's not difficult to imagine the conventionally handsome, broad-shouldered Ric as the captain of the hometown football team, with main squeeze Rene as the head cheerleader.

"Once I started casting for a film," said Apostolof, "word of mouth would start going out. I don't remember if [Rene] called me or I called her. [Rene and Ric] were in the business, I was in the business, we met. It was inevitable. Rene was a very fine actress. Very cooperative. Very professional."[14]

Rene began exotic dancing in May 1975. She said she decided that she really wanted to know who her audience was, and to perform personally for them. She succeeded in drawing a crowd every night at Lee Witten's Ivar Burlesque Theatre off Hollywood Boulevard. During that time, she also joined the Screen Actors Guild, appeared in TV movies and commercials, and played a slave in the X-rated *Flesh Gordon* (1974, dir. Michael Benveniste and Howard Ziehm). She also went to Europe to do a play with a stage touring company.

Although some X-rated stars were running away from abusive or dysfunctional homes, Rene had plenty of familial support. While her mother happily accompanied her to personal appearances, her father allegedly took inordinate pride in his daughter's exhibitionist career as a stripper and porn star, unconcerned with how it might affect his status as a member of the local Chamber of Commerce. Or so the story goes. Rumor has it that Rene would even croon "My Heart Belongs to Daddy" in her act and bring the old man out on stage at the Ivar. Bond's biographer John Harrison is doubtful about this story:

> Considering how youthful and innocent Rene looked, I would not be surprised if the Ivar hired someone to act as her father, just to play up the youth angle. The story about her father turning up with work colleagues is likely just that—a story to promote the show and help sell tickets, and tie-in with the act. It's all tied-in with that weird daddy-daughter fantasy that seemed a popular theme in adult entertainment at the time.[15]

In the early to mid-1970s, the carnal contessa Rene had two marriages go south on her, both to adult film stars. She and Lutze split in '72, and a 1973 rebound marriage to Tony Mazziotti stalled three years later. But the work continued. Always. Dozens of pictures a year. Magazine spreads, too. By the time Ronald Reagan took office as president of the United States and announced that it was "morning again in America," Rene had passed her 30th birthday and dropped off the porno radar. The days of the 35mm theatrical porn film were over by then anyway, and a new generation of young turks with VHS cameras had arrived to glut the market with cheaply produced, narrative-free porno flicks.

Meanwhile, Rene Bond re-remarried, this time to a nice-looking fellow named Lonnie Levine with no apparent connection to show business, let alone the smut racket. She and Lonnie appeared as gleeful, grinning contestants on the 1985–86 syndicated game show *Break the Bank*. The Levines' episodes—a winning streak that netted a cool $9000 in cash and prizes—most likely occurred in '86, as Joe Farago had already replaced *Match Game*'s Gene Rayburn as host. The program identified Rene as a bankruptcy specialist rather than an actress.

The former Ms. Bond had seemingly abdicated her showbiz throne for a more humdrum but dependable life in the private sector. She was puffy-faced, permed and polyester-clad by then and looked more suited to a church bake sale than a porn set. But the famous megawatt smile was still there, and the eyes were as bright and expressive as ever. Unfortunately, she couldn't keep it together. A decade after *Break the Bank*, Rene Bond, 45, was dead from cirrhosis of the liver.

Drop-Out Wife (1972)

> My husband gives me an A
> for last night's supper,
> an incomplete for my ironing,
> a B plus in bed.
> My son says I am average,
> an average mother, but if
> I put my mind to it
> I could improve.
> My daughter believes
> in Pass/Fail and tells me
> I pass. Wait 'til they learn
> I'm dropping out.
> —Linda Pastan, *Marks* (1978)

The next film for director Apostolof and writer Wood was considerably more timely and political, an attempt to comment on the sexual and social mores of the early 1970s. *Drop-Out Wife* had a title and a premise that reflected the trends of the era, a time when more women sought liberation and sexual satisfaction outside of the confines of marriage and the traditional family. But viewers should not get the idea that *Drop-Out Wife* is any kind of feminist statement. In fact, the chauvinism of Apostolof and Wood is evident throughout. Essentially, this is a story about the so-called "swinging" scene and the ruinous effect it was having on American Womanhood.

At the time this movie was made, the term "drop-out wife" was very much on the public's mind. She has since been largely forgotten, but a Seattle woman named Wanda Adams was one of the cultural lightning rods of 1972. A married mother of three, Adams was infamous for her decision to "abandon" her family and live her own life, moving into a ramshackle old house with two other women. After amicably divorcing her husband, she took custody of her daughter but not her two sons.

Wanda's story wasn't unique. She was just one of many women who, emboldened by the burgeoning women's rights movement during those turbulent years, decided to reject traditional female roles and question the institution of marriage. No one knew the exact number, but venerable CBS News estimated that there could be between 30,000 to 100,000 such cases in the U.S.[16]

What set Wanda apart from the others was her initial willingness to talk to the press about her unorthodox living arrangements. She thus became the *de facto* face of the phenomenon. On March 17, 1972, Adams appeared on the front cover of *Life*, which sensationally called her "Dropout Wife" and dubbed her story "A Striking Current Phenomenon," both in bold red letters, subtly reminding us of Hester Prynne. (*Life* most likely got the "Dropout" tag from counterculture guru Timothy Leary's resounding 1967 edict "Turn on, tune in, and drop out.") Wanda did her best to present herself not as an irresponsible libertine but as a sensible, intelligent woman who was simply not satisfied by her marriage and her circumscribed role as a wife and mother. The public, however, saw red and sent her Bible quotes and death threats.

Things got worse after a 1973 profile on CBS' *60 Minutes*, also entitled "Drop-Out Wife," in which a grim, unsympathetic Mike Wallace questioned Wanda with barely concealed hostility. The segment also featured Wanda's remarkably agreeable ex-husband Don, and portrayed him as a wholesome, hard-working, all–American father who showed no bitterness at all toward his former spouse. Having refused alimony or child support, Wanda was then on welfare after losing her job at North Seattle Community College due to public outrage over her "immorality." One can almost hear the arguments that must have broken out in living rooms across America in the wake of that inflammatory *60 Minutes* episode.

Apostolof took notice of the phenomenon and called his old buddy Wood to help him work on the project. The two men were apparently eager to capitalize on the runaway housewife fad, exploiting it while simultaneously passing judgment upon it in the grand tradition of exploitation. They took a serious, socially relevant topic and distorted it to the point that it was nearly science fiction by the time they were through. If you believe this movie, women were abandoning their homes and husbands in droves so that they could booze it up, attend orgies and go on wild blind dates with libidinous strangers.

Chapter 11. The Master of Mayhem (1972–1978)

Just so the movie didn't completely give itself over to misogyny, Apostolof and Wood made its discarded husband a clueless, selfish, sometimes abusive jerk. The wife therefore has a good reason for ditching him, but she doesn't get a free pass, because she's banging drunken strangers while neglecting her kids. In a way, Apostolof and Wood were hedging their bets by making everyone in the movie pretty awful.

Not unreasonably, Apostolof preferred to work with competent, dependable professionals, both in front of and behind the camera. But his two favorite leading ladies, Marsha Jordan and Rene Bond, were absent this time around. Instead, the star of *Drop-Out Wife* was comely brunette Angela Carnon (aka Priscilla Lee, Gloria Jane Medford and Angela Field), a model and actress whose film career was pretty much what one might expect: a lot of softcore flicks from the late 1960s to the early '80s. Chronologically, her career neatly overlaps that of Rene Bond. And just like Bond, Carnon did land a couple of legit films, including *The Last Married Couple in America* (1980, dir. Gilbert Cates) with Natalie Wood and George Segal. Carnon married a fellow adult performer, Norman Fields, with whom she appeared in several films, including *Wheeler* (1975, dir. Jack Collins and Jim Feazell), *Poor Cecily* (1974, dir. Lee Frost), *Video Vixens!* (1974, dir. Henri Pachard) and, yes, *Drop-Out Wife*. Angela and Norman don't have any scenes together, though, in this one. Their union didn't last, but neither did Norman's four other marriages.

Most important to Apostolof, Carnon was an attractive, competent actress who was willing to do explicit nudity and yet could still handle Wood's twisted dialogue. Her professionalism won her the admiration of other adult filmmakers, including producer Jacques Descent (1937–2018), who was among the first to hire her. He recalls,

> Angela was a nice girl and would not consider X stuff. I had heard that she did some XXX [films] with her husband or partner afterward, but I did not see that. It was the same thing with [Rene] Bond, same start then a lot of XXX [rated films] after her tits job. These girls were all from [Hal Guthu's] troupe. I shot her in *Watch the Birdie ... Die!* in 1967–68, a time when there was very little open X material. It was the first 35mm widescreen color film to be released, and it played the whole of the drive-in movie theaters chains, mostly as a second feature when in those days a major studio feature plus a low-budget or second-run film was the norm to keep patrons in the drive-ins for four hours.[17]

Apostolof later recalled what it was like to work with Carnon:

> Sometimes the nudity has nothing to do with the artistic ability of the actor or actress. Angela happened to be a very good actress, very receptive to direction, attentive to what I told her. She realized I was trying to help her. The screenplay, I changed a couple of things during shooting to fit her personality. It's one thing when you imagine a character and something else—the magic moment, I call it, when you see it on the set before you start shooting and it becomes real.... [E]verybody has certain idiosyncrasies, which as a director it's my job to watch for and capture them on screen.[18]

The cast of *Drop-Out Wife* included several Apostolof stock players: Harvey Shain (who also served as Apostolof's assistant director on this one), gap-toothed starlet Terri Johnson and golden-haired stud Chris Geoffries. Among the unbilled performers grinding against each other in the orgy scenes were Ric Lutze and the legendary stripper and adult performer Candy Samples. *Drop-Out Wife* was shot by Robert Caramico, working under the alias R.C. Ruben. Composer Jaime Mendoza-Nava provided another part–Latin, part–Muzak score. This time, he was billed as J. Mendozoff, a pseudonym that sounds like an over-the-counter sleep aid.

In almost equal measures, *Drop-Out Wife* is compelling and appalling. Sometimes, a movie invites the question "Who was this made for?" And it's tempting to ask that question here, too, except for the fact that Apostolof had a very definite target audience for his movies, a group uncharitably but hilariously described by Rob Craig in his book *Ed Wood, Mad Genius: A Critical Study of the Films* as "socially retarded men who were comfortable masturbating in a public venue."[19]

One can only imagine what the "raincoat brigade" thought of *Drop-Out Wife*. On the one hand, the film is replete with female nudity and simulated sex. But on the other, its male characters are all portrayed quite negatively, and many minutes of screen time are devoted to women earnestly discussing their personal problems with each other. The film also contains a truly traumatic flashback sequence in which dissatisfied husband Jim (Chris Geoffries) cruelly slaps his very pregnant wife Peggy (Carnon), causing their baby to be stillborn. As in many Apostolof films, the characters do a lot of drinking, but the ugly specter of alcoholism is really never made an issue the way it is in, say, *The Divorcee*.

Drop-Out Wife tells the story of Peggy, a miserable housewife with two young children, who are seen only briefly via photos. (Apostolof used pictures of his own kids Polly and Susan, much to their embarrassment.) In desperation, Peggy leaves her stressed-out businessman husband Jim because the two have no sexual chemistry and spend all their time arguing. She goes to stay with her friend Janet (Terri Johnson), a swinging single who lives in a high-rise apartment and is balling one of her many short-term boyfriends (Norman Fields) as the movie begins. Janet is more than pleased to have Peggy stay with her, and the two women spend a lot of time sitting at the dinner table hashing out Peggy's problems.

The movie includes flashbacks to several significant moments from Peggy and Jim's marriage, most of which unsurprisingly revolve around sex. Since the couple's marital woes largely stem from their lack of sexual compatibility, most of their attempts at intercourse are unsuccessful and frustrating. To balance it out, there are several scenes in which Janet sets Peggy up on blind dates, and we watch the drop-out wife have sex with some obnoxious strangers, including a loudmouth pilot (Douglas Frey, sometimes billed as Douglas Fray) who refers to himself in the third person as "Captain Roger" and makes silly jet-plane–type motions in bed. Some of these scenes end with Peggy finding out that her "date" is either married or engaged, which is a downer for her, but at least our title character seems to be having fun before getting the bad news.

Peggy's surreal flashback to her traumatic miscarriage is easily the movie's most notable scene. At this point in the film, we have just witnessed the almost–Biblical conception of Peggy and Jim's third child. Already burdened with two daughters and unable to have sex in their own bedroom, they make love out on the lawn during a thunderstorm. At the climax, Peggy moans, "Oh my God! Number three!" Apostolof then cuts to the three of spades being laid down on a kitchen table. We are in Janet's kitchen now. She and Peggy are playing cards while noirish lighting comes in through the blinds.

Janet calls men "the most disgusting, mixed-up creatures the Creator ever put on this crazy, mixed-up planet," but says she doesn't really hate them. "After all," she says, "someone has to go out and pay the bills while we stay home and take care of the house

Chapter 11. The Master of Mayhem (1972–1978) 185

and the brats." Again, this is not a movie that is interested in challenging traditional gender roles.

Apostolof now zooms in on an ashtray as the screen goes blurry, transporting us to a different kitchen—the one Peggy and Jim once shared in the suburbs. These kinds of transitions are common not only for *Drop-Out Wife*, but for many other Apostolof movies. The camera will zoom in on a particular object, often a light source such as a candle, a lamp, or a chandelier, until it goes out of focus and ends the scene. Or, conversely, a scene might start with a blurry image that then crystallizes into something recognizable.

Apostolof now gives the audience an almost absurdly stereotypical image of a housewife in her domicile. Peggy putters unproductively around her kitchen while wearing a plaid housecoat, fuzzy slippers and giant pink hair curlers. She is in her third trimester. Jim pulls up to the family's modest-looking suburban house in a modest-looking car. The scene was shot in front of the house at 3456 Rowena Avenue where Apostolof used to live. Clad in a gray suit, Jim enters the kitchen and sets his briefcase on the counter. Peggy tries to kiss him, but he pushes her away, saying he doesn't find her attractive. Their dialogue is melodramatic and strained with long, dramatic pauses, very much like what you'd find on a soap opera. The score and the camera angles are very soapy, too. Only the sexually explicit dialogue lets us know that this isn't a daytime TV show. The language throughout *Drop-Out Wife* is harsher and more vulgar than Apostolof's other productions, and the film abounds with full frontal nudity. Even Apostolof felt that in the movie, "there are certain scenes where I thought I went too far. I had one disadvantage, which is that with a zoom lens I don't see through the camera. So there were a couple of things that came out without me knowing it."[20] According to Apostolof, *Drop-Out Wife* was banned in Japan not only because of its full frontal nudity but also because of its story.

In the flashback, Jim slaps Peggy across the face. She drops to the kitchen floor and writhes in agony. He storms out. She holds her stomach and screams in pain. Cut to a flashing red light. A siren wails on the soundtrack. There's some nighttime footage showing an ambulance driving through what seems to be a very busy commercial district with lots of neon signs. Peggy is now either on a gurney or a hospital bed. Her bandaged head rests on a white pillow as she wriggles and squirms under the covers. The scene is lit by a flashing red light, which intermittently illuminates Peggy's horrified face. The corners of the screen are dark. In the red light, we see the silhouette of a lifeless infant being held upside down. A shadowy hand slaps the child three times without a response as Peggy looks on in panic. We hear stern, authoritative male voices discussing the case with grim finality. The baby is dead, they say, but maybe they can save the mother.

This downbeat sequence fundamentally changes the tone of *Drop-Out Wife* and casts a pall over everything that happens subsequently. It is not merely unsexy but anti-sexy. From here on out, we know that sex equals trouble. Peggy even spells it out when she says that it was Jim's cock that got them into this situation. The villain of the movie is the penis itself. That's probably not the message that horny middle-aged male moviegoers were hoping to hear.

The third act of *Drop-Out Wife*, especially its final scene, is a dramatic departure from the rest of the movie, leading author Rob Craig to speculate that it was imposed on Wood by Apostolof. By this point in the story, the swinging lifestyle has taken its toll on Peggy, who looks in the mirror behind Janet's well-stocked bar and assesses her own reflection harshly: "You've aged ten years in a month!" Very tentatively, Peggy picks up the phone and calls Jim. To say the least, the call is a disaster. Jim is irate, calls Peggy an unfit mother, and informs her that he's suing her for divorce and custody of the children. Peggy, distraught, is comforted by Janet, who throughout the film has expressed her dubious philosophy that one should constantly live in the present and not worry about the past or the future.

Janet and Peggy decide to have some "fun," which means hanging out in a dank, musty piano bar

A color one sheet for *Drop-Out Wife*.

and schmoozing with a bunch of sleazeball lounge lizards, including Howard (Duane Paulsen) and Larry (Harvey Shain). The latter announces that the bar is closing and that it's now "motel time." He and Howard escort Janet and Peggy back to a truly heinous-looking room with two double beds. After making love with their respective dates (and each other's dates), the men suggest that Peggy and Janet "make it" with each other. Peggy is no stranger to lesbian sex, but she's reluctant to go to town on her best friend. Janet's game, though: "Maybe I've always wanted to make it with my best friend." Peggy exits in disgust, her friendship with Janet ended in an instant.

In the film's bewildering finale, Peggy walks through a playground and sees the happy children there. We hear her echo-drenched inner monologue: "I wonder what my two little daughters are doing right now. I left them … and for what? To be free? To live? Truly live, I thought! What a joke! They're what's real! Maybe … maybe I can go back! They've got to take me back! We'll make it work this time! I just know we will!"

Nothing about her husband's neglect and abuse is brought up. It's a disheartening conclusion to a disheartening film.

The Class Reunion (1972)

> "There's a new frame collecting a lot of attention around the British movie-club circuits. To say nothing of our own mail-bag. A brunette for a change. Or she was until we decided to photograph her in Hollywood as the first in a series of Cinema Xciters. The name is Bond. Rene Bond. A sassy little Los Angelean making hay galore, and much else besides, in the skin flick trade with such recent credits as Country Cuzzins, Below the Belt, Jekyll and Hide [sic] and Harry Novak's title of '72: Please Don't Eat My Mother. *Latest Bonded import, see page 64, happens to be one of her first,* Class Reunion, *and includes a moment to remember. Rene, the nudie-queen in the making, in the arms of Marsha Jordan, the den mother of the exploitation industry. A similar confrontation with Uschi Digart [sic] has to be in the cards…"*—Cinema X magazine, issue 55, 1973

The next Apostolof-Wood film turned out to be a sequel of sorts to *College Girls*, even though that film had not performed spectacularly well for Apostolof. He took some of his characters from that movie and followed them into their boozy, stress-plagued adult years. This was more familiar territory for Apostolof and Wood. In *The Class Reunion,* which predates *The Big Chill* (1983, dir. Lawrence Kasdan) by over a decade, some former college classmates spend a weekend at a hotel reminiscing, drinking and having lots of unprotected, conscience-free sex, all while trying to figure out where their lives are going.

Apostolof's 1970s films are bolder and more explicit than his 1960s output; occasionally the language in *Drop-Out Wife* is downright crude. But they're still tame compared to what was hitting the market at the time. Even with its token attempt at social and political relevance, a film like *The Class Reunion* was already obsolete by the time it reached theaters, post–*Deep Throat*. Apostolof claimed to have been bored and unimpressed by Damiano's film. Besides, even though *Deep Throat* attracted reams of free publicity, it also brought on additional legal headaches. And Apostolof definitely didn't want any of those.

Whatever twisted logic guided Ed Wood in the co-writing of this screenplay, Apostolof's priorities as a director are never in doubt. The film starts with another close-up of Marsha Jordan in the shower, lovingly polishing her breasts to a high shine. The sequence is so similar to the beginning of *The Snow Bunnies* that some viewers may accuse Apostolof of reusing old footage. But a comparison shows that these scenes are shot from different angles and use different music.

The Class Reunion was filmed in early 1972 in Los Angeles. Structurally, this film is rather eccentric. Like a James Bond movie, it begins with a pre-credits sequence that has very little to do with the rest of the film. After emerging from the shower and painstakingly drying herself off, Jordan receives from the mailman an invitation to a class reunion. Bafflingly, Jordan's character is called Rose Cooper in this scene but is identified as Jane mere seconds later in the opening title sequence. It doesn't matter anyway, since top-billed Jordan disappears entirely from the film after the credits. The prologue vaguely establishes that "the class of '69" from "the old alma mater" is getting back together for a weekend.

The Class Reunion was shot by Robert Caramico. The opening scene was filmed at Apostolof's place at 4055 Tujunga Avenue in North Hollywood where he was living with his third wife Shelley and where his youngest son Christopher was born. The rest of the movie takes place at a hotel whose decor is typical of the era—lots of murky earth tones, dark wood paneling, shag carpeting. The reunion kicks off in the hotel's French Room, merely a dimly lit bar where the main characters down a lot of bourbon. The class of '69 amounts to about eight people by this movie's reckoning. From a distance, one might guess them to be typical lounge lizards on the make, hoping to find someone to accompany them upstairs for some fun. There's nothing particularly nostalgic or collegiate about the gathering.

The ringleader of the event is the satyr-like Charlie (Harvey Shain), a self-described "lowly account executive" who has arrived at the hotel without an escort and is eager for mischief. This is the fraternity brother and "king of kicks" that Shain had played in *College Girls,* only a few years older now. Winsome, buck-toothed blonde Liza (Terri Johnson) has been torching for Charlie since college and still gets "goose pimples" when she thinks of him. Athletic, all–American Harry (Ric Lutze) is now a football coach in Iowa and can't get over how everyone's matured since college. Slender, troubled brunette Rosie (Starline Comb aka Starlyn Simone) is married, but her rich, older husband Jim is away on one of his frequent business trips. Fluff (Sandy Carey, taking over a part played by Gee Gentell in the original film) is the class slut, plain and simple. Rosie counsels her to keep her panties on and her legs crossed, but we all know Fluff will not be heeding that advice, as she quickly sets her sights on the even-more-improbably-named Wimpy Murgatroyd (Fred Geoffries aka Christopher Geoffries, filling-in for Randy Lee in the first film), a sturdy-looking lummox with platinum hair. Flamboyantly gay Tom (Ron Darby) and lipstick lesbian Thelma (Rene Bond) are married and acting as one another's beards. He's satisfied with the arrangement; she isn't. While he bats his eyelashes and flirts with every man in sight, she sulks in the corner.

More so than Apostolof's other feature films, *The Class Reunion* recycles existing footage in weird and almost arbitrary ways. Early in the proceedings, for instance, the boozy bonhomie of the French Room is suddenly threatened by a noisy political demonstration outside. Young, shaggy-haired folks are marching down the street next to the hotel to protest the war in Vietnam. To represent this student uprising, Apostolof has bluntly inserted some newsreel footage of an April 1972 anti-war demonstration in Los Angeles. His characters are supposedly seeing this action through a window in the bar. The establishing shot of the hotel shows the facade of the landmark Century Plaza Hotel.

Class Reunion's main characters are in their early twenties and should probably be social liberals at this stage in their lives, but this film was created by two fortysomething conservatives, one a staunch anti–Communist (Apostolof), the other a highly patriotic ex–Marine (Wood), and the script reflects their stodgy, reactionary views. The college graduates therefore react to these young ruffians as if they were members of a hostile alien species. Wimpy snorts: "Nothing like those street apes ever happened when we were their age! You know, to think, I helped pay their school tax!" Harry, too, is incensed. "The only principles they've got is called sex. S-E-X with a double X!"

Charlie, to his credit, is more lenient toward the kids and reminds his classmates that they too used to engage in some kinky, reckless behavior. To prove his point, he invites the reunion attendees up to his hotel room to watch some supposed "home movies" from his "frat rat" days. (In those pre–VCR years, that meant he had to bring a projector and movie screen with him to the hotel.) The films indeed show that the gang used to participate in orgies, apparently in full view of a movie crew. This footage is lifted from *College Girls*, including that memorable shot of Harvey Shain jumping off a balcony while high on LSD.

The reunion attendees are shown nodding and giggling at Charlie's movies, as people tend to do when watching old films of themselves, but things get a little uncomfortable when the rape scene from the earlier movie is shown. Perhaps Apostolof should have been more careful about the footage he chose to repurpose.

In any event, Charlie suggests that he and the gang have another orgy for old time's sake, and without any further prodding, all the other characters immediately disrobe and start crawling all over each other on the hotel floor. The only abstainers are limp-wristed, lisping Tom and sullen, pouty Thelma. In essence, the film's two homosexual characters are not allowed to join in these heterosexual reindeer games. They're not missing much, though, since this must be one of the most passion-free orgies in movie history. The only real eroticism occurs when Rene Bond, forced to watch from the sidelines, strips and fondles herself while gazing sadly at her nude, writhing classmates.

From there, *The Class Reunion* is merely a series of sexual interludes. In a typical Apostolof scenario, reminiscent of sequences from *Motel Confidential* and *Suburbia Confidential*, hapless Wimpy finds himself unable to get away from the sexually insatiable Fluff, who keeps dragging him back into bed for round after exhausting round of aerobic intercourse.

In the movie's most regrettable sequence, the one highly likely to make modern-day audiences cringe, stereotypical "fag" Tom finds himself duped by a couple of con artists, Bruce (Con Covert) and Henrietta (Flora Weisel), who have a very impractical sexual blackmail scam going. Again, this is highly reminiscent of a plot point from *Motel Confidential*. Apostolof was freely borrowing from his earlier movies. ("Oh, yes! I milked this scene over and over again," Apostolof used to brag.[21]) Meanwhile, Liza (whose name is pronounced Lisa) finally gets her chance to rendezvous with Charlie.

Rosie, the unfortunate young woman whose absent husband Jim is a good provider but a lousy lover, participates in the two most meaningful and interesting sex scenes. The first is her tender and erotically charged lesbian encounter with jumpsuit-clad Thelma, who uses the opportunity to bash the opposite sex: "[Men] don't care what a woman likes or dislikes! They just wanna get their own climax and go home!"

The film's climax, which blessedly takes place outside the dreadful-looking hotel, brings Rosie back to the safe and familiar world of heterosexuality by pairing her with bland nice guy Harry. "You're so kind and masculine," Rosie gushes, before the leisure-suited Lothario makes sweet love to her in a Garden of Eden-esque public park. "It's just like out of a storybook! So beautiful!" Harry enthuses. The scene was shot at

A color one sheet for *The Class Reunion*. Apostolof managed to sneak the name of Valentine Enterprises, the company that he used to produce the film, onto the cover of the yearbook.

the picturesque Fern Dell, a woodsy glen at the lower end of Western Canyon in Griffith Park. The place was a favorite of Apostolof and he would often take his children fishing in the creek with homemade fishing poles. Because of its charming beauty, Fern Dell has long been a popular filming location for films such as Rudolph Valentino's *The Young Rajah* (1922, dir. Phil Rosen), *Star Trek II: The Wrath of Khan* (1982, dir. Nicholas Meyer) and, most recently, *La La Land* (2016, dir. Damien Chazelle).

The Class Reunion premiered on June 21, 1972. The movie's pressbook said:

> *The Class Reunion* is a strong film in the tradition of sex and what sex stands for and if the antiquated missionary position is impossible for some then they must seek out and investigate other ways. *Class Reunion* investigates most of those other ways. Some will love this story while others turn purple, but all will leave the theatre with something new in their minds … and there is little doubt but what they have learned something about their own welfare.

In July 1973, an obscure newspaper called *Psychic Review,* published by one Baron Von Brenner, printed a profile of Ed Wood in which among many other things, it said: "*The Class Reunion*, the original story & screenplay written by Eddie, is now under consideration for achievement by the Academy of Motion Picture Arts & Sciences, and he's beside himself with joy."

Baron Von Brenner himself was a curious character: An ex-sheriff, an ordained minister, a self-described "master hypnotist," he claimed to be "the only man who ever hypnotized Adolf Hitler." Von Brenner was a friend of Ed Wood, Criswell and John Agar, so, naturally, he caught the attention of Rudolph Grey, who asked Apostolof about him. The latter denied knowing anything about neither Von Brenner nor *Psychic Review* even though he had a copy of the newspaper in his archives. Apostolof claimed,

> No, I don't know of any newspaper called *Psychic Review*. And even if I have read it at the time, I would have had a good laugh. To begin with, it wasn't an original story and screenplay by Eddie, but by both of us. [*The Class Reunion*] is one of the films I shot *simultaneously*.[22] I wrote the story to confirm with stock footage I had from *College Girls* which was in black and white and built a story about the same class, years later. I had to make sure that the sets of each picture was the same as the other and when I was in the theatrical distribution, made sure that the two films were never shown together. It didn't have much dialogue because both pictures were tailor-made for the sex-oriented market. Eddie had nothing to do with the production—he was too drunk to even consider him, not to mention that Bob Caramico would not shoot with him around.[23]

Nineteen seventy two was the same year that Rene Bond and Ric Lutze broke up, and it's interesting that Starline Comb beds both of them in *The Class Reunion*. During their romantic interlude, which is scored with syrupy violins, Rosie and Harry take a moment to ponder the larger issues of life. "It seems like life has cheated us out of all the things we like best," says Rosie. "Take me, for example. I like sex, and what do I get? An old, impotent, rich husband! What's happened with us, Harry? Where did all those years go? We had so much fun in college!" Harry, on the other hand, just accepts life as it comes to him. He feels that Rosie is miserable because she asks too many questions, and adds, "If there's gotta be a reason, we'll find out sooner or later."

The two lovers then undress and make love in this serene, pastoral setting. Original sin has been cleansed away by the sunshine and fresh air, and Harry and Rosie are naked and beautiful and free in the glorious natural world outside the dark, sleazy hotel. *The Class Reunion* ends with an enigmatic yet sweet and hopeful exchange between Rosie and Harry.

"Ah, it's so wonderful here!" she exclaims. "I wish I could stay forever!"

"Yeah," agrees Harry. "Life is so wonderful, and you're so beautiful! Maybe that's the reason, the only reason! Well, there'll always be another class reunion."

This sentimental moment is strangely reminiscent of Judy Garland's "There's no place like home" speech from the end of *The Wizard of Oz* (1939, dir. Victor Fleming). Considering the other Apostolof-Wood films of this vintage, it's a remarkably sunny way to end an often depressing motion picture.

The Cocktail Hostesses (1973)

> "*You pay for the drinks ... they do the rest!*"—tagline for *The Cocktail Hostesses*

The standard line on Stephen C. Apostolof is that his career sputtered out in the 1970s and that his films from that era were not financially successful or at least not financially successful enough to keep him in business. Indeed, he was broke and out of movies entirely by the decade's end. But 1972 was one of his best years. Aside from expecting his first child with Shelley, he was busy working on a couple of movies, often shooting back to back or even simultaneously in order to cut down on production costs. The year also marked the seventh anniversary of the founding of his company

Stephen Apostolof, Rene Bond, and an unknown person at the seventh anniversary party of A.F.P.I. Productions.

A.F.P.I. Productions. So, on September 22, Apostolof threw a lavish cocktail party, hosting more than 100 personalities in the film business at the Riviera Room (formerly the Los Feliz Brown Derby). The assemblage included bank managers, producers, distributors and actors and actresses, including Harvey Shain, Marsha Jordan and Rene Bond.

Ed Wood and Criswell were also there. Among the producers were Daniel B. Cady, Chris Warfield, Don Davis, David F. Friedman and Larry Price. Michael Kraike, who ghostwrote *Suburbia Confidential*, and Herb Niccolls who wrote *Journey to Freedom* also attended. Out-of-town distributors included Al Weiner from Orbit Films, Dallas, Marvin Miller from Toronto, and Jerry Purcell from the Western states region. Edward Mayhew from the Bank of America and Harry Geyer from Crocker Citizens Bank represented the financial community.[24]

Actor David Ward (1932–2017), who played bit parts in Apostolof's *Cocktail Hostesses* and *Drop-Out Wife*, recalls the night when Apostolof and Wood indulged in a bit of old school Hollywood revelry at a historically significant location: "Steve Apostolof was having a big party before they shot *Cocktail Hostesses* and *Drop-Out Wife*, and Apostolof rented a room at Michael's, which is a pretty ritzy place up on Los Feliz and Hillhurst. Rene Bond, the porno queen, everybody connected with these pictures was there. And Eddie, who wrote the screenplays, wanted me to go along, because he knew I didn't drink, and he was planning to get drunk, stinking drunk, and he wanted me to drive him home."[25]

Herb Niccolls puts his arm around his pal Stephen Apostolof at the party. David Ward and Ed Wood are visible in the background.

Stephen Apostolof, Ed Wood (second from left), and Shelley Apostolof (far right) at the party.

Apostolof hobnobs with his former *Orgy of the Dead* star Criswell. The woman between them is unidentified.

Chapter 11. The Master of Mayhem (1972–1978)

The evening Ward describes was the source of several photographs in which Apostolof looks dapper, Bond looks perky, and Wood simply looks drunk. The Riviera Room, the restaurant in question, was known as Michael's Los Feliz Inn from the 1960s until the early '90s and was located on the site of the fourth and last-surviving Brown Derby restaurant. The Derby chain is central to the Apostolof-Wood mythology. The Los Feliz property was sold to an entity known as CMC Asset Investments in August 2012, narrowly escaping the wrecking ball. In its heyday, the restaurant had a derby-shaped sign on the roof. The domed portion of the building was taken over by a Chase bank branch.

According to Rudolph Grey's *Nightmare of Ecstasy: The Life and Art of Edward D. Wood, Jr.,* Ed's more practical wife Kathy considered the low-paying Apostolof movies to be a waste of time and felt that her husband would be better off cranking out more books and stories for Bernie Bloom at Pendulum Publishing. In fact, Ed continued writing lurid faux-educational textbooks, articles and pornographic short stories for such Pendulum imprints as SECS (Sex Education Correspondence School), Edusex and Gallery during this time. But Wood and Apostolof didn't want to quit what they had going.

Perhaps if Apostolof could have secured financing, he and Ed would have done several more movies in the same vein as the existing ones from 1972 to 1976. There are several unproduced Wood screenplays from this era whose titles tell you all you need to know about their contents: *The Teachers, The Basketballers, The Airline Hostesses.* You don't need to read them to guess that they respectively concern teachers, basketballers and airline hostesses screwing their brains out. (A typically coy logline for *The Teachers*: "Junior college students soon learn the best method to achieve high grades from their instructors.") Only *The Basketballers* has been positively identified as a collaboration with Apostolof, but all three sound like they fit the SCA mold.

With their next film, Apostolof and Wood continued to explore the sleazy side of American life, both in the boardroom and the barroom. What sets *The Cocktail Hostesses* apart from other SCA films of this era is that it's a starring vehicle for Rene Bond. She'd been in Apostolof films before, but always as a supporting or ensemble player. This time she was center stage, playing a young woman who decides to abandon secretarial work in favor of the exciting world of cocktail waitressing.

Other than that, *The Cocktail Hostesses* is very typical of Apostolof-Wood 1970s output. Once again, it features a lot of pasty-skinned Californians half-heartedly pretending to hump each other in blandly ugly bedrooms, motel rooms and living rooms, while easy listening–style music drones in the background. Same actors. Same props. There's even the same busty blonde on the poster, coquettishly hiding her nipples from our view. Some of the same basic shots and dialogue from Apostolof's previous movies reappear here, too.

The Cocktail Hostesses plays like a feature-length tribute to Mark Twain's famous maxim "Write what you know." If there was one realm that Apostolof and Wood knew by 1973, it was cocktail lounges. The cast, too, was familiar. Alongside Rene Bond, the film featured the usual SCA regulars: Duane Paulsen, Chris Geoffries, Douglas Frey, Terri Johnson, Norman Fields (unbilled despite a prominent role), Ric Lutze and Harvey Shain. Harvey again worked both in front of and behind the camera on *The Cocktail Hostesses. Drop-Out Wife* bit player Lynn Harris was elevated to the status of supporting actress in *The Cocktail Hostesses*. She had previously worked on such films as *Love Feast* (1969, dir. Joseph Robertson), *Take It Out in Trade* (1970, dir. Ed Wood) and *The Only House in Town* (1970, dir. Ed Wood), as well as Apostolof's *Office Love-In, White Collar Style* (1968).

Composer Jaime Mendoza-Nava again used the moniker J. Mendozoff. This was his last film with Apostolof, though he would continue working in movies until 1985, with credits including *The Town That Dreaded Sundown* (1976, dir. Charles B. Pierce) and *A Boy and His Dog* (1975, dir. L.Q. Jones). He passed away in 2005 at the age of 79. Cinematographic duties were handled by Robert Caramico, using his trusty R.C. Ruben pseudonym.

The bulk of *The Cocktail Hostesses* was shot in the last week of October 1972. Some exterior scenes had been filmed at the end of March of the same year. Most of the action takes place in an unnamed cocktail bar. The place has an obvious Irish theme, with glowing neon tubes fashioned into shamrocks as well as the long-stemmed pipes and flat-topped hats associated with leprechauns. The sign advertising COCKTAILS in bold red letters is in close proximity to an ever-burning torch, suggesting the fires of Hell.

Inside, the waitresses wear skimpy, revealing versions of Irish Renaissance dresses with absurdly low necklines and high hemlines, plus puffy sleeves bedecked with shamrocks.

The many lengthy sex scenes play out against backdrops indistinguishable from those seen in *Drop-Out Wife* and *The Snow Bunnies*. Viewers who watch these movies back to back may come to recognize particular pieces of wall art and other set decorations. And always, there are the oppressive, gray paneled walls that look like something out of a Soviet Gulag.

A major reason for the homogeneity of *Drop-Out Wife* and *The Cocktail Hostesses* is that they were filmed simultaneously and utilized the same sets. This was apparently an ill-advised

A color Belgian one sheet for *The Cocktail Hostesses*.

attempt at efficiency on Apostolof's part. He later regretted the plan, as he explained in a 1998 interview with Something Weird Video founder Mike Vraney. "I got the idiotic idea to make two pictures simultaneously. *The Cocktail Hostesses* and *Drop-Out Wife*. Not back to back, simultaneously," said Apostolof. "It was a nightmare for my editor. I had some of the same actors playing different parts in both films, although they both had different leading ladies, Rene Bond and Angela Carnon. I made sure never to book those two pictures together."[26]

Ultimately, *The Cocktail Hostesses* is less substantial and affecting than other SCA films of the period. The sociopolitical commentary of *Drop-Out Wife* and *The Class Reunion* is almost entirely absent here, and there is no bright, cheerful mountain scenery to offset the sleaziness as there was in *The Snow Bunnies*. No, *The Cocktail Hostesses* starts in a fallen world of horny men and mercenary women and remains there for its entire 76-minute running time. In contrast to the diluted and dandified mixed drinks being served on screen, there is nothing in the script to sweeten or mute the sleaziness of this story, nor is there any evidence of artfulness or nuance in the filmmaking.

If there is a second level on which this movie can be appreciated, it comes from looking at it from a feminist perspective. In the story of "career girl" Toni Rice, there is a submerged parable about a young, obviously bright woman who uses her surgically enhanced body to attain what she wants, i.e., financial independence, in a male-dominated world. Toni unhappily acknowledges the chauvinism that keeps her a wage slave and a sex slave, but she does not directly challenge the patriarchy or try to change the system in any meaningful way. Instead, she pragmatically accepts the reality of her situation and employs her feminine wiles to extract money and gifts from weak-willed men. In doing so, she raises a pertinent question: If women can use sex to manipulate men, then where is the true source of power in our society—the penis or the vagina? This probably wasn't what Helen Reddy was thinking when she sang "I Am Woman," the feminist anthem that hit #1 in America in December 1972 (between the making of *Hostesses* and its eventual release), but in the Apostolof universe, it's the best one can expect.

At first glance, Apostolof seems to have returned to the stamping grounds of *Office Love-In*. The film begins on a typical Friday afternoon in the L.A. office of a tycoon named Henderson (gaunt, haggard Norman Fields), who is enthusiastically boffing his buxom secretary Toni (Bond, wearing a terrible blonde wig) on a lumpy beige couch across from his heavy oak desk. This is clearly an ongoing relationship, but when Henderson and Toni finish their lovemaking and start donning their clothes, their conversation is jarringly impersonal and detached. That is, until the subject of money comes up.

Henderson compliments Toni on being "perfectly delightful" and complains about his own unsatisfying home life. But he won't get divorced: "She'd clean me out!" (The twice-burned Apostolof works in a few digs at California's lopsided divorce laws.) Toni is upset that she still makes only $86.91 a week. Henderson's alibi is that "things haven't been going so well lately" and that the company's supposed success is "only on paper." He asks her to be patient for just a little longer. But Toni's patience is running out quickly.

Later, still fuming at home, Toni tells her roommate Jackie (Terri Johnson, blank as ever) about her humiliating job. "I've been poked, probed, sodomized and debauched!"

Toni declares. "Keep punching that clock from nine to five," Jackie responds, "and that's all you're ever gonna get. And when you're old and gray, you can say you chalked up a lot of clock time." But Jackie has a better way: Toni can join her as a cocktail hostess in a nearby bar.

In this movie, the job description of a hostess falls somewhere between barmaid and hooker. During their regular shifts, these ladies are expected to serve drinks to wealthy men, and then service these guys sexually in their free time. Every last woman in this movie is fine with that arrangement. In addition to her salary, Jackie earns $30 a night in tips, and the previous night she made $50 more for having "the most delightful time with an out-of-town buyer." When Toni admits that this amounts to more than she makes in a week, Jackie asks her, "Why don't you ball where you can get something substantial for your time and money?" Toni is reticent, but Jackie assures her that the job is "strictly legit." It's simply that "smart girls" can make "important contacts" at such a place.

There's a bit more hemming and hawing on Toni's part (she's too "mad" and "tired" to go to the cocktail bar that night), but in the very next scene our heroine arrives at Jackie's workplace. There she meets congenial bartender Larry (Harvey Shain) and gets a look at Millie (Lynn Harris), "one of our top waitresses around here." She then goes to interview with the boss (Chris Geoffries, whimsically clad in a red-and-white polka-dotted robe, tan slacks and a green ascot) in his cozy, den-like office, which has a fireplace and a couch but no desk, phone, filing cabinets or any other business accessories. With only a modicum of pressure ("Let's see what you have to offer my customers!"), the boss convinces Toni to disrobe and have sex with him about a minute after they first meet. Needless to say, she gets the job.

One blurry dissolve and an establishing shot later, Toni is at last wearing the ridiculous "Irish" uniform and slinging overpriced drinks to the bar's wealthy clientele. One man, a successful diamond importer (drink of choice: gin and tonic), makes a "date" with her. Later, after they've had sex, the diamond importer asks our protagonist about her career choice. Toni is philosophical: "I just figured that life had more to offer me than four walls and a typewriter and a boss with big, roving hands that always wanted to take but never wanted to dig into his pockets and give." Very much echoing the sentiments of the characters in *The Snow Bunnies*, Toni makes it plain that she is not interested in any "permanent arrangement" with the diamond importer and just wants to enjoy "the time we have together."

Seemingly no SCA film of this vintage would be complete without a shocking scene that completely negates any attempt at eroticism. In this film, a pervert overhears Millie telling Toni and Larry that she's done for the night. He follows her to the parking lot where he accosts her, drags her into his own car and rapes her. Here, as nowhere else in the film, Jaime Mendoza-Nava's score is tense and unnerving. But Apostolof does one of his characteristic 180-degree turns and cuts back to the bar, where blond-haired piano man Tom (Douglas Frey, also wearing an ascot) pumps out the usual lounge-lizard Muzak for the contented customers. Then it's back to the nightmarish rape scene, and the horror movie music resumes. Millie's rape goes on for several long minutes of screen time, with the assailant thrusting away without mercy and his victim screaming in agony.

And then we return to the safe, sedate atmosphere of the bar, where smarmy Tom sets up an after-hours three-way with Loraine and Jackie, promising to pay the girls 50 bucks from his tip jar. The juxtaposition is alarming and meaningful. As the patrons of the lounge enjoy the smoothed-out piano jazz and numb themselves with alcohol, they are blissfully unaware that a young woman is being traumatized and degraded in the parking lot, yards away from where they are seated.

Certainly, the behavior of the rapist should make viewers seriously reconsider the sexual bartering that goes on inside the bar, where women are routinely "rented" for the evening by guys like Tom. Disturbingly, when Loraine says she'll have to ask Jackie about the proposed *ménage à trois*, Tom says, "Don't ask her. Tell her." This is a world where saying "no" is not an option for women. If guys can't buy it, they'll just take it. In the subsequent sex scene, Tom proves his selfishness by balling Jackie while all but ignoring Loraine. When it's Loraine's turn for some action, Tom first has her perform fellatio on him. "Suck it!" he orders. "Let me feel those lips!"

Hands down, however, the movie's most maddening scene happens next, as Toni walks to the parking lot and finds that her car, a white VW Bug, won't start. Larry the bartender happens along and offers to help. At first, Toni is scared when a man approaches her. "I couldn't help thinking about poor Millie and that rapist," she says. But Larry is utterly unsympathetic: "Aw, she's a tough kid. Besides, what's a little screw to her? She'll be back by the end of the week. She has to. Tom Southern's giving another one of his big parties at our place." Tom, by the way, is a wealthy customer with a fondness for cocktail waitresses and orgies.

Toni is not absolutely appalled at this conversation, though she should be. Larry takes Millie's agonizing and dehumanizing ordeal and calls it "a little screw," then says that the poor woman has less than a week to recover because she's expected to prostitute herself to yet another rich big shot customer. Then, after pretending to help but not actually doing anything of value, Larry has the gall to sexually proposition Toni in the very spot where the rape occurred. This is the script's way of setting up a tryst between Larry and Toni.

A sequence like this tests the likability of any actor, even Harvey Shain. Fortunately, Larry the bartender regains some of his vulnerability and Toni some of her integrity during a post-coital conversation on the floor of Larry's apartment. Like the diamond importer, Larry wants to make his fling with Toni "a permanent thing." Toni's gentle but firm response is the same as before: "Look, I'm a free soul, and when I ball somebody, it's because I want to, when I want to." She just wants to "take it as it comes." This is a significant moment because it shows that Toni, who has been obsessed with money through the whole movie, treats the wealthy diamond importer exactly the same way she treats the working class bartender. She does not, therefore, believe in sexual discrimination based on income.

At Tom Southern's big party, Jackie, Toni, Loraine and the now-recovered Millie are waiting tables. Millie does not mind when one gentleman sticks his nose directly down her cleavage. The other Tom (the ascot-wearing pianist) is providing the soundtrack, while Larry is back behind the bar. The free-spending Southern is, in modern parlance, "making it rain" at the club, so much so that Toni and Jackie lament Los Angeles' two a.m. curfew, which will put an end to the $5 and $10 tips. Larry is dubious: "Sometimes I think you girls are on the take." Jackie rationalizes: "Why not, if he's on the giving end?" Larry tells them not to worry; Southern's moving "the whole schmear" to his place.

Apostolof's fans should know where this is all heading: yet another listless orgy scene in a nondescript hotel room. While a blond-haired piano player makes music in the corner, the ten or so partygoers dutifully undress and start pawing each other. (Interestingly, during this sequence, Rene Bond canoodles with Ric Lutze, who would have been her ex-husband by the time this movie came out.) Once again, just as in previous Apostolof films, a woman who has been maltreated by men takes comfort in the arms (and legs) of another woman. In this case, rape survivor Millie has a heart-to-heart chat with sensitive co-worker Loraine. They don't seem to mind that an orgy is happening all around them as they have their intimate *tête-à-tête*.

Millie describes her terrifying encounter with "that rapist bastard" and says she wishes she'd had a knife to protect herself. Loraine, in typical Apostolof-Wood fashion, delivers a condemnation of the masculine gender: "They're all bastards. The only thing men are good for are what they keep in their wallets. Anything else about 'em can go to hell!"

The women retreat to a private bedroom, where they talk about the drinks and sex toys Mr. Southern has thoughtfully provided for his guests. Loraine then whips out a vibrator and declares, "This way, lonely girls don't have to depend on men for their satisfaction." From there, the scene develops into a lesbian lovemaking session with dialogue nearly identical to that of the big Rene Bond-Starline Comb tryst from *The Class Reunion*. "Men are all animals," says Loraine as she undresses Millie. "They're not interested in what a woman likes or dislikes. They're just simply interested in getting their own guns off and going home. You know, have you ever thought about how much a woman gives and how little she gets in return? All men think about is their own selfish pleasures." This is almost word-for-word the same as a speech given by Rene Bond's Rosie in the previous film. And just like Rosie, Loraine plays a maternal role with her partner. "Tell Mama what it is that you want," Loraine purrs. "Tell her. She'll give you everything that she has to give." Only the use of the comically buzzing vibrator distinguishes this scene from the parallel one in *The Class Reunion*.

The orgy in the main room drones on for several more uncomfortable minutes, during which someone shouts from off-screen, "Hey, everybody! Let's have some fun!"—a vague exclamation that the others interpret as a signal to congregate together on the floor in carnal abandon. Finally, the movie remembers its main character, Toni, and follows her into yet another private bedroom. This time she is accompanied by the founder of the feast, Tom Southern. At first, he wants Toni to pleasure him orally, and she obliges. But like seemingly all of Rene Bond's on-screen male partners, Southern is unable to achieve an erection. His alibi: "I just don't dig it that much."

What the rich man really wants is for the pretty young cocktail hostess to spank him. At first, Toni is incredulous, but Southern swears he is sincere. And so, seeing no real harm in it and wanting to please her client, Toni spanks him. This he digs. ("More! Harder!") The popularity of spanking as a sexual fetish is rooted in the desire to create a feeling of helplessness, which to some individuals is an aphrodisiac. Tom Southern, however, is definitely "topping from the bottom" here, i.e., nominally taking a submissive role but remaining in control of the situation the whole time. He soon demonstrates his total dominance over Toni. Once he is erect, he forcefully takes the waitress from behind like an animal.

It's significant that this room has leopard-print sheets on the bed and implements of war (a shield with crossed swords) on the wall, while Jaime Mendoza-Nava's score becomes unusually percussive and aggressive. In one shot, the camera is placed behind a fern, giving us the impression that we are watching two creatures mating in the jungle.

After this delirious scene, the film returns to the comparatively tame cocktail lounge, where the exhausted Toni and Larry are slogging through another dull shift. At least Toni has a souvenir from her evening of debauchery—a bracelet made from 18-karat gold and diamonds. ("That Tom Southern doesn't fool around!" Toni ironically declares.) Our heroine believes she's in for just another slow night at the bar, until one of her customers turns out to be Mr. Henderson (his drink of choice: a Manhattan). The "chance encounter" is no accident. He has tracked her down because he misses her. She's surprisingly receptive. Toni tells Henderson he can phone her after work. ("It's your dime.") That night, she invites him to her apartment, and he comes running.

What's notable in this sexual interlude is that, for once, Toni is the aggressor, the one taking the lead and guiding the man. And Apostolof has one last surprise in store for us. After making love, Henderson and Toni discuss their relationship while still in bed. He starts by making the kind of offer that Toni has already turned down twice in this movie: "I'd sure like to make this a permanent arrangement, Toni." When Toni asks her about his wife, he says, "Well, she never knew then. There's no reason for her to find out now." Besides, Henderson wants to continue his relationship with Toni "more than anything else in the world." Toni agrees, but she has some conditions, namely $86.91 a week. "And that, my dear cocksman, is our permanent arrangement," Toni says with finality. She and Henderson make love to end the film, with her on top.

It's not exactly a great moment in the women's liberation movement. But for an Apostolof movie, this ending is subtly revolutionary. Consider the fact that *The Cocktail Hostesses* was filmed at the same time as *Drop-Out Wife*, which ends with poor Angela Carnon running back to her abusive, negligent, just-plain-horrible husband. *The Cocktail Hostesses* also concludes with the reunion of the central couple, but this time the woman is re-entering the relationship on her own terms, not the man's.

By studying the body language and vocal inflections of the last scene of this movie, the viewer can really see how the balance of power has shifted drastically from where it was at the beginning, when Mr. Henderson was riding Toni like a pack animal in his office. Now he's in her lair, crumpled up like a rag doll, and she's the one on top and calling the shots. Presumably, she will continue working with Jackie at the cocktail bar as usual and will only rendezvous with Henderson on Fridays. She hasn't gotten a pay raise from her old boss, but she's getting the same amount of money while putting in a lot fewer hours. And she can use that extra time to work as a waitress while having "dates" with other men on the side.

The Cocktail Hostesses premiered on December 6, 1972, in Kansas City, Missouri. The pressbook was designed by illustrator Chester "Chet" Collom (born in 1927), who would also create the posters for Apostolof's *Snow Bunnies* and *Fugitive Girls*. It says: "Director A.C. Stephen once again proves he can mix the light touch with heat for volcano effect."

Another boastful SCA Distributors trade ad's artwork exactly mirrored that of the theatrical poster for *The Cocktail Hostesses*, except that the titular hostess (nude but for a pair of hot pants) is carrying a tray containing an overstuffed money bag garnished with stacks of paper currency. The screaming headline bragged of the film's smash success in Boston: "$31,060.00 at Lowe's West End Cinema" and backed up this claim with a reproduction of a congratulatory May 24, 1973, Western Union telegram to Apostolof from one Sumner Meyerson of the "New England Motion Picture Distributors": "COCKTAIL HOSTESSES NOW IN ITS 5TH WEEK AT EN LOEW'S WESTEND CINEMA BOSTON A 500 SEAT HOUSE GROSS BUSINESS TO DATE $31,060 NEW ENGLAND GROSSES TERRIFIC 76

A color one sheet for *The Cocktail Hostesses*, featuring art by Chet Collom.

PLAY DATES IN FIRST 3 MONTHS OF RELEASE NEW PLAY DATES INCREASING DAILY SEND US MORE PICTURES OF THIS CALIBRE AND WE WILL BE VERY HAPPY." The ad urged exhibitors: "$$$$ Book It Today for Big Profits $$$$" and helpfully included a list of Apostolof's other "films in current release," including such Ed Wood–scripted titles as *Orgy of the Dead*, *The Class Reunion*, *Drop-Out Wife* and *The Snow Bunnies*. Potential buyers were advised to contact Al Weiner's Orbit Films at its Indianapolis or Chicago locations.

Fugitive Girls (1974)

"*In the Ed Wood–scripted* Fugitive Girls, *Wood and director A.C. Stephens [sic] give Quentin Tarantino a run for his money.*"[27]—Paul Brenner, contactmusic.com

For decades, the desire of heterosexual men to see women locked up, chained and subjugated (usually by other women) has created its own special niche in the exploitation industry. This kind of entertainment arguably first appeared in the dime paperbacks and men's magazines of the 1950s, including *Women in Prison*, *Human Detective*, *Detective World* and *Women in Crime*. Certainly there had been depictions of incarcerated women in popular culture before this, including such films as *Hold Your Man* (1933, dir. Sam Wood) and *Ladies They Talk About* (1933, dir. Howard Bretherton and William Keighley), but these were relatively genteel. Hollywood kept churning out stories of imprisoned women throughout the 1940s and '50s, sometimes setting the action in reform schools, as in *So Young, So Bad* (1950, dir. Bernard Vorhaus), and World War II internment camps, as in *Two Thousand Women* (1944, dir. Frank Launder).

Even so, the movies had yet to latch onto what made the pulp stories so popular with men: an emphasis on lurid sexuality at the expense of realism. One problem was the strictness of the censorship laws. But those standards began to relax during the 1960s, paving the way for the women-in-prison film as we know it today. It is possible, though not substantiated, that the first director to truly take advantage of the new freedoms in a women's prison setting was Jesus "Jess" Franco, whose *99 Women* (1969) featured recognizable stars such as Herbert Lom and Mercedes McCambridge as well as the nudity, violence and elements of sado-masochism that would become the subgenre's hallmarks. The undisputed master in this category, though, was an American—legendary exploitation director Jack Hill, who set the pace with his drive-in classics *The Big Doll House* (1971), *The Big Bird Cage* (1972) and *Switchblade Sisters* (1975).

In other corners of the filmmaking world, the standard women-in-prison movie (or WIP) mutated into a few highly specialized sub-subgenres, including Nazisploitation flicks set in German concentration camps and "jungle prison" films, usually set in South America or Southeast Asia. Stephen Apostolof's buddy David F. Friedman was heavily into the Nazi stuff, producing such well-known examples of the form as *Love Camp 7* (1969, dir. Lee Frost) and *Ilsa, She Wolf of the SS* (1975, dir. Don Edmonds).

On the exploitation ladder, a WIP movie would have been at least a rung or two higher than, say, *The Cocktail Hostesses* or *The Class Reunion*. As such, it could have reached some venues where Apostolof's previous films were not welcome. It could be marketed as an action film, not just a sex film. For such a project, Ed Wood was a perfect collaborator, since he had plenty of experience with female-centric crime fiction. He had written about all-girl gangs in his screenplay for the surprisingly successful *The Violent Years* (1956, dir. William Morgan) as well as his novels *Devil Girls* (1967) and *Hell Chicks* (1968).

The next Apostolof-Wood film was a radical break with the last few, containing much more action, violence and location footage. With *Fugitive Girls,* also known as *Five Loose Women,* the pair decided to tackle one of the most popular subgenres in the history of cinema, the WIP film. Naturally, though, they did so in their own inimitable style.

True to form, Apostolof and Wood's *Fugitive Girls* script contained many of the standard WIP trappings: an innocent newcomer who serves as our viewpoint character; a tough lesbian inmate who runs the place and has eyes for the newbie; catfights and lesbian sex scenes; and an escape attempt that results in the deaths of several characters.

In *Fugitive Girls,* innocent Dee (newcomer Margie Lanier) drives her sleazy boyfriend (Joe Pepe) to a Los Angeles liquor store, unaware that he intends to rob the place. He shoots the owner, pushes Dee out of the car and drives off. As witnesses run toward the store, Dee lies in the parking lot. After the credits, it is revealed that she has been arrested, tried and convicted for her part in the fatal robbery and is being taken to a minimum-security institution identified only as "Correctional Facilities for Women."

In her new home, Dee meets bull-dyke ringleader Kat (Tallie Cochrane), foul-tempered Sheila (Donna Young), racist Southern belle Toni (Rene Bond) and honky-hating soul sister Paula (Jabie Abercrombie). Toni knows where some stolen money is stashed, and Kat and the others have been planning to escape the camp, retrieve it and split it four ways. Sheila tells the scared, lonely Dee that Kat "runs this place," and that night Kat proves her dominance by forcing Dee to participate in lesbian sex acts.

A color one sheet for the X-rated 1975 version of *Fugitive Girls* called *Five Loose Women.*

The prison break happens very early in the movie, so the rest of the running time is devoted to what happens to the five girls while they're on the run. For starters, they encounter a group of hippies (including Gary Schneider, Maria Arnold, Douglas Frey, Janet Newell and Eve Orlon) who are initially friendly but then antagonistic. Members of a biker gang (including Con Covert and Armando Federico) are unfriendly right from the start. Other folks they meet along the way include a motorist (Harvey Shain) who unwisely stops to offer them a ride; a loony caretaker named Pop (Ed Wood) who tries to turn them in; and a terrified housewife (Nicole Riddell), whose husband was crippled in Vietnam. Eventually, internal tensions destroy the group. Kat is killed, while Sheila and a newly exonerated Dee are taken into custody. That leaves archrivals Toni and Paula, who actually do recover the money but are chased by the cops toward a gravel quarry, where the predictably violent conclusion plays out.

Fugitive Girls was shot by Guy Nicholas (1933–2017), a half–Bulgarian, half–Greek cameraman and a good friend of Apostolof. Born in the small mountain town of Florina in Northern Greece, he had known Apostolof since 1962, but *Fugitive Girls* marked their first time working together. Nicholas also played a sheriff's deputy in the final scene. The reason for this casting decision: Apostolof just had a police uniform that fitted Guy well. Nicholas went on to shoot Apostolof's final film, *Hot Ice*.

Casting-wise, Apostolof went with a mixture of old and new faces. Two of his most dependable stock players, Rene Bond and Harvey Shain, were again given prominent roles; Douglas Frey and Con Covert returned in smaller parts. The rest of the actors, male and female, have exactly the kind of résumés one might expect: five to ten very productive years in exploitation and sexploitation films of the 1970s, then nothing else. Many of these actors had worked together before and would work together again, suggesting that the sex film industry was insular and close-knit. Marsha Jordan observed, "It's like a close family thing; everybody's friends, and everybody knows each other. A lot of times you'll be working on the same films with more or less the same people, and it gives you a sense of being more relaxed because you know how they're gonna be."[28]

Indeed, the same titles turn up again and again in their filmographies: *The Dicktator* (1974, dir. Perry Dell), *The Dirty Mind of Young Sally* (1973, dir. Bethel Buckalew), *Country Doc* (1976, dir. Corry Phelps), *Hot Connections* (1973, dir. James Hong), *Beach Blanket Bango* (1975, dir. James Bryan), etc. A surprising number of *Fugitive Girls* cast members wound up in the aforementioned *Ilsa, She Wolf of the SS*. There you'll find Donna Young, Nicole Riddell, Janet Newell, Eve Orlon and Gary Schneider.

Of the newcomers to SCA, the most intriguing was Tallie Cochrane (1944–2011), a 5'3" Memphis-born spitfire who played the girl gang's tough-as-nails lesbian leader, Kat. *Fugitive Girls* was just one assignment in an exciting and varied career that spanned nearly 20 years. Tallie never worked with Apostolof or Ed Wood again. Several years before her death from cancer, she gave an informative and entertaining interview to the *Chateau Vulgaria* blog, during which she reminisced about *Fugitive Girls*: "They took us to a shut-down Boy Scout camp where we filmed that whole thing. A girl named Margie Lanier, who was new, was in that with me. She was a genuine klutz and had all of us laughing all day and all night. Steve Apostolof would try and direct us moving around the woods by telling us to 'move like spaghetti.' He was such a joke. We had a good time."[29]

The other major casting news from *Fugitive Girls* was that Ed Wood plays at least three roles in the film, perhaps out of sheer convenience. Eddie was more involved with the making of *Fugitive Girls* than he had been with any of Apostolof's films since *Orgy of the Dead*. Under his oft-used pseudonym Dick Trent, Wood was also Apostolof's assistant director on this one. Apostolof called Wood a "jackass of all trades" and gave him a variety of chores. One of Ed's tasks was to deliver cigars to Apostolof. Wood's fans will instantly recognize his voice in the pre-credits sequence as a witness to the liquor market robbery. His lines sound semi-improvised: "There's no doubt she was with him! We'll call the police, but the guy in there is bleeding to death! Somebody call an ambulance!"

Apostolof, wearing his signature white shoes, prepares to direct an action scene from *Fugitive Girls*. Meanwhile, Tallie Cochrane stretches out her muscles; Douglas Frey is on Apostolof's left.

The real fun, though, starts at about the 40-minute mark when Wood appears as Pop, the scatterbrained old geezer who works at an isolated, lonely airstrip with only a dog for company. Wearing denim overalls and a red short-sleeved shirt with a strange-looking red hat to match, he appears disheveled and befuddled. His hair is long and stringy, he sports a wicked five-o'clock shadow, and his nose is as red and shiny as that of W.C. Fields. He's bloated and out of shape, but not quite as bad as he looked in *Love Feast* (1969, dir. Joseph Robertson).

Wood was obviously having a lot of fun with the part, and the character emerges as one of the film's most memorable elements. Wood re-emerges at about the 69-minute mark as a sheriff who takes Sheila and Dee into custody and tells the latter that her boyfriend confessed everything when he was caught, thus putting her in the clear. Here, Eddie is clean-shaven, has his unruly hair tucked up into his sheriff hat, and sports a rather snazzy pencil mustache. He's hardly the Errol Flynn lookalike who starred in

Glen or Glenda, but he looks better here than he had in years. Eddie even narrated the film's terrific, hyperbolic trailer.

Apart from the prologue, most of *Fugitive Girls* was filmed outside of Los Angeles, but not that much outside. A behind the scenes still from the production identifies the filming location as Frazier Park, an unincorporated village about 73 miles north of L.A. It was shot in a couple of weeks in October 1973. Steve Apostolof had gone several times to Three Falls, the now-defunct Boy Scout camp where it was filmed: "That's how Dad knew about it. I worked there one weekend during the shoot and got to enjoy meeting Ms. [Rene] Bond in the communal dining hall at breakfast. She could tell how uncomfortable I was and added to it by discussing her upcoming lesbian scene she was going to shoot that day. I think she had fun teasing me."[30]

Apostolof worked his cast and crew until they were ready to drop. Maybe to compensate for the long and tiring hours, he hired a French chef who made crêpes suzette in the morning. The cast and crew loved them so much they didn't want to leave when the filming was over.

On *Fugitive Girls*, Apostolof had access to both an airstrip and a working gravel quarry. It seems likely that he and Wood wrote the script around these available filming sites. Apostolof stayed with his cast and crew at the camp premises and in two trailers. He recalled:

> One is for the girls. The other trailer Eddie and I take. The White House we call it. So I sleep here and Eddie sleeps on the other side of the trailer. The first night, the fuse blows up, the electricity is off, I couldn't see in front of me, and the girls and everyone are freezing the ass 'cause it was so cold. But it didn't bother Eddie. In the morning I wake up and see Eddie in a long nightgown, with stubble and a red hat and coat made out of sheepskin. I said, "Eddie, I look at you dressed like that, I wanna scream. You're upsetting me to look at you. Let's just cut the bullshit, okay…"[31]

In sharp contrast to previous Apostolof-Wood sexploitiation films from the early 1970s, which relied heavily on ugly studio sets, *Fugitive Girls* takes place almost entirely out of doors. While this gives the film a bit more visual variety, it also presented a series of challenges. Plenty of the scenes in the script supposedly take place at night, but these sequences were clearly filmed using the so-called "day-for-night" technique and then the film was corrected during post-production to create the illusion of darkness.

There are some intriguing shots of Los Angeles at night during the opening sequence. We get some more of Apostolof's customary footage of the Sunset Strip, including a billboard for the American rock band Rare Earth playing at the Anaheim Convention Center on February 26, 1972, and a glimpse of the long-gone Sunset Apartments (8440 Sunset Boulevard), current site of the Mondrian hotel and a hip nightspot called Skybar. The liquor store robbery was filmed at the still-existent liquor market at the corner of Magnolia and Cahuenga. The place was found by Wood, and Apostolof rented it for $250. Apostolof:

> Dick Damon, who was my soundman, him and Eddie were fellow boozers. Which I wouldn't allow during work. I keep Bulgarian hours: 14 hours, 18 hours…. It's three o'clock in the afternoon someplace…. So we went on location to a liquor store to shoot the sequence with the robbery … and Dick and Eddie are like cats in a supermarket. Their tongues are hanging. Saliva running down. And Eddie comes to me and says, "Poppy, why don't you do me a favor? When the truck comes to take the equipment, would you lock us in? No one'll notice…" I said, "You son of a bitch, you'll drink the whole store and I won't find you for six weeks, cause you'll be in the basement with beards down to your knees!"[32]

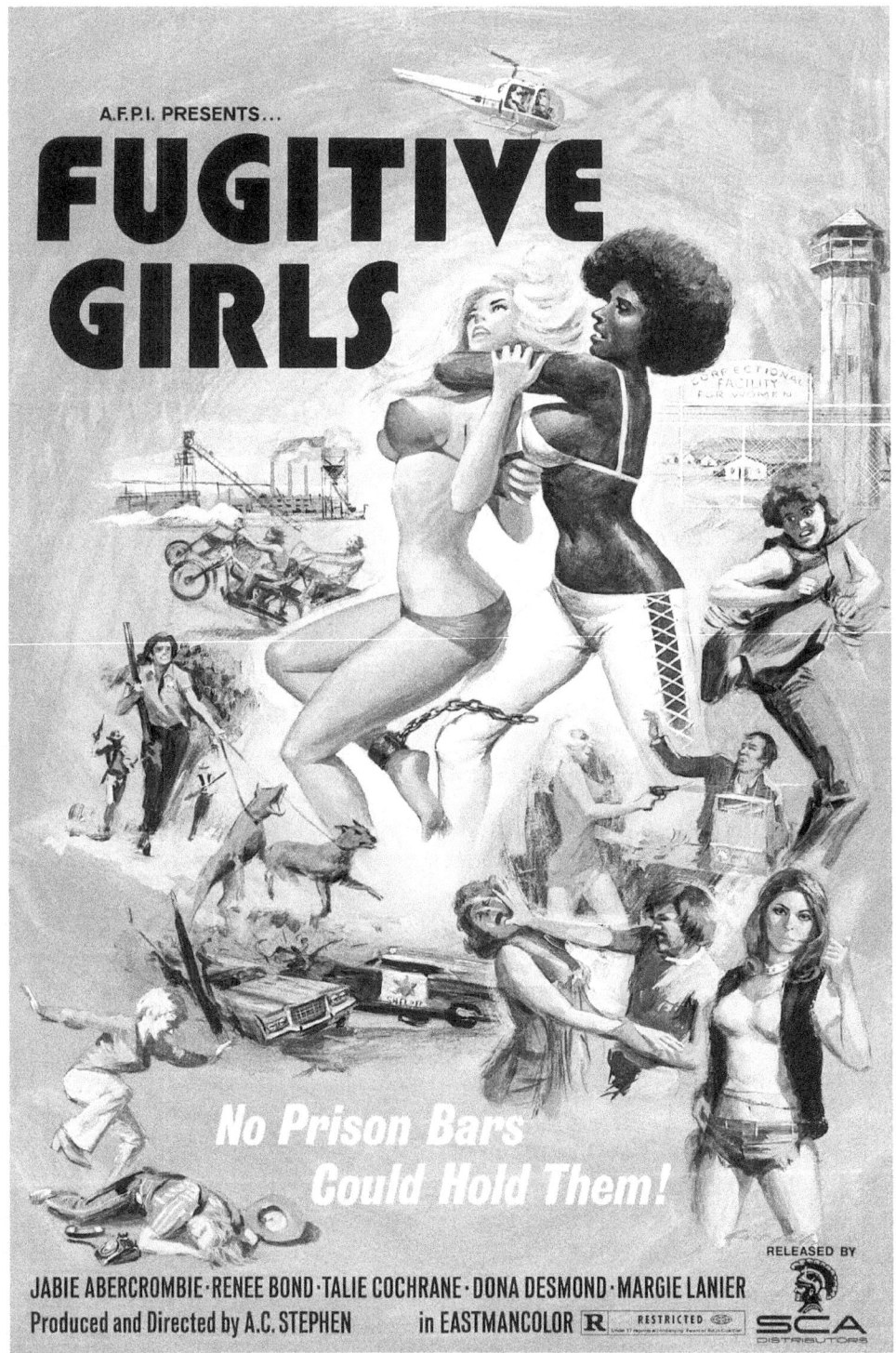

A color one sheet for *Fugitive Girls*, with art by Chet Collom.

After the liquor store scene was shot, Apostolof got a surprising extra bill for $500: Someone from the store accidentally turned off the ice cream freezer to turn on the film lights. "Eddie, what kind of friends do you have?" Apostolof asked angrily. "Steve, the owner is a very cool guy—he gives me booze on credit," replied Wood. In the end, Apostolof had no choice but to pay the bill.[33]

Fugitive Girls was the end of the long working relationship between Apostolof and set designer Budd Costello. According to Apostolof's son Steve, the two had a falling-out because Costello used fake receipts for gasoline reimbursements.

Despite its technical inconsistencies, *Fugitive Girls* is surprisingly satisfying, involving, and even a bit suspenseful. Films like *The Class Reunion*, *The Cocktail Hostesses*, *The Snow Bunnies* and *Drop-Out Wife* could easily blur together in a viewer's mind. Take away each film's particular gimmick (e.g., the skiing in *The Snow Bunnies*), and they're basically indistinguishable from one another. *Fugitive Girls* marks a definite change of pace, even though the movie begins with a sequence that's straight out of one of those other films. The first shot is of a neon motel sign. Then it's yet another first-blurry-then-clear shot of some questionable motel drapes, accompanied by generic Muzak on the soundtrack. The camera pans down to show some discarded clothes as well as a carpet that looks like it was made from Oscar the Grouch. Pan over to the hideous orange-and-gold bedspread and at last we find our lovers, in flagrante delicto.

As the scene begins, Dee's boyfriend drains the last of the Scotch. Dee offers to get more from a liquor store a couple of blocks away, but her lover has a different idea. He says he has his "own special liquor store across town" where he can "sign for" his purchases without cash. He even turns down Dee's offer of $20 cash, which should probably be Dee's first clue that something isn't right here. Apparently, this was the couple's first time making love after over a month of dating. The boyfriend compliments Dee on her soft skin. "Everything about me is soft," she says in a very prophetic line. Throughout the film, Dee will be the naïve ingénue, offering a contrast to the hardened criminals around her. It's significant that Dee only has sex with men she truly loves. In an Apostolof film, that practically makes her a nun.

Dee and her man head to the liquor market. This scene leads directly to the fateful robbery in which her boyfriend, the man she says she loves, betrays her for a bottle of Scotch. Once again, as in previous SCA films, men are constantly letting down the women who care about them. That's a crucial theme in *Fugitive Girls*.

As the plot progresses, the audience will learn more about these women and their negative relationships with men. Except for Toni, every convict is there because of some no-good guy. Sheila was a drug-smuggling stewardess whose male partner let her take the fall. Paula castrated her pimp. Kat murdered hers, even though her pimp was also her husband. ("His mistake ... was that he turned me onto chicks. And I dug it!") Kat never lost her resentment for the male of the species.

After the main title sequence, which looks exactly like the opening credits from all SCA films from this era (big yellow letters superimposed over swirling colors, courtesy of Greg Van der Veer), the movie finally gets to the women-in-prison stuff. True WIP connoisseurs should be forewarned that this particular entry does not really deliver the goods that they are probably expecting. For instance, sadistic and corrupt guards are a hallmark of this subgenre, yet there is not a single guard in the entire movie. There are several references to "Old Hazel," a sentry who agrees to help the girls escape in return for a cut of the money, but Hazel is never once even glimpsed on camera.

Everyone knows that a proper WIP movie has to contain at least one gratuitous shower scene. A few minutes into this movie, several of the girls (including Rene Bond) are summoned to the showers, but we don't go with them. Instead, we stay in the barracks as Sheila shows Dee how to make her bed. Apostolof was obviously lacking two major elements that any director of a WIP film really needs: women and a prison. What he had was exactly five actresses, some denim work shirts and blue jeans, and a defunct Boy Scout camp. Instead of a "women behind bars" flick, this is more like a "women behind screen doors" flick.

The script's hard-boiled dialogue is amusing. Apostolof had native Californian Rene Bond play her character, Toni, as a stereotypical Southerner who speaks with a drawl. Perhaps it was to intensify her rivalry with black inmate Paula. In one scene, Toni starts bragging about the money she has stashed away. But Paula isn't impressed: "Honeychile, ain't no money in the world gonna make white trash no more than white trash!" Toni's response is swift: "Shut your big mouth, you black bitch!"

This sets up a racially charged Paula-Toni rivalry that will escalate for the rest of the movie and eventually cause a fed-up Kat to bark, "I'm getting sick and tired of this rainbow trip, so you two just cool it!" Any viewer who wants to turn *Fugitive Girls* into a drinking game should take a slug every time Paula says "white trash." In another scene, she says that Toni would "screw a cockroach if it turned you on." Toni disagrees: "Cockroaches are black, and I don't go black!"

In keeping with the conventions of WIP films, *Fugitive Girls* has a scene in which a butch lesbian (Kat) forces a straight woman (Dee) to have sex with her. But this part is more depressing than erotic. Dee is lying in her cot, sobbing loudly, when an underwear-clad Kat gets out of her bed and climbs into Dee's and proceeds to spoon with her and caress her. Dee resists, but Kat will not be denied. "All I have to do is force you," she says. "And I've got all the help I can use." She gestures around the room, suggesting that the other female prisoners are under Kat's command.

Under those grim circumstances, it's probably for the best that the big escape scene happens 15 minutes into the movie. Fortunately, this leads to one of the film's strangest and funniest interludes, namely the escaped girls' extended encounter with the hippies living in a makeshift desert commune. Apostolof and Wood were middle-aged men when they made *Fugitive Girls*, and neither one had any clue about American youth culture. That explains why these hippie characters are at least half a decade out of date—not that they would have been realistic for any year. We first see them at night, when they are playing a cretinous approximation of folk music and dancing around a campfire. Some crude, faux-Indian designs are painted on sheets behind them. At least two of the girls are topless (more unmotivated Apostolof-ian female nudity), and most of these characters go by silly nicknames like Bat, Presser, Calico and Tears. "They call her Tears because she cries an awful lot," explains Bat, who wears a ludicrous mesh shirt. The hippies generously invite the convicts to share the fire and the booze. (Presser asks Kat, "Hey, prison lady, want some red?" She proceeds to shotgun it.)

There's some discussion of the sex situation in the hippie camp, during which Kat makes sure to point out that Dee is "taken." (Dee is unperturbed by this.) But it's too late and the girls are too tired for any hanky panky.

The next morning, relations between the fugitives and the hippies rapidly go downhill. None of the prison escapees like the "organic tea," which they just think is bad coffee. And they refer to the group's vegetarian food as "seaweed" that must have been raised in "dung." Presser steps forward to defend the tribe's cuisine in a pompous and pretentious manner: "When we eliminated ourselves from the establishment, we eliminated all of their ways. And that includes their food styles." After some more talk about organic food (the fugitives still aren't sold on the concept), the hippies say that the girls need not fear the authorities. "We know how to use these," says Presser, wielding a chain. For some reason, this sets Kat off, and she calls the hippies "a bunch of filthy freaks."

This does not go over well, and eventually the conversation turns to the hippies' lack of hygiene. "Don't any of you ever take baths?" Dee asks innocently. Bat's typically preachy response: "Water's for growin' things. It's for drinking. We shouldn't pollute it with such things as our body waste!" Then his tone grows darker, as Presser hands him the chain: "However, gentle people as we are, name-calling like that can only lead to broken bones and open skulls, lady!" Kat announces that she's more than ready for a showdown, should it come to that. When she asks why these supposedly "gentle" people need to show so much muscle, Presser semi-coherently explains that all non-conformists need to be able to defend themselves.

Weirdly, among this ramping-up of tension between the two groups, Bat suggests that the fugitives trade clothes with the hippie chicks so as to avoid detection. More unmotivated nudity follows. Presser and Bat ogle the girls as they undress and make lewd remarks about them. Kat finally snaps. She karate chops Bat and then menaces Presser with his own chain. Presser's response to this is an Ed Wood line for the ages: "Oh, good Christ! A lesbian!" Defeated, the hippies let the fugitives leave with the clothes. But it's not much of a victory for our gals. The borrowed duds are infested with lice and are terribly itchy and uncomfortable. Live and learn, ladies.

Next is a semi-comical vignette involving Ed Wood's cranky old caretaker, Pop. As the scene begins, Pop receives a telephone call from the sheriff warning him about the escaped prisoners. Pop responds (in a silly hillbilly-type voice), "Lemme tell ya somethin', sheriff. If I see five pretty broads comin' my way at my age, you can bet I'm gonna call on you for help!" After this, some grungy bikers harass poor Pop at the airfield because "he services those croppers [crop dusters] but he won't service our choppers."

The movie returns to its titular anti-heroines, who have decided to hijack a car. Using scantily clad Sheila as bait, they flag down a passing horny motorist (Harvey Shain) who has no idea that he's stepped right into their trap. The girls steal his car, plus his wallet and watch, then tie him up and leave him in the desert—but not before they force him to have sex with several of them. This scenario is imported directly from Wood's script for *The Violent Years*. ("You sure took that white boy like a sex-starved pussycat!" Paula gleefully says to Toni after the deed is done.) In later scenes, we'll see Harvey—whose ankles and wrists have been bound together—hopping around the desert in his boxer shorts until he's rescued by the cops. He was an awfully good sport to take this uncomfortable and degrading role for his old pal Apostolof.

Ed Wood (center, with hat) as the hapless gas station owner Pop in *Fugitive Girls*. Wood also portrays a sheriff in the film and provides the voice of a witness during a robbery scene.

The gals take off in their stolen car (a clunky-looking brown 1968 Cadillac Coupe de Ville) but realize to their dismay that the thing is out of gas. Their search for a working gas pump takes them to Pop's airfield, which in turn leads to the epic, long-anticipated meeting of Ed Wood and the fugitive girls. Eddie plays this scene with real community theater panache, turning Pop into what Bart Simpson might call a "grizzled 1890s prospector." When an impatient Kat instructs Pop to pump the gas a little faster, he responds, "Hey, young lady, this here ain't no big city gas pump!"

Pop's fate is sealed when he excuses himself from their company, supposedly to use the rest room but really to phone the sheriff. This wouldn't be so bad, except that he makes this call just a few feet away from the girls in plain sight and uses perhaps the loudest rotary phone in movie history. Kat rips the phone out of the wall and brains him with it. ("I was gonna pay you cash, too!" she says ruefully.) The last time we see Pop, he is bloody and unconscious on the ground. His ultimate fate is anyone's guess.

The fugitive ladies head back out on the road, where they are harassed by the same bikers who were bothering Pop earlier. After a brief rumble, the ladies are victorious. ("Men'll just never learn," says Kat.) The girls' next move is to find a farmhouse where they might locate clothes and guns. ("I thought you said there wasn't going to be any killing!" says goody-two-shoes Dee. "Why don't you mind your own business?" Kat replies.) They locate a promising-looking domicile and break in. This turns out to be one of the most surreal and unnerving sections of the film. They find the clothes they want (including "skimpy undies," a classic Wood touch) but decide to break into the

Chapter 11. The Master of Mayhem (1972–1978)

house anyway. At first, the homeowners are shown to be sound asleep. The lady of the house (Nicolle Riddell) is sprawled out like a lifeless rag doll in her recliner while her husband is slumped over in his wheelchair a few feet away. As Rob Craig aptly points out in his book *Ed Wood, Mad Genius*, these two people look like they might already be dead. But then the wife's eyes open wide in total terror, and she immediately wakes up her slumbering hubby Phil. Phil recognizes these five ladies as the escaped prisoners and threatens to call the cops.

But Kat has other ideas. She's commandeered the couple's only gun, and she wants the wife to make coffee for them. The husband reluctantly tells her to comply. ("See how your man backs down when you put him in his place?" Kat gloats.) The hubby explains to Kat that he was paralyzed by shrapnel in Vietnam. Kat, utterly without sympathy: "Tough." While Sheila supervises the coffee-making, Toni turns on the TV, "trying to find the news to see what they have to say about us." But there's nothing to be found, so Toni steers the conversation in a new direction: What is Kat going to do with Dee? Kat suggests that she'd be happy to take her on if Kat is done with her. ("Hallelujah!" exclaims Paula. "White trash is turnin' lez!" Take another drink.)

Toni notices that the female homeowner is "kinda cute," and the scene takes a disturbing left turn. While Sheila holds the woman's arms behind her back, Toni rips her clothes off. This is highly reminiscent of the notorious "Singin' in the Rain" scene from *A Clockwork Orange* (1971, dir. Stanley Kubrick), as is the fact that the male homeowner, Phil, is in a wheelchair with a blanket on his lap. In his DVD commentary for *Fugitive Girls*, Z-grade filmmaker Ted Newsom scoffs at the idea that Apostolof and Wood could have been referencing the Kubrick film, but it's well within the realm of possibility. *Clockwork* was not some obscure art film, let's remember. It was a major release from Warner Brothers and the seventh highest-grossing movie of 1972. It even made the cover of *Mad* magazine. Apostolof and Wood would certainly have been aware of it and had very likely seen it since they both kept tabs on popular culture.

Soon all of the girls except Kat and Dee are taking part in the woman's sexual humiliation, as the impotent husband sits off to the side, bawling and begging them to stop: "Please! I'll do anything! Take my car! Take my money!" Kat loses her patience with the man, knocks over his wheelchair and starts kicking him. Quick-thinking Dee grabs the gun and shoots and kills Kat. (Kat's last words: "Look, you don't want to shoot me!") Dee manages to hold Sheila at gunpoint, but Toni and Paula slip away and hop into the stolen car. The sheriff (Ed Wood) arrives on the scene, arrests Sheila, and tells Dee that she has been cleared of all charges, but that she still has to go to the police station to tell her story.

Now it's down to Paula and Toni, who speed towards "the old Carson shack" where the money is stashed. Toni tells Paula that she's still only entitled to a fourth of the cash. ("Damned lousy white trash!" replies Paula. Take another drink.) The ladies recover the briefcase full of cash, but the cops are hot on their tail. A car chase ensues, and it's surprisingly well-filmed and paced, except for one shot in which it's obvious that the two actresses, Jabie Abercrombie and Rene Bond, are sitting in a non-moving car. And you'll have to excuse the fact that Toni makes the same speech about how she and Paula have to "bury the hatchet about our personal differences" twice in the span of roughly five minutes.

Belgian poster art for *Fugitive Girls*.

The two fugitives ditch the Cadillac and take off on foot toward a gravel pit. Sheriff Ed Wood follows them, accompanied now by a deputy. "We can't shake the pigs!" laments Paula. "There's only one way of stopping them," says Toni, "and that's if they find a body!" With that, she smacks her ex-partner upside the head with the briefcase full of money. And it is here, only five minutes before the end of the movie, that *Fugitive*

Girls gives viewers the big catfight scene they've been waiting for since the opening credits. This epic tussle ends when Toni tosses her rival over a railing, and Paula falls to her instant death.

But the cops are still in pursuit of our one remaining fugitive, and we get some almost artsy, backlit shots of Wood and his partner walking around on the scaffolding between the facility's giant towers. Rene Bond frantically scampers back into the woods, where her briefcase opens and the money goes flying everywhere. Sobbing, she tries to collect the scattered bills, but it's no use. Wood's deputy (Guy Nicholas) has caught up with her and has a gun trained right at her head.

All in all, *Fugitive Girls* stands as a high-water mark in the canon of Apostolof-Wood movies and may be the best-made of their collaborations, though it is nowhere near as thematically bizarre or visually arresting as *Orgy of the Dead*. Like most of Apostolof's early 1970s films, its color palette is dominated by muddy earth tones. *Fugitive Girls* is much more exciting and well-paced than *Orgy of the Dead*, largely because it has a conventional screen story with a beginning, middle and end. Plus, it has some truly quotable dialogue, like this line delivered with aplomb by Tallie Cochrane: "You repeat one word you heard in here, and I'm gonna cut your tits off!"

Fugitive Girls was rated R and premiered with 20 copies on March 15, 1974, in Richmond, Virginia, at the Town and Booker T. theaters. It opened in Washington, D.C. soon afterwards. The film was distributed by Phil Glazer through his Baltimore-based company Associated Pictures. *Fugitive Girls* became one of Apostolof's most popular movies and in 1975 he recut a new X-rated version called *Five Loose Women* which contained scenes the other did not.

The Beach Bunnies (1976)

"These Bunnies Keep On Hoppin'!"—tagline for *The Beach Bunnies*

After giving the world their approximation of a women-in-prison movie, Apostolof and Wood decided to attempt another classic subgenre of exploitation, the beach movie. Counterintuitive as this might seem, the preeminent beach bunny in American popular culture was created by an author from a landlocked European country: Austrian-born writer Frederick Kohner (1905–1986) wrote the highly successful novel *Gidget, the Little Girl with Big Ideas* in 1957, taking inspiration from his daughter Kathy, who grew up in Malibu and immersed herself in the town's thriving surf scene. Kohner's book spawned a series of sequels (1959–68), three movies (1959–63) and a TV sitcom (1965–66), which lasted but a single season before becoming a syndication perennial.

Other beach-themed Hollywood youth films of the era included *Where the Boys Are* (1960, dir. Henry Levin) and *Beach Party* (1963, dir. William Asher). Bottom-feeding Crown International got into the beach game later in the decade with *Never Steal Anything Wet* (1967, dir. Lee Sholem). In the 1970s and '80s, the sandy subgenre became disreputable, with an increased emphasis on T&A and drug-and-booze–fueled shenanigans, e.g., *Malibu Beach* (1978, dir. Robert J. Rosenthal) and *The Beach Girls* (1982, dir. Bud Townsend), both Crown releases.

Apostolof waited until early 1976 before dipping his toe into the ocean, so to speak. But his sun and surf flick, *The Beach Bunnies*, was a little different from the kind of thing Crown was doing. Crown's beach movies tended to focus on high school and college age characters, spring breakers, while Apostolof's movie, like all his other 1970s movies, was firmly ensconced in the darker, more sordid world of adults: grown-ups with jobs and responsibilities, hoping to drown their problems in sex and alcohol for a few precious days. While characters in Crown's beach flicks chugged beers at rowdy house parties, the characters in *The Beach Bunnies* sipped cocktails at dimly lit piano bars and complained about their dull day jobs. In an early scene, two of the bunnies even talk about their depressing workplaces.

As one might guess from the title, *The Beach Bunnies* was only a slight rewrite of Apostolof's previous *The Snow Bunnies* (1972). Each of these movies is about a single woman who goes on vacation to a resort and takes three of her friends along with her, ostensibly so they can all meet available guys and have lots of sex. The two films are structured along very similar lines. Each one begins with a prologue explaining why the frustrated heroine needs to get away. Then there's a standard SCA credit sequence and some travelogue-type driving footage. The protagonist and her friends arrive at the hotel, undress, and split up for separate storylines. In scene after scene, the women hook up with horny guys in tacky hotel rooms. Along the way, there's a horrifying, anti-erotic sequence in which one of the main characters is raped or beaten by men. The women reunite as their vacation winds down, and the movie ends with another driving sequence like the one at the beginning. In all these respects, *The Beach Bunnies* follows the template of *The Snow Bunnies*.

And just like *The Snow Bunnies*, *The Beach Bunnies* is a combination of location footage and studio footage. The studio stuff—mainly hotel rooms, as indicated above—is virtually indistinguishable from *Drop-Out Wife*, *The Cocktail Hostesses*, *The Snow Bunnies* and *The Class Reunion*. The sets are constructed from the same materials and feature the same props as those other films. In particular, there is a gigantic, splotchy, green and white curtain that closely resembles a slice of moldy Wonder Bread. It absolutely dominates any scene in which it appears, as it dwarfs the actors. And once again, the familiar gray-paneled walls appear. *The Beach Bunnies* has more visible boom mics than most other SCA films, though this may be a result of the films being improperly matted for home video.

The one visible highway sign in *The Beach Bunnies* identifies the filming location as Leo Carrillo State Park Beach. Actor Carrillo was best known for playing the role of sidekick Pancho in a number of Cisco Kid films and a popular syndicated TV series (1950–56); he was also a conservationist who served on the California Beach and Parks commission for 18 years. The state park named in his honor is located west of Malibu on the Pacific Coast Highway and has been a filming site for many prominent motion pictures, including *Grease* (1978, dir. Randal Kleiser), *The Karate Kid* (1984, dir. John G. Avildsen) and, appropriately, *Gidget* (1959, dir. Paul Wendkos). It is also a popular spot for fishing, swimming, surfing and beachcombing.

Other exteriors seen in *The Beach Bunnies* include a hotel with a distinctive elevator on the outside of the building, a large ranch-style beach house on a hill overlooking the Pacific, and a swinging cocktail lounge on 5061 Sunset Boulevard called the Cameo

The female stars of *The Beach Bunnies* (left to right): **Linda Gildersleeve, Mariwin Roberts, Brenda Fogarty, and Wendy Cavanaugh.**

Room, famous for its double-time cocktail hour and specialties like brook trout, frog legs, guinea hen and crêpes suzette.

As with *Fugitive Girls*, *The Beach Bunnies* has a cast consisting of both SCA regulars and some fresh faces. Apostolof loyalist Harvey Shain was back as his assistant director and as an actor, this time sporting bushier hair and a bristly mustache, making him look rather like comedian Avery Schreiber. Also returning: Con Covert of *The Class Reunion* and *Fugitive Girls* and Cory Brandon and Rick Cassidy, both of *Drop-Out Wife*. Apostolof gave himself a cameo as a piano player in a bar scene and got to show off his skill at the tickling the ivories.

The four main actresses, however, were newcomers to SCA. Playing the central role of gossip magazine editor Elaine Street was Brenda Fogarty, then about a year into a five-year stretch of strictly softcore films. Fogarty was not your typical skin flick bimbo, however. Somewhat resembling Cloris Leachman in *The Last Picture Show* (1971, dir. Peter Bogdanovich), she had genuine acting chops and a warm, naturalistic screen presence. After her half-decade in movies, she remained active in theater, penning a one-woman show called *The Lesbian Monologues* and appearing in YouTube videos under the direction of acting teacher Charles Tentindo. "Apostolof always wore a big hat. In *The Beach Bunnies* he liked doing one or two takes. He was busy shooting fast. He ran a show," remembers Fogarty, who's now retired from acting and works as a realtor in Long Beach, California.[34]

Texas-born beauty Mariwin Roberts (1948–2017) made her film debut in *The Beach Bunnies*. She went on to be *Penthouse* magazine's Pet of the Month in April 1978 and did a few more R-rated sex comedies before leaving showbiz to become an artist. Linda

Gildersleeve and Wendy Cavanaugh also debuted here, thus embarking on similarly undistinguished careers in low-budget skin flicks. Gildersleeve seems to have earned a little extra pocket money as a pinup model. Apostolof must have been impressed with these ladies, because he brought Roberts, Gildersleeve and Cavanaugh back for his next and final film, *Hot Ice* (1978).

Among the film's notable male talent was Robert Bullock, then just embarking upon a two-decade career in porn that would include *Genital Hospital* (1987, dir. Bianchini Floriani), *My Bare Lady* (1989, dir. Scotty Fox) and *The Last Condom* (1990, dir. Anthony Spinelli). Marland Proctor, who goes uncredited here despite playing a pivotal role as movie star Rock Sanders, previously appeared in *Lady Godiva Rides* and *The Divorcee*. He eventually clawed his way up to roles on such TV shows as *The Rockford Files*, *Quincy M.E.*, *Fantasy Island*, *Hunter* and more.

By far, however, the most famous cast member, male or female, in *The Beach Bunnies* was Johnny Fain (born in 1943), hilariously billed here as John Aquaboy. This renowned California surfer parlayed his success on the waves into a nearly 20-year film career as an actor and stuntman, including an appearance in (you guessed it) *Gidget*. He also played doomed ranch hand Shorty Shea in the TV movie *Helter Skelter* (1976, dir. Tom Gries). Fain seems to have dropped out of public life since the 1970s, but he has occasionally resurfaced to comment on the physical toll of being a surfer and to eulogize one of his colleagues. He does a little surfing here, but it is brief and unimpressive. You'd never guess he was once considered "one of the four aces of Malibu."[35]

As a film, *The Beach Bunnies* is alternately enervating and intriguing. After the

Surf god Johnny Fain and Linda Gildersleeve pose with a longboard in *The Beach Bunnies*.

welcome change of pace provided by *Fugitive Girls*, it was a return to the same old same old for Apostolof. Once again, the script was merely an excuse for a lot of nudity and simulated sex. Were it not for Ed Wood's contributions to the script, it is probable that *The Beach Bunnies* would be entirely forgotten in the 21st century. And yet the film is not without its charm. Take, for instance, the infamous opening scene, which sets up the wafer-thin plot. After a typical establishing shot of a phallic skyscraper, Apostolof cuts to the interior of what's supposed to be the office of *Blue* magazine editor Elaine Street (Fogarty). Elaine's sitting behind her desk in a white wicker chair that definitely looks like patio furniture. She's wearing a rust-colored polyester pantsuit that sets the tone for the outfits we'll see throughout the movie. Behind her is that notorious green and white curtain, which Apostolof has previously used in scuzzy motel rooms in his other movies.

As the scene begins, Elaine is angrily lecturing a guilty-looking reporter (played by a non-speaking, unbilled actor) who has a skeevy-looking porno mustache and wears a tacky blue suit with a black bowtie. As she yells at him, he looks like a child being scolded by his mother. The film begins with an extended monologue of pure rage, which Brenda Fogarty handles with aplomb. "Great Scott!" she exclaims. "You want something done around this place, you have to do it yourself!"

What did he do that was so terrible? Well, apparently, he was supposed to file a story about macho movie star Rock Sanders (Marland Proctor), but all he's managed to dig up is an unsubstantiated and possibly libelous rumor that Rock has had "a sex transplant performed on him" in Denmark and is going to marry his effeminate agent Bruce Collins (Con Covert). Elaine also mentions that Rock is "ready to star in SCA's new film *Tidal Wave 2000*." That line allowed Apostolof to work in a clever plug for his own production studio. Elaine makes it clear that she isn't interested in mere conjecture and hearsay. She needs the facts: "I've got to know if Rock Sanders has a cock!" she yells, in the movie's most memorable line.

She dismisses the shamed reporter, telling him to cover a dog show. Then Elaine's own boss, distinguished J.B. (Cory Brandon billed as Correy Brandon), strides in. He's not happy about this Rock Sanders situation either, but Elaine says she has a plan. Rock is currently staying at a place called the Silver Cove Lodge. She'll check into the place herself, bringing along three friends as "sex decoys." And if that doesn't work, she promises to use her own "sex charms" on Rock. In an echo of the previous SCA films *Office Love-In* and *The Cocktail Hostesses*, it's revealed that Elaine and J.B. have a sexual relationship in the office. Though nothing is shown, it's implied that the female reporter is occasionally expected to fellate her boss.

The prologue is probably *Beach Bunnies*' dramatic and comedic highlight, and it occurs in the first five minutes. After the theme song, Elaine and her pals go to the Silver Cove Lodge, where Elaine tries repeatedly to get close enough to Rock to determine whether or not his penis is still attached. Essentially, the script requires Elaine to act like Wile E. Coyote from *Looney Tunes* or Lucy Ricardo from *I Love Lucy*. The desperate reporter comes up with one ridiculous scheme after another to spy on him, but they all fail miserably. That is, until the end when she finally has sex with him and gets a definitive answer to her question.

Rock's sexuality is really never in doubt, though, because Marland Proctor plays his part in such an obviously masculine way. Elaine's strange statement about using her three friends as "decoys" is ultimately meaningless, since Lorrie (Roberts), Sheila (Gildersleeve) and Bonnie (Cavanaugh) have *no* impact on the main plot. After the introduction, each young lady gets her own individual, largely self-contained subplot.

Poor Elaine spends the majority of the running time trying and failing to get near Rock's crotch in a series of increasingly wacky gambits. At first, she simply pretends to be Rock's "cousin" and calls the front desk for his room number. The clerk isn't buying it. ("What a faggot!" she complains in defeat.) She finally gets the number by screwing a bellboy (Robert Bullock, in an amusing debut). At least she gets the room number: 714. But when she calls Rock's room, she gets cigarette-holder-clutching Bruce Collins, who shoots her down immediately, saying in a sing-song voice, "It is my happy, happy duty to inform you that we do not give interviews." Click.

That's when the Lucy Ricardo–Wile E. Coyote gene kicks in. Elaine pays a maid $50 for her uniform and enters Rock's room. She tries to peep on him when he's in the bathroom, only to be caught (again) by Bruce. The next day, Elaine spots Rock on the beach and tries to get his interest by pretending to be attacked by a shark. Why a shark? Well, this was the year after *Jaws* (1975, dir. Steven Spielberg) broke box office records. This plan also flops. Rock just sits on the beach, staring in amusement, while a Japanese tourist dives into the ocean to "save" Elaine.

Stereotypes are here in full force. Of course, the Asian tourist has a giant camera around his neck. His companion, played by a non–Asian actress, is clad in a kimono and carries around a silk parasol, as if she's dressing up like a geisha for a costume party. As the well-meaning Japanese fellow carries a protesting, kicking-and-screaming Elaine out of the water, Rock delivers the "punchline" for this silly scene: "God, I've gotta learn how to swim sometime!"

But our intrepid reporter is far from finished! Her next plan involves standing outside Rock's room with a fire extinguisher and yelling, "There's a fire! Everybody out of the building!" In all the confusion, Elaine grabs the crotch of—can you guess?—Bruce Collins, who is suitably offended. ("You bitch!") Dejected, Elaine sits on the hallway floor, spraying foam from the fire extinguisher as Hanna-Barbera–type music plays on the soundtrack.

While all this is going on, the three other women cruise for guys at nearby beaches and bars. Sweet, shy "computer analyst" Sheila begins a rather chaste courtship with golden-haired surfer boy and trust fund layabout Dennis Coleman (Johnny Fain). That night, she and the Big Kahuna have a boring dinner at a boring-looking restaurant and talk about how boring they are. (He: "Life with the jet set just isn't my bag." She: "I know what you mean! Now, my friends, they thrive on the fast life.") The actors seem to run out of dialogue before the scene ends, but Apostolof's camera just stays on them, smiles frozen on their faces.

Over at the Cameo Room, featuring the ten talented fingers of Stephen C. Apostolof at the piano, Lorrie and Bonnie get hit on by lounge lizards Dave (Rick Cassidy) and Chris (Harvey Shain), who wear garish polyester outfits and dub themselves "two of the most fantastic studs in town." Dave gets Lorrie and Chris gets Bonnie. That's pretty much how it stays for the rest of the movie, except for one scene in which Dave and Chris double-team Lorrie in a hotel room with all the enthusiasm of motorists exchanging insurance information. The boys waste no time in following through on their sexual innuendos. Mere moments after meeting, Chris and Bonnie are canoodling on the former's catamaran. At least Dave and Lorrie have the decency to drag themselves back to a hotel room.

Unfortunately for the movie, Sheila's subplot takes a nasty left turn at this point. The redheaded computer analyst confides to Elaine that "there wasn't a bed scene" between her and Dennis. Elaine tells her friend to "stop being such a prude," lest she wind up "an old maid." This is foreshadowing. Sheila agrees with Elaine, who is the Marsha Jordan-esque mother figure to the group, and goes out for a walk on the beach. One of Apostolof's jarring dusk-to-dark jumps later, Sheila is strolling along the beautiful shore of Leo Carrillo when she's stopped and harassed by a trio of fairly clean-cut-looking surfers—Coolie, Tenpipe and Hickory—who look like stand-ins for the Beach Boys circa 1963. Later, Sheila will refer to these fellows (totally inaccurately) as "hippies," which shows you just how out of touch Apostolof and Ed Wood were with the counterculture, a movement that had been dead for several years by the time this movie came out.

Following a disturbing trend in the Apostolof-Wood films, Sheila—the nicest character in the story—is gang raped by the three young men. They strip her, then take turns forcing themselves on her. In an absolutely unforgivable twist, Sheila ends up enjoying the "sex" she's having, making this movie even less sensitive than *The Cocktail Hostesses*.

The next morning, both Bonnie and Elaine recognize that something is wrong with Sheila. With only a little coaxing, she reveals that she was raped. She says that she screamed, but only "at first." Then, she admits, "I was enjoying everything they were doing to me. I really did!" Elaine assures Sheila that there's nothing wrong with enjoying sex, but suggests "there's a right way and a wrong way." Sheila says she will report the men who raped her, even though the experience turned out to be her sexual awakening. The next exchange could have come from any number of Apostolof films.

"Just remember one thing," Elaine says. "All men are out for the same thing!"

"I know!" responds Sheila. "But I'll tell you one damn thing for sure! I'm gonna screw every one of them, before they screw me! And it's gonna start tonight!"

At that point, Sheila gets a call from Dennis, asking for a date. She accepts. Elaine warns her not to wear herself out before "the big beach party tomorrow night," and the three women end the scene giggling like schoolgirls at a slumber party. Perhaps here, viewers can see some evidence that Wood and Apostolof were operating at cross purposes in their co-creation of this screenplay, as Wood manages to include some of his typical quasi-feminist dialogue about how men are "bastards" who want to use women for sex. Modern viewers may also wonder why Apostolof included traumatic rape scenes in what was supposed to an easygoing beach comedy.

After an out-of-nowhere three-way between Chris, Dave and Lorrie, Apostolof cuts to another one of Sheila and Dennis' dinner dates. Again, alcohol comes to the forefront. "Mmmm," enthuses Sheila, "cognac just warms me all over!" Linda Gildersleeve sports a Farrah Fawcett hairdo in this scene. This was the year that gave us both Farrah's iconic poster and TV's *Charlie's Angels*.

Regrettably, this scene also confirms that the rape was indeed intended as a sexual awakening or initiation for Sheila. "Somehow," Dennis notes with appreciation, "you've really changed!" All he knows is that she's more affectionate now, sloppily French kissing him, and shimmying out of her dress in record time. When Dennis and Sheila finally hit the (pink satin) sheets, a veteran viewer of SCA films will easily notice that the decor of his supposedly posh beach house looks exactly like the cheapskate hotel rooms where our heroines are staying, right down to those dreaded gray square panels on the wall.

At last, the film reaches its conclusion: a beach party attended by almost all the characters. Apostolof makes a fairly clever transition into this scene, zooming in on a candle during Dennis and Sheila's romantic tryst and cutting from that to a bonfire. One flame leads to another. For the most part, this sequence is light on dialogue and extremely heavy on bongo music. There are at least two bongoists on hand at the beachfront bacchanal—one who seems really into it, and one who's just kind of going through the motions. For reasons known only to the actor, Johnny Fain wears a Day-Glo orange and yellow wizard's robe to this affair.

Elsewhere, Chris dons his ugliest polyester shirt yet, plus mustard yellow shorts. Harvey Shain proves in this scene that he was no dancer, but he's obviously having a lot of fun anyway, looking like a drunken relative at a wedding reception. After a few minutes of watching a bunch of uncoordinated actors flailing around on the sand, a lone dancer—a busty, dark-skinned, raven-haired beauty in a pink bikini—becomes the center of attention. In a way, it's a return to the dance routines from *Orgy of the Dead*, except that this woman does not remove her swimsuit.

Eventually Apostolof resumes the plot. A late-arriving guest at the party, Rock Sanders, stumbles over Elaine, causing her to drop her drink; he offers to buy her another one. (From who? This is a beach party!) Elaine and Rock's relationship escalates quickly, from sharing a drinking glass (She: "It's kind of like kissing by proxy!" He: "Why by proxy?") to screwing on the beach. All this is possible because Rock has finally slipped away from the watchful eye of Bruce Collins. ("That guy follows me around like a warden!" laments Rock.) At last, our intrepid gal reporter gets indisputable evidence that Rock's genitals are still very much attached to his body. "Oh, god, it's big!" she exclaims.

Perhaps to maintain a sense of democracy among the cast, Apostolof occasionally cuts away from the Rock-Elaine tryst to show the furious coupling of Chris and Bonnie and the just-as-eager fornication of Lorrie and Dave. Apostolof must have thought the audience had seen enough of Sheila and Dennis by this point.

The next day, Elaine and the gang pile into their Cadillac Eldorado and head for home. Apostolof gives us a brief glimpse of the car's bumper sticker: "If You're Horny, Honk." Like its companion movie *The Snow Bunnies*, *The Beach Bunnies* ends with an almost unconscionably long driving scene as our title characters pull out of the hotel parking lot, drive down a fairly busy stretch of road, and finally merge onto the highway. At least here, there's some attempt at humor, because lots of other cars honk their horns when the girls drive by.

Fugitive Girls and *The Beach Bunnies* were released at a time when the market for Apostolof's brand of erotica was drying up. According to David F. Friedman, the problem he and other producers were facing was that major American newspapers resisted sexploitation movies. In the early 1970s, for instance, The *Los Angeles Times* banished

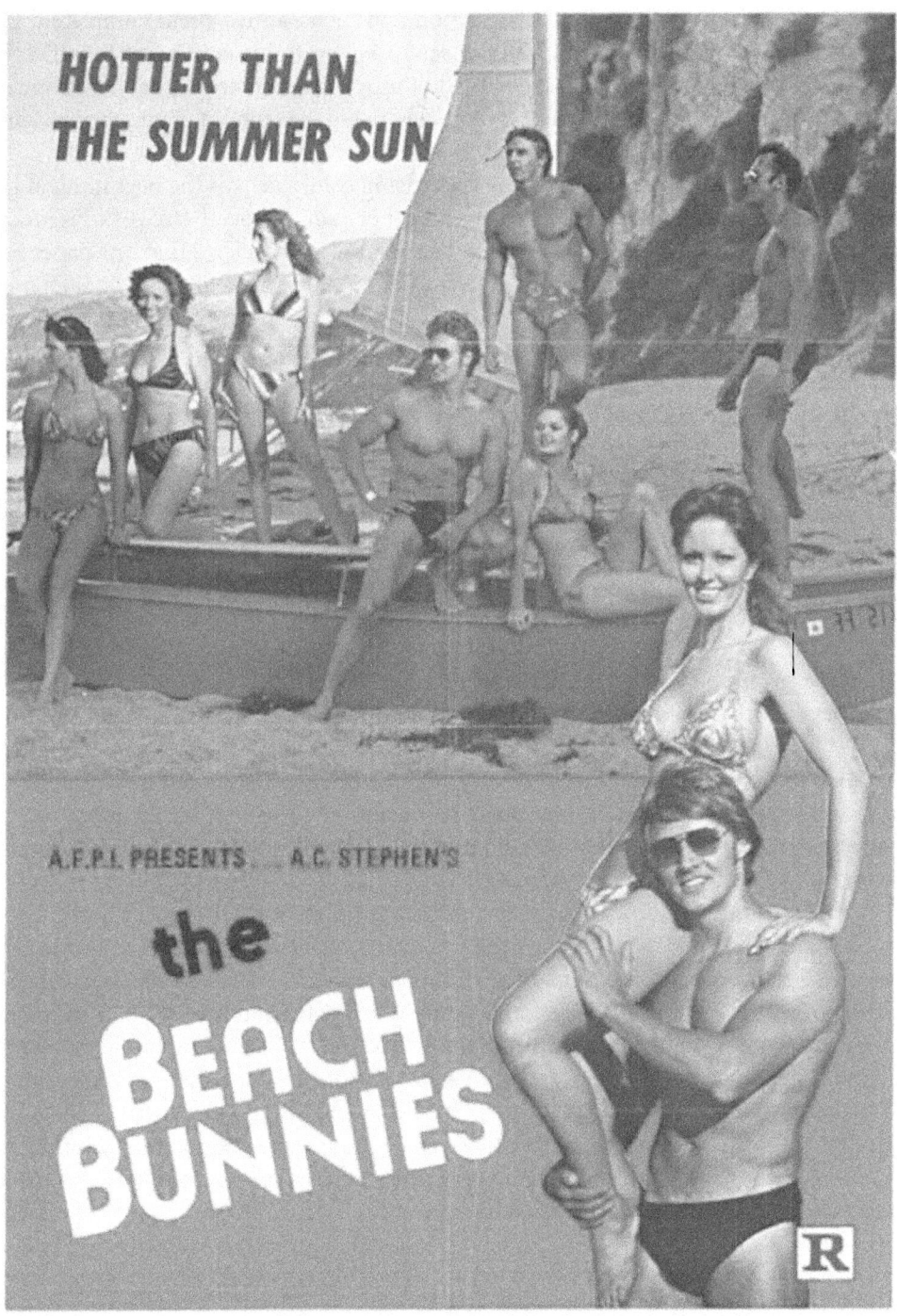

A color one sheet for *The Beach Bunnies*.

sexploitation ads to their own special section and then banned them completely. On August 23, 1977, publisher Otis Chandler sent a memo to his employees in which he announced that the newspaper's special "adult movie" section would be discontinued. That same year, *The New York Times* severely restricted the amount of ad space given to adult-oriented films.

"When the *L.A. Times* stopped the advertising cold, that was the beginning of the end for the [California-based] Pussycat and other [adult movie] circuits," Friedman said in an interview with exploitation film historian Eric Schaefer. "That one paper had more than anything else to do with it. In New York, it didn't make that much difference. In New York, the trade came from people just walking by, bums stumbling into the theaters. But in L.A., no one walks, everybody drives. The *[L.A.] Times* had circulation of a million, the [*Los Angeles Herald Examiner*] paper only 200,000. Without the ads in the *Times,* it really began to hurt things." Friedman recalled that even when Pussycat tried to advertise their cinemas as the place with the freshest popcorn in Los Angeles, the *L.A. Times* still refused to publish their ads.[36]

Another important reason was the decline of roadside drive-in theaters. These were crucial venues used by Apostolof and other sexploitation producers and directors. Even in the hyper-conservative Bible Belt, for instance, Apostolof's movies played for years at drive-ins to great success. According to Apostolof, "The Bible Belt down south was my biggest market. All the drive-ins. The Carolinas. Georgia. The drive-ins were where my prints got burned up. They would open at 6:00, and, because it was still light out, they had the projectors cranked way up and they just burned the hell out of my prints."[37]

But the drive-ins occupied a lot of land, and when cities started expanding, that land suddenly took on new value. Business owners were willing to pay more money per acre than any drive-in theater could make. So a lot of these theaters closed to make room for new commercial development.

Along with the decline of drive-ins, the late 1970s also saw the rise of home video. In November 1975, Sony introduced the first commercially available VCR in the U.S., using its Betamax technology. The LV-1901 model came in a massive teakwood console, complete with a 19" color TV set, and retailed for $2495 (around $11,000 in today's money). Sony co-founder Akio Morita boldly declared that it would launch a revolution in watching video at home. To survive, many producers and directors were forced to make serious compromises with their movies, including cutting them so as to obtain the coveted R rating. Faced with these challenges, some sexploitation filmmakers defected to the blossoming but shadowy world of hardcore pornography. Apostolof refused to make that transition. Apostolof:

> Later on, it became crazy when hardcore came in, and that's when I got out. They were making book when I was gonna make hardcore, but I said nope. I bumped into [attorney] Stanley Fleishman and he said, "Steve, when the hell are you gonna make a good hardcore picture? Show them that it could be done!" I said, "Never!" All my friends were making them, but that's their department. I have my own standards, my own morality. I can go so far. I do not criticize people who went over there, that's their business. It's also my business what I make.[38]

Apostolof's son Steve further explained his father's position on the matter:

In the early '70s, there was a shift in the way the adult films were made. Dad's movies were titillating. They showed breasts. The actresses would come out, wearing underwear. It wasn't pornography. Dad's movies were something that fitted in his family ideal. He wasn't ashamed of making them. But to make films that were pornography, that were showing actual copulation, actual full-frontal nudity, that was a line he just didn't want to cross.[39]

According to Shelley Apostolof, apart from his moral standards, Apostolof refused to go into hardcore films because of the connection between the porn industry and the American Mafia: "Steve went to a meeting with some financiers in Miami, Florida. He came home and said they are Mafia. So he didn't want to go to the bed with Mafia that was slowly getting over the industry. I told him if he do it, I'd divorce him. I didn't want the Mafia, the FBI coming and knocking down our doors for pornography."[40]

For example, in the early 1970s, Anthony "Big Tony" Peraino, a Colombo crime family mobster, financed *Deep Throat*. When the film became a hit, he began to blackmail theater owners for 50 percent of the revenue from ticket sales. To make sure they wouldn't be ripped off, the mobsters would send their own people to count heads and then report on the attendance of each screening. Peraino used the *Deep Throat* revenues to build a financial empire, which according to FBI included ownership of garment companies in New York and Miami and investment companies. Peraino's brother Joseph, meanwhile, distributed another very successful pornographic film, *The Devil in Miss Jones* (1973, dir. Gerard Damiano).

"I saw only one hardcore movie, *Deep Throat*," said Apostolof. "Here again, I saw it at the Pussycat Theatre because I was waiting for another screening. I was bored stiff. Bored stiff. Then I went to see *The Devil in Miss Jones* but that, to me, was a very interesting picture. A very well-done picture. Too bad it had hardcore in it."

Apostolof didn't have kind words for the hardcore pornographers whom he called "a bunch of chicken-shits"[41]: "I'll tell you a secret. A couple of 'our own' started the revolution. And that's what killed us. The hardcore. It ruined the market. Why should a fellow see my film when he can see everything in a hardcore for the same price? Unfortunately, some people among us saw the moola and dove in."[42]

So if Apostolof wasn't willing to make hardcore and his beloved drive-ins were disappearing, what was left for the veteran producer to do? Retirement loomed on the horizon. But before packing it in for good, the 48-year-old Apostolof attempted his most ambitious and uncharacteristic film yet.

Hot Ice (1978)

> "I was not very proud of what I was making. It was right before the so-called sexual revolution and the morals of America were quite disapproving. Later on, everybody used to ask me why I didn't make hardcore movies. I have nothing against hardcore movies or the people who made them but I, personally, just didn't want to get into that."—Stephen C. Apostolof[43]

Waterloo. Little Big Horn. Bay of Pigs. *Hot Ice*. That's about the size of it when it comes to Apostolof's final film, a seemingly innocuous diamond heist comedy that turned out to be a career-ending fiasco.

Like many of the great miscalculations of history, the movie was born of overreaching ambition. "He wanted so bad to get into the mainstream," reports Shelley Apostolof, "that he did that *Hot Ice*." Part of the pressure to make a mainstream movie might have come from Shelley. She referred to sexploitation films as "sickening" and to Apostolof's audience as "perverts."[44]

Apostolof's response was to go after a broader audience, following the lead of MGM's mega-popular James Bond franchise. Never mind that the price tag for producing a Bond movie was doubling with each new entry as ticket buyers' appetite for spectacle increased—from $7 million for *The Man with the Golden Gun* (1974, dir. Guy Hamilton) to $14 million for *The Spy Who Loved Me* (1977, dir. Lewis Gilbert). Naturally, the Bond films were turning hefty profits on those hefty budgets, but this franchise was definitely following one of the golden rules of business: You have to spend money to make money.

Theoretically, at least, *Hot Ice* made some sense in the film marketplace of the late 1970s. After all, Apostolof was capitalizing on America's obsession with caper films, a trend that began in the 1950s and underwent a renaissance in the '60s. Several years earlier, *The Sting* (1973, dir. George Roy Hill) with Paul Newman and Robert Redford had been an unparalleled success, winning seven Oscars and becoming a box office smash hit with $160 million (around $800 million today) in receipts. Films like *Kelly's Heroes* (1970, dir. Brian G. Hutton), *The Hot Rock* (1972, dir. Peter Yates) and *Diamonds* (1975, dir. Menahem Golan and Arik Dichner) made crime look fun and turned characters who would normally be villains into heroes.

But Apostolof didn't have the resources to be competitive in the mainstream with an action-adventure film. His son Steve recalled his dad's financial woes during the Me Decade: "As the 1970s rolled on, he didn't have product to sell. He couldn't get investors that wanted to invest in his movies because the return just wasn't gonna be there."[45] Shelley agrees that money was a major problem for the film: "He made a mistake by trying to get into the mainstream with such a low budget."[46]

Christopher remembers the devastating consequences of his father's error:

> Steve had taken out a third mortgage on his home. It was the last large home that he owned in Studio City on Sarah Street. And that was it. We lost the house. We couldn't afford to put the picture out, and it tanked. And Steve was always one movie away from basically bankruptcy. Each film was funding the next. It had always started like that, from *Orgy of the Dead*, all the way through. I mean, all the pictures that everybody knows. He made enough money to make the next picture, and when that cycle stopped, it was over. Steve had no savings, and that was it.[47]

After *Hot Ice*, Apostolof never produced or directed another motion picture. It was also the last production on which Ed Wood ever worked. In essence, then, two legendary film careers ended here. Christopher still has many boxes of *Hot Ice* posters. At least this was a film in which the director could take obvious pride. It was the first film since *Journey to Freedom* (1957) in which Apostolof used his real name in the credits.[48]

While *Hot Ice* turned out to have pretty grim consequences for Apostolof, the making of this movie was not an unhappy experience. It was another family affair, partially filmed at Apostolof's ski resort of choice, California's lovely Mammoth Mountain, where Apostolof had done *The Snow Bunnies* a few years previously. As mentioned earlier, Apostolof was buddies with a hotel owner in Mammoth, a fellow Bulgarian-American

One of the two versions of the color one sheet for *Hot Ice*, Apostolof's disastrous diamond heist flick.

named Mike Mikhailof. Instead of calling the site by its real name, Apostolof's script referred to the resort as the Matterhorn Ski Lodge, possibly to keep the location of the place vague. In *Bunnies*, remember, the resort was supposed to be in Canada. Apostolof's first lieutenant, Harvey Shain, was along for this final project, as an actor and a casting director.

Production for *Hot Ice* began in August 1976 and lasted 27 days. Apostolof and his crew shot in the town of Mammoth Lakes, California, as well as near Big Bear Lake in the San Bernardino Mountains, 100 miles northeast of L.A. The location filming continued for two weeks, amid stubbornly cold and rainy weather. When the location shooting ended, Apostolof and his crew headed to Hollywood to shoot the studio scenes at a soundstage at the historic Mutual–Don Lee Studios on the corner of Vine Street and Fountain Avenue. The studio was near the Hollywood Ranch Market, a 24-hour grocery store whose aisles were haunted by many actors, including the decrepit Criswell and his one-time *Plan 9* co-star Vampira.

Harvey Shain remembers a comical bedroom scene in which he had to pretend to be a bullfighter. It turned out to be a real workout for the actor: "Steve made me swing a blanket around and dance. And I figured, 'Ahh, this is fine, doing it for two or three minutes.' And he just keeps the camera rolling. And I'm about ready to have a heart attack!"[49] Apostolof did yell "Cut!" before poor Harvey could go into cardiac arrest.

Hot Ice's interior sets should look familiar to anyone who's seen Apostolof's other movies. The man sure did love his bright yellow paint. Mercifully, the film does not feature the exact same walls, furniture and other props that were used endlessly in SCA films from 1972 to 1976. Here again, though, the director took many of his props directly from the Apostolof homestead. Christopher Apostolof reports, "Half of the family's furniture is in *Hot Ice*. That French provincial headboard in the hotel scenes was Mom and Dad's headboard from the Sarah Street house."[50]

Hot Ice was shot by Apostolof's friend Guy Nicholas, who had previously shot *Fugitive Girls*. The cast again consisted of a mix of Apostolof veterans and newbies. Among the former was Shain, touchingly given top billing in this final Apostolof film. (His film and TV career kept going for decades after that.) Several cast members from *The Beach Bunnies* (1976) were back, Mariwin Roberts, Rick Cassidy and Linda Gildersleeve returning as members of the rowdy, hard-partying Matterhorn Ski Club. Best known as the ex-husband of porn queen Rene Bond, Ric Lutze (who had worked for both Apostolof and Ed Wood several times) was another member of this fictional club and got to do some serious onscreen slaloming in the process. Rounding out the cast was Fred Spencer, who had previously appeared in *The Human Tornado* (1976, dir. Cliff Roquemore), an entry in Rudy Ray Moore's *Dolemite* series.

Doing some stunt work on the slopes was Apostolof's oldest son, Steve. "I had a small part in that," he remembered fondly. "I got to play the first aid man. Great! Just how perfect was that? I did not realize how annoying shooting a film could be. First, our asses froze, and second, we were doing the same thing again and again. But at least the snowmobiles were fun."[51]

Two of the main female roles were played by actresses whose careers amounted to almost nothing: adorable brunette Teresa Parker and Farrah-haired blonde Patti Kelley (real name Patti Clifton). Cast-wise, the big news is the presence of sturdy film and

Patti Kelley strikes a seductive pose in a promotional photograph for *Hot Ice*.

TV actor Max Thayer, billed here under the name Mike Thayer. Max, who took his stage name from the Harold Robbins novel *The Carpetbaggers,* went on to appear in such big-time films as *Pearl Harbor* (2001, dir. Michael Bay), *The Man Who Wasn't There* (2001, dir. Joel and Ethan Coen) and *S.W.A.T.* (2003, dir. Clark Johnson), not to mention TV's *Dallas* and *Simon & Simon*. In the early 1980s, after a couple of roles in low-budget Filipino movies, he became a B-movie action star. At the time of *Hot Ice*, his most prominent credit was *Ilsa, Harem Keeper of the Oil Sheiks* (1976, dir. Don Edmonds), in which he got second billing behind Ilsa herself, Dyanne Thorne. With his cleft chin, Marlboro Man mustache, and easy charm, Thayer definitely gives this movie a boost, like a big leaguer brought in as a ringer on a triple-A team. He and co-star Patti Kelley have a nice, *Hart to Hart*-esque chemistry, too.

Thayer remembers, "Steve was a very dynamic person. To me, he looked like a lion tamer in a circus. He always controlled the situation and knew what he wanted. He was the director! His emphasis was very funny. [*Imitating Apostolof's husky voice:*] 'Come

Apostolof massages Teresa Parker's foot on the set of *Hot Ice* while Max Thayer and cameraman Guy Nicholas watch.

on! Let's shoot the damn thing!' Boom! Boom! Boom! I liked him a lot. We got along really well."[52]

Thayer was born on June 18, 1946, in Detroit. At 19, he joined the army and served a three-year hitch before heading to Hollywood to pursue acting in 1969. "At that time, I didn't know anything about acting," he admits. "I didn't know anything about movies, about Hollywood."[53] Taking his inspiration from Steve McQueen in *Bullitt* (1968, dir. Peter Yates), the naïve young Thayer applied for a job as an actor at MGM, only to be laughed out the office. He joined an experimental theater troupe and performed street theater in Venice, California. By the end of the 1970s, he was finally landing some film roles.

Thayer got paid $100 a day for *Hot Ice*, a standard rate for a starring role in a low-budget, non-union movie. "I just couldn't believe this was happening to me," he says. "They were paying me as an actor. I was surrounded by pretty women. We had good wine and good food. When you take part in Apostolof's film, this is the standard. You always get good food and good wine!"⁵⁴

Thayer owed this relatively plum role to Harvey Shain, with whom he appeared in *Planet of Dinosaurs* (1977, dir. James K. Shea). That obscure sci-fi film (a loose adaptation of Arthur Conan Doyle's 1912 novel *The Lost World*) featured badly animated dolls as its monsters. As luck would have it, Harvey was serving as the casting director on *Hot Ice*, a job for which he was paid $1500. Because of his previous connection to Harvey, Thayer showed up at a *Hot Ice* casting session at Apostolof's office on 3518 West Cahuenga Boulevard, initially reading for a relatively small part as a bartender. According to Thayer,

> I started reading the lines, but suddenly Steve interrupted me and turned to the other guy present at the casting and said, "Let's get him to read the lines of Winford Farthington!" Ten minutes later, I got the role."⁵⁵
>
> I had to start somewhere but had no ties in the film business. I was coming from nowhere, and I was just trying to get some work done. *Ilsa, Harem Keeper of the Oil Sheiks* was my first movie. I did not have the privilege of choosing my roles, so I was very happy when they offered me a role in it. I was very excited until the movie came out on screen. Then I watched it and said, "Good Lord!" *Ilsa* is like a tattoo. You can't get rid of it, you can just try to keep it hidden." With *Hot Ice*, the situation was quite different; there was nothing of the blood and torture of *Ilsa*. *Hot Ice* was just innocent fun and a perfectly legitimate way to become an actor."⁵⁶

"Fun" is the operative word here. For Apostolof, *Hot Ice* was an excuse to mix business with pleasure. During the day, he and his actors would ski and ride snowmobiles. In the evening, he'd take the cast to dinner. Thayer was particularly impressed with Apostolof's sense of style: "After a day of shooting, we would always go out for dinner. Steve was ordering, and he always knew what wine goes with which food, how the meals should be prepared. He was quite continental and sophisticated in this respect."⁵⁷

"Steve liked to eat out, he liked the good food, he liked good wine," confirms Harvey Shain. "He always gave you the impression that he knew what to order in a restaurant. He had a continental charm. And of course women fell for that, they liked Steve. Even though he wasn't that good-looking. Ha ha ha! Well, he was okay."⁵⁸

One evening, Thayer went skiing with Apostolof's son Steve, contrary to the rules of most film productions. Normally, this sort of thing wouldn't be allowed out of fear that the main actor could get injured, and that would disrupt the shooting schedule. As might be expected from a low-budget production such as *Hot Ice*, some of the actors had to perform their own stunts. None of them had ever ridden a snowmobile before. Thayer knew how to ride a motorcycle, a skill that later helped him land a role in *Do It in the Dirt* (1979, dir. Joe Tornatore), a dirt-biking film starring Frank Sinatra, Jr., so the always inventive Apostolof made him change his clothes and play two roles. "That's how I found myself in the absurd situation that in one of the scenes I'm chasing myself with a snowmobile in two consecutive shots," explains Thayer. This was hardly a first for Apostolof. In *Orgy of the Dead,* Pat Barrington played two roles and so at one point, her character watched herself dancing.

There is some debate over Ed Wood's involvement in *Hot Ice*. Officially, he is listed in both the opening credits and the pressbook as Apostolof's assistant director. In an interview with the website *Nanarland*, Thayer mentions Wood's "attempt at acting," which corresponds with what filmmaker Ted Newsom says during the introduction to the DVD version of *Hot Ice*.[59] According to Newsom, Apostolof maintained that Ed Wood had no input whatsoever in the script. Eddie simply came in to do a cameo, Apostolof insisted. But no evidence of this can be found in the finished film. Apostolof clarified:

> [Ed] was the assistant director and I also wanted him to play the small part of a janitor who almost interrupts a jewel heist. We shot his scene in the morning and I was lining up the shot and looking through the lens when Eddie starts making all this noise—blonk! blonk!—hitting the set and banging around a bucket and big, heavy mop he was carrying. I said, "Eddie, what are you doing?! You're going to wake up the dead!" Then I saw his eyes and knew he was drunk as a skunk. I said, "How can you be drunk at ten o'clock in the morning?!"[60]

Apostolof had no choice but to call a taxi and send Wood home. The role of the janitor was then given to Robert Kanters, a film distributor and a close associate of Apostolof, hired as a set photographer. "Next morning," Apostolof remembered sadly, "[Ed] came to me crying…. It's a sickness. It was so hard for him. I was so sorry when he died."[61]

For what it's worth, Wood did list *Hot Ice* among his writing credits on his self-curated résumé.[62] It is unlikely, though, that Apostolof would have denied Wood proper writing credit on this final movie. In the finished film, Apostolof shares credit for the script with two other writers. The first is his wife Shelley, who is credited as S.B. Cooper, based on her maiden name of Shelley Barbara Cooper. Shelley had also been an associate producer on *Fugitive Girls*, *Drop-Out Wife* and *The Beach Bunnies* as well as a production coordinator on *The Snow Bunnies* and *The Class Reunion*. The other credited author is Pam Eddy, who co-wrote Ted V. Mikels' *The Doll Squad* (1973) and worked as a script supervisor on exploitation films from 1969 to 1979; this was her first and last movie with Apostolof.

In *Hot Ice*, a husband-and-wife con artist team (Thayer and Kelley) decide to hide out from Interpol by visiting a remote ski lodge under stolen identities, posing as wealthy socialites Winford and Charlotte Farthington. At the hotel, they learn that temperamental rock star Diamond Jim is performing at the resort and keeps a quarter-million dollars in diamonds in a safe behind the main desk. Even though they're on vacation and trying to lay low, they can't resist such a target and steal the "ice"[63] by using a rather amazing gadget: a fake jewelry case that can secretly record the numbers of a combination lock.

This presents a major crisis for poor, put-upon Victor (Harvey Shain), a nervous, bumbling innkeeper who decides to play detective and recover the gems himself, thus sparing the hotel's reputation. Victor is so worried about the goings-on at his hotel that he is oblivious to the fact that his wife Danielle (Parker) is having an affair with her ski instructor (one-film wonder Bob Anderson) and *another* with Winford, who distracts her with sex while Charlotte steals the diamonds. Everything gets sorted out in a wacky snowmobile chase, and the film concludes with an award ceremony, along with a tag that optimistically or naively sets up a possible sequel.

As befits an Apostolof movie, the consumption of alcohol is a major motif. The

Director of photography Guy Nicholas guides a camera operator during the filming of the nude dance scene in *Hot Ice*.

characters occasionally express their love of cognac, and several scenes revolve around a bar called Kelly's, where a few female Ski Club members get so tipsy that they strip down to their underwear in the middle of the dance floor. One poor damsel gets so hammered that she falls down in the snow on her way back to the lodge and has to be rescued.

Whether or not Ed Wood was involved in the creation of the screenplay, *Hot Ice* still has plenty of the odd, stilted dialogue that fans of Apostolof's 1970s movies have come to know and love. Take, for instance, an early scene in which Victor and Allan are shamelessly eyeing some sexy ski bunnies in the lobby before being caught by Danielle, who herself is shamelessly cheating on Victor. Their conversation consists mostly of clumsy exposition. (A sample line from Allan: "Being Diamond Jim's manager, I always have to take care of his valuables!") It almost sounds as if it were written in another language and then clumsily translated into English.

But the movie's single best line belongs to Victor, who berates a shiftless underling named Charlie (Richard Bergman, whose twitchy, giggly performance deserves to be studied). When Charlie says he can't pick up one of the hotel's wealthy guests because the cast on his leg (a fake, we'll soon learn) prevents him from driving, Victor's line is one for the ages: "Hmm! You know, you young guys are all the same! I mean it! You come here for one reason and one reason only ... bummin' around, booze and broads!"

Even though Apostolof was attempting to ape the James Bond franchise, *Hot Ice* more closely resembles the long-running TV series *The Love Boat* (1977–87). The Matterhorn ski lodge is analogous to the *Pacific Princess,* the famous cruise ship—an isolated, slightly exotic location where people from various walks of life frolic and interact. *Hot Ice* merely lacks *Love Boat*'s budget and bottomless well of guest stars. It makes up for those elements by adding just enough sex and nudity to warrant an R rating. Matterhorn staffers Victor, Danielle and Charlie are counterparts to the crew of the *Pacific Princess*. Kelly's is just a more raucous version of the bar presided over by *Love Boat*'s Isaac Washington (Ted Lange). Characters like the Farthingtons and Diamond Jim are very much like the roles given to the guest stars on the TV series.

Hot Ice's mildly smutty jokes would be very much at home in a *Love Boat* episode, too. Take, for instance, the scene in which Danielle tells Victor that she's going to a ski lesson with her instructor, Erik, and says, "He thinks my form is improving!" Cut to Erik and Danielle in bed together. "Your form is really improving!" enthuses Erik. Ba-dum-bum!

Since this is an Apostolof film, there is more nudity than one would expect in a typical diamond heist film, but it's important to note how careful Apostolof was here to distinguish *Hot Ice* from his previous softcore sex romps. The one big nude scene takes place at the bar and involves a trio of female skiers (including Linda Gildersleeve from *Beach Bunnies*) getting a little stewed and showing some skin on the dance floor. Just breasts this time, nothing below the waist. And there's not even a hint of any hanky panky in this scene. It's just some good old-fashioned drunken exhibitionism, divorced from any sexual context. In the bedroom scenes, the characters go out of their way to keep their naughty bits under wraps. So *Hot Ice* has both nudity and sex, just not together. It's a testament to this film's wholesomeness that porn star Ric Lutze never even takes his sweater off and is actually a little embarrassed by the antics of the topless ladies.

The catchy but slightly cheesy score for *Hot Ice*, which contributes to its made-for-TV feel, is credited to Richard McCurdy. "*Hot Ice* was scored from a stock library," remembers McCurdy. "I supervised the selection and edited the cues to picture. The sound post-production was done at the Quality Sound Studios on Melrose Avenue."[64] According to McCurdy, Apostolof failed to pay him in full for his services.

Hot Ice includes some familiar pieces of stock music, including Alan Tew's "The Detectives," which serves as the opening credit theme, and Dennis Farnon's "King Conga," which underscores a comedic bedroom scene with Harvey Shain. Cartoon fans will recognize "King Conga" from such Nickelodeon series as *The Ren & Stimpy Show* and *SpongeBob SquarePants*, while "The Detectives" was often used on the BBC sketch comedy show *The Two Ronnies*.

Meanwhile, a shadowy organization called the Chasin-Shooter Group provided the movie's title song, which is crooned by Diamond Jim in a lounge to a smallish audience of tourists, plus the twangy ballad "Call Me Anytime." Unlike a real James Bond movie, *Hot Ice* does not have an elaborate, lengthy title sequence.

Besides *The Love Boat*, the other big cultural touchstone evoked by *Hot Ice* is the classic comedy *The Pink Panther* (1963, dir. Blake Edwards), starring Peter Sellers as heroically clumsy Inspector Clouseau. Apostolof may have wanted to make a Bond movie, but he seemingly followed the Clouseau template much more closely. According to his daughter Polly, "he loved that movie."[65] In *Hot Ice*'s very first scene, Charlotte and Winford are in their hotel room planning their next caper, which would have taken them to Rome, when they are confronted by Giroux (Jean-Claude Smith), a mustachioed, French-accented, trenchcoat-wearing Interpol agent. They let him into the room because they think he must be a bellboy. The impeccably mannered Giroux also turns out to be quite gullible, and our heroes are easily able to trap him in a clothes closet within just a few seconds of his big entrance. After the credits, Giroux is never seen again, so the Clouseau role is filled—quite ably—by klutzy hotel-manager-turned-detective Victor.

The similarities between *The Pink Panther* and *Hot Ice* go on and on. The original Clouseau film takes place in an exclusive ski resort and involves the theft of a valuable diamond. Just as Peter Sellers' diligent-yet-clueless Clouseau is unaware that his wife (played by French model-actress Capucine) is having an affair with the film's suave thief (David Niven), Victor is oblivious to the fact that *his* wife Danielle is carrying on with the swaggering Winford. The main comedic set piece from *Hot Ice*—a drawn-out, farcical sequence in which Victor arrives home earlier than expected, forcing Winford to hide in a closet while ski instructor Erik hides under the bed—is something straight out of a Blake Edwards movie. Coincidentally, Vincent Barbi, one of Apostolof's regulars, had the minor uncredited role of a gangster in *The Pink Panther*.

Like Peter Sellers' indefatigable investigator, Harvey Shain's character in *Hot Ice* takes himself very seriously but is looked upon as a bumbling idiot by everyone else, including Charlie who mocks him the second he leaves the room. Victor and Inspector Clouseau also share a penchant for injuring themselves. The fact that Shain ends this movie being hailed as a hero while encased in a full body cast is straight out of the Edwards-Sellers playbook. Victor's naiveté—analogous to Sellers' too-trusting nature in the Panther sequel *A Shot in the Dark* (1964, dir. Blake Edwards)—is demonstrated when he catches the Farthingtons red-handed with the diamonds and just assumes that they "found" them. (He's still convinced that they're classy millionaires.)

From a technical standpoint, *Hot Ice* is plagued with problems from start to finish. It contains more visible more boom mics—and boom mic shadows—than the average SCA film. At one point, there is even a boom mic at the bottom of the screen, pointing up at the actors. And even though *Hot Ice* was Apostolof's most lavish production in the 1970s, it still contains some of the same visual mismatches and unconvincing driving scenes as his cheaper movies. His directorial techniques hadn't really changed much since the 1960s. Haphazard zooms are plentiful here, and Apostolof certainly never lost his fondness for ending a scene with the image going blurry or starting a scene with a blurry image that then comes into focus.

Despite the movie's lack of commercial viability, Apostolof was obsessed with promoting *Hot Ice* and tried relentlessly to get the film distributed for years afterward, even as late as 1983. In pursuit of this goal, he used to haunt the office of a Los Angeles company called Manson International which distributed some of his previous films. Manson had its headquarters at 9145 Sunset Boulevard in the Aladdin Building, a nondescript two-story structure whose only distinction was a big brass Aladdin's lamp hanging over the entrance. Apostolof all but begged Manson boss Edmund Goldman to pick up *Hot Ice*. Todd Tranner, who worked in Manson International's shipping department at the time, recalls:

> [Apostolof] was a habitual visitor to Manson, often bringing a box of "stinkweed" cigars for Ed, which Ed would dispose of as soon as Steve was out of sight. Manson distributed such A.C. [Stephen] works as *Class Reunion, Snow Bunnies, Fugitive Girls* and *Lady Godiva Rides*, with its trailer narration: "Filmed on two continents ... in Hollywood!" Steve was presently trying to get Edmund to pick up his latest title, *Hot Ice*, a caper film with intended and unintended comic overtones, that unique A.C. Stephen blend. As I recall, it had almost no nudity, which didn't help the sale.[66]

Manson International was trying to elevate its corporate image at the time, so they were reluctant to acquire a shaky property like *Hot Ice*. Apostolof was having great difficulty selling the picture, as he openly confessed to Tranner and another Manson employee. According to Tranner, Apostolof was certain that *Hot Ice* was "his greatest film and possibly the last one his buddy Eddie Wood was capable of working on." Apostolof was concerned about Wood. "I'm worried about the son of a bitch. He just drinks and watches TV. If Manson distributes *Hot Ice*, it'll help Eddie," said Apostolof.[67] Such a deal never happened.

Like Rudolph Grey, Wood's most prominent biographer, Tranner grew up on the East Coast and was a big fan of Wood's *Bride of the Monster* (1955) and *Plan 9 from Outer Space* (1957). He watched these films every time they played on Zacherley's *Chiller Theatre*, a Saturday night showcase for classic horror movies on New York's Channel 11 WPIX. And so, intrigued, he asked Apostolof to bring Wood with him on his next visit to the Manson offices. He also suggested that all of them have lunch at the Cock'n Bull, a mock British tavern across the street, where they could "discuss the tender side of the 'The Super Swedish Angel' Tor Johnson," who'd appeared in a few Wood films. "Steve said Wood never leaves his chair unless he falls off it," remembers Tranner. "I pleaded some more and Steve said, 'If Manson distributes my *Hot Ice*, I'll bring Eddie to lunch.'"[68]

After Apostolof left Manson's premises, Tranner's colleagues described Wood to him as "a transvestite drunk" and said they didn't want him anywhere near the office. From that moment on, whenever they saw a distressed female on the street, they suggested that Tranner take her to lunch as it might be Ed Wood. It was akin to a popular joke from the 1920s: "Don't step on that spider, it might be Lon Chaney," referring to the great silent star.

Tranner recalls that the ribbing continued "up to the day in '78 when a despondent Apostolof came into the office and told us Eddie was dead. Steve mused, 'If Manson had picked up *Hot Ice*, maybe Eddie would still be alive and we could have lunch. That's something to think about.'"[69]

Wood's final years were anything but happy ones. According to Apostolof, Wood could not live in normal neighborhoods because he and his wife Kathy often quarreled violently and neighbors always complained about them. Apostolof himself was often the subject of their arguments. Kathy called Apostolof "the Bulgarian bastard"[70] and was certain that he was taking advantage of her naïve, gullible husband. In truth, working on the SCA films was probably giving the low-spirited Wood a reason to live in the 1970s. On some level, perhaps even Kathy knew that.

"Our relationship with Kathy was one of love-hate," said Apostolof. "One day she would be like, 'Oh, Steve! I'm so sorry, the house is such a mess.' I go there the next day and she would start bitching, 'You bastard! You use Eddie and you don't pay him enough!'"[71]

David Ward, a close friend of Wood and an actor in two of Apostolof's movies, remembers one of those terrible fights: "Kathy was complaining about Apostolof and Eddie happened to be nearby, so he said, 'Shut up, Kathy,' but she continued to fret. Then Ed just grabbed her head and slammed it into the wall."[72]

Apostolof's third wife Shelley also couldn't stand Wood. "My mother banned Eddie from coming to our house," Christopher Apostolof remembers. "She thought he was weird. I know that Ed came to my baby shower together with Criswell, who gave me a baby blanket. I still have the guest list and the gifts."[73]

The year 1978 proved to be a pivotal one for Apostolof in multiple ways. Not only did it mark the release of his final movie, *Hot Ice*, it was also the year that he lost one of his most loyal associates. On December 10, Ed Wood died at the age of 54 of heart disease. Years of drinking had ruined his body, and he and Kathy had been evicted from their Yucca Street apartment and were living with actor Peter Coe at 5636 Laurel Canyon Boulevard in North Hollywood.

Apostolof saw Wood's death coming. "Eddie wouldn't go to a doctor," he said. "Partly because of laziness or procrastination. I know it sounds silly, but it's the truth. Also he didn't want to hear the truth about himself. He did not like steak because he had no teeth. He just had neglected himself."[74]

Wood's health habits appalled Apostolof:

> He was like a drug addict. The most important thing was to procure drinking, and even the food was not so important. The bastard was eating dog food, and it was just very embarrassing. We'd go to a diner and eat hamburgers. Eddie loved hamburgers and fries. But he would take a hamburger and pour ketchup all over it. I told him, "Eddie, for heaven's sake, stop it! The waiters are giving us an evil eye!" He'd squeeze out the whole bottle and smile. He was putting ketchup on everything, including the chocolate cake.[75]

Some feel that Apostolof's creative decline after the late 1970s was due to Wood's death, since Wood wrote or co-wrote nearly all of Apostolof's later movies. Film critic Greg Goodsell sees it differently:

> I don't think Apostolof lost his muse when Ed Wood died. I think Apostolof just got sick of the whole thing. Let's not forget that there were sexploitation movies that failed to find their audience [when originally released]. Russ Meyer's *Faster, Pussycat! Kill! Kill!* may be a cult film today, but at the time, it was filmed for pennies and brought no money initially. Stephen Apostolof kept Ed Wood busy, but from what I know of Ed Wood's life, he was on his way out anyway. He was an end stage alcoholic. And in his last films, he doesn't look that good. He was on the way out.[76]

In an interview with Mike Vraney and James Elliot Singer,[77] Apostolof said,

> In the last few years of his life, Eddie lived with help from his friends. He could not keep any job. He was always drunk as a skunk. I'd give him something to write, he wouldn't do it. You have to

understand, I liked him a lot. Otherwise I wouldn't tolerate him. But his condition worsened progressively. He was getting together with drunkards who would start drinking today and will stop next week. People like John Agar. Do you know how these people looked? Like mummies! People like Aldo Ray, who acted in a porn movie. He looked like Porky Pig. Red![78]

The producer also explained his peculiar working relationship with Wood:

> He was a production director in several films. Whenever I made a movie, Eddie was with me. It was a tradition. He never stole or misused a single dollar in his life. Eddie was the most honest man I've ever known. But Eddie had no clue how to handle money. At the end of the month, he comes to me and cries, "Boss, can you borrow me 41 dollars and 13 cents?" I say, "Shit, Eddie! Why do you need exactly 43 dollars and 13 cents?" And he explains, "So much for the water, so much for the electricity, so much for the gas."[79]

Apostolof knew first-hand how bad things had become for Wood. "Ironically, I talked to Eddie a day or two before his death, and he was worried that he had been thrown out of his apartment on Yucca Street, which was a terrible place." Apostolof learned of Wood's passing a couple of hours after it happened. "Kathy Wood called me immediately," he said. "She told me that Ed died while watching TV. She had to tell me what happened because some friends asked and wanted to organize his funeral. I think that Eddie had always wanted to be buried as a bride."[80]

After learning of Wood's death, Apostolof called Criswell, but the famed prognosticator knew nothing about the funeral. Apostolof claims that when he tried to connect with Kathy Wood later that day, she seemed to disappear and he never saw or heard from her again.

Wood was cremated at the Utter McKinley Mortuary at 6240 Hollywood Boulevard (appropriately, the place where Bela Lugosi's funeral was held in 1956). His ashes were scattered in the Pacific Ocean near Malibu. Since Kathy did not allow Apostolof to attend the memorial service, he didn't even know that Wood had been cremated. He only learned about his friend's ultimate fate in 1984, when the topic came up during a conversation with Rudolph Grey in an interview for *Nightmare of Ecstasy: The Life and Art of Edward D. Wood*.

In his conversations with Grey, Apostolof said that Wood would often discuss the subject of death with him. Death was an omnipresent subject for Wood, not just in his films but in his short stories and books as well. A perfect example is his 1967 novel *Death of a Transvestite*, the tale of cross-dressing hitman Glen Marker, who winds up on Death Row and has only one last wish—to die in drag. Apostolof said, "In his book *Death of a Transvestite*, I think Ed described his own funeral. I had a sneaky feeling that maybe he didn't want anybody to be at his funeral. Because, even if he was cremated, they dress you, and he wanted to be dressed as a bride."[81]

According to the obituaries published a couple of days after Wood's demise, he was "buried" the day after he died. Criswell, Paul Marco, Buddy Hyde, David Ward and of course Kathy Wood attended the memorial service, which was led by ordained minister David De Mering, who had played co-pilot Danny in *Plan 9 from Outer Space*.

"Eddie often joked, who would go first, me or him," reminisced Apostolof. "I wanted to do something for him as a friend, like leaving a bottle of liquor in his coffin. Because that's what we did when [cameraman] Bill Thompson died. Bill loved black rum, so we put a bottle of 120 proof Jamaican in his casket."[82]

Apostolof says he even considered building a small memorial to Wood at the Brown Derby restaurant in Los Feliz. After their first meeting there in the mid–1960s, they continued to haunt the place in the ensuing years. According to Rudolph Grey, Wood genuinely liked Apostolof and felt close to him, something even Kathy Wood admitted. Apostolof told Grey:

> I know she liked me. Because I was the only producer who tolerated him. I also liked him, don't get me wrong. But he did a few things, without malice, simply because he had not thought about it. Like when he took the fucking photos from *Orgy of the Dead*. I had albums and albums with photos and he took them all. Why? To go and make $400. It would have cost $5 to make copies, and I would have been very happy to give them to him.

Ultimately, Apostolof mused to Grey, "Eddie was loyal to me and I was loyal to him. The only thing I regret is that I did not know about his funeral."

Part Three

The Last Mile to El Diablo (1979–2005)

Chapter 12

In Exile
(1979–1986)

In December 1978, a 29-year-old New Yorker named Lawrence Bianca attended a midnight screening of *Glen or Glenda* at the Thalia Theatre on Manhattan's Upper West Side. That unusual film, the most personal work of Bianca's favorite director Ed Wood, had been a TV staple when Bianca was growing up in the early 1960s. That "fateful day," as Bianca would call it later, changed his life forever. The young man—who'd been a part of the flourishing New York post-punk scene of the late 1970s under the pseudonym Rudolph Grey—began a massive research project about Wood. His findings led to the 1992 publication of *Nightmare of Ecstasy: The Life and Art of Edward D. Wood, Jr.*, a major biography of the idiosyncratic director. Grey ultimately emerged as the main driving force behind the revival of interest in Ed Wood's films.

A few months earlier, on the opposite coast, a frustrated and broke Ed Wood was living in one of L.A.'s most deprived neighborhoods, his alcoholism and numerous career setbacks having doomed him to poverty. Though he didn't live to see his films take on newfound notoriety in the 1980s and beyond, he did get a taste of his posthumous fame when he learned by letter that there would be a retrospective of his career in New York.

"Someone back East was having an 'Ed Wood Day' and were going to show his films, and when he got that letter, he was just ... thrilled," remembered Phil Cambridge, an artist who had worked with Wood at Pendulum Publications. "I mean, he brought it into work, and he read it to me twice and said, 'You read it!' I read it. He said, 'Isn't that nice that somebody remembers me, that someone thinks of me?' And Ed Wood, to me, had always been this old drunk who wrote porn."[1]

Wood died of a heart attack on December 10, 1978. Grey failed to meet him in time, which intensified the mystery surrounding his idol. Grey spent more than a decade feverishly collecting information about Wood's life and career. He sold his collection of posters of classic American films and borrowed money in order to continue his research. He interviewed dozens of Wood's colleagues, friends and relatives. Those conversations formed the basis of *Nightmare of Ecstasy*, which in turn became the inspiration for Tim Burton's 1994 biopic *Ed Wood*.

One of Grey's interview subjects was, naturally, Stephen C. Apostolof, whom Grey contacted by mail. In a letter dated April 7, 1984, Grey wrote:

Dear Mr. Apostoloff [sic],

    I am doing a book on the late Ed Wood Jr., which will basically be composed of interviews. The book is a serious one and will hopefully balance the scales as to the nonsense that has been written about Mr.

Wood. I will be in Los Angeles hopefully in a few weeks and would very much like to speak to you about your films and your association with Ed Wood. According to my research Ed worked on the story and/ or screenplay for the SCA films: Snow Bunnies, The Hostesses (Cocktail Hostesses), Dropout Wife [*sic*], Beach Bunnies, Hot Ice, Suburbia Confidential, Fugitive Girls *(I seem to recognize Ed Wood in the pressbook stills) and* Orgy of the Dead.

I would be very pleased if you consent to do an interview, your help would be invaluable to this project. I am also curious as to the current film projects of "A.C. Stephen."

Yours,
Rudolph Grey

Apostolof was more than happy to help Grey. He probably saw it as a chance to set the record straight. Finally, someone was interested in his version of the story as well as in the "current film projects of A.C. Stephen." Apostolof and Grey forged a friendship that would last more than 20 years.

In truth, Apostolof was also in dire need of attention by the time he received Grey's letter. His own career had taken a precipitous plunge by the end of the 1970s. The market for his brand of softcore erotica was rapidly evaporating, and *Hot Ice* proved that Apostolof could not breach the mainstream. By the time he turned 50 in 1978, it appeared that he had already outlived his usefulness in the movie world. But he still had a family to support and bills to pay. Things looked grim. According to his son Steve:

In 1979, Dad had taken out a second mortgage on the house on Sarah Street to process and distribute *Hot Ice*, but it hadn't worked out too well. The movie hadn't made much money. The video market was starting up, but the X-rated market was selling, not soft nudie films. Although the house had gone up in value, Dad's credit, a lack of income, and double-digit interest rates made a refinance impossible.[2]

Apostolof had no other choice but to sell the house. It went on the market in late 1979 with an asking price of $250,000 (the home is valued at over $2 million today). He was hoping for a quick sale, but the house lingered on the market for months. Luckily, he was able to borrow some money from a friend to spruce the house up a bit. He also hired a Studio City realtor named Mort Allen. Probably fooled by Apostolof's appearance and his Greek-sounding name (or perhaps intentionally, in order to lure potential buyers), Allen wrote in the real estate ad that the house was owned by "a Greek movie mogul" and "his starlet wife." This seemingly innocuous mistruth provoked an unexpected reaction from the Bulgarians at the St. George Eastern Orthodox church in Los Angeles. Christopher Apostolof: "They were furious. They said that Dad denied his Bulgarian roots, that he's pretending to be a Greek, that sort of bullshit. Dr. Matthew Jeikoff got angry at my father and said to him, 'Are you ashamed to say you're Bulgarian?' Dad's reaction was, 'What the hell are you talking about?! I've never seen this agent. I'm just trying to sell the house!'"[3]

After a few more months on the market, the house was sold to *General Hospital* actress Jackie Zeman. Apostolof had lost his home but was out of trouble financially. He received a good chunk of money in cash to live on, if not as lavishly as before. His son Steve Apostolof remembers:

Dad was classic house poor. He had a home that he owed less than $100,000 that was worth $250,000 or more back then, but he didn't have two nickels to rub together. I think his combined mortgages were about $900 a month, and after the sale he rented a condo for $1700 a month or almost twice that. The deal with Jackie had Dad carrying paper [i.e., retaining the mortgage] and supplied a semi-regular income for several years.[4]

After selling the house, Apostolof moved to a place south of Ventura Boulevard in Sherman Oaks, just behind Coldwater Canyon. It had been owned by one of his friends. After about nine months there, the Apostolofs moved to Encino, this time to a condo across the street from Lake Balboa Park.

In 1983, Apostolof rented a house in Westlake Village, a town of 10,000 people that straddles the Los Angeles and Ventura County line. Tucked in the foothills of the Santa Monica Mountains and just a short drive from Malibu's beaches, Westlake Village is known for its affluence and seclusion. It's considered one of the wealthiest communities in the greater Los Angeles area. Apostolof rented a 2500-square-foot home in a cul-de-sac neighborhood known as The Cove. In this tidy residential community, everything was very well maintained and rules were enforced.

Christopher:

> I think Dad saw Westlake as that idealized vision of suburban life. Thirty minutes to the beach, thirty minutes to the Valley, green lawns, the works. This condo was different from the house on Sarah Street, which was the "Hollywood producer" side of things. Who buys a house with a putting green and a guest house and a damn cutting and screening room? Only "Hollywood" does that. The problem with Westlake was one of pure boredom. And it was all new money. So, a lot of people spending money and a lot of drugs. A lot of parents working 12-hour days. And a lot of bored teenagers. Makes for a bad mix.[5]

The family's dream life Westlake Village quickly faded under the hot California sun. Christopher again: "There were a ton of cocaine problems in town and just some general drama, so we moved back to the San Fernando Valley for a couple of years to this total shithole in North Hollywood across the street from my school. We lived in this horrible second floor apartment directly above the landlord, who hated that we had a piano."[6] By 1984, Apostolof's financial situation was so dire, his family had to resort to using food stamps.

"I remember driving for fifteen miles, making sure that nobody that knew us will see us using food stamps," remembers Christopher. "Dad was so proud and that proudness was his downfall. He refused to take work for the studios. He was A.C. Stephen."[7]

But reality was closing in. Apostolof's platitudes were of little comfort to his family, especially as his old movies from the 1960s and '70s weren't generating much income any more. According to Christopher, "My dad used to say, 'Films are like a bag of flour. Shake it and something comes out.' One night, my mother got pissed off and said, 'Steve, can we just get a scoop and take some flour?' And she was right. There was nothing left to scoop out of the bag. Just shaking the crumbs and getting the dust. That was all left."[8]

In 1985, thanks to financing obtained through his attorney Harold A. Abeles, who had gone into investment banking, Apostolof was able to buy a Westlake Village condo at 1192 Landsburn Circle. "We saved enough cash after some junior high kids chased me home from school with a knife, and we moved back to the condo in Westlake," says Christopher.[9]

But real estate was never Apostolof's strong point. "Dad, never one to read the fine print, didn't realize that the loan had a pre-payment penalty that extended 36 months," explained Steve Apostolof. "He sold the condo in less than two years and got stuck for better than ten grand."[10]

While Apostolof spent the early 1980s largely out of the public eye, Ed Wood was making a startling comeback from beyond the grave. Rudolph Grey wasn't the only one interested in Wood. In 1980, film critics Michael and Harry Medved published a book called *The Golden Turkey Awards*, in which Wood's *Plan 9 from Outer Space* (1957) was called the Worst Film of All Time, based on more than 3000 ballots from readers, while Wood himself was given the Worst Director award. While its take on Wood seems outdated and unfair today, *The Golden Turkey Awards* nevertheless played a major role in turning Wood into a cult filmmaker during the Reagan years. Wood's ironic fame was largely based on smug condescension, including widespread mockery of his cross-dressing, but it kept his films in the public eye.

In the months following the publication of the Medveds' book, *Plan 9* continued to gain popularity, and in August 1980, the first Ed Wood Fest was held at the restored, historic Vista Theatre in West Hollywood. It was attended by three of Wood's closest companions, all of whom had appeared in his films: Conrad Brooks, Paul Marco and Criswell. Incognito among the audience were actors Warren Beatty and Diane Keaton, a sign that something important was happening.[11] The *Los Angeles Herald Examiner* wrote that *Plan 9* was becoming a cult film, not unlike *The Rocky Horror Picture Show* (1975, dir. Jim Sharman) had become a couple of years earlier. Keith Henry Schroeder, manager of the Vista, said he would show *Plan 9* just once because the rejuvenated cinema was "too fragile" to withstand the crowds of fans gathering up to see "the worst movie of all time."[12]

The Ed Wood phenomenon continued to gain strength in the coming months, with several festivals devoted to his films in various countries, including Australia. On May 23, 1981, the University of Southern California in Los Angeles held its first Ed Wood retrospective, screening five of his features along with numerous shorts and outtakes. Some observers even praised Wood as an *auteur* filmmaker.

"America's true *auteur* is Ed Wood," declared filmmaker Andrew Solt, co-director (with Malcolm Leo) of the 1982 compilation film *It Came from Hollywood,* featuring bizarre clips from vintage B-movies, including Ed's. "He wrote, produced and directed *Glen or Glenda* and starred in it as the transvestite. Now, can you get any more *auteur* than that?"[13] Solt's film included an entire Wood tribute segment hosted by comedian John Candy.

Eventually, as Wood's posthumous profile kept rising through the 1980s and '90s and his movies began to circulate again, his former colleague Apostolof finally started receiving some overdue recognition of his own. But this would take a while. At first, the general public didn't seem to know who exactly Apostolof was. In 1987, for example, the eighth issue of the underground magazine *Magick Theatre* (devoted to "Film Esoterica & Weird Science") ran a lengthy review of *Orgy of the Dead* which posited a crackpot theory of its own: Stephen C. Apostolof ("a relatively obscure filmmaker whose previous credits are so far unknown") never existed; the name was merely one of Wood's many professional aliases. Writer Raymond Young went on to speculate that the seven films Apostolof made after *Orgy of the Dead* were, in fact, directed by Ed Wood. Young wrote:

> One may scoff at the theory of Wood and Stephens [sic] being one in the same, but consider the possibilities.[…] Aside from camerawork more fluid than, say, *Bride of the Monster*, ample close-ups and

cutting, and scenes which appear to have been rehearsed (something Wood's 1950s budgets wouldn't allow), the dialog, delivery, situations and "denouements" have that unmistakable Woodian feel to them. If the seven post–*Orgy of the Dead* pictures are by Wood, then a significant discovery has been made—but not only in terms of celluloid. They would mark an incredibly productive point in Wood's life between writing and directing (with an actual crew), admirable in determination and drive. Yes, it may be schlock; but any man who can knock out seven films and about ten novels within ten years should get some positive recognition.[14]

Yes, strange as it may sound, some people actually thought Apostolof and Wood were one and the same. Cult film critic Greg Goodsell elaborates: "Ed Wood used a lot of pseudonyms, and a lot of people said, 'Hey, that's probably one of Ed's pseudonyms!' But it wasn't! Apostolof was a very proper, straight-shooting guy and kept a very low profile, so many people just got in their heads that this was just another pseudonym for Ed."[15]

Once Apostolof stopped making films in the late 1970s, he lost touch with a lot of his showbiz friends and collaborators. Criswell died in 1982. He was the last person from the cast of *Orgy of the Dead* Apostolof ever saw. Marsha Jordan moved to Fresno and married a wealthy businessman. She kept in touch with Apostolof through occasional Christmas postcards. The actress passed away in 2013. Rene Bond got out of the porn business, married and started working in a bank. The only person with whom Apostolof stayed in touch was Harvey Shain, who got out of the film industry and returned to his theatrical roots, making a couple of national tours with the horror musical *Little Shop of Horrors* and the perennial *West Side Story*.

Back in the mid–1960s, when Ed Wood penned his semi-autobiographical advice guide *Hollywood Rat Race*, he had made a bold prediction regarding his most famous work with Apostolof: "Our newly released *Orgy of the Dead* will be a pleasant surprise; it was filmed using a widescreen process and exciting color. It could well become a classic in its field."[16] Wood's book was not published until 1998. By then, his prediction had indeed come true, but it took a couple of decades.

The person who helped turn *Orgy of the Dead* into "a classic" was one Martin Margulies, better known as Johnny Legend, a rockabilly musician, occasional actor and wrestling manager. Growing up, Legend had been a close friend of the legendary Tor Johnson, of *Plan 9 from Outer Space* fame, even hanging out at the actor-wrestler's home. He'd met Ed Wood during a visit to the home of *Famous Monsters of Filmland* founder Forrest J Ackerman in the 1960s. "He was nice," remembers Legend, "and he accused me of being the first Ed Wood fan."[17]

Legend was destined to meet Apostolof, too. "I first tracked Steve down around 1972 when Ed Wood was still alive, and there was no conceivable market for the film at that time," Legend recalls. "Then, ten years later, I found him again, told him now we can do something with the film, and single-handedly dragged him kicking and screaming into the cult universe."[18]

At first, Apostolof was not particularly thrilled by the prospect of reviving *Orgy of the Dead*, which he considered one of his weakest films. His initial reaction was to point out that he had produced more than a dozen adult films superior to *Orgy*. Nevertheless, Legend was instrumental in the revival of interest in Apostolof's films in the 1980s. He managed to convince Rhino Entertainment, a Los Angeles–based novelty and nostalgia reissue label, that *Orgy* needed to be rediscovered, released on video, and put back into theaters.

"Our most notorious release was *Orgy of the Dead*, a little-seen movie written by

Apostolof shakes hands with Johnny Legend during the Ed Wood Fest organized by Rhino Home Video in 1988. The person between them is Richard Foos, one of the founders of Rhino Records.

the world's worst director, Ed Wood," Harold Bronson, co-founder of Rhino Records, remembered. "It required considerable detective work from Martin [Margulies] to track down *Orgy*'s producer, Stephen Apostolof. Contrary to public opinion, Apostolof considered Ed 'a great filmmaker and a great man.' Unlike some of Ed's more interesting bad movies, this one is little more than strippers dressed as ghouls disrobing in a graveyard set. Wood adapted it from his, ahem, novel."[19]

And so, in April 1985, almost two decades after its premiere, *Orgy of the Dead* had a "re-premiere" at the Nuart, an art deco theater opened in the early 1940s and a staple of the Los Angeles arthouse scene since the 1970s. Apostolof attended this screening. Johnny Legend: "That was the night Steve finally understood the cult and Ed Wood audience for the film and announced that he had no idea that he had accidentally made a 'grand comedy.' That stayed with him because during the last ten years when I would run into him at events or the American Film Market, he was always pitching the *Orgy of the Dead* sequel, script in hand."[20]

Legend wasn't the only alternative musician to embrace Apostolof's films. Around 1985, some of the old SCA titles were sold as bootlegs by Howie Pyro, a 25-year-old veteran of the punk scene. Pyro was a friend of Sid Vicious (and one of the last people to see the former Sex Pistols bassist alive) and had been a founding member of the glam punk band D Generation. In Pyro's own words, he started an "early video empire" after finding Apostolof's *Fugitive Girls* in the porno section of a video store in 1985. Pyro posted an ad proclaiming "RARE LOST ED WOOD FILM!" in *Fangoria*, the most prominent horror publication in the world back at the time.

"The whole thing brought in so many people I knew in the past, like Lux Interior, and people I met later on, like Larry Hardy and Haunted George," says Pyro. "I couldn't handle the responsibility when it got too big for me to deal with alone. I thank the dark lord that Mike [Vraney] came along and did what he did, better than anyone else ever could or would, still to this day."[21]

In 1990, Mike Vraney (1957–2014) founded Something Weird Video, a Seattle-based company that specializes in reissuing vintage exploitation and sexploitation films, particularly those from the 1960s and '70s. While perhaps most closely associated with the movies of Herschell Gordon Lewis and Doris Wishman, Something Weird Video also handled many of Apostolof's films. In the late 1990s, the company put out a series of VHS tapes called *The Erotic World of A.C. Stephen*. Later, when DVD supplanted VHS, Vraney's company issued DVD-R versions of the Apostolof films.

In the 1980s, Apostolof was busy selling other producers' films, but he was still a creative person at heart, and he never truly gave up on the idea of being a filmmaker. Rudolph Grey says, "He had all these projects, movies he wanted to do through the years, which he could never get the money for. Films like *Savage Fugitives, Terrorist Girl, State of Fear* and, of course, *Orgy of the Dead II*."[22]

Of the unrealized Apostolof films, a thriller called *State of Fear* (also known as *Agent Orange*) might be the most intriguing. The screenplay, written in the early 1980s, involves an American military truck which crashes; the leaking nerve gas turns the troops into zombies that wreak havoc on a camp with counselors and kids in the wilderness. Apostolof allegedly was inspired by Agent Orange and the U.S. herbicidal warfare program during the Vietnam War.[23]

Apostolof's son Steve described *State of Fear* as "kind of horror, but there's reality there. Nerve gas gets all over the place. Dad had the whole idea, but it would have been really tough at that time to put that together. It was a location shoot. It had kids in it. It wasn't an adult film at all. It would probably be rated R, because there's lot of gore in it."[24]

"Things are the same here in sunny California," Apostolof wrote to Rudolph Grey in August 1986. "Am busy with all kinds of things, primarily with distribution and foreign sales (which I HATE) but what can you do, we all have to eat and smoke those big cigars."[25]

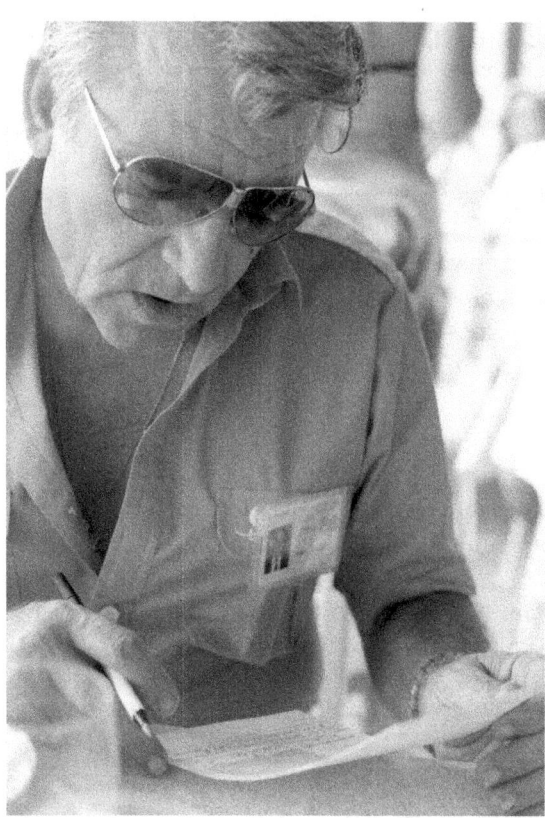
Apostolof examines a document at the 39th Cannes Film Festival in 1986.

In the 1980s, Apostolof started

working with Conrado "Boy" Puzon (born in 1949), a Philippine distributor who bought cheaply made Filipino films through his company F. Puzon Film Enterprises, then refurbished and dubbed them into foreign languages and sold them to video and film distributors around the world. Apostolof represented Puzon's company and sold its films at various film markets such as Marché du Film and MIPCOM (Cannes), MIFED (Milan) and American Film Market (Los Angeles). Some of the films that Apostolof was selling in the mid–80s were *The Firebird Conspiracy* (1984, dir. Jun Gallardo and Vittorio Romero) and the Anthony Alonzo starrer *W Is War* (1983, dir. Willy Milan).

The *State of Fear* and *Savage Fugitives* projects caught the attention of Vestron Video. Based in Stamford, Connecticut, the company was one of the pioneers in the home video market. In the mid–1980s, it started making its own films: *Dirty Dancing* (1987, dir. Emile Ardolino), *Earth Girls Are Easy* (1988, dir. Julien Temple) and *Blue Steel* (1990, dir. Kathryn Bigelow).

"The people from Vestron read the scripts and now they want me to submit to them the budgets, tentative casts, etc.," Apostolof wrote to Grey. "It is a pain in the ... but what can I do, I must prepare these items for them, who knows, maybe something will break through.... In the meantime I'm keeping everything crossed ... fingers ... hands ... balls ... don't want to take a chance on this one."[26]

None of the projects got funded, but Apostolof kept working on *State of Fear* in the years to come. Christopher Apostolof maintains it was the last screenplay his father ever worked on. "He had actually broken that whole script down," says Christopher. "Nowadays, we think of that with computers, but of course, Steve didn't use computers. Back in the day, he actually used to break things down with breakdown boards, and every strip [of paper] is actually a different scene that's going to be shot for all the dailies."[27]

Apostolof was constantly revising the *State of Fear* screenplay. He started writing it around 1983 and one of the roles was supposed to be played by Christopher, who was taking acting lessons. As Christopher grew, his father would alter the screenplay, adapting it to suit an older actor. Christopher: "I had three roles in *State of Fear* over the years. Originally, I was the kid in peril, then I went to camp counselor, then later I was going to be one of the military commanders. Poor Dad worked on that script for years. He really felt like it was something he was going to be able to get made."[28]

Apostolof's finances simply didn't allow for an ambitious project like this. The filmmaker had been forced to take his Social Security at age 59 because he wasn't working and had no money. "If you took it at 59," Christopher explains, "you lost half of your money. But he was so broke at that point so he had to take it as soon as he could. And of course, he didn't have retirement. It was literally a state pension."[29]

Chapter 13

The Resurrection (1987–1997)

> "Orgy of the Dead suggests Flaming Creatures or Inauguration of the Pleasure Dome as envisioned by someone whose hallucinogens of choice are airplane glue and Ripple."—J. Hoberman, *The Village Voice*[1]

On February 25, 1987, the eve of his 59th birthday, Stephen C. Apostolof received a gift for which he had been waiting more than three decades. After spending two-thirds of his life as an immigrant, he finally became a citizen of the United States, the country where he'd spent most of his adult life. The event was cause for a modest family celebration. His daughter Polly made a special plate inscribed "To Our Favorite Citizen" and got all her siblings to sign it.

That same year, Apostolof was invited to present *Orgy of the Dead* at the Tokyo International Fantastic Film Festival—an unofficial but very popular part of the Tokyo International Film Festival, established two years earlier. The official Japanese premiere was organized by a company called GAGA Communications, which had purchased the overseas distribution rights to *Orgy of the Dead* from Rhino, the official American distributor, in 1986. The Japanese company decided to distribute the "eccentric" (in their own words) film theatrically, convinced this would boost video sales. Apostolof boasted that the Japanese ordered 6000 videotapes of the film in advance. As excited as he was, though, he was still a bit skeptical of his film's late-blooming success. "They are entering *Orgy of the Dead* in the competition and I have a funny feeling that I might get some stupid award or something like that for a film that I made over 20 years ago," Apostolof wrote to his friend Robert Kanters in June 1987.[2]

A week before leaving for Japan, Apostolof met his old pal, *Orgy of the Dead* cameraman Robert Caramico, and shared the good news. But, as Apostolof remembered, Caramico was worried that his past was coming back to haunt him. "He cried, 'Don't you dare mention my name while in Japan!' I told him, 'Don't worry, Mr. Rubin, I won't!' 'Robert Rubin' was the pseudonym Caramico used when he shot *Orgy of the Dead*. At the time he was shooting the TV series *Dallas* and didn't want anyone to know that he was doing these movies. I totally understood him."[3]

The trip was a proud moment in Apostolof's long career. He left for Japan on September 23, 1987, via Singapore Airlines and landed at Tokyo's Narita International Airport, where he was met by GAGA representative Ken Hirosava. For the next week, all of Apostolof's needs were met. He was accommodated at Roppongi, a deluxe hotel near

Tokyo Tower, and was provided with a translator for his entire stay. All he was obliged to do in return was make himself available for press conferences during his visit.

The Japanese premiere of *Orgy of the Dead* generated a wave of publicity with reviews in *Playboy* magazine (Japan) and influential publications such as *Studio Voice* and *Heibon Punch*. GAGA spent around 2 million yen (about $17,000 in today's money) promoting *Orgy*. It ballyhooed the film with small paper fans depicting a boy wearing a blue kimono with the *Orgy* logo. They also hired a troupe of dancers wearing bandanas emblazoned with the film's title. The dancers drummed and danced their way through the streets of Tokyo as a Buddhist priest chanted. Never one to shy away from a bit of fun, Apostolof

Apostolof poses with a Buddhist monk in front of the Kaminarimon, one of the two large entrance gates leading to the ancient Buddhist temple Sensō-ji in Asakusa, Tokyo.

danced right along with them. Apostolof proudly recalled, "The film was screened from a very good copy on a big screen, and it looked like a million dollars. The president of GAGA joked, 'When I die, I want to be buried with some of those beauties.' I told him, 'Be careful what you wish for, because, you know, they turn into skeletons with the sunrise.'"[4]

During his stay in Tokyo, Apostolof seriously considered making *Orgy of the Dead II*. He discussed the idea with the GAGA representatives, who were more than enthusiastic. "This time we can make it international," enthused Apostolof. "We'll include a Japanese, a Swedish, an American, South American, Indian, etc."

The Japanese moneymen wanted horror host Cassandra Peterson aka Elvira, Mistress of the Dark to play the Empress of the Night. Apostolof started dreaming big and envisioned Cesar Romero or Vincent Price replacing the late Criswell. "Better hurry, because they're not getting any younger," joked Rudolph Grey.

Neither was Apostolof, unfortunately. The *Orgy* sequel, subtitled *The New Generation*, never happened in his lifetime. Apostolof started working on the script in the early 1980s and dedicated it "to Eddie Wood and Criswell." It was full of ironic self-references and nods to sci-fi franchises like *Star Trek* and *Star Wars*. The idea for the sequel stayed with Apostolof for the rest of his days.

Initially, the action in *Orgy of the Dead II* was supposed to take place in the sea or in an ancient Indian burial ground, complete with totem poles. But then Apostolof decided to shift the action to Mars in the year 3000. The film begins with a mission to the Red Planet, a routine trip that goes wrong when the shuttle explodes, just like how Bob and Shirley's Chevrolet Corvair crashed into the cemetery in the original film. Apostolof planned to use the same four main characters from *Orgy*, but this time instead of being tied to the cemetery gates, Bob and Shirley were going to be enclosed in an electric cell, where they couldn't move but only sit. The set of *Orgy of the Dead II* was supposed to be all white, very similar in appearance to the planet Krypton in *Superman: The Movie* (1978, dir. Richard Donner). But Apostolof's Mars would not be covered in snow, as Donner's Krypton had been. The ever-grandiose Apostolof envisioned his film ending with a triple sunrise—bad news for the creatures of the night!

"I will not talk about [*Orgy of the Dead II*]. I'll just say that it'll take place in a similar setting as the first one but will be very philosophical in many, many ways," Apostolof said in an interview included in the DVD extras of the Rhino Home Video edition of *Orgy of the Dead*, released in 2004. "I'm taking a poke at us. At society. As human beings. What we do. How we do it. It'll start with something happening with a little spaceship or a probe. And there'll be very good discussions between the 'guests' and 'the Emperor.'"

Apostolof envisioned *Orgy of the Dead II* as being more substantial than the original, discussing issues such as teenage suicides, the drug problem, and the gangs terrorizing New York. The film was going to end with the Emperor of the Night addressing the viewers: "We are you and you are us!"

But the sequel would

A cover for the 2004 Rhino Home Video DVD edition of *Orgy of the Dead*. Note the prominence of Ed Wood's name.

resemble the original in many ways, too. "There'll be dancing in it," Apostolof clarified. "There's nothing wrong with dancing. Dance is one of the most primitive expressions of the human being. Even dogs dance in their own way. So there will be dancing in it. It just won't be 90 minutes of dancing and 10 minutes of dialogue."[5]

As for the fact that two decades had transpired since the first film, Apostolof was apparently unconcerned. He explained,

> Getting a new Criswell will be easy. I'll have Johnny Legend be in charge of finding a new Criswell look-alike. And I have a fantastic ending. Right now I have a treatment for *Orgy of the Dead II*. And I'm concentrating on who the people are. Because in the first *Orgy*, the characters were barely introduced. For example, the girl who worshipped gold is turned into gold. The bride who murdered her husband now lives with his skeleton. And so on. This time, I'll show what happened, in a flashback, why he or she is the way they are. Also, what do you know about the Wolfman and the Mummy? What's their relationships? What is the sex of the Mummy? Is the Mummy a man or a woman? I'm gonna show that the mummy is a girl.[6]

The original *Orgy of the Dead* was released on video in Japan on October 21, 1987. Apostolof sold the broadcasting rights for the film to Nippon Columbia Co. for five years, agreeing on a 60 percent split in the company's favor. In the meantime, the film started playing at several theaters, including Nakano Masashino Hall, Nagoya Cinematheque, Jab 70 Hall and Osaka Apple Theater. In March 1988, Apostolof received the first sales reports for the film, which brought a total net profit of $5106 (around $10,000 in today's money).

Orgy's popularity continued to grow. On April 26, 1988, Rhino organized an Ed Wood festival called Woodstock at the Nuart Theatre and hired *Golden Turkey Awards*

Nuart Movie Theatre marquee advertising Rhino's Ed Wood festival with a mistaken middle initial.

co-author Harry Medved to host it. The program included *Glen or Glenda*, *The Violent Years* and *Orgy of the Dead*, which was billed as Wood's "only full color masterpiece." The next day, Johnny Legend presented his *Sleazemania!*, a compilation that included Apostolof's *College Girls*. Apostolof was once again on hand to present the film.[7]

"In those days, you could sell almost anything," says Arny Schorr, who was running Rhino's video division at the time. "Video stores were still opening, retailers were more willing to take quirky releases and *Sleazemania!* was quirky. But films always sold better than compilation videos and it helped *Orgy of the Dead* which was sold as a rough follow-up of *Plan 9 from Outer Space*."[8]

In 1989, excerpts from *Orgy of the Dead* were included in *The Incredibly Strange Film Show*, a series of British-made documentaries hosted by Channel 4's Jonathan Ross. The show focused on cinematic oddities, mostly of the low-budget variety. Other directors showcased on the series included John Waters, Doris Wishman and Herschell Gordon Lewis. Ross' series also included episodes about Mexican wrestling films and Hong Kong horror. Apostolof's films were starting to gain an unexpected new audience among connoisseurs of the bizarre.

In 1990, exactly 25 years after it was made, *Orgy of the Dead* finally had its official British premiere at Scala, a thousand-seat repertory theater opened in 1920 in the King's Cross area of London. Invited to present the film, Apostolof left from Los Angeles on May 23, his two suitcases weighed down with film cans. *Orgy* was being screened as part of the Edward D. Wood Festival, the first U.K. fest dedicated to the life and career of the "worst director of all time." Ten years earlier, in November 1980, Michael Medved had visited Scala while promoting his *Golden Turkey Awards* book and had presented *Plan 9 from Outer Space* and *Glen or Glenda*. The U.K. premiere of *Orgy of the Dead* was part of the promotion for the 1990 video releases of *Orgy* and Ed Wood's own *Night of the Ghouls* (1959) by a company called Mondo Video.

The festival was organized by eccentric musician Bal Croce, whose goal was to clear Ed Wood's name from the ridiculous label the Medveds had given him a decade earlier. Croce was a vocalist in a British psychobilly band called the Sting-Rays and owner of the Psychotronic video store in London, where one could find copies of obscure films such as Ray Dennis Steckler's *The Incredibly Strange Creatures Who Stopped Living and Became Mixed-Up Zombies!!?* (1964) and *Rat Pfink a Boo Boo* (1966).

"We were just trying to think of more and more ridiculous things that we could put on, things that were more than just cinema," says Croce, a fan of vintage B-movies whose company released its own home video edition of *Plan 9*. Educating the public was Croce's motivation behind creating the festival. "We really wanted to set the record straight," Croce claims.[9] To that end, they invited Apostolof to the event.

"Apostolof assumed he would be staying in a top West End hotel, but he ended up in [writer] Marc Isted's flat," jokingly remembers Damon Wise, a contributing editor to *Empire* magazine who helped organize the event.[10]

"Steve Apostolof was quite a character," Croce remembers. "He had a white silk suit, gold rings, and smoked Havana cigars. He was about five foot high and spoke in a very thick Bulgarian accent."[11]

At 9:00, Saturday night, May 26, 1990, Apostolof, "everything you'd ever imagined a low-budget exploitation freak to be"[12] and "dapper in a natty *Our Man in Havana* number,"[13] was called up on stage to answer questions posed by the audience. Bal Croce presented Apostolof as "a nudie Bulgarian director," which irked the filmmaker a bit. "I told them to stop making such a big deal about where I was born," Apostolof said. "Everyone is born somewhere! […] We're all Americans here."[14]

The evening was a success. "*Orgy* went down a storm," remembers Jane Giles, who was the programmer at the Scala from 1988 to 1992. "A.C. Stephen's accent got in the way of him talking audibly about anything, but he was very jolly and signed our file copy of the programme."[15]

"So, a bramah time was had by all," remembered author Howard Lake. "Even Apostolof quoting Schopenhauer at turgid length and spelling my girlfriend's name wrong on the programme couldn't diminish it."[16]

While on stage giving his lecture, Apostolof couldn't resist telling the famous story of his first meeting with Ed Wood at the Brown Derby. The people in the audience might not have known what he was talking about. Bal Croce recalls,

> We didn't think we'd have any problems, but we didn't bank on his accent, which was very thick. And he just stood there for about half an hour, just [*imitates Apostolof's heavy accent*], "Oh, yes, ho ho ho! Eddie Wood! Eddie Wood! And the camera, and the film…" Nobody understood him. And then he had a load of trailers for his films, which he confided in me that he'd spent a lot of time putting it together himself especially. The first one came up with no problems. The second one, he'd spliced it in upside down and back-to-front, which got a good cheer and made him walk out of the theater in disgust. I had to go after him and bring him back, but that was all right. It was a good night.[17]

Even before Tim Burton's *Ed Wood* hit movie screens in the fall of 1994, documentaries about Wood started springing up like toadstools after a rainstorm. Naturally, Apostolof participated in several, appearing every inch the suave, well-dressed movie producer of yore. In 1992, he was one of the talking heads in *Flying Saucers Over Hollywood: The Plan 9 Companion* (1992, dir. Mark Patrick Carducci), a modest but informative direct-to-video production about Wood's most famous film. It was another opportunity for Apostolof to tell the story of his infamous Brown Derby meeting with Wood, the one where Wood appeared wearing an angora sweater, boots and a three-day beard. Apostolof also participated in the documentary *Ed Wood: Look Back in Angora* (1994) and supplied some behind the scenes 16mm footage of the making of *Orgy of the Dead*. Its director Ted Newsom remembered, "Arny Schorr, the head of Rhino's video department, called me and said, 'How would you like to do an Ed Wood documentary? We will call it *Ed Wood-stock*.' The Tim Burton film was coming out, so we got a $10 million ad campaign for nothing."[18]

Apostolof wrote in a letter to Rudolph Grey, "They gave it a more serious attempt in showing Eddie in a good light, which I knew they will. One of the reasons I gave them the footage of the behind the scenes shots. Incidentally, more than half of it was superimposed over some negative, which was shot before and in lots of the scenes we had trouble. As lousy as it is, I am glad I have it because it recorded at least some of the pondomonium [*sic*], which was going on set, at times."[19]

Feeling that momentum was on his side, especially with all the attention Ed Wood was receiving in the early 1990s, Apostolof optimistically pitched his *Orgy of the Dead* sequel to GAGA. The company had completed its first American film, a little-remembered horror comedy called *The Jitters* (1988, dir. John M. Fasano), and was getting more and more into production. Apostolof also tried to interest GAGA in distributing *Fugitive Girls,* perhaps his second most bankable film after *Orgy.* But after screening it, CEO Kenji Okuhira politely declined.

Meanwhile, distributors were eternally trying to screw Apostolof out of money. The last Japanese sales reports for *Orgy of the Dead* arrived in June 1988. The Japanese were trying to get Apostolof to pay for the cost of making copies of the movie. Still in all, after those expenses and further censorship fees were deducted, *Orgy*'s total revenue still amounted to 532,322 yen, 40 percent of which (about $3500 in today's money) went directly to Apostolof. Not bad for a film that was then over a quarter-century old. But even this was not enough to keep the filmmaker afloat. And so, in 1992, Apostolof made the decision to get out of the film business altogether. He was willing to sell the rights to his movies, including film negatives and press materials. He wrote to his old distributor from Manson International, Michael Goldman, "I would like to sell outright all of these films to a serious buyer, including the negatives and video masters as well as all advertising for a set cash price. After all these years I have decided to concentrate more on MAKING films, rather than selling them."[20]

When Stephen C. Apostolof stowed away on the cargo ship that took him from Bulgaria to Turkey in 1948, he essentially lost contact with his homeland and the existence he had known as a youth. That part of his life seemed forever closed off to him, never to be reopened. But, over the decades, there were occasional breakthroughs. In early 1988, for instance, Apostolof reunited for first time with his brother Stavri, who flew from Sofia to Los Angeles. The two had not laid eyes on each other in four decades.

Then, in January 1994, the seemingly impossible happened: Apostolof finally re-

In a family photograph dated April 10, 1993, Stephen Apostolof holds his newborn granddaughter Chelsea.

Chapter 13. The Resurrection (1987–1997)

Stephen Apostolof and his brother Stavri on the It's a Small World ride in Disneyland in Anaheim, California, in 1988.

turned to Bulgaria for the first time since his escape. So much had happened in the ensuing four and a half decades, including the death of the filmmaker's father, but the political climate had finally changed enough in the Balkan nation that he could visit. It was time for Apostolof to make peace with the past. Not all of his fellow Bulgarian émigrés were so bold. Even after the fall of Communism and the 1989 regime change in Bulgaria, Mike Mikhailof and Boris Kutchukov kept their distance from the old country. Having long ago been convicted of high treason, they still feared being arrested if they ever returned.

Apostolof boarded a flight from Los Angeles, stopping first in Frankfurt, Germany, before arriving in Sofia. There, he stayed in the home of his brother Stavri. This was Apostolof's first time in the Bulgarian capital. While there, he visited Sofia's magnificent Alexander Nevsky Orthodox Cathedral, named for the Russian prince and saint.

But Apostolof's main goal in returning to his native land was to inspect the Boyana film production complex, built in 1962, during the Communist regime. He wanted to produce a spy thriller that took place in Istanbul and planned to shoot some of the scenes in the capital Sofia, whose streets resembled those of the Turkish metropolis. "His visit in 1994 was a location scouting for a completely different company," says Christopher Apostolof. "He was just doing some side work and they were paying him to go out there. He ended up staying with his brother and that way he could keep the *per diem*. You know, a nice little chunk of money."[21]

One of Apostolof's business partners was Dino Dinev, a fellow Bulgarian émigré and film producer whose reputation was, at best, dubious. Apostolof barely suspected

Back in his homeland for the first time in decades, Stephen Apostolof relaxes at his brother's home in Sofia, Bulgaria.

that his partner had a turbulent past. Dinev was running a film distribution company in France called Pyrine Film by then, but before getting into the motion picture business, he had his fair share of problems with the law. In 1978, the 38-year-old Dinev was the first person ever arrested and subsequently released in connection with the infamous Bulgarian Umbrella murder in London, which claimed the life of dissident Bulgarian writer Georgi Markov. The incident was named for the poison-tipped umbrella that had been used as the murder weapon. Dinev was suspected of perpetrating the heinous act, but this has never been proven. (Allegedly he told the judge, "We Bulgarians kill with a brick, not an umbrella.") He was convicted on charges of industrial espionage for the Soviet Union and Bulgaria and spent three years in a prison in Melun, a commune in north-central France.

Boyana, however, proved to be a bust. "The studio was crumbling down, and when my dad saw it he quickly forgot about his plans to shoot a film there," remembers Christopher.[22] Instead, his father headed for Burgas, where he visited relatives and friends he'd not seen in ages. He was very unhappy to see that his childhood house had fallen into disrepair. While in Burgas, Apostolof had his photo taken by Armenian photographer Mesrob Engibarov, who was well-known in the city for his striking black-and-white portraits in the tradition of the glamorous Parisian studio Harcourt.

While in town, Apostolof met with some of his childhood friends, including Krum Mollov and Dr. Mikhail Koldamov. According to Koldamov, Apostolof hadn't changed much while away from his home country; he still remembered the old jokes and sayings from his childhood. Apostolof also met some of his fellow ex-inmates from his stint in prison. At the labor union building in Burgas, he attended a meeting of Bulgarians oppressed by the Communists. Also in attendance was Mollov, with whom he'd fought the Communist regime as a teenager. "I sat next to him," remembered Mollov. "He looked at me, but he didn't recognize me [at first]. Then he started crying. He didn't know what had happened to me in prison. He was very elegant, wearing a suit, but I found him unchanged, the same joker with an open soul."[23]

January 1994 proved to be a pivotal month for Apostolof in another way, because that was also when California's San Fernando Valley suffered a magnitude 3.6 earthquake. The geological disturbance was so severe that its reverberations were felt as far away as Las Vegas. Northridge was the most devastating earthquake to struck America since the one that hit San Francisco in 1906.

Apostolof was thousands of miles away in Bulgaria when the earthquake hit, leaving his wife Shelley and son Christopher to fend for themselves during the disaster. Christopher tells what that was like: "We were living in Reseda, just off of Lindley Boulevard and Roscoe Boulevard, which is about two miles from California State University, Northridge, where the parking literally collapsed, just folded over. So the whole thing was just destructive!"[24]

The earthquake hit at 4:30 in the morning, meaning Shelley and Christopher were still in bed. Christopher again:

> I had a buddy of mine from high school who had come to hang out, and he was staying at our place. I'd fallen asleep on the couch in the living room. Shelley was there, of course, sleeping in the bedroom. And I'm having this dream that Edward James Olmos is in this total *Miami Vice* set-up, and he's grabbing the front of my jacket, screaming at me, "You fucked up!" And I'm going, "Captain, it's not what you think!" And I wake up, but I'm still moving, bouncing around on this couch. All hell was breaking loose! My friend was in my bedroom. He'd fallen asleep on my bed playing video games. Luckily his head was where his feet were supposed to be, because these big bookshelves on either side of my bed had collapsed where his head should have been. It wasn't rolling waves, but a violent shaking. It was just unbelievable![25]

Shelley and Christopher suddenly found themselves in a frightening, surreal situation. "So at this point, water is out, phones are out, power is out, and we're just freaking out," reports Christopher. "It was the middle of the night, so we all huddle in the house, try to get some sleep, wake up next morning, start putting the house back together. Phones were down for about two days. Steve was trying to get in touch with us; he couldn't. Me and my buddy had walked up the street, and there was a lot of price gouging. People were charging $5 for a small bottle of water and $20 for a pack of cigarettes. It was nuts!"[26]

It soon became apparent how widespread the destruction had been. Christopher saw firsthand what an impact the earthquake had on his mother and her family:

> Two days after the earthquake, Shelley's brother Dave and his wife called us because their apartment building has been red tagged and they were forced to leave, so they came to stay with us. And then, the next morning, Shelley just freaked out. She started pacing around the house like a caged animal. She grabs all of her stuff, a checkbook and a bank card. She looks at me and she goes, "Honey, I love you, but I gotta get out of here. I can't stay here." She puts all of her stuff in her car and she goes, "Call me when your Dad gets home," and she leaves.[27]

Shelley had decided to head east to Las Vegas to get away from Reseda, a journey that took her almost 24 hours. "She got to Vegas and collapsed on her mom's front porch," remembers Christopher. "They ended up calling an ambulance. And she left all of us, her brother, her sister-in-law, me, and my two friends with no money, no car, no nothing. We were just stuck. My brother Steve came with his car and dropped off some food and money. Dad had finally gotten in touch. There were no flights coming to Los Angeles, so he couldn't get in. It was such a strange moment."[28]

Northridge proved to be the breaking point for Apostolof. When he finally returned from Bulgaria, he knew that his life in California could not continue. Shelley was adamant about abandoning the Golden State for good. "Steve got back and decided to move to Las Vegas," Christopher recalls.[29] Shelley had given her husband an ultimatum: "You can have a divorce, you can do whatever you want, but I'm never going back to California."[30] Christopher and his father had to make a choice: stay in California or join Shelley in Nevada. The filmmaker opted for the latter. Christopher: "I looked at Steve saying, 'We don't have to go.' Dad looked back and said, 'Son, we have to.'"[31]

Shelley talks about her decision to abandon California:

We were right in the epicenter, and I said, "I'm not gonna stay here anymore." Glass broke everywhere. The wall unit for the air conditioner was flying over me. I could have been killed! I got in my car and said, "Anybody want to go with me to Las Vegas?" And nobody wanted to leave. So I packed my clothes, and I left for Vegas. And every time I would go by the ramps, the ramps would close, so that nobody could get in and out because of the structural damage. But I got it all the way to Las Vegas. I said, "I'm not going back ever again to Los Angeles."[32]

Steve and Shelley found a three-bedroom apartment in Las Vegas. Apostolof's friend Guy Nicholas, who was also living there, helped the two by putting some of their possessions in storage at Ultra Light, his film lights company.

The Apostolofs' new life in Vegas did have some unexpected side effects. "We both got fat together because of the buffets," remembers Shelley, referring to the famously cheap food available in the gambling Mecca. "They were five bucks."[33] Apostolof was a natural for the town in other ways as well. "He liked to gamble," says Shelley. "He liked the party life. He did that in his past, too."[34]

Christopher says, "I went to Los Angeles for about eight months. When I came back, they have moved from the three-bedroom to one bedroom and I was sleeping in the dining room at that point."[35]

Tim Burton's quirky black-and-white biopic *Ed Wood* premiered on September 23, 1994, at the 32nd New York Film Festival at Lincoln Center. The film opened in 693 American cinemas in October 1994 and severely underperformed at the box office, despite critical acclaim and a cast teeming with well-known actors like Bill Murray. It earned only $1.9 million in its first weekend and a total of $5,887,457 during its initial run, against a budget of $18 million. But the film, released through Disney subsidiary Touchstone Pictures, has become an enduring favorite in the ensuing decades, thanks to VHS, DVD and Blu-Ray releases.

"*Ed Wood* is a great movie, but it's depressing to watch," maintains film critic Greg Goodsell. "Hollywood produces films about artistic failure, and nobody goes to see them."[36] Goodsell cites such examples as *The Producers* (1967, dir. Mel Brooks), the story of a disastrous Broadway show, and *Waiting for Guffman* (1996, dir. Christopher Guest), a mockumentary about a laughable small town play. The makers of these films, Goodsell says, "expect people to come and laugh, but no one goes to see them because they are about failure. Failure is a great topic, but it isn't something we want to watch in a movie, because we already have enough failures in our own lives."³⁷

Despite the box office letdown, *Ed Wood*'s reviews were quite enthusiastic. Burton was nominated for a Golden Palm award at the Cannes Film Festival, and there were Oscars for Martin Landau (Best Supporting Actor for his portrayal of Bela Lugosi) and for makeup artist Rick Baker, who designed Landau's prosthetic makeup along with Ve Neill and Yolanda Toussieng. Apostolof watched *Ed Wood* with Christopher in Las Vegas. He declared the film "confusing" and "pathetic."³⁸ Most of all, he felt the movie misrepresented Ed Wood, a man he'd known for years. "There was a scene especially where Eddie meets Maila [Vampira] Nurmi, and he's on his knees begging her to be in his picture—that was not Eddie," said Apostolof.³⁹ He also said the movie "made Eddie look like a star-struck kid. Okay, Eddie was a movie-struck kid, he really liked the cinema, but not to a point of stupidity, because Eddie was anything but a stupid man."⁴⁰

Part of Apostolof's negative reaction stemmed from personal resentment: He was unhappy that no one from Tim Burton's team had bothered to talk to him or other people who used to know Ed Wood. Apostolof criticized the script by Scott Alexander and Larry Karaszewski, based on Rudolph Grey's *Nightmare of Ecstasy*, as "very shallow."⁴¹ While Grey's book spans Wood's entire life and career, the film only covers about a decade, beginning in the late 1940s (the premiere of his 1948 play *The Casual Company*) and ending in the late 1950s (the premiere of *Plan 9 from Outer Space*). Wood and Apostolof didn't even meet until the '60s. People who actually knew Wood in the '50s, including Paul Marco, Conrad Brooks and Kathy Wood, were consulted by the filmmakers.

"If I'd directed or produced, I would have concentrated more on the characters," Apostolof declared. "They concentrated on the relationship with Bela, and Bela was not a nice guy, because he was a dope addict. They made it as if Eddie and Bela were using each other, which in a sense was right. But the relationship was entirely different. [...] There were all kinds of funny incidents in Eddie's life which could have been put in, but they made it too pat."⁴²

Apostolof also had some unkind words for director Burton:

> [He] doesn't understand anything that an independent filmmaker has to go through, all the improvisations that you have to do. It's very easy to have $10 million and make a film—that's the easiest thing in the world. The key is to take $200,000 and make a film that looks like $10 million. Obviously the director, whatever his name was, he never made a small one, everything is technical things, special effects. So, I did not like the picture.⁴³

In fact, Burton had established his reputation with innovative short films like *Vincent* (1982) and *Frankenweenie* (1984). On the *Ed Wood* DVD commentary, he explained that he was drawn to the project because of the critical drubbing received by his debut feature, *Pee-wee's Big Adventure* (1985). He felt he could relate to Wood, whose movies got reviews that were similarly dismal.

"We laughed a lot [watching *Ed Wood*], but my father's laughter was bitter," remembers Christopher.⁴⁴ Apostolof was most irritated by the epilogue, which declared that Wood "kept struggling in Hollywood, but mainstream success eluded him. After a slow descent into alcoholism and monster nudie films, he died in 1978, at the age of 54." Apostolof was offended that Burton had referred to his most popular film *Orgy of the Dead* simply as a "monster nudie film." Never mind that Apostolof himself had once doubted the value of *Orgy*, until Johnny Legend changed his mind. Steve Apostolof:

> When all the hype came with *Ed Wood*, with the Johnny Depp movie, that was a big deal. And here's one of Dad's contemporaries that has been turned into an icon. Johnny Depp starring as Ed Wood?! Come on! I think that was a blow to Dad. I think Dad would have loved the attention. Dad would have loved the accolades even if the accolades were making fun of what he did. That is why Dad loved to go to the conventions when *Orgy of the Dead* hit it. There was this overseas market for *Orgy of the Dead* because of the connection with Ed Wood. And Dad got to go to Great Britain. Dad got to go to Japan.[45]

A spokesman for Feral House, the publisher, said Touchstone Pictures paid $250,000 for the rights to *Nightmare of Ecstasy*.[46] Rudolph Grey received additional $10,000 as a consultant, but says that Burton never used his services. In fact, Burton kept Grey away from the film set. At the end of 1993, Grey was on the set of *Ed Wood* in Los Angeles when Burton spotted him and instructed his staffers to take him out.

While *Ed Wood* was being cast, some people associated with Wood tried to secure roles in the film, occasionally to no avail. Harvey Shain said,

> If anyone deserved to be in this film, that was me. I knew Ed Wood. I must have been involved in six or seven films based on his screenplays, shot by Steve Apostolof. But my agent could not get me a role in the film. When you're an actor in Hollywood, your agent has to have something called clout. In other words, he has to have an impact! And my agent didn't. I was very disappointed that I got no part in this film. I spent a week on the phone trying to arrange any role. I did not care what role, it could have been only one line.[47]

David Ward, one of Wood's closest friends and actor in two of Apostolof's films, managed to snare a small role thanks to Wood's widow Kathy, who lobbied for him. Ward can be seen briefly in the background in the slaughterhouse scene when Johnny Depp is dancing after completing *Bride of the Monster*. The scene is one of the most memorable in the picture, with star Johnny Depp in full drag, complete with blonde wig, gyrating wildly to exotic organ music provided by Korla Pandit, the turban-wearing cult musician who had been a multimedia sensation in his own right in the 1950s. "Johnny Depp invited me to his trailer and began picking my mind about Eddie's mannerisms," remembers Ward, who had no doubt seen the real Ed Wood in drag on numerous occasions.[48]

Apostolof became obsessed with Wood's posthumous glory and collected every article he could find on him. In the mid–1990s, he even sent an inquiry to a bibliographic database called InfoTrac and printed everything that had ever been published about Wood on the internet to that point.

Curiously, Apostolof refused to take part in *The Haunted World of Edward D. Wood, Jr.* (1995, dir. Brett R. Thompson), a stylish documentary with unusually high production values. Alan Doshna served as the film's associate producer and historian, and presented an overview of Wood's strange career. Part of Doshna's research for the project included attending a late 1980s Ed Wood festival at the Vista Theatre. *Orgy of the Dead* was on the bill that night, and Apostolof made an appearance, breaking out the old anecdotes, including the time he covered Pat Barrington in gold paint. Jokingly or not, the director said he made the actress "look like a million dollars." Doshna remembers Apostolof as being "very friendly" that evening.[49]

When Doshna attempted to recruit Apostolof for the documentary a few years later, however, their telephone conversation did not go so well. The Bulgarian filmmaker apparently did not understand what Doshna wanted him to do, which was to film an interview about Ed Wood at a soundstage on Santa Monica Boulevard in Hollywood. Doshna explained the project over and over, but the conversation went in circles. Doshna finally gave up, and the documentary proceeded without Apostolof. The production team did manage to recruit such notables as Maila "Vampira" Nurmi, Dolores Fuller, Paul Marco and others to appear, but Apostolof was the one that got away. Doshna speculates, "Rudolph Grey had told us that Apostolof had an antipathy for Wood due to *Orgy* overshadowing his other work in popularity, so it is likely that this was a major factor in his declining our offer, although he did discuss his work with Ed in [the documentary] *Flying Saucers Over Hollywood*. Perhaps once was enough for Stephen."[50]

Chapter 14

State of Fear
(1998–2005)

German-born psychoanalyst Erik Erikson (1902–1994) was most famous for his theory of personality, which divides life into a series of distinct stages, each marked by its own unique conflict. The final struggle, faced by those 65 and up, is that of integrity vs. despair. When a man looks back on his life and his accomplishments, can he take pride in what he has achieved and feel satisfaction? Or is he haunted by what he did and what he failed to do when he was in his prime?

These were the issues that Apostolof faced in the final years of his life. His movie career had ended in disappointment in the late 1970s, but he'd still managed to amass an impressive body of work over the course of two productive decades. His films had even been rediscovered and re-released on multiple occasions in the 1980s and '90s thanks to such series as *Saturday Night Sleazies* from Rhino Home Video, which spanned three volumes in 1990 and 1991, and *The Erotic World of A.C. Stephen* from Something Weird Video.

If there was a downside to the delayed attention that *Orgy of the Dead* received in the 1980s and '90s, it was that the lion's share of the credit for the movie went to Ed Wood and not the film's director and producer, Stephen C. Apostolof. The problem intensified when Wood's life was used as the basis for a Disney-produced biopic starring Johnny Depp. Apostolof was finding himself relegated to the role of a footnote in the Wood saga.

A story that Roger Ebert was fond of quoting concerns an actor playing the gravedigger in a production of *Hamlet*. Asked to summarize the plot of the play, the actor said, "It's about this gravedigger who meets a prince."[1] Was Apostolof doomed to be the gravedigger to Wood's prince? This would have been intolerable to the proud Bulgarian, especially since he considered Wood to be an utterly hopeless director.

"He was kind of jealous of Ed Wood, that he got so much attention," Shelley Apostolof observes.[2] His son Christopher agrees: "I think he found the whole Ed Wood thing confusing. Ed became popular for all the wrong reasons and Steve never understood it."[3] Apostolof scoffed, for instance, when he was canonized in 2000 as the "patron saint of the pornographers" at a fan website called *The Church of Ed Wood*.

After his biopic, Ed Wood's legacy seemed secure. But what was to become of Apostolof? By the mid-1990s, his family was in a state of flux. After spending about a year in Las Vegas with his parents, Christopher decamped for a new life in North Carolina in 1996. In 1997, Shelley landed a job in Tacoma, so she and Apostolof moved from Nevada to Washington. The couple found a modest one-bedroom apartment in Federal Way, located in the booming Seattle metropolitan area. But the move did not suit Apostolof, who pined for the sunshine of Los Angeles. According to Christopher,

> Steve hated it in Washington! Seattle was really beautiful, but it was always dark, always cloudy, always rainy. I believe he was one of those people that had SAD, seasonal affective disorder, a type of depression that's related to changes in seasons. When it started raining and was gloomy for a few days, he would literally start to get depressed. Literally, you could put just some sunlight on the guy or take him to the beach and all of a sudden he's happy. I really believed he suffered from that because he'd just call me and say, "Son, it's so depressing here."[4]

In 1997, Apostolof underwent quadruple bypass heart surgery and had an arterial stent implanted at St. Joseph Medical Center in Tacoma. After the operation, his daughter Polly went to Federal Way for a week to take care of him as Shelley was working and couldn't take time off. According to Polly, "The health issues he had and having to follow Shelley with her menial jobs bothered him a lot. But even though he was encouraged to change his habits, he never did. And this would continue for the rest of his life. He said he could quit smoking if he wanted, but he didn't want to. He said this was one of the last pleasures in life for him."[5]

Further changes lay ahead. In 1998, Alaska Airlines offered Shelley a job in Los Angeles, so they moved back to California for a couple of months. This time, they settled in Playa del Rey, three miles north of Los Angeles International Airport. But this move, too, was short-lived. This time it was Shelley who was unhappy, mainly due to her job. "Shelley decided she needed to stop working a high stress job," remembers Christopher. "She was on a lot of antidepressants. She had a breast reduction surgery. She just couldn't handle the pressure of the work she was doing."[6] Shelley was working for the weight and balance crew at Alaska Airlines. She had a lot of responsibility, and it just didn't sit well with her. She couldn't handle the stress and the pressure. So the company offered her to move to the call center in Tempe, Arizona.

In November 1998, Steve and Shelley moved yet again, this time to a two-bedroom apartment in Mesa, a suburb located about 20 miles east of Phoenix. They were now residents of the Villa Fiesta complex, originally built in 1986. For a man like Apostolof, who was used to the exciting, fast-paced life of a Hollywood producer, this was a disheartening change. Villa Fiesta was a soul-crushing locale. The place certainly had a negative effect on Apostolof. And, once again, the climate was not to his liking. He was sweltering in the merciless Arizona heat.

"It's too hot. It's desert. He lived in Las Vegas prior to that. At least Las Vegas is more exciting," observes Apostolof's daughter Susan, who maintains that her father "never cared for Arizona." She could tell that her father was depressed when she called him on the phone, despite the fact that he would always put on a cheerful disposition for her benefit. "It broke my heart," she says.[7]

As Apostolof explained to Rudolph Grey, "It's nice here in September and October. But the summer is brutal! I didn't realize this until I moved here. When I came here in November it was great, it was just wonderful. But from June to September it's hell, and now with all the winds and the monsoon it's downright intolerable." Indeed, when compared to the subtropical Mediterranean climate of Los Angeles, Mesa seemed like a portal to hell. Apostolof:

Sometimes the temperatures reach 116°F. Perhaps the only other place which is hotter is Death Valley. One day I got really angry and decided to show my wife something. Around 4:00 in the afternoon, I took an egg. I went to the parking lot in front of our house and cracked it on the asphalt. Lo and behold, a few minutes later the egg got cooked. I took my wife to see it, and she said, "Now put some salt and pepper on it and eat it."

The *State of Fear* project might have been one of the few things keeping Apostolof going during those last few years. "Up until the last week of his life," says Christopher, "Steve was actually working on both *State of Fear* and *Orgy of the Dead II*, which he had really envisioned to be definitely a comedy or what he called 'campy.' And, of course, what he also called 'a good movie, son, for ticket-sellers,' which, of course, were tits for him."[8]

Christopher recalls that his father had some definite plans for shooting the film. "After going to Bulgaria in 1994, he wanted to shoot *State of Fear* [there] because of the forest and all the old Cold War military installations.[9]

"Dad's last hope to make a new picture was Arny Schorr when he was at Rhino," says Christopher. "Arny really liked Steve, so he was trying to find a way to finance *Orgy of the Dead II* or *State of Fear*."[10]

According to Schorr,

Steve and I shared a deep appreciation for each other, as people, as professionals, enormous mutual respect. He was sort of my cool uncle, charming, witty, funny, an endless source of incredible stories and anecdotes—I wish I could remember them. And he was so elegant in that European way. Blue shirts with white collar and cuffs, always elegant but it never felt forced.[11]

Shelley also remembers Apostolof laboring on *State of Fear*. "He was revising it and constantly making it new. But it was getting him nowhere." She blames herself somewhat for her husband's malaise after moving to Arizona. "It was my fault that he did that. He wanted to be with me, and I didn't want to be in California."[12] Daughter Susan observed how her father changed after the final move. "He just got very depressed in Mesa. He didn't like it. He wouldn't go out, and he wouldn't do anything. He wouldn't pursue it."[13]

One of the most unusual byproducts of Wood's posthumous fame was *I Woke Up Early the Day I Died* (1998, dir. Aris Iliopulos), a star-studded feature film based on one of Wood's unproduced screenplays. Wood had been working on the script, notable for its total lack of dialogue, for well over a decade.

The project began life as *Silent Night* or *The Night of Silence* back in the early 1960s. By 1974, it had taken on the title *I Woke Up Early the Morning I Died*. The plot concerned a madman who escapes from a sanitarium and goes on a crime spree. Rudolph Grey describes *I Woke Up Early* as "quintessential Ed Wood with its thematic obsession with death, graveyards, burlesque and the grotesque."[14] Wood often dreamed of making this film himself, and even had some actors in mind for certain parts (Aldo Ray, John Carradine and John Agar among them). Criswell plugged the project as late as mid-1974 thus: "Lloyd Lindroth, the Harpist's Bazaar, will score the new film *I Woke Up Early* for Columbia, the new Edward D. Wood film."[15] The unfilmed screenplay was one of the few items Wood managed to save when he was evicted from his final apartment on Yucca Street in December 1978.

Apostolof claimed to own the rights to this screenplay and planned to mount his own production of *I Woke Up Early the Day I Died*. He maintained that he saw the potential of the script back in the '70s and bought it from Wood. In fact, Apostolof claimed to have been working on the screenplay of *I Woke Up Early the Day I Died* after his return from Tokyo International Fantastic Film Festival in 1987. Apostolof also maintained he was working on it with Wood when the latter died in 1978. "Eddie and I talked about the script," he said. "I told him, 'Eddie, it would be a very boring movie if there's no action in it. Plus, someone has to talk because everyone will fall asleep.' This is what I changed in the script when I rewrote it."[16]

Apostolof's claims have some legitimacy. Son Christopher says, "The only time I ever remember actually seeing Eddie was at Steve's offices at the Taft Building [in Hollywood]. Eddie had come over trying to sell a script again, which turned out to be *I Woke Up Early the Day I Died*, which Dad actually owned the rights to. I have the receipt for the purchase."

When *I Woke Up Early* finally went before the cameras in the late 1990s, Greek-born artist Aris Iliopulos was at the helm. Despite the neophyte director's lack of feature filmmaking experience, the project managed to attract a large, varied cast of Hollywood notables, including Billy Zane, Eartha Kitt, Tippi Hedren, Christina Ricci, Sandra Bernhard, Karen Black, John Ritter and Conrad Brooks. This was when Tim Burton's *Ed Wood* was still fresh in people's minds, so plenty of stars wanted to be part of the unusual project. The end result plays like a cross between a high-fashion shoot and a very long music video. The film received mixed reviews and had only a very brief run in theaters before largely dropping out of sight. Apostolof, for one, was not worried about having lost control of the film: "Big deal! I don't want to associate with failure. And this film is definitely a failure," Apostolof wrote in a letter to Grey. "These people are terribly stupid. They pay for a fantastic cast and then hire a Greek filmmaker, who previously made two commercials and a half. I could be easily found. Why didn't they call people who know how to do these things?"

Apostolof was disappointed to learn that the director had used an earlier version of the script, minus his added dialogue. "They used the old version of the script, written by Eddie. That's why the film is so boring," Apostolof remarked. He was even more surprised to find out that Iliopulos had made a comedy out of Wood's ostensibly serious screenplay. "Not that Eddie didn't have a sense of humour," explained Apostolof. "On the contrary! But the screenplay is not funny at all. It's a very serious story. The producer would be lucky if he manages to get even five cents back."

Apostolof turned out to be right. *I Woke Up Early* was screened at the 23rd Toronto International Film Festival and at the Second Annual B-Movie Film Festival in Syracuse, New York, where it won six awards. Shortly after that, however, the film was withdrawn from distribution due to copyright problems. It received little to no support from mainstream critics, and box office receipts were negligible.

Apostolof took some comfort in the film's utter failure, knowing that he had dodged a bullet. "The film played for one week in a small New York theater, long enough to qualify for Oscar," he remarked in a letter to Grey.[17] "They hoped to cash in on the popularity of Ed, but they had no idea what they're doing. I read horrible things about the film, and I don't want to watch it. I know they used my opening scene with the nurse." Apostolof even took issue with the fact that Wood's widow had been awarded a brief cameo, asking rhetorically, "What actress is Kathy Wood?"

Part of his distaste for *I Woke Up Early* might have been a case of sour grapes. By the late 1990s, Apostolof was unable to get any film projects going, despite his lengthy showbiz résumé. "He was a director for 20 years," observes Christopher. "What do you do from now on? Send your résumé to the studios? How exactly does it work? [During his heyday] Steve was always offered projects, found the money, and was doing another film. But times were different."[18]

Apostolof kept tabs on the movie industry, and one film in particular caught his attention. On July 14, 1999, Artisan Entertainment released *The Blair Witch Project* (1999, dir. Daniel Myrick and Eduardo Sánchez), a so-called "found footage" horror film about three film students who travel to a small town to shoot documentary about the Blair Witch, a legendary local murderess, but lose their way in the woods. The film's budget was only $60,000 but it made $248.6 million at the box office, becoming the tenth highest-grossing film in America that year.[19] Apostolof was in awe.

"The film totally blew his mind!" Christopher remembers. "A budget of a couple of tens of thousand dollars? A bunch of kids lost with their cameras in the woods? Simply genius! My dad said, 'We can totally do this!' I told him, 'Yes, Dad, but it's already done.'"[20] Apostolof was not too far wrong here, though, as similar "found footage" horror films have abounded in the ensuing years.

Another film that Apostolof loved was the Nia Vardalos romantic comedy *My Big Fat Greek Wedding* (2002, dir. Joel Zwick), a surprise sleeper hit. "He watched it three times a day for several months. He loved the storyline, and the fact it was made so cheap intrigued him from a financing standpoint," says Christopher.[21]

That eternal time-waster, television, never provided much fascination for Apostolof. Though he kept up with the news and would occasionally enjoy a rerun of *M*A*S*H* or *The Benny Hill Show*, he wasn't the couch potato type. The infernal device was always on, though, because of Shelley's compulsive viewing habits. "It bugged him," says Christopher. "He would rather read a book."[22]

The Dying of the Light

The new century brought with it new heartbreak for Apostolof. On April 14, 2001, noted Beverly Hills attorney Harold A. Abeles, one of Apostolof's best friends for decades, died at his home in Los Angeles after a lengthy battle with cancer. He was 74. "When Harold died, it hit Dad hard. He was one of his last friends from back in the day," says daughter Susan.[23]

"It was a big loss for Steve," says Christopher Apostolof. "He needed money to start a film—Harold would find it. In recent years, Dad could not get any credit. So Harold was the one who always managed to help him."[24]

While in Mesa, nearly 400 miles from Los Angeles, Apostolof barely kept in touch with the people he'd known in the movie industry. One exception was producer David F. Friedman, with whom he often talked on the phone and exchanged holiday cards. Another was Harvey Shain. The two would talk on the phone at least once a week, with their conversations often lasting hours. Sometimes Harvey mailed Apostolof cigars.

Stephen C. Apostolof with his friend, exploitation movie kingpin David Friedman, in Los Angeles in December 1990.

Another person with whom Apostolof kept in touch was Conrado "Boy" Puzon, the Philippine distributor for whom he worked in the 1980s. They stopped working together in the early 1990s, but kept in touch afterwards. One day in 2002, Apostolof got the news that Conrado has passed away. He was devastated. "Steve and Puzon got along really, really well," remembers Christopher. "He was just of those people Steve enjoyed being around. Puzon dying affected him almost as much as Harold [Abeles] dying."[25]

In a bizarre twist of fate, it turns out that Puzon, unbeknownst to Apostolof, was alive and well and to this day lives in Manila.

In his waning years, Apostolof spent long hours on the phone with Rudolph Grey, who trawled him for stories related to Ed Wood, but somehow their conversations always circled back to two topics: death and Apostolof's woeful financial state. "Half of my friends are gone," Apostolof told Grey in 2001. "My distributor Jerry Balsam passed away two years ago. My lawyer is not around any more and to be in film business today, one needs a good lawyer. It's pretty depressing."

Apostolof's sister Lila died in June 2002. His first wife Joan, 77, passed away on February 9, 2003. Despite their acrimonious divorce, the two did see each other occasionally, according to Christopher.

The years were taking a toll on Apostolof. "He had no friends left," says Shelley Apostolof. "But he wouldn't go out and make new friends either. Because he was like the top two percent brain-wise. He was so smart that people couldn't keep up with him. But around here, he found no intelligence. And so he gave up."[26]

The death of Apostolof's friends and relatives may have made him realize his own death was fast approaching. Christopher again:

> When Harold Abeles died, that was beyond difficult for Steve. Harold was one of those few people that could keep up with Steve. Extremely smart man! They were constantly in touch. It was either a phone call or fax. And every couple of months, there was a package of cigars that Harold managed to get from Cuba via Canada. Harold dying was definitely this moment when Steve just went, "Holy shit! I'm getting old. All my friends are dying. This sucks."[27]

In a 2014 *Huffington Post* article, writer Carol E. Wyer discussed so-called "Grumpy Old Man" syndrome, i.e., the reasons that older men become disagreeable.[28] By the age of 70, a man's testosterone levels have dropped to half the levels of his prime, and he might be dealing with numerous health problems. These medical factors, combined with a lack of goals or aspirations, might make a man irritable or depressed. Apostolof apparently succumbed to this phenomenon in his final years.

"He definitely had this 'old grumpy man' thing going," reports Christopher. "'Oh, son, my back hurts, my knee hurts, my head hurts.' That kind of thing."[29] Apostolof's daughter Polly felt that her father should fraternize with other people his age in one of the so-called social centers, where he could have coffee and pastries, play cards and watch television; but Apostolof didn't feel old, so he preferred hanging out with young people. Sometimes he stayed with Christopher's friends until early in the morning, drinking and telling old stories about Hollywood. Christopher:

> Dad always kept late hours, he was always up until two, three, four in the morning. Until he died. That was his favorite time. He'd just sit in his office and read. He was reworking breakdowns for *State of Fear* and *Orgy of the Dead II* and trying to figure out how he can get them made. That was very important to him, to still have an office. He had brought that big, olive green desk that he had at his office at Sunset Boulevard in the 1970s. That was part of his self-respect and his demeanor, to continue his business acumen.

In Mesa, Apostolof was isolated from all the things he'd known back in Los Angeles—his friends, his church and the company of other Bulgarians. Christopher says that none of the filmmaker's old cronies visited him in Arizona, though Harvey Shain did help him from time to time with small amounts of money. Apostolof ventured back to Los Angeles every couple of months and saw his friends then, occasionally enjoying a lunch or dinner with Harvey at a one-time Hollywood industry haunt, the Formosa Cafe. Back in the 1960s, Apostolof had an office not far from the place. But Apostolof's friends never visited him in Mesa. "In that apartment," says Christopher, "he would have never invited anybody, bluntly. His pride wouldn't have allowed that."[30]

The Bulgarian church had long been the hub of Apostolof's social life in California, but this pattern was not repeated in Arizona. "We went to a couple of Sunday masses in the Orthodox church in Phoenix. It was nice, but it wasn't St. George," says Christopher. "The church for Steve was more than religion. This was part of the Bulgarian Club, part of their identity being away from the home country."[31]

Apostolof visited the Bulgarian church in Los Angeles one last time in the early 2000s. Christopher:

We were sitting on the second floor and everybody was like, "Oh, it's good to see you," blah blah blah. But everyone was kind of standoffish. It was very strange. It's me, Dad and the priest Father Damian and the old, old guard. And everybody else is on the other side of the room. One of the guys got very drunk and took a swing at the guy who sings at the church and punched him in the mouth. So I grabbed the guy and took him across the room. Everything calms down, Steve comes to me and asks if everything is okay. "This is insane! What the hell! That's why I don't want them to be able to drink at the church any more!" He wanted to cut the booze off. So I'm standing at the balcony, smoking a cigarette when I suddenly hear from downstairs: "Hey, you! Foreigner! You stay out of our business!" I said, "Foreigner?! You son of a bitch! I was the first kid ever baptized in this church!" Steve looked at me and said, "I'm not coming back here..."

But there were also some happy memories in Arizona, even during those arid final years. In October 2001, Christopher moved back to Mesa with his then wife. "We moved in with Steve and Shelley," he relates. "My ex left in February 2002. Around that time, John Miller, a very good friend of mine, had gotten laid off from his job in Boston and he had come out to Mesa and moved in with me, Shelley and Steve. Me and John were roommates living in that one bedroom apartment for years."[32]

Miller became a key figure in the Apostolofs' lives. He was born to Russian parents who emigrated to Texas in the 1960s. His father, a dock worker, had died in an accident. Christopher met John at the St. John's Military School in Salina, Kansas, and they clicked instantly. Apostolof, too, took a liking to John and in a sense adopted him. He was the father figure John had looked for.

Ultimately, Christopher and John ended up getting an apartment together in the same Villa Fiesta complex, just a couple buildings over from Steve and Shelley. This proximity allowed for some latter-day father-son bonding. "I was with him every day in the last years of his life, which was fantastic. I was the last child, so I grew up with him," Christopher says. "Once I met my second wife Dana and we got married, Dad actually spent a lot of time at our place. He'd always just be sitting, having a drink, talking with all kids, telling stories. Just having a good ol' time."[33]

The End of the End

Like many people in their twilight years, the once flamboyant Apostolof fell into a comfortable if drab and predictable rut. According to Christopher, the ex-filmmaker rarely deviated from his daily routine: wake up early, sit with a cup of coffee, smoke a cigarette, and catch up with the latest headlines from his home country through a Bulgarian website called news.bg. Apostolof was both amazed by technology and skeptical of it at the same time. So while he regularly surfed the internet, he was not always able to let go of the past. Christopher said, "He had the same two Adler typewriters from the 1960s, and he still had these things in the '90s. And he was trying to get parts for these things to keep them working. He liked the computers but whenever he wanted to write something, he used a typewriter. Talking about teaching an old dog a new trick. He loved the feeling of the old IBM Selectric typewriters which had something called a beam spring key which makes this sound *cha-ching*!"[34]

By the new millennium, screenwriters had long since switched to software platforms like Final Draft and had ditched their typewriters, but here Apostolof remained

Exiled to Mesa, Arizona, Apostolof uses his son Christopher's old computer to break down one of the scripts he was working on in the early 2000s.

dubious. "My son told me about a program that can teach you how to write scripts. This is ridiculous!" Apostolof told Rudolph Grey.

Meanwhile, Apostolof's health was deteriorating. He'd never exactly been a health nut, and he wasn't about to change his old habits, such as smoking, even if they were taking years off his life. In May 2000, he was supposed to attend the Cannes Film Festival as a representative of Something Weird Video to pick some new films for the company to distribute on video. He was offered first class airfare, accommodations, per diem expenses and $1500 a week. But in March, Apostolof had a minor stroke, the first in a series, so Mike Vraney, the CEO of Something Weird Video, called off the trip.

Christopher scoffs at the idea that his dad would change his habits because of a setback like this. That just wasn't the man's style. In August 2005, when Apostolof suffered another minor stroke, Christopher drove him to Banner Desert Medical Center, a hospital in Mesa. The filmmaker's children were naturally alarmed, but Apostolof tried to put them at ease. Polly Apostolof remembers, "I was in New York with my daughter April for her 13th birthday when I learned Dad had a stroke. I called him immediately in the hospital from Times Square. He sounded very happy, he was flirting with the nurses. He was in the best of moods."[35]

Polly flew back to California and then to Arizona, but by the time she arrived, Apostolof had suffered a second, massive stroke and lost consciousness.

"Dad loved chocolate," says John Miller, an honorary member of the Apostolof clan. "The last thing I gave him before he passed away was a Snickers. He said, 'Yani, go and bring me a Snickers. I can't breathe.' I told him he needs to worry more about his

Cover for the 2017 French DVD edition of *Orgy of the Dead* from Bach Films.

Ed Wood vs. Quentin Tarantino, a cartoon mashup by American artist Mitch O'Connell. The book Vampira is reading is *Orgy of the Dead* (courtesy Mitch O'Connell).

life, but what am I to do? I brought him a Snickers and he ate it. Then he put the oxygen mask back and that was the last time I saw him."[36]

In the next few days, the Apostolof kids converged on Mesa. By then, Apostolof was intubated. Two days later, they collectively approached the doctor to get a picture of their father's condition. The prognosis was grim. Polly Apostolof:

The doctor showed us an X-ray of Dad's brain, and at least half of it was filled with blood. We knew then there's no coming back. We decided at that point to turn off the machines helping him to breathe. We brought in a Catholic priest who gave Dad last rites. As we were doing this, we got his brother Stavri on the phone with him. He was crying and talking to Dad as we turned off life support.[37]

Apostolof, tenacious to the end, kept breathing even without mechanical assistance, forcing his family to take additional steps. "At that point, hospital staff decided we needed to move him to a hospice facility," Polly says. "An ambulance transported him to a beautiful place—Hospice of the Valley in Chandler, Arizona. We made him comfortable in a bed and hospice staff slowly administered morphine and he slipped away after several hours."

Stephen C. Apostolof—scourge of the Communist Party, father of five, husband of three, self-proclaimed "executive filmmaker" (as he ostentatiously added to his already-personalized SCA California license plate) and visionary behind films such as *Orgy of the Dead*, *The Divorcee* and *Motel Confidential*—died on August 14, 2005. He was 77.

No newspaper published an obituary. The one public announcement of his demise was a brief message posted by his daughter Polly on the now defunct IMDb message board for *Orgy of the Dead*. It simply said:

Would like to let everyone know that my father, the director, producer and writer for *Orgy*, has died today. He was 77. Although he was dead serious at the time of the making of this movie, over the years he learned to laugh at himself and the mistakes that were made. It was unintended camp, and he wore it on his sleeve. We grew up with Eddie Wood as our weird "uncle," and wore the costumes [from the film] for Halloween.... We've had several versions of an *Orgy II* script, and perhaps the time is right.... R.I.P. Dad.... Criswell will be up there waiting at the gates with a glass of Scotch.... And yes.... I can't watch the silly thing without fast forwarding it either ... definitely the worst movie ever made. I'm so proud.[38]

In some respects, Apostolof's death came as a surprise to his family. "He was doing pretty well, I would say. It was totally shocking to die in a hospital as he did. I mean, his stroke was completely unexpected," says Christopher.[39]

Like a low-rent version of Charles Foster Kane, the tycoon protagonist of *Citizen Kane* (1941, dir. Orson Welles), Apostolof spent his final days in isolation and inertia, rudderless and without purpose. Far removed from Hollywood and the filmmaking life he'd known, the ex-producer lost the will to carry on. "The last three months of his living," says Shelley, "he said he wanted to die. And he talked himself into dying. Three months later, he was dead. It's sad that such a talented man surrendered at the end."[40]

Not everyone believes in this version of events, however. "I understand that the life in Mesa was not great, but he had a strong will to live," insists Polly. "He had his children and grandchildren. The fact that he kept breathing on his own even after they switched off the machines shows that up until the very end, he had a strong will to live."[41]

Christopher looks back on this era of his father's life with bitter regret. "He was living in some two-bedroom apartment in some shithole in Mesa, Arizona. And the last thing he ever told me was, 'Son, don't let me die here.' And I failed him! I never told anybody that!"[42] The filmmaker's youngest son still gets choked up thinking about those days, regretting both what was done and what was left undone.

Apostolof's body was cremated at Paradise Memorial Crematory in Scottsdale,

A 2016 color poster for Peepshow Menagerie's burlesque *Orgy of the Dead*.

Arizona on August 16. "I went to go pick up his ashes," says Christopher, "and they hand me this maroon plastic box! It didn't even had hinges. It was like Tupperware, just a snap lid. And I was like 'Oh, my God!' I'm driving home, kind of in shock at this point."[43]

On the way back home, Christopher stopped at his father's favorite cigar shop, where one of his friends was working at the time. "My buddy looked at the box. 'Is that it?' he asked. Then he added, 'Man, this is so wrong!' and pulled out a laminated cigar box from behind the counter."[44] He put his father's ashes in the box and has kept them there ever since.

The bittersweet irony of the situation wouldn't have been lost on Apostolof. The Bulgarian who started his career in Hollywood at a time when a person needed "a screenplay, a Cadillac and a cigar" to be a producer, found his final resting place in a shiny cigar box. But there is a degree of cosmic justice in Apostolof's ultimate fate. When Christopher left Arizona and moved to Las Vegas for good, he took the cigar box containing his father's remains with him.

"I finally got him out of Arizona like I promised," says Christopher.[45]

Appendix:
The Immoral Artist
(unused story outline)

What follows are two story outlines for *The Immortal Artist*, a sexploitation film Stephen C. Apostolof planned to make in the early 1960s. The influence of Russ Meyer's *The Immoral Mr. Teas* is obvious here, though an Indian dance sequence presages *Orgy of the Dead*. On April 8, 1961, Apostolof mailed a copy of this outline to himself as a cheap way of establishing a copyright. It was postmarked on April 10 in Los Angeles. The author included a letter, typed on official-looking SCA Productions stationery, explaining that he was the sole author of the work. Apostolof's grammar and spelling have been preserved here to give the reader some insight into the filmmaker's writing style. These documents were kept in Apostolof's archives and are being presented to the public for the first time.

"The Immoral Artist"
by Stephen C. Apostolof

The art museum–Mecca for the artists, is visited by many people to enjoy the beauty of the old masters work. Many young painters also are going there to study the technique of the great masters. On this particular afternoon a busload of young students are visiting the museum. The uniformed guide shows them around, explaining each particular painting the story involved when the paricular [sic] painter painted them. "What you see here," says the guide, pointing to a painting, "is the work of a genius, his imagination and above all his self expression. A painter paints what he sees, that's what makes a great painter." Those words are herd [sic] by a young painter, Peter, who is painting a copy of the statue of Venus. The guide moves to another painting down the hall, but his words made a big impression on our hero, how true were those words, to paint what you see, not somebody else but what YOU see. All these years he has tried [sic] to capture his thoughts and to be able to express them on the canvas. But where did that lead him, nowhere. Even now, right this moment what is he doing, copying someone else's style; putting down what somebody else saw long, long time ago. No ... this is not what he wants, he wants to paint what he sees. Why not give it a try ... yes, why not? He tears off the sheet he was painting, puts a new one and starts to make a new scetch [sic] of the statue. All of a sudden there is a new life in the heart of the painter. As if a new world is being seen for the first time in his life. He sees the same old statue which he has seen so many times in a new light

The beautiful woman, which was so cold and distant before, all of a sudden became real. He sees her come back to life, the face is a beautiful one, the lips so fresh and inviting, as a matter of fact, he sees her as God created her ... in the nude. Feverishly he starts to put down on paper what he sees and not before very long he has the whole statue on his sketchbook. Thsi [*sic*] unusual sketch attracts the attention of many visitors and particularly of an elderly couple. The man is enjoying what he sees, but the lady is realy [*sic*] angry. She calls the museum attendant, who trows [*sic*] our hero out.

FADE OUT

FADE IN

It is a beautiful morning day. on the beach. There is the general activity going on. PETER is seen coming down from a little sand dune towards the beach. He carries his sketchbook in one arm and a beach umbrela [*sic*] under the other. Two little boys are running around the sand bothering everybody with their noise and especially with a magnifying glass. They are burning holes on umbrelas [*sic*], newspapers, magazines and even people. PETER selects a secluded spot and makes himself comfortable. Next to him is a beautiful girl, who is taking a sun bath. He couldn't help it but to admire her well build [*sic*] anatomy. Not before very long she decides to take a swim in the ocean. Peter couldn't resist the temptation to paint the beautiful nymph. He starts to paint ... and you guesed [*sic*] it ... he sees her in the nude. He is so preocupied [*sic*] with his painting that he doesn't notice the two little rascals, who did point their magnifying glass on him: to be more specific on the lower part of his body. With a sudden jurk [*sic*] he jumps from off his chair and with shouts chases the two rascals.

FADE OUT

FADE IN

We see PETER'S car going on a mountain road towards the medows [*sic*] bellow [*sic*]. Peter is in a happy mood enjoying the wonderful vuiw [*sic*] around him. Not before very long he arives [*sic*] at the medow [*sic*]. He walks to a fence, where there are several cows on pasture. He takes his sketchbook out and starts to draw a sketch of a particular cow that attracted his attention. Not before very long he starts to see this particular cow in a very peculiar way. He sees her as a beautiful readhead [*sic*], but with only one exeption [*sic*] her head; the body is that of a woman but the head of a cow. He can't beleave [*sic*] his eyes, but that is what he sees and naturly [*sic*] that is what he paints. His thoughts are suddenly being interupted [*sic*] by laughing voices comming [*sic*] from the river bellow [*sic*]. He can't resists [*sic*] the temtention [*sic*] and he gets up and goes down the river to investigate. When he comes down to the river he is delighted with what he sees. In front of him in the water are several women taking a bath in the river. They are having a time of their life enjoying the cool mountain water swimming, playing and slashing each other. They are not aware of the presence of the stranger. Peter is anxious to capture the beautiful scenary [*sic*] in front of him, but this is almost imposible [*sic*]. He tryes [*sic*] to paint one girl, then another and he couldn't posible [*sic*] concentrate on what he sees. He is hiden [*sic*] behind the tall grass and nobody can see him. After many attempts to paint he gives up and enjoys the scenary [*sic*] in front of him. But like everything else that is good, this too does not last for very long. The farmer is approaching from nowhere carrying a rifle in his hands and surprises our hero in the moddle [*sic*] of the act. Peter has no other choice but to run as fast as he can. The farmer chases him as far as the car and Peter barely manages to drive of [*sic*] back to the big city.

FADE OUT

FADE IN

It is late at night when Peter arrives back to his room. He starts to undres [*sic*] but sudenly [*sic*] his attention his focused on the window across his room. There like a cameo is the silluet [*sic*] of a woman who is undresing [*sic*] to go to bed. He couldn't resist the temptation of watching. He turns off his light and enjoyes [*sic*] the scenary [*sic*]. Not before very long the light across the window turns off, obviously the leady [*sic*] went to bed, and our hero dissapointed [*sic*] goes to his own bed. But even here he has no rest. He just falls asleep and like in a nightmare all the previous day's scenes come back to life. He dreams of the girls all those beautiful girls he saw during the day, but somehow they take a new dimension. He feels hot … so very hot as if he is on the top of a fire…. We dissolve to a camp of INDIANS. Peter is fastened on the poll [*sic*] and around him is the fire, he is going to burn … but wait where is everybody. there seems to be only the girls from the river, dressed in indian outfits and beating the drums. All of a sudden there is the girl from the Ocean coming out from a teppee [*sic*] and she starts to dance to the rittum [*sic*] of the drums. She dances and dances and when he looks at her closely she has almost nothing on. The fire is getting hotter and hotter, he hardly can stand it any more. Then all of a sudden the drums stop, the beautiful dancer falls on the ground … the chew is coming from another tepee holding a tomahawk in his hand and starts comming [*sic*] closer and closer towards him. Peter is helples [*sic*], he tryes desperatly [*sic*] to free himself from the ropes, but it is impossible. The chief comes closer and closer he has the same face as the farmer with the gun in the medow [*sic*]. The indian girl tries to beg the chief to spare his life, but the chief brushes her aside and starts comming closer and closer, and closer…. Peter wakes up with a scream, only to find that he is in the safety of his room and this was only a bad dream. He is perspiring very heavily and turns around on the other side and goes to sleep.

FADE OUT

FADE IN

It is late in the afternoon when Peter drives to a Hamburger place. On the way down he notices a girl waiting for the bus in front of a busstop [*sic*]. He turns his car around and starts to sketch the girl's figure and face. He works very fast because he expects the bus to come very [*sic*] moment and she may leave. A small crowd gathers around him watching him paint. But there is something dreadfully wrong. What he sees is not what she actually wears. For the first time in a long time he sees the girls clothed; as a matter of fact too clothed. He paints her with a coat, a rain coat in the middle of the summer, even a hat, what she actually has is only a blouse and a pair of slacks. This is too much…. When finally her boy friend arrives on the scene, (she was waiting for him, not for the bus) he tells him that the sketch is not like the girl. "What is wrong with it?" asks Peter. "Oh, nothing wrong with the face, but where do you SEE this clothes on her?" This is too much, he realizes that now he starts to see things too clothed, and the hell with all this. He tears the sketchbook off as we…. FADE TO THE END.

April 8, 1961
Hollywood, California

SECOND VERSION:

The Immoral Artist
by S.C. Apostolof

PETER the young painter is a man of unusual talents and not a very bad painter. Somehow he laks [sic] what some people call inspiration. He seeks it everywhere in this wide world. After all there are so many things that a young painter can do. The world is full of things that he can see and transfer on his canvas, but … he sees only the beauty in the world and what is more beautiful than a young girl…. So he sees only the beautiful girls around him.

What is more important to a painter, money, security, glamour or maybe fame and recognition … of course none of this. The most important thing in the world for our friend is self expression. To paint things as they are as HE SEES THEM, as he understands them as he can paint them, this is what he is triving [sic] to acheave [sic].

So far so good, but what does PETER sees [sic], he sees only the object of his painting just AS THEY ARE. Sometimes this [sic] objects are to their bare minimums, e.g., bare naked as mother nature had made them.

This particular point of view of his puts him in all kind of situations, but somehow he manages to come on top. He sees his inspiration everywhere. On the beach, on the farm, in the mountains even in the Mecca of the artist–The museum. The whole world of his is full with nothing but beauty, but what a beauty … all those lovely bear [sic] naked women.

Not before very long this becomes an obsession with him, an obsession which he can no longer endure. After all he has no peace all day long painting all those girls and he is dreaming for the rest which he will have at night in the quietness of his room. But somehow this is not possible Even in his own room the rest which he needs so badly does not come as easy as one may think. The [sic] begin with there is the sweet little thing across the apartment and in those warm summer nights she seems to need lots of fresh air and her window is always open. What a better thing to do on a warm summer night but take a shower … and that is exactly what she is doing. Night after night she is bothering him with this [sic] activities of hers. After all how long can a healthy man take of all this…. He can not help it but this is becoming his one ring circus, a one woman show, a private chanel [sic] on his big T.V. screen. Inevitably just when he wants the show to continue she will turn off the light switch and he'll have to stop the enjoing [sic] viewing [sic] and go to bed. But even there he can not find peace he is having "nightmares" All those beautiful girls from the past are coming back to life and he waking up having all kinds of dreams.

Somehow he must get rid off all this nonsense, but how, this is the big question. Maybe a new change of scenery or even a new climate. Oops did I say a new climate the poor guy even in Alaska it will be cold for everybody but not for him. There must be a way.... How about inviting one of those cutie [*sic*] to his apartment for a glass of wine, but no such luck.

One day while walking down the street he sees a beautiful girl waiting in front of a building. He starts to paint it, but something is very wrong, what he sees is not what the girl is. He sees her FULLY CLOTHED and what she actually has is only a blouse and a pair of short pants. Finally he is cured and this is it. The poor boy, now he is just like everybody else.

April 8, 1961
TO WHOM IT MAY CONCERN:

This document dated this eight [*sic*] day of April 1961 was written by the undersigned, Stephen C. Apostolof. It was written and enclosed with this outline of an original screenplay tentatively entitled "THE IMMORAL ARTIST."

This document is written and signed by the undersigned with only one purpose in mind—the protection of the motion picture, television, radio, literary and now known or unknown mediums rights.

Stephen C. Apostolof

Timeline

1903 May 18: The opening of a new port in Burgas, Bulgaria, marks the city's debut on the world stage. Among those drawn to the city are Stephen C. Apostolof's father and maternal grandfather.

1907 August 18: Jeron Charles Criswell King (aka The Amazing Criswell) is born in Princeton, Indiana.

1915 Apostolof's older sister Vesa is born.

1919 Apostolof's older sister Lila is born. June 29: Herbert F. Niccolls, screenwriter of *Journey to Freedom*, is born.

1920 September 3: Apostolof's older brother Stavri is born.

1924 October 10: Future collaborator Edward D. Wood, Jr., is born in Poughkeepsie, New York.

1925 December 1: Jaime Mendoza-Nava, composer of the score of *Orgy of the Dead* and many other Apostolof movies, is born in La Paz, Bolivia. December 30: Joan Mary Higgins, Apostolof's first wife and mother of his first four children, is born in Toronto.

1926 June 22: Dimitri Yordanov, Apostolof's friend from Paris, is born in Sofia, Bulgaria.

1928 February 25: Apostolof is born Stefko Christov Apostolov in Burgas, Bulgaria. May 16: Apostolof's friend Boris Kutchukov is born in Yambol, Bulgaria.

1932 June 7: Donald A. Davis is born in Florida. December 6: David Ward is born in New York, New York. December 10: Robert Caramico is born in New York, New York.

1933 May 1: Guy Nicholas, Apostolof's friend and cameraman of *Fugitive Girls* and *Hot Ice*, is born in Florina, Greece. July 23: Fawn Silver is born in Los Angeles, California.

1936 February 10: Marsha Jordan is born in Gadsden, Alabama.

1937 Apostolof's leading man, Harvey Sheldon Shain, is born in New York City.

1938 Apostolof enrolls at the Deutsche Schule in Burgas, where he studies German.

1939 October 16: Pat Barrington is born Patricia Annette Bray in Charlotte, North Carolina.

1941 Apostolof joins *Brannik*, a Bulgarian youth league.

1944 *Brannik* disbands. Apostolof's mother Polyxena, 45, dies of heart disease. April 8: Ric Lutze is born in Indiana. September 5: The Soviet Union declares war on Bulgaria. September 9: The Red Army enters the country, which falls under Communist control. October 7: Tallie Cochrane is born Lillian Rose Cochrane in Memphis, Tennessee.

1945 Apostolof meets Boris Kutchukov, who will be a close friend for decades. He joins up with a group of anti–Communist conspirators who attempt to blow up a Standard Petroleum factory and sabotage an election. September 12: Apostolof and three other conspirators are arrested. December 20: A court sentences Apostolof to two years, two months and 20 days in prison.

1946 March 8: Apostolof enters prison. April 4: Apostolof's second wife Patricia Jeanne Rudl is born in Flint, Michigan.

1947 March 21: Apostolof's future wife Shelley is born Barbara Rachelle Cooper in Coral Gables, Florida.

1948 January 14: Apostolof is released from prison. March 3: Apostolof escapes his homeland of Bulgaria by stowing away on a cargo ship. The ship takes him to Istanbul, Turkey. March 6: Bulgaria enacts a new law depriving escapees of their citizenship. May 24: Mariwin Roberts is born in Fort Worth, Texas. December: Apostolof leaves Turkey and travels by train to France, ostensibly to join the French Foreign Legion. He does not enlist and leaves for Paris.

1949 March 15: Apostolof runs into his Bulgarian friend Boris Kutchukov in Paris. Apostolof decides to emigrate to Canada.

1950 July 1: Apostolof receives his transit visa and departs for Canada by ship. In Toronto, he meets his first wife, nurse Joan Mary Higgins. October 11: Actress Rene Bond is born in San Diego, California.

1951 Apostolof begins working for the Canadian National Railway. October 14: Maria Patricia Apostolof, the first child of Stephen C. Apostolof and Joan Higgins, is born in Canada and given up for adoption. November 4: Apostolof marries Joan in Toronto.

1952 May 28: Apostolof and Joan depart Canada by train to go to the United States. Several days later, they arrive in Los Angeles.

1953 Apostolof and Boris Kutchukov form a Bulgarian Club. November: Apostolof joins the tabulating department at 20th Century–Fox.

1954 April: Apostolof leaves Fox. May: He becomes an auto parts salesman. December: He lands a job in the production department at the ABC television network.

1955 January: Apostolof departs ABC and meets the future backers of his autobiographical film *Journey to Freedom*. March 27: Steve and Joan's second child, Paula Christine Apostolof, is born in Los Angeles. April: Apostolof forms Cosmopolitan Pictures Co. with Harry Keatan.

1956 February 20: Apostolof drops out of Cosmopolitan. August: He and others found SCA Productions, and production on *Journey to Freedom* begins. December: Apostolof attends a charity screening of *Journey to Freedom* in Washington, D.C. Unrealized projects include *Jeanne*, *7 Rue Pigalle* and *From Out of the Darkness*.

1957 Apostolof completes a banking course and begins working at Bank of America. Joan contracts polio. June 21: *Journey to Freedom* is released. October 1: Steve and Joan's third child, Stephen Christie Apostolof, is born in Los Angeles.

1958 Unrealized projects include *Monster from the Grave* and *Man from the Moon*. Apostolof applies unsuccessfully for U.S. citizenship.

1959 November 26: Steve and Joan's fourth child, Susan Joanne Apostolof, is born in Los Angeles.

1960 June 17: Joan becomes a naturalized American citizen. November: Apostolof welcomes his first daughter, Maria, back to the family after her adoptive mother dies. Unrealized project: *The Plot to Destroy the Earth*. December 8: Apostolof, Dr. Matthew Jeikoff and a small group of Bulgarian emigrants found St. George, the first Bulgarian Eastern Orthodox Church in Los Angeles.

1961 Unrealized project: *The Immoral Artist*.

1962 Apostolof meets Guy Nicholas, who will become his friend and a cameraman on his later films.

1963 Steve and Joan begin divorce proceedings, with Apostolof accusing his wife of trying to poison him. October 22: William C. Thompson dies in Los Angeles, California. December: Their divorce becomes final.

1964 Apostolof leaves Bank of America. May: His children are sent to live with their mother.

1965 September: Apostolof makes his directorial debut with *Orgy of the Dead*. It is the first of his films to be scripted by Ed Wood. Apostolof meets Jaime Mendoza-Nava, who will be the composer on many of his films. October 2: Criswell promotes *Orgy* on *The Tonight Show Starring Johnny Carson*. Apostolof meets Patricia J. Rudl, who will briefly become his second wife.

1966 Mid-July: Production on *Suburbia Confidential* begins. September 4: Apostolof marries secretary Patricia J. Rudl in Las Vegas. November 16: *Suburbia Confidential* premieres in Baltimore.

1967 January 19: Apostolof buys a script called *Quickie*. The resulting film, *Motel Confidential*, is released later that year. February 25: Patricia J. Rudl leaves Apostolof. May 10: *Bachelor's Dream* is released. August 25: Apostolof's divorce from Patricia becomes final. November 10: *Motel Confidential* premieres at the Monica Theatre in Los Angeles.

1968 January 12: Apostolof buys a story tentatively called *College Kicks* from his friend Herbert F. Niccolls. April: Production of *Office Love-In, White Collar Style* begins. August 14: *College Girls* is released. September: Production on *Lady Godiva Rides* begins. November: Production of *The Divorcee* begins. November 4: *Office Love-In, White Collar Style* is released.

1969 Apostolof meets his third wife, Shelley. January 13: Apostolof is among the founders of the Adult Film Association of America. March: *Lady Godiva Rides* is released. April: *The Divorcee* is released.

1970 The President's Commission on Obscenity and Pornography cites Apostolof Film Productions as one of "the most important producer-distributors or distributors in the exploitation industry." July 22: Apostolof's SCA Mini Art Theatre opens for business in Santa Monica; it closes several months later.

1971 February 14: Apostolof marries his third wife, Shelley. Apostolof buys a home in Studio City. May 12: Tor Johnson dies in San Fernando, California.

1972 Apostolof reunites with Ed Wood for a string of films, including *The Snow Bunnies*, *Drop-Out Wife* and *The Class Reunion*. February: Shooting of *The Snow Bunnies* begins. March: Shooting of *The Cocktail Hostesses* begins. June 12: Gerard Damiano's hardcore pornographic film *Deep Throat* is released to great success and controversy, changing the adult film industry. July: Apostolof is called as a prosecution witness in the obscenity trial of his friend, Don Davis. October: Shooting of *The Cocktail Hostesses* continues.

1973 March 18: Christopher David Apostolof, the only child of Stephen Apostolof and his third wife Shelley, is born. August 9: *The Cocktail Hostesses* is released. October: Shooting of *Fugitive Girls* begins. Christo, Apostolof's father, dies in Bulgaria.

1974 July 13: *Fugitive Girls* is released.

1975 Apostolof edits a new X-rated version of *Fugitive Girls*: *Five Loose Women*.

1976 *The Beach Bunnies* is released.

1977 August 23: The *Los Angeles Times* stops accepting ads for adult movies.

1978 January: Production on *Hot Ice* begins. The film, Apostolof's last, is barely released that same year. December 10: Ed Wood dies at the age of 54 in Los Angeles.

1979 Apostolof sells his home to actress Jackie Zeman and moves to Sherman Oaks.

1980 *The Golden Turkey Awards* is published, naming Ed Wood as the worst director of all time and bringing him posthumous stardom.

1981 May 23: The University of Southern California in Los Angeles holds its first Ed Wood retrospective.

1982 September 23: Don Davis dies in Los Angeles. October 4: Criswell dies in Burbank.

1983 Apostolof and his family move to a rented house in Westlake Village. April 20: Herbert F. Niccolls dies in Los Angeles.

1984 April 7: Ed Wood biographer Rudolph Grey contacts Apostolof by letter. May: Dr. Matthew Jeikoff dies in Los Angeles.

1985 February 25: Apostolof becomes a U.S. citizen. April: Thanks to Johnny Legend, *Orgy* re-premieres at the Nuart in Los Angeles. September 23: Apostolof travels to Japan to present *Orgy of the Dead* at the Tokyo International Fantastic Film Festival. October 21: *Orgy* is released on video in Japan. Unrealized projects from this time include *Orgy of the Dead II*.

1986 Japanese company GAGA Communications purchases the overseas distribution rights to *Orgy of the Dead* from Rhino, the official American distributor.

1987 GAGA Communications releases *Orgy of the Dead* on video and distributes the film in a selected number of Japanese cinemas as part of the promotion strategy.

1988 Forty years after his escape from Bulgaria, Apostolof reunites with his brother Stavri in Los Angeles. April 26: Rhino Video organizes Woodstock, an Ed Wood festival at the Nuart. The program includes Wood's *Glen or Glenda* and *The Violent Years* and Apostolof's *Orgy of the Dead*. The next day, Johnny Legend presents his *Sleazemania!*, a compilation that includes Apostolof's *College Girls*.

1990 Mike Vraney establishes Something Weird Video, a Seattle-based company specializing in reissuing vintage exploitation and sexploitation films from the 1960s and '70s. The company would handle many of Apostolof's films. The first volume of Rhino Home Video's *Saturday Night Sleazies,* including *College Girls,* is released. May 26: *Orgy of the Dead* premieres in England as part of an Ed Wood festival.

1991 Two additional volumes of *Saturday Night Sleazies,* including *Bachelor's Dream, Lady Godiva Rides, Motel Confidential* and *Office Love-In*, are released.

1994 January: Apostolof returns to Bulgaria for the first time in decades. January 17: The devastating Northridge earthquake hits the San Fernando Valley. Because of this disaster, Apostolof leaves California and moves to Las Vegas. September 23: *Ed Wood* premieres at the 32nd New York Film Festival at Lincoln Center.

1996 June 2: Rene Bond dies in Los Angeles.

1997 October 18: Robert Caramico dies in Santa Clarita, California.

1998 November: After living in various places, Apostolof and his wife Shelley settle in Mesa, Arizona. Unrealized projects include *State of Fear*, a thriller.

1999 April 25: Apostolof's distributor Jerome "Jerry" Balsam dies.

2000 February 27: Hal Guthu dies in a rather mysterious fire in Los Angeles. His death is ruled a suicide by gunshot.

2001 March 9: Apostolof's Parisian friend Dimitri Yordanov dies in Carrara, Italy. April 14: Harold A. Abeles dies in Los Angeles. May 9: James E. Myers dies in Bonita Springs, Florida.

2003 February 9: Apostolof's first wife Joan dies in Henderson, Nevada.

2004 Rhino releases *Orgy of the Dead* on DVD, complete with an Apostolof interview.

2005 May 31: Jaime Mendoza-Nava dies in Woodland Hills, California. August 14: Stephen C. Apostolof dies at the age of 77 in Chandler, Arizona. August 16: He is cremated in Scottsdale, Arizona. His ashes are given to his son Christopher.

2006 May 2: Apostolof's friend Stéphane Groueff dies in Southampton, New York.

2007 April: British film magazine *Sight & Sound* lists Apostolof among the most prominent figures in the sexploitation genre.

2011 May 21: Tallie Cochrane dies in Panama City, Nevada. August 27: Eve Brent dies in Sun Valley, California.

2013 June 3: Marsha Jordan dies in Fresno, California.

2014 September 1: Pat Barrington dies in Fort Lauderdale, Florida.

2016 April 22: Boris Kutchukov dies in Kostenets, Bulgaria.

2017 August 4: Mariwin Roberts dies in Camarillo, California. August 23: David Ward dies in Los Angeles. November 17: Apostolof's son Steve dies in Chatsworth, California. December 23: Guy Nicholas dies in Las Vegas, Nevada.

Filmography

Journey to Freedom (1957) 60 minutes. Directed by Robert C. Dertano. Written by Herbert F. Niccolls, based on an original story by Stephen C. Apostolof. Produced by Apostolof with Stafford B. Harrison. Edited by Robert Dertano. Cinematography (B&W) by William C. Thompson. Music by Joseph Zimanich. Cast includes Jacques Scott, Geneviève Aumont, Tor Johnson and Eve Brent (under the name Jean Ann Lewis). Cameo by Apostolof. Also known as: *Escape to Freedom* (working title), *The New Refugee* (working title).

Orgy of the Dead (1965) 82 minutes. Directed by Stephen C. Apostolof. Written by Edward D. Wood, Jr. Produced by Apostolof with William Bates, L.S. Jensen and Neil B. Stein. Edited by Don Davis. Cinematography (color) by Robert Caramico. Music by Jaime Mendoza-Nava. Cast includes Criswell, Fawn Silver, William Bates, Pat Barrington, Lou Ojena, John Andrews, Nadejda Dobrev, Rene De Beau, Lorali Hart, Stephanie Jones, Dene Starnes, Coleen O'Brien, Bunny Glaser, Mickey Jines, Barbara Nordin and Texas Starr. Also known as: *The Ghoulies* (working title), *Nudie Ghoulies* (working title), *Orgy of the Damned* (working title), *Ghouls and Dolls* (working title), *Orgy of the Weirdos*, *Party of the Dead*, *Revels of the Dead*.

Suburbia Confidential (1966) 82 minutes. Directed by Stephen C. Apostolof. Written by Apostolof (as Jason Underwood) (claimed); actual author was Michael Kraike. Produced by Apostolof with Don Nagel. Cinematography (B&W) by Robert C. Wilson (replacing the fired Robert Caramico). Music by Jaime Mendoza-Nava (as Igor O'Gigagusky). Cast includes George Cooper, Gary Kent, Lolita Williams, Hidie Shnee, Janice Kelly, Brandy, Lou Ojena, Mark Crowe, Don Jones and Hugh Hooker. Also known as: *Neglected Wives* (working title), *Suburban Confidential*.

Bachelor's Dream (1967) 33 minutes. Directed by Stephen C. Apostolof. Written by Apostolof (as Jason Underwood). Produced by Apostolof. Cinematography (B&W and color) by Robert C. Wilson. Music by Jaime Mendoza-Nava (as Igor O'Gigagusky). Cast includes Abner Bidle, Andrea Cooper, Bunny Glaser, Nadejda Dobrev, Barbara Nordin, Coleen O'Brien and Shirley Wood. Also known as: *Naked Dreams of the Naughty Nerd*.

Motel Confidential (1967) 85 minutes. Directed by Stephen C. Apostolof. Written by Mark Desmond (as Mark Del Monde). Produced by Apostolof with Don Nagel. Cinematography (B&W) by Robert Caramico (as Robert Ruben). Music by Jaime Mendoza-Nava (as Igor O'Gigagusky). Cast includes Harvey Shain, Milton Kaye, Dora Lorber, Bunny Glaser, Coleen O'Brien, Barbara Nordin, Lou Ojena (as Louis Ojarof), Shirley Wood, Belinda Newton, Andrea Cooper, Eva Love, Ruby Perl, Carlton Price, James Jeans, Didi Seider, Elena Green, Stefanie Murphy, Don Davis and Conchita Gonzalez. Also known as: *Quickie* (working title).

College Girls (1968) 65 minutes. Directed by Stephen C. Apostolof. Written by Bruce Mitchell (pseudonym of Herbert F. Niccolls). Produced by Apostolof. Cinematography (B&W) by Robert Maxwell. Music by Jaime Mendoza-Nava (as Igor O'Gigagusky). Cast includes Harvey Shain, Marsha Jordan, Sean O'Hara, Randy Lee, Moose Howard, Capri and Dianna Rosano (as Dionna Rosano). Also known as: *College Kicks* (working title), *College Girls Confidential*.

Office Love-In, White Collar Style (1968) 82 minutes. Directed by Stephen C. Apostolof. Written by J.T. Casey (pseudonym of Taggart Casey). Produced by Apostolof with Casey. Cinematography (B&W) by Robert Caramico (as Robert Ruben). Music by Jaime Mendoza-Nava (as Igor O'Gigagusky). Cast includes Harvey Shain, Kathy Williams, Marsha Jordan, Hugh Thelman, Clete Bennett, Michael DiRosa, Lynn Harris, Ray Cyr, John Bealey and Sheri Jackson (as Colleen Murphy). Also known as: *Sex in the Office*, *Office Love-In*, *Office Girls*.

Lady Godiva Rides (1969) 105 minutes. Directed by Stephen C. Apostolof. Written by Apostolof (as Jason Underwood) (claimed); actual author was Victor McLeod. Produced by Apostolof with Kevin S. Brent and H.Z. Patrick. Cinematography (color) by Robert Caramico (as R.C. Ruben). Music by Jaime Mendoza-Nava (as Igor O'Gigagusky) and Sons of the Keystone Kops. Cast includes Marsha Jordan, Harvey Shain, James E. Myers, Mark Desmond (as Mark Del Monde), Liza Renay, Mary Bauer, Elizabeth Knowles, Deborah Downey and Bob Kendal. Cameo by Apostolof. Also known as: *Lady Godiva*, *Lady Godiva Rides Again*, *Lady Godiva Meets Tom Jones*.

The Divorcee (1969) 90 minutes. Directed by Stephen C. Apostolof. Written by Apostolof (as Jason Underwood) (claimed); actual author was James Henderson. Produced by Apostolof. Cinematography (color) by Robert Caramico (as R.C. Ruben). Music by Jaime Mendoza-Nava (as Igor O'Gigagusky). Cast includes Marsha Jordan, Deborah Downey, Lloyd Nelson (as Lloyd Bilson), Liza Renay, Robert Wielie, James E. Myers (as James Meyer), Marland Proctor (as Marlan Proctor) and Mark Desmond. Also known as: *I, a Divorced Woman* (working title).

The Snow Bunnies (1972) 86 minutes. Directed by Stephen C. Apostolof. Written by Apostolof with Edward D. Wood, Jr. Produced by Apostolof. Cinematography (color) by Allen Stone. No music credit. Cast includes Marsha Jordan, Rene Bond, Harvey Shain, Terri Johnson, Sandy Carey, Starline Comb, Ron Darby, Mark Desmond, Christopher Geoffries and Ric Lutze. Cameos by Stephen and Shelley Apostolof.

Drop-Out Wife (1972) 82 minutes. Directed by Stephen C. Apostolof. Written by Apostolof with Edward D. Wood, Jr. Produced by Stephen C. Apostolof with Shelley Apostolof (as S.B. Cooper). Cinematography (color) by Robert Caramico (as R.C. Ruben). Music by Jaime Mendoza-Nava (as J. Mendozoff). Cast includes Angela Carnon, Christopher Geoffries, Terri Johnson, Douglas Frey, Duane Paulsen, Harvey Shain, Rick Cassidy, Norman Fields, Ric Lutze, Cory Brandon, Candy Samples, Sandy Dempsey and Lynn Harris. Also known as: *Pleasure Unlimited*, *The Sensuous Wife*.

The Class Reunion (1972) 85 minutes. Directed by Stephen C. Apostolof. Written by Apostolof with Edward D. Wood, Jr. Produced by Apostolof. Cinematography (color) by Allen Stone. Music by Jaime Mendoza-Nava. Cast includes Marsha Jordan, Harvey Shain, Sandy Carey, Rene Bond, Ric Lutze, Starline Comb, Christopher Geoffries, Con Covert, Ron Darby and Flora Weisel.

The Cocktail Hostesses (1973) 76 minutes. Directed by Stephen C. Apostolof. Written by Apostolof with Edward D. Wood, Jr. Produced by Apostolof. Cinematography (color) by Robert Caramico (as R.C. Ruben). Music by Jaime Mendoza-Nava (as J. Mendozoff). Cast includes Rene Bond, Norman Fields, Terri Johnson, Starline Comb, Lynn Harris, Christopher Geoffries, Douglas Frey, Ric Lutze, Duane Paulsen and Harvey Shain. Also known as: *The Hostesses* (working title), *Intimate Confessions of the Cocktail Hostesses*.

Fugitive Girls (1974) 95 minutes. Directed by Stephen C. Apostolof. Written by Apostolof with Edward D. Wood, Jr. Produced by Apostolof with Shelley Apostolof (as S.B. Cooper). Edited by Tony Mora (as Louigi Rogatoni). Cinematography (color) by Guy Nicholas. No music credit. Cast includes: Rene Bond, Jabie Abercrombie, Tallie Cochrane, Harvey Shain, Douglas Frey, Con Covert, Donna Young, Maria Arnold, Nicole Riddell, Janet Newell, Eve Orlon, Gary Schneider, Margie Lanier and Ed Wood. Also known as: *Five*

Loose Women, Hot on the Trail, Women's Penitentiary VIII.

The Beach Bunnies (1976) 90 minutes. Directed by Stephen C. Apostolof. Written by Apostolof with Edward D. Wood, Jr. Produced by Stephen C. Apostolof with Shelley Apostolof (as S.B. Cooper). Cinematography (color) by Robert Caramico (as R.C. Ruben). No music credit. Cast includes Brenda Fogarty, Harvey Shain, Con Covert, Cory Brandon (as Correy Brandon), Rick Cassidy, Mariwin Roberts, Linda Gildersleeve, Wendy Cavanaugh (as Wendy Cavanough), Robert Bullock, Johnny Fain (as John Aquaboy), and Marland Proctor. Cameo by Apostolof. Also known as *Sun Bunnies, Red Hot and Sexy* (UK title).

Hot Ice (1978) 94 minutes. Directed by Stephen C. Apostolof. Written by Stephen C. Apostolof with Shelley Apostolof (as S.B. Cooper) and Pam Eddy. Produced by Stephen C. Apostolof with Shelley Apostolof (as S.B. Cooper). Editing by Ben Andrew. Cinematography (color) by Guy Nicholas. Music by Richard McCurdy and the Chasin-Shooter Group. Cast includes Harvey Shain, Max Thayer (as Mike Thayer), Mariwin Roberts, Rick Cassidy, Linda Gildersleeve, Ric Lutze and Fred Spencer.

Note: For all films from *Orgy of the Dead* to *The Beach Bunnies,* Apostolof is credited as A.C. Stephen. All running times are approximate. Due to the adult nature of most of these movies, they have been edited to various lengths for theatrical and home video releases. The running times are merely intended as a general guideline and are not meant to be taken as exact.

Unrealized films include: *Tangier, The Immoral Artist, The Plot to Destroy the Earth, Monster from the Grave, Man from the Moon, The Man with the Glass Eye, Jeanne, From Out of the Darkness, 7 Rue Pigalle, 69 Rue Pigalle, The Basketballers, The Airline Hostesses, The Teachers, Orgy of the Dead II* (aka *Orgy of the Dead, Part II: The New Generation*), *Savage Fugitives, Terrorist Girl,* and *State of Fear.*

Lost or non-existent films claimed by Apostolof include: *Five Stations to Hell, Crazy Circle* and *The Last Mile to El Diablo.*

In addition to its own films, SCA Distributors also released *Wrong Way* (1972), directed by Ray Williams and produced by Ron Kelly. The cast includes Apostolof regulars Ron Darby and Starline Comb.

Chapter Notes

Epigraphs

1. Tim Elliott, "Dad Made Dirty Movies, Friday, December 9," *The Sydney Morning Herald*, December 08, 2011, http://www.smh.com.au/entertainment/tv-and-radio/dad-made-dirty-movies-friday-december-9-20111201-1o8lt.html
2. Walt Hackett, "Bulgarian Refugee Apostolof, 28, Making Big Stir as New Director," *Lansing State Journal*, January 6, 1957.
3. Jimmy McDonough, *Big Bosoms and Square Jaws: The Biography of Russ Meyer, King of the Sex Film* (London: Vintage, 2006).

Prologue

1. Stephen C. Apostolof, interview by Mike Vraney and James Elliot Singer, May 1998.
2. Rudolph Grey, *Nightmare of Ecstasy: The Life and Art of Edward D. Wood, Jr.* (New York: Feral House, 1992).
3. "Lesson 19: The First Saints of Wood. Where Reverend Steve and the Board of Woodian Reverends Announce the First List of Holy Woodian Saints!" August 24, 2000, http://lessons.edwood.org/L19.html
4. Randall Clark, *At a Theater or Drive-in Near You: The History, Culture, and Politics of the American Exploitation Film* (New York: Garland, 1995).

Chapter 1

1. Johnston McCulley, *The Mark of Zorro* (Oxford: Macmillan Education, 2008).
2. Christopher Apostolof, interview by Jordan Todorov, March 1, 2016.
3. Yordanka Ingilizova, "Burgas Man Conquers Hollywood with Erotica and Horror," *Chernomorski Far* (Burgas), July 10, 2007.
4. Ibid.
5. Ibid.
6. Ibid.
7. Ibid.
8. Ibid.
9. The Union of Bulgarian National Legions, formed in 1993, was a right extremist organization in Bulgaria that maintained links with National Socialist Germany.
10. Spas Raikin, *Rebel with a Just Cause: A Political Journey Against the Winds of the 20th Century*, Vol. 2 (Sofia, Bulgaria: Pensoft Publishers, 2001).
11. Yordanka Ingilizova, "Burgas Man Conquers Hollywood with Erotica and Horror," *Chernomorski Far* (Burgas), July 10, 2007.
12. Kasket—a Russian cap, somewhat similar to a combination cap, but made of felt.
13. Boris Kutchukov, interview by Jordan Todorov, June 3, 2008.
14. Frank Henenlotter, Johnny Legend, Peter Clark and Mark Isted. "Stephen C. Apostolof: Bulgarian Nudie Director," *Psychotronic Video*, 1990.
15. Goryani—an active guerrilla resistance against the Bulgarian Communist regime. It began immediately after the 1944 coup d'état, and reached its peak between 1947 and 1954. It is known to have been the first organized and longest lasting anti-Soviet armed resistance in Eastern Europe.
16. Indictment 236/45 г. on the inventory of First examining magistrate at the District Court of Burgas.
17. Ibid.
18. Ibid.
19. Yordanka Ingilizova, "Burgas Man Conquers Hollywood with Erotica and Horror," *Chernomorski Far* (Burgas), July 10, 2007.
20. Boris Kutchukov, interview by Jordan Todorov, June 3, 2008.
21. Ibid.
22. Kina Apostolova, interview by Jordan Todorov, September 12, 2005.
23. Christopher Apostolof, interview by Jordan Todorov, December 1, 2006.

Chapter 2

1. Fikret Adil, *Asmalımescit 74 (Bohem hayatı)* (Istanbul: İletişim Yayınları, 1993).
2. Major Gilbert E. Bursley to Stephen C. Apostolof, August 21, 1948, Istanbul, Turkey.
3. Major Zinovi Pechkoff, *The Bugle Sounds: Life in the Foreign Legion* (Uckfield, England: The Naval & Military Press, 2000).
4. Boris Kutchukov, interview by Jordan Todorov, June 3, 2008.

Chapter 3

1. Ginette Kutchukov, interview by Jordan Todorov, May 2, 2010.
2. Boris Kutchukov, interview by Jordan Todorov, June 3, 2008.
3. *Ibid.*
4. *Ibid.*
5. *Ibid.*
6. Ginette Kutchukov, interview by Jordan Todorov, May 2, 2010.
7. Boris Kutchukov, interview by Jordan Todorov, June 3, 2008.
8. Ginette Kutchukov, interview by Jordan Todorov, May 2, 2010.
9. *Ibid.*
10. Actually Count Lobanov died in the so-called Camp C, founded in late 1947 as a division of Department II (counterintelligence) of the Bulgarian State Security Services. The camp was located in the old Pazardzhik Prison and it was only known to the prime minister of Bulgaria Georgi Dimitrov, Minister of the Interior Anton Yugov, the director of the People's Militia Russi Christozov and heads of the counterintelligence department. Families of the people sent to Camp C didn't know what happened to their loved ones—whether they made it to the free world or were killed at the border.
11. Stéphane Groueff, *My Odyssey* (New York: Writers Advantage, 2003).
12. *Ibid.*
13. Dimitar Spisarevski (1916–1943) was a Bulgarian fighter pilot known for taking down an American bomber by ramming it during the bombing of Sofia in World War II.
14. Boris Kutchukov, interview by Jordan Todorov, June 3, 2008.
15. *Ibid.*
16. Boris Kutchukov, interview by Jordan Todorov, June 3, 2008.
17. Ginette Kutchukov, interview by Jordan Todorov, May 2, 2010.
18. Boris Kutchukov, interview by Jordan Todorov, June 3, 2008.
19. *Ibid.*
20. *Ibid.*
21. Walt Hackett, "Bulgarian Refugee Apostolof, 28, Making Big Stir as New Director," *Lansing State Journal*, January 6, 1957.
22. *Who's Who in the West*, Vol. 11 (Chicago: A.N. Marquis, 1968).
23. "Apostolof and Cooper Vows Solemnized," *Los Angeles Times*, March 15, 1971.
24. Paul Anisef and Lanphier, C. Michael. *The World in a City* (Toronto: University of Toronto Press, 2003).

Chapter 4

1. Polly Apostolof, interview by Jordan Todorov, August 8, 2016.
2. Barbara Higgins Graham, interview by Jordan Todorov, July 11, 2016.
3. Susan Schmideler, interview by Jordan Todorov, February 3, 2016.
4. Steve Apostolof, interview by Jordan Todorov, April 12, 2016.
5. Barbara Higgins Graham, interview by Jordan Todorov, July 11, 2016.
6. Steve Apostolof, interview by Jordan Todorov, April 12, 2016.
7. Susan Schmideler, interview by Jordan Todorov, February 3, 2016.
8. Polly Apostolof, interview by Jordan Todorov, April 27, 2019.
9. Barbara Higgins Graham, interview by Jordan Todorov, July 11, 2016.
10. Steve Apostolof, interview by Jordan Todorov, April 12, 2016.

Chapter 5

1. Michael Faust, "Shock Cinema Talks with Sexploitation Auteur A.C. Stephen a.k.a. Stephen Apostolof," *Shock Cinema*, 1999.
2. Christopher Apostolof, interview by Jordan Todorov, December 1, 2006.
3. Kevin Starr, *Golden Dreams: California in an Age of Abundance, 1950–1963* (New York: Oxford University Press, 2011).
4. *Ibid.*
5. Boris Kutchukov, interview by Jordan Todorov, June 3, 2008.
6. *Ibid.*
7. Steve Apostolof, interview by Jordan Todorov, July 18, 2017.
8. Ginette Kutchukov, interview by Jordan Todorov, May 2, 2010.
9. Stephen C. Apostolof, interview by Mike Vraney and James Elliot Singer, May 1998.
10. *Ibid.*
11. Barbara Higgins Graham, interview by Jordan Todorov, July 11, 2016.
12. Stephen C. Apostolof, interview by Mike Vraney and James Elliot Singer, May 1998.
13. *Ibid.*
14. Steve Apostolof, interview by Jordan Todorov, April 12, 2016.
15. Stephen C. Apostolof, interview by Mike Vraney and James Elliot Singer, May 1998.
16. *Ibid.*

Chapter 6

1. "Rode on Back of Wild Lion, Lives to Tell It," *Rochester Democrat and Chronicle*, March 30, 1928.
2. Darryl F. Zanuck, "20th-Fox Production Chief Cites Studio's Own Impressive Roster of 'New Faces,'" *Variety*, January 3, 1951.
3. "'Brave' Young Man with Ideas," *Motion Picture Herald*, December 8, 1956.
4. Stephen Apostolof and Joseph Rome, "Pro and Con. The Question: Will the Televising of Old Films Endanger the Careers of Long-Established Stars?" *The Film Daily*, November 13, 1956.

5. Marie Torre, "Out of the Air," *The Evening Review* (East Liverpool, Ohio), September 30, 1958.
6. Charles Denton, "Dancers Find TV Show Work Nightmare of Labor," *The Cincinnati Enquirer*, October 12, 1958.
7. Apostolof meant the film *Gun Girls* (1957), directed by Robert C. Dertano.
8. A quote from the pressbook of *Journey to Freedom*.
9. Daniel E. Slotnik, "Eve Brent, Played Jane in Tarzan Movies, Dies at 81," *The New York Times*, September 7, 2011.
10. Erskine Johnson, "New Film Comedy Will Be Lampoon on 'Spellbound,'" *The San Bernardino County Sun*, May 15, 1951.
11. Stephen C. Apostolof, interview by Mike Vraney and James Elliot Singer, May 1998.
12. *Ibid*.
13. "'Freedom' to Assist Hungarian Refugees," *Variety*, December 14, 1956.
14. Stephen C. Apostolof, interview by Mike Vraney and James Elliot Singer, May 1998.
15. *Ibid*.
16. Richard Maurice Hurst, *Republic Studios: Beyond Poverty Row and the Majors* (Lanham, MD: Scarecrow Press, 2007).
17. "Journey to Freedom," *Motion Picture Exhibitor*, July 10, 1957.
18. Walt Hackett, "Bulgarian Refugee Apostolof, 28, Making Big Stir as New Director," *Lansing State Journal*, January 6, 1957.
19. Stephen C. Apostolof, interview by Mike Vraney and James Elliot Singer, May 1998.
20. Christopher Apostolof, interview by Jordan Todorov, December 1, 2006.
21. "Movieland Events," *Los Angeles Times*, December 25, 1956.
22. "Estabrook Tale to Be Filmed," *Los Angeles Times*, November 15, 1956.
23. "Apostolof Scouting," *The Hollywood Reporter*, November 11, 1956.
24. Stephen C. Apostolof, interview by Mike Vraney and James Elliot Singer, May 1998.
25. *Ibid*.
26. Christopher Apostolof, interview by Jordan Todorov, December 1, 2006.
27. "L.A. Producer Plans 14 Films Yearly Here," *Toronto Daily Star*, September 27, 1958.
28. *Ibid*.
29. "Russians Don't Have Anything Against Miss Monroe," *The Bakersfield Californian*, August 28, 1956.
30. *Ibid*.
31. "An Open Letter to Michael Todd," *Daily Variety*, August 22, 1956.
32. Steve Apostolof, interview by Jordan Todorov, April 12, 2016.
33. Christopher Apostolof, interview by Jordan Todorov, December 1, 2006.
34. *Ibid*.
35. Susan Schmideler, interview by Jordan Todorov, January 30, 2017.
36. *Ibid*.

Chapter 7

1. Shelley Apostolof, interview by Jordan Todorov, December 3, 2006.
2. Maria Apostolof, interview by Jordan Todorov, April 27, 2019.
3. Susan Schmideler, interview by Jordan Todorov, February 3, 2016.
4. Steve Apostolof, interview by Jordan Todorov, April 12, 2016.
5. *Ibid*.
6. *Ibid*.
7. *Ibid*.
8. *Ibid*.
9. Shelley Apostolof, interview by Jordan Todorov, December 3, 2006.
10. Susan Schmideler, interview by Jordan Todorov, January 30, 2017.
11. Steve Apostolof, interview by Jordan Todorov, April 12, 2016.
12. *Ibid*.
13. Polly Apostolof, interview by Jordan Todorov, August 8, 2016.
14. Susan Schmideler, interview by Jordan Todorov, January 30, 2017.
15. *Ibid*.

Chapter 8

1. Michael Faust, "Shock Cinema Talks with Sexploitation Auteur A.C. Stephen a.k.a. Stephen Apostolof," *Shock Cinema*, 1999.
2. Stephen C. Apostolof, interview by Mike Vraney and James Elliot Singer, May 1998.
3. *Ibid*.
4. *Ibid*.
5. *Ibid*.
6. *Ibid*.
7. *Ibid*.
8. John Andrews (1941–1991), who played the Wolfman in *Orgy of the Dead*, said he was given the cape after he walked into the costume department of Universal Studios, allegedly introducing himself as "Bela Lugosi, Jr.," and asking if they had any clothes worn by his father. Andrews later traded the cape to the collector Clark Wilkinson for complete sets of lobby cards from all of Lugosi's movies. Clark described the cape as made of black satin and having a gold colored lining with a burn mark and measuring 28 feet across. It was made to order by Western Costume Co. for Universal-International Pictures.
9. In *Orgy of the Dead* Criswell reprises exactly his opening speech from Ed Wood's unreleased *Night of the Ghouls*.
10. Michael J. Weldon, *The Psychotronic Encyclopedia of Film* (London: Plexus, 1989).
11. Michael Faust, "Shock Cinema Talks with Sexploitation Auteur A.C. Stephen a.k.a. Stephen Apostolof," *Shock Cinema*, 1999.
12. *Ibid*.
13. Stephen C. Apostolof, interview by Mike Vraney and James Elliot Singer, May 1998.

14. Susan Schmideler, interview by Jordan Todorov, February 3, 2016.
15. Stephen C. Apostolof, interview by Mike Vraney and James Elliot Singer, May 1998.
16. *Ibid.*
17. *Ibid.*
18. Jeron Criswell King, *Criswell Predicts Your Next Ten Years* (New York: Grosset & Dunlap, 1971).
19. Stephen C. Apostolof, interview by Mike Vraney and James Elliot Singer, May 1998.
20. Greg Goodsell, interview by Jordan Todorov, August 28, 2017.
21. Stephen C. Apostolof, interview by Mike Vraney and James Elliot Singer, May 1998.
22. *Ibid.*
23. Jeron Criswell King, "Criswell Predicts (An Accurate Glimpse of the Future)," *The Bridgeport Post*, September 5, 1965.
24. Stephen C. Apostolof, interview by Mike Vraney and James Elliot Singer, May 1998.
25. *Ibid.*
26. *Ibid.*
27. Nadejda Dobrev, interview by Jordan Todorov, May 6, 2010.
28. Laura Schiff, "*Orgy of the Dead*—Ed Wood's Post-'Plan 9' Legacy: Bonding Spirits and Strippers—in Color!" *Femme Fatales*, June 1998.
29. Stephen C. Apostolof, interview by Mike Vraney and James Elliot Singer, May 1998.
30. *Ibid.*
31. *Ibid.*
32. *Ibid.*
33. Ted V. Mikels, interview by Jordan Todorov, July 29, 2016.
34. Stephen C. Apostolof, interview by Mike Vraney and James Elliot Singer, May 1998.
35. Steve Apostolof, interview by Jordan Todorov, April 12, 2016.
36. *Ibid.*
37. Stephen C. Apostolof, interview by Mike Vraney and James Elliot Singer, May 1998.
38. *Ibid.*
39. *Ibid.*
40. Pat Barrington was supposedly discovered by William Rotsler after he perused some *Orgy of the Dead* publicity material and subsequently appeared in several of his films.
41. Stephen C. Apostolof, interview by Mike Vraney and James Elliot Singer, May 1998.
42. *Ibid.*
43. *Ibid.*
44. *Ibid.*
45. *Ibid.*
46. *Ibid.*
47. *Ibid.*
48. *Ibid.*
49. *Ibid.*
50. *Ibid.*
51. *Ibid.*
52. *Ibid.*
53. *Ibid.*
54. *Ibid.*
55. *Ibid.*
56. Michael Faust, "Shock Cinema Talks with Sexploitation Auteur A.C. Stephen a.k.a. Stephen Apostolof," *Shock Cinema*, 1999.
57. Stephen C. Apostolof, interview by Mike Vraney and James Elliot Singer, May 1998.
58. Frank Henenlotter, Johnny Legend, Peter Clark and Mark Isted, "Stephen C. Apostolof: Bulgarian Nudie Director," *Psychotronic Video*, 1990.
59. The screenplay of *7 Rue Pigalle* follows the Parisian police inspector Goulet (the role was supposed to have gone to John Bealey) who is tracking down the killer of a number of strippers with the help of a Texas sheriff named Tex Strong (William Bates) and a female impersonator (T.C. Jones).
60. *7 Rue Pigalle*, accessed March 3, 2018, http://www.knowitalljoe.com/wp-content/uploads/2014/03/Rue-Pigalle.pdf
61. The cover of *Parisian Passions* reads "by J.X. Williams," a house name for Sundown/Corinth, however the inside title page states Wood's real name.
62. Stephen C. Apostolof, interview by Mike Vraney and James Elliot Singer, May 1998.
63. *Ibid.*
64. Forrest J Ackerman, interview by Jordan Todorov, December 5, 2007.
65. Stephen C. Apostolof, interview by Mike Vraney and James Elliot Singer, May 1998.
66. Frank Henenlotter, Johnny Legend, Peter Clark and Mark Isted, "Stephen C. Apostolof: Bulgarian Nudie Director," *Psychotronic Video*, 1990.
67. David F. Friedman and Don DeNevi, *A Youth in Babylon: Confessions of a Trash-Film King* (Buffalo, NY: Prometheus Books, 1990).
68. Stephen C. Apostolof, interview by Mike Vraney and James Elliot Singer, May 1998.
69. Simon Strong, "Sous la páve, le plàge!: Lesbian Vampires Vs the Situationist International," *Senses of Cinema*, April 2004, http://sensesofcinema.com/2004/feature-articles/lesbian_vampires_vs_situationist_international/
70. Michael Faust, "Shock Cinema Talks with Sexploitation Auteur A.C. Stephen a.k.a. Stephen Apostolof," *Shock Cinema*, 1999.
71. Forrest J Ackerman, interview by Jordan Todorov, December 5, 2007.
72. Earl Kemp, interview by Jordan Todorov, May 6, 2012.
73. Earl Kemp, "The Bela Tolls for You," *E*I*12-* (Vol. 3 No. 1), February 2004, http://efanzines.com/EK/eI12/index.htm

Chapter 9

1. Dean J. DeFino, *Faster, Pussycat! Kill! Kill!* (London: Wallflower Press, 2014).
2. "The Curious Craze for Confidential Magazines," *Newsweek*, July 11, 1955.
3. Lewis Mumford, *The City in History: Its Origins, Its Transformations, and Its Prospects* (New York: MJF Books, 1989).
4. Stephen C. Apostolof, interview by Mike Vraney and James Elliot Singer, May 1998.

5. *Ibid.*
6. *Ibid.*
7. *Ibid.*
8. *Ibid.*
9. Gary Kent, interview by Jordan Todorov, April 17, 2012.
10. Stephen C. Apostolof, interview by Mike Vraney and James Elliot Singer, May 1998.
11. Gary Kent, interview by Jordan Todorov, April 17, 2012.
12. *Ibid.*
13. *Ibid.*
14. *Ibid.*
15. Stephen C. Apostolof, interview by Mike Vraney and James Elliot Singer, May 1998.
16. *Ibid.*
17. *Ibid.*
18. Michael Faust, "Shock Cinema Talks with Sexploitation Auteur A.C. Stephen a.k.a. Stephen Apostolof," *Shock Cinema*, 1999.
19. Stephen C. Apostolof, interview by Mike Vraney and James Elliot Singer, May 1998.
20. *Ibid.*
21. *Ibid.*
22. Judith Crist, "Bumping the Grinds," *New York*, March 10, 1969.
23. Stephen C. Apostolof, interview by Mike Vraney and James Elliot Singer, May 1998.
24. *Ibid.*
25. Christopher Apostolof, interview by Jordan Todorov, June 13, 2017.
26. Harvey Shain, interview by Jordan Todorov, December 5, 2006.
27. *Ibid.*
28. Polly Apostolof, interview by Jordan Todorov, February 17, 2017.
29. Steve Apostolof, interview by Jordan Todorov, April 12, 2016.
30. Stephen C. Apostolof, interview by Mike Vraney and James Elliot Singer, May 1998.
31. *Ibid.*
32. Michael Faust, "Shock Cinema Talks with Sexploitation Auteur A.C. Stephen a.k.a. Stephen Apostolof," *Shock Cinema*, 1999.
33. Mora is credited under the names Luigi (or Louigi) Rogatoni for his work on Apostolof's films.
34. Michael Faust, "Shock Cinema Talks with Sexploitation Auteur A.C. Stephen a.k.a. Stephen Apostolof," *Shock Cinema*, 1999.
35. Polly Apostolof, interview by Jordan Todorov, August 8, 2016.
36. Susan Schmideler, interview by Jordan Todorov, January 30, 2017.
37. Steve Apostolof, interview by Jordan Todorov, April 12, 2016.
38. Harvey Shain, interview by Jordan Todorov, December 5, 2006.
39. Harvey Shain, interview by Jordan Todorov, December 5, 2006.
40. Stephen C. Apostolof, interview by Mike Vraney and James Elliot Singer, May 1998.
41. *Ibid.*
42. *Ibid.*
43. *Ibid.*
44. *Ibid.*
45. Edward H. Clarke, *Sex in Education: Or, a Fair Chance for the Girls* (Boston: James R. Osgood and Company, 1873).
46. Tom Lisanti, *Glamour Girls of Sixties Hollywood: Seventy-Five Profiles* (Jefferson, NC: McFarland, 2008).
47. "Gerald Priestland in San Francisco," *British Broadcasting Corporation*, December 19, 1969.
48. Harvey Shain, interview by Jordan Todorov, December 5, 2006.
49. Christopher Apostolof, interview by Jordan Todorov, December 1, 2006.
50. Harvey Shain, interview by Jordan Todorov, December 5, 2006.
51. *Ibid.*
52. *Ibid.*
53. Frank Henenlotter, Johnny Legend, Peter Clark and Mark Isted, "Stephen C. Apostolof: Bulgarian Nudie Director," *Psychotronic Video*, 1990.
54. Harvey Shain, interview by Jordan Todorov, December 5, 2006.
55. *Ibid.*
56. Stephen C. Apostolof, interview by Mike Vraney and James Elliot Singer, May 1998.
57. Harvey Shain, interview by Jordan Todorov, December 5, 2006.
58. Ted V. Mikels, interview by Jordan Todorov, July 29, 2016.
59. Kenneth Turan and Stephen F. Zito, *Sinema: American Pornographic Films and the People Who Make Them* (New York: Praeger, 1974).
60. *Ibid.*
61. Stephen C. Apostolof, interview by Mike Vraney and James Elliot Singer, May 1998.
62. *Ibid.*
63. *Ibid.*
64. *Ibid.*
65. Kenneth Turan and Stephen F. Zito, *Sinema: American Pornographic Films and the People Who Make Them* (New York: Praeger, 1974).
66. Harvey Shain, interview by Jordan Todorov, December 5, 2006.
67. Stephen C. Apostolof, interview by Mike Vraney and James Elliot Singer, May 1998.
68. Michael DiRosa, interview by Jordan Todorov, March 7, 2017.
69. Stephen C. Apostolof, interview by Mike Vraney and James Elliot Singer, May 1998.
70. C. Wright Mills, *White Collar: The American Middle Classes* (Oxford, UK: Oxford University Press, 1951).
71. Stephen C. Apostolof, interview by Mike Vraney and James Elliot Singer, May 1998.
72. Jeffrey Sconce, *Sleaze Artists: Cinema at the Margins of Taste, Style, and Politics* (Durham, NC: Duke University Press, 2007).
73. Michael Faust, "Shock Cinema Talks with Sexploitation Auteur A.C. Stephen a.k.a. Stephen Apostolof," *Shock Cinema*, 1999.

Chapter 10

1. Stephen C. Apostolof, interview by Mike Vraney and James Elliot Singer, May 1998.
2. Harvey Shain, interview by Jordan Todorov, December 5, 2006.
3. *Ibid.*
4. *Ibid.*
5. Steve Apostolof, interview by Jordan Todorov, February 27, 2017.
6. *Ibid.*
7. Harvey Shain, interview by Jordan Todorov, December 5, 2006.
8. *Ibid.*
9. "Sons of the Keystone Kops," *Psychedelicized*, accessed May 15, 2017, http://psychedelicized.com/playlist/s/sons-of-the-keystone-kops/
10. Stephen C. Apostolof, interview by Mike Vraney and James Elliot Singer, May 1998.
11. In fact, the documents show Apostolof paid $15 to Ojena.
12. Steve Apostolof, interview by Jordan Todorov, February 27, 2017.
13. "Video Units, Cable Make for Blue Movie Boom," *Vidette-Messenger of Porter County* (Valparaiso, Indiana), March 8, 1982.
14. Stephen C. Apostolof, interview by Mike Vraney and James Elliot Singer, May 1998.
15. *Ibid.*
16. "Sex In Movies," *The Raleigh Register* (Beckley, West Virginia), October 28, 1969.
17. *Ibid.*
18. Stephen C. Apostolof, interview by Mike Vraney and James Elliot Singer, May 1998.
19. *Ibid.*
20. *Ibid.*
21. Harvey Shain, interview by Jordan Todorov, December 5, 2006.
22. Kenneth Turan and Stephen F. Zito, *Sinema: American Pornographic Films and the People Who Make Them* (New York: Praeger, 1974).
23. Stephen C. Apostolof, interview by Mike Vraney and James Elliot Singer, May 1998.
24. *Ibid.*
25. *Ibid.*
26. Shelley Apostolof, interview by Jordan Todorov, December 3, 2006.
27. *Ibid.*
28. *Ibid.*
29. *Ibid.*
30. *Ibid.*
31. *Ibid.*
32. Steve Apostolof, interview by Jordan Todorov, April 12, 2016.
33. Shelley Apostolof, interview by Jordan Todorov, December 3, 2006.
34. *Ibid.*
35. Steve Apostolof, interview by Jordan Todorov, April 12, 2016.
36. "Apostolof and Cooper Vows Solemnized," *Los Angeles Times*, March 15, 1971.
37. Christopher Apostolof, interview by Jordan Todorov, March 1, 2016.
38. Stephen C. Apostolof, interview by Mike Vraney and James Elliot Singer, May 1998.
39. *Ibid.*
40. *Ibid.*
41. Christopher Apostolof, interview by Jordan Todorov, March 16, 2017.
42. Shelley Apostolof, interview by Jordan Todorov, December 3, 2006.
43. "Richard Nixon: Statement About the Report of the Commission on Obscenity and Pornography—October 24, 1970," *The American Presidency Project*, accessed June 11, 2017, http://www.presidency.ucsb.edu/ws/?pid=2759
44. Frederick H. Wagman and William B. Lockhart, *Technical Report of the Commission on Obscenity and Pornography V. 3* (Washington, D.C.: U.S. Government Printing Office, 1971).
45. Greg Goodsell, interview by Jordan Todorov, August 28, 2017.
46. "Radford Man Found Guilty in Film Case," *The Progress-Index* (Petersburg, Virginia), July 3, 1966.
47. David Welling and Jack Valenti, *Cinema Houston: From Nickelodeon to Megaplex* (Austin: University of Texas Press, 2011).
48. "Movies Said Traffic Hazard," *The Amarillo Globe-Times*, February 26, 1970.
49. Melissa Mathison, "Harry Reems, King of the Porno Actors, Finds Himself in Deep Throes," *People*, June 21, 1976, http://people.com/archive/harry-reems-king-of-the-porno-actors-finds-himself-in-deep-throes-vol-5-no-24/
50. Stephen C. Apostolof, interview by Mike Vraney and James Elliot Singer, May 1998.
51. *Ibid.*
52. "Skin Flicks on Trial Drawing Crowd to Memphis Courtroom," *Kingsport News*, October 10, 1975.
53. Jacqueline Marino, "Sex on the Run: The Memphis Religious Right prepares to launch a new attack on adult entertainment," *Memphis Flyer*, April 2, 1998, https://www.memphisflyer.com/backissues/issue476/cvr476.htm

Chapter 11

1. Stephen C. Apostolof, interview by Mike Vraney and James Elliot Singer, May 1998.
2. Ted V. Mikels, interview by Jordan Todorov, July 29, 2016.
3. Steve Apostolof, interview by Jordan Todorov, April 12, 2016.
4. Stephen C. Apostolof, interview by Mike Vraney and James Elliot Singer, May 1998.
5. *Ibid.*
6. Steve Apostolof, interview by Jordan Todorov, April 12, 2016.
7. Harvey Shain, interview by Jordan Todorov, December 5, 2006.
8. Shelley Apostolof, interview by Jordan Todorov, December 3, 2006.

9. Michael Faust, "Shock Cinema Talks with Sexploitation Auteur A.C. Stephen a.k.a. Stephen Apostolof," *Shock Cinema*, 1999.
10. Greg Goodsell, interview by Jordan Todorov, August 28, 2017.
11. John Harrison, interview by Jordan Todorov, November 22, 2017.
12. "Graduate's Career," *Newhall Signal and Saugus Enterprise*, December 3, 1976.
13. *Ibid.*
14. Stephen C. Apostolof, interview by Mike Vraney and James Elliot Singer, May 1998.
15. John Harrison, interview by Jordan Todorov, November 22, 2017.
16. "Drop-Out Wife," *CBS News*, August 17, 1973, https://www.cbsnews.com/videos/drop-out-wife/
17. Jacques Descent, interview by Greg Javer, March 4, 2017.
18. Michael Faust, "Shock Cinema Talks with Sexploitation Auteur A.C. Stephen a.k.a. Stephen Apostolof," *Shock Cinema*, 1999.
19. Rob Craig, *Ed Wood, Mad Genius: A Critical Study of the Films* (Jefferson, NC: McFarland, 2009).
20. Michael Faust, "Shock Cinema Talks with Sexploitation Auteur A.C. Stephen a.k.a. Stephen Apostolof," *Shock Cinema*, 1999.
21. Stephen C. Apostolof, interview by Mike Vraney and James Elliot Singer, May 1998.
22. Apostolof directed *The Class Reunion* and *The Snow Bunnies* simultaneously.
23. Stephen C. Apostolof to Rudolph Grey, November 11, 1995, Las Vegas, NV.
24. "Los Angeles," *Boxoffice*, October 2, 1972, W-2.
25. Rudolph Grey, *Nightmare of Ecstasy: The Life and Art of Edward D. Wood, Jr.* (New York: Feral House, 1992).
26. Stephen C. Apostolof, interview by Mike Vraney and James Elliot Singer, May 1998.
27. "Fugitive Girls Review," Contactmusic.com, January 9, 2015, http://www.contactmusic.net/film/review/fugitivegirls
28. Kenneth Turan and Stephen F. Zito, *Sinema: American Pornographic Films and the People who Make Them* (New York: Praeger, 1974).
29. "Tallie Cochrane Interview," *Chateau Vulgaria*, October 14, 2012, http://plantweed.blogspot.de/2012/10/tallie-cochrane-interview.html
30. Steve Apostolof, interview by Jordan Todorov, September 18, 2017.
31. Frank Henenlotter, Johnny Legend, Peter Clark and Mark Isted, "Stephen C. Apostolof: Bulgarian Nudie Director," *Psychotronic Video*, 1990.
32. *Ibid.*
33. Stephen C. Apostolof, interview by Mike Vraney and James Elliot Singer, May 1998.
34. Brenda Fogarty, interview by Jordan Todorov, June 16, 2016.
35. Matt Warshaw, *The Encyclopedia of Surfing* (Orlando: Harcourt, 2005).
36. Jeffrey Sconce, *Sleaze Artists: Cinema at the Margins of Taste, Style, and Politics* (Durham, NC: Duke University Press, 2007).
37. Stephen C. Apostolof, interview by Mike Vraney and James Elliot Singer, May 1998.
38. Michael Faust, "Shock Cinema Talks with Sexploitation Auteur A.C. Stephen a.k.a. Stephen Apostolof," *Shock Cinema*, 1999.
39. Steve Apostolof, interview by Jordan Todorov, April 12, 2016.
40. Shelley Apostolof, interview by Jordan Todorov, December 3, 2006.
41. Stephen C. Apostolof, interview by Mike Vraney and James Elliot Singer, May 1998.
42. *Ibid.*
43. *Ibid.*
44. Shelley Apostolof, interview by Jordan Todorov, December 3, 2006.
45. Steve Apostolof, interview by Jordan Todorov, April 12, 2016.
46. Shelley Apostolof, interview by Jordan Todorov, December 3, 2006.
47. Christopher Apostolof, interview by Jordan Todorov, March 1, 2016.
48. Apostolof also used his real name in the promotional materials for *The Divorcee*, a film he was especially proud of.
49. Harvey Shain, interview by Jordan Todorov, December 5, 2006.
50. Christopher Apostolof, interview by Jordan Todorov, March 1, 2016.
51. Steve Apostolof, interview by Jordan Todorov, April 12, 2016.
52. Max Thayer, interview by Jordan Todorov, May 18, 2012.
53. *Ibid.*
54. *Ibid.*
55. *Ibid.*
56. *Ibid.*
57. *Ibid.*
58. Harvey Shain, interview by Jordan Todorov, December 5, 2006.
59. "Max Thayer," *Nanarland*, accessed October 14, 2017, http://www.nanarland.com/interview/interview-maxthayervo-max-thayer-en.html
60. Stephen C. Apostolof, interview by Mike Vraney and James Elliot Singer, May 1998.
61. *Ibid.*
62. Fred Olen Ray, "Edward D. Wood Jr, interview," *Cult Movies #11*, 1993.
63. Hot Ice—criminal slang for stolen diamonds or diamonds to be gotten rid of quickly.
64. Richard McCurdy, interview by Jordan Todorov, October 7, 2017.
65. Polly Apostolof, interview by Jordan Todorov, February 18, 2018.
66. "The Other Manson Family or Bottom Feeding in the Overseas Distribution Aquarium—An Exploitative Memoir," *World Cinema Paradise*, June 7, 2014, http://worldcinemaparadise.com/2014/06/07/the-other-manson-family-or-bottom-feeding-in-the-overseas-distribution-aquarium-an-exploitative-memoir/
67. *Ibid.*
68. *Ibid.*
69. *Ibid.*

70. Rudolph Grey, *Nightmare of Ecstasy: The Life and Art of Edward D. Wood, Jr.* (New York: Feral House, 1992).
71. Stephen C. Apostolof, interview by Mike Vraney and James Elliot Singer, May 1998.
72. David Ward, interview by Jordan Todorov, May 7, 2010.
73. Christopher Apostolof, interview by Jordan Todorov, March 1, 2016.
74. Stephen C. Apostolof, interview by Mike Vraney and James Elliot Singer, May 1998.
75. *Ibid.*
76. Greg Goodsell, interview by Jordan Todorov, August 28, 2017.
77. Stephen C. Apostolof, interview by Mike Vraney and James Elliot Singer, May 1998.
78. Ray appeared in the pornographic film *Sweet Savage* (1979, dir. Ann Perry, Charles Samples (uncredited)), in a non-sexual role. Ironically, this is the only role for which he ever won an award—Best Actor from the Adult Film Association of America.
79. Stephen C. Apostolof, interview by Mike Vraney and James Elliot Singer, May 1998.
80. *Ibid.*
81. Rudolph Grey, *Nightmare of Ecstasy: The Life and Art of Edward D. Wood, Jr.* (New York: Feral House, 1992).
82. Stephen C. Apostolof, interview by Mike Vraney and James Elliot Singer, May 1998.

Chapter 12

1. Rudolph Grey, *Nightmare of Ecstasy: The Life and Art of Edward D. Wood, Jr.* (New York: Feral House, 1992).
2. Steve Apostolof, interview by Jordan Todorov, April 17, 2017.
3. Christopher Apostolof, interview by Jordan Todorov, December 1, 2006.
4. Steve Apostolof, interview by Jordan Todorov, April 17, 2017.
5. Christopher Apostolof, interview by Jordan Todorov, June 30, 2017.
6. *Ibid.*
7. Todorov, December 1, 2006.
8. *Ibid.*
9. Christopher Apostolof, interview by Jordan Todorov, June 30, 2017.
10. Steve Apostolof, interview by Jordan Todorov, March 17, 2017.
11. Beatty is purported to have sponsored the *Glen or Glenda* 1981 reissue by Paramount while he was working there making *Reds* (1981).
12. "Friday Night at the Movies," *Los Angeles Herald Examiner*, August 25, 1980.
13. Paul Scanlon, "Attack of the Killer Turkeys," *Rolling Stone*, December 9, 1982.
14. Raymond Young, "Movieguide: Review-O-Rama (*Orgy of the Dead*)," *Magick Theatre*, 1987.
15. Greg Goodsell, interview by Jordan Todorov, August 28, 2017.
16. Edward D. Wood, Jr., *Hollywood Rat Race* (New York: Four Walls Eight Windows, 1998).
17. Justin Bozung, "The Most Interesting Man in the World, Johnny Legend," December 17, 2013, http://blog.tvstoreonline.com/2013/12/interview-most-interesting-man-in-world.html
18. Johnny Legend, interview by Jordan Todorov, September 9, 2010.
19. Harold Bronson, *The Rhino Records Story: Revenge of the Music Nerds* (New York: SelectBooks, 2013).
20. Johnny Legend, interview by Jordan Todorov, September 9, 2010.
21. Howie Pyro, interview by Jordan Todorov, April 15, 2016.
22. Rudolph Grey, interview by Jordan Todorov, December 10, 2009.
23. From 1961 until 1971 the U.S. military dropped more than 19 million gallons of toxic chemicals—defoliants or herbicides, including Agent Orange—on 4.8 million Vietnamese.
24. Steve Apostolof, interview by Jordan Todorov, April 17, 2017.
25. Stephen C. Apostolof to Rudolph Grey, August 10, 1986, Los Angeles, CA.
26. *Ibid.*
27. Christopher Apostolof, interview by Jordan Todorov, June 30, 2017.
28. *Ibid.*
29. *Ibid.*

Chapter 13

1. "Wood Primeval," *The Village Voice*, July 30, 1985.
2. Stephen C. Apostolof to Robert Kanters, June 25, 1987, Westlake Village, CA.
3. Stephen C. Apostolof, interview by Mike Vraney and James Elliot Singer, May 1998.
4. *Ibid.*
5. Frank Henenlotter, Johnny Legend, Peter Clark and Mark Isted, "Stephen C. Apostolof: Bulgarian Nudie Director," *Psychotronic Video*, 1990.
6. *Ibid.*
7. "Rhino Film Festival Opens Tonight at Nuart," *Los Angeles Times*, April 22, 1988, http://articles.latimes.com/1988-04-22/entertainment/ca-1836_1_film-festival
8. Arny Schorr, interview by Jordan Todorov, December 11, 2017.
9. "Bal Croce Talking 'bout Incredibly Weird Psychotronic Movies!!!" July 23, 2013, accessed May 15, 2017, https://www.youtube.com/watch?v=kA-WLIO7Ng8&feature=youtu.be&t=94
10. Damon Wise, interview by Jordan Todorov, April 24, 2017.
11. "Bal Croce Talking 'bout Incredibly Weird Psychotronic Movies!!!," July 23, 2013, accessed May 15, 2017, https://www.youtube.com/watch?v=kA-WLIO7Ng8&feature=youtu.be&t=94
12. Howard Lake, "Are You Ready…. For Eddie?" *Sheer Filth #9*, 1990.
13. *Ibid.*
14. Michael Faust, "Shock Cinema Talks with Sex-

ploitation Auteur A.C. Stephen a.k.a. Stephen Apostolof," *Shock Cinema*, 1999.

15. Jane Giles, interview by Jordan Todorov, April 24, 2017.

16. Howard Lake, "Are You Ready.... For Eddie?" *Sheer Filth #9*, 1990.

17. "Bal Croce Talking 'bout Incredibly Weird Psychotronic Movies!!!!," July 23, 2013, accessed May 15, 2017, https://www.youtube.com/watch?v=-kA-WLIO7Ng8&feature=youtu.be&t=94

18. Ted Newsom, interview by Jordan Todorov, December 9, 2017.

19. Stephen C. Apostolof to Rudolph Grey, November 11, 1995, Federal Way, WA.

20. Stephen C. Apostolof to Michael Goldman. May 1, 1990.

21. Christopher Apostolof, interview by Jordan Todorov, December 1, 2006.

22. *Ibid*.

23. Yordanka Ingilizova, "Burgas Man Conquers Hollywood with Erotica and Horror," *Chernomorski Far* (Burgas), July 10, 2007.

24. Christopher Apostolof, interview by Jordan Todorov, June 11, 2017.

25. *Ibid*.
26. *Ibid*.
27. *Ibid*.
28. *Ibid*.
29. *Ibid*.

30. Shelley Apostolof, interview by Jordan Todorov, December 3, 2006.

31. Christopher Apostolof, interview by Jordan Todorov, June 11, 2017.

32. Shelley Apostolof, interview by Jordan Todorov, December 3, 2006.

33. *Ibid*.
34. *Ibid*.

35. Christopher Apostolof, interview by Jordan Todorov, June 11, 2017.

36. Greg Goodsell, interview by Jordan Todorov, August 28, 2017.

37. *Ibid*.

38. Michael Faust, "Shock Cinema Talks with Sexploitation Auteur A.C. Stephen a.k.a. Stephen Apostolof," *Shock Cinema*, 1999.

39. *Ibid*.
40. *Ibid*.
41. *Ibid*.
42. *Ibid*.
43. *Ibid*.

44. Christopher Apostolof, interview by Jordan Todorov, December 1, 2006.

45. Steve Apostolof, interview by Jordan Todorov, April 12, 2016.

46. Richard B. Woodward, "Their 15 Minutes," *The New York Times*, October 3, 1993.

47. Harvey Shain, interview by Jordan Todorov, December 5, 2006.

48. David Ward, interview by Jordan Todorov, May 7, 2010.

49. Alan Doshna, interview by Joe Blevins. March 24, 2017.

50. *Ibid*.

Chapter 14

1. Roger Ebert, "Backbeat Movie Review & Film Summary (1994) | Roger Ebert," April 22, 1994, http://www.rogerebert.com/reviews/backbeat-1994

2. Shelley Apostolof, interview by Jordan Todorov, December 3, 2006.

3. Christopher Apostolof, interview by Jordan Todorov, March 1, 2016.

4. *Ibid*.

5. Polly Apostolof, interview by Jordan Todorov, April 28, 2019

6. Christopher Apostolof, interview by Jordan Todorov, March 1, 2016.

7. Susan Schmideler, interview by Jordan Todorov, January 30, 2017.

8. Christopher Apostolof, interview by Jordan Todorov, March 1, 2016.

9. *Ibid*.
10. *Ibid*.

11. Arny Schorr, interview by Jordan Todorov, December 11, 2017.

12. Shelley Apostolof, interview by Jordan Todorov, December 3, 2006.

13. Susan Schmideler, interview by Jordan Todorov, January 30, 2017.

14. Rudolph Grey, *Nightmare of Ecstasy: The Life and Art of Edward D. Wood, Jr.* (New York: Feral House, 1992).

15. Jeron Criswell King, "Criswell Predicts (An Accurate Glimpse of the Future)," *The Bridgeport Post*, May 26, 1974.

16. Stephen C. Apostolof, interview by Mike Vraney and James Elliot Singer, May 1998.

17. Apostolof is mistaken. To be eligible for Academy Awards consideration in most categories, a feature-length film will need to complete a qualifying run of at least seven consecutive days in Los Angeles, not in New York.

18. Christopher Apostolof, interview by Jordan Todorov, December 1, 2006.

19. Trey Williams, "Blair Witch Tries to Live Up to 1999 Original and Continue Horror Films Success," *MarketWatch*, September 17, 2016, https://www.marketwatch.com/story/blair-witch-tries-to-live-up-to-1999-original-and-continue-horror-films-success-2016-09-15

20. Christopher Apostolof, interview by Jordan Todorov, December 1, 2006.

21. *Ibid*.
22. *Ibid*.

23. Susan Schmideler Apostolof, interview by Jordan Todorov, March 16, 2017.

24. Christopher Apostolof, interview by Jordan Todorov, December 1, 2006.

25. Christopher Apostolof, interview by Jordan Todorov, March 1, 2016.

26. Shelley Apostolof, interview by Jordan Todorov, December 3, 2006.

27. Christopher Apostolof, interview by Jordan Todorov, March 1, 2016.

28. Carol E. Wyer, "The Age at Which Men Officially Become Grumpy," *The Huffington Post*, May 08,

2014, http://www.huffingtonpost.com/carol-e-wyer/men-and-grumpiness_b_5266944.html

29. Christopher Apostolof, interview by Jordan Todorov, March 1, 2016.
30. *Ibid.*
31. *Ibid.*
32. *Ibid.*
33. *Ibid.*
34. *Ibid.*
35. Polly Apostolof, interview by Jordan Todorov, April 28, 2019.
36. John Miller, interview by Jordan Todorov, December 2, 2006.
37. Polly Apostolof, interview by Jordan Todorov, April 28, 2019.
38. "R.I.P," accessed April 01, 2019, https://moviechat.org/tt0054240/Orgy-of-the-Dead/58c723a05ec57f0478ecd458/RIP
39. Christopher Apostolof, interview by Jordan Todorov, March 1, 2016.
40. Shelley Apostolof, interview by Jordan Todorov, December 3, 2006.
41. Polly Apostolof, interview by Jordan Todorov, April 28, 2019.
42. Christopher Apostolof, interview by Jordan Todorov, March 1, 2016.
43. *Ibid.*
44. *Ibid.*
45. *Ibid.*

Bibliography

Books

Adil, Fikret. *Asmalımescit 74 (Bohem hayatı)*. Istanbul, Turkey: İletişim Yayınları, 1993.

Anisef, Paul, and C. Michael Lanphier. *The World in a City*. Toronto, Canada: University of Toronto Press, 2003.

Bartley, Nancy. *The Boy Who Shot the Sheriff: The Redemption of Herbert Nicholls, Jr.* Seattle: University of Washington Press, 2015.

Benshoff, Harry M. *Monsters in the Closet: Homosexuality and the Horror Film*. Manchester, UK: Manchester University Press, 1998.

Blake, Peter. *God's Own Junkyard: The Planned Deterioration of America's Landscape*. New York: Holt Rinehart and Winston, 1979.

Bougie, Robin. *American XXX Movie Posters: 1970 to 1985*. Guildford, UK: FAB Press, 2015.

Boyreau, Jacques. *Trash: The Graphic Genius of Xploitation Movie Posters*. San Francisco: Chronicle Books, 2002.

Bronson, Harold. *The Rhino Records Story: Revenge of the Music Nerds*. New York: SelectBooks, 2013.

Clark, Randall. *At a Theater or Drive-in Near You: The History, Culture, and Politics of the American Exploitation Film*. New York: Garland, 1995.

Clarke, Edward H. *Sex in Education: Or, a Fair Chance for the Girls*. Boston, UK: James R. Osgood, 1873.

Craig, Rob. *Ed Wood, Mad Genius: A Critical Study of the Films*. Jefferson, NC: McFarland, 2009.

Criswell, Jeron. *Criswell Predicts Your Next Ten Years*. New York: Grosset & Dunlap, 1971.

Daley, Brittany A., and Stephen J. Gertz. *Sin-A-Rama: Sleaze Sex Paperbacks of the Sixties*. Port Townsend, WA: Feral House, 2016.

DeFino, Dean J. *Faster, Pussycat! Kill! Kill!* London: Wallflower Press, 2014.

Feaster, Felicia, and Bret Wood. *Forbidden Fruit: The Golden Age of the Exploitation Film*. Baltimore: Midnight Marquee, 1999.

Friedman, David F., and Don DeNevi. *A Youth in Babylon: Confessions of a Trash-Film King*. Buffalo, NY: Prometheus Books, 1990.

Geltzer, Jeremy. *Dirty Words and Filthy Pictures: Film and the First Amendment*. Austin: University of Texas Press, 2016.

Gorfinkel, Elena. *Lewd Looks: American Sexploitation Cinema in the 1960s*. Minneapolis: University of Minnesota Press, 2018.

Grey, Rudolph. *Nightmare of Ecstasy: The Life and Art of Edward D. Wood, Jr.* New York: Feral House, 1992.

Groueff, Stéphane. *My Odyssey*. New York: Writers Advantage, 2003.

Hayes, David C. *Muddled Mind: The Complete Works of Edward D. Wood, Jr.* Shreveport, LA: Ramble House, 2006.

Hurst, Richard Maurice. *Republic Studios: Beyond Poverty Row and the Majors*. Lanham, MD: Scarecrow Press, 2007.

Lisanti, Tom. *Glamour Girls of Sixties Hollywood: Seventy-Five Profiles*. Jefferson, NC: McFarland, 2008.

Martin, Len D. *The Republic Pictures Checklist: Features, Serials, Cartoons, Short Subjects, and Training Films of Republic Pictures Corporation, 1935–1959*. Jefferson, NC: McFarland, 2006.

McCulley, Johnston. *The Mark of Zorro*. Oxford, UK: Macmillan Education, 2008.

McDonough, Jimmy. *Big Bosoms and Square Jaws: The Biography of Russ Meyer, King of the Sex Film*. New York: Three Rivers Press, 2005.

Medved, Harry, and Michael Medved. *The Golden Turkey Awards: The Worst Achievements in Hollywood History*. New York: Berkley Books, 1981.

Mills, Charles Wright. *White Collar: The American Middle Classes*. Oxford, UK: Oxford University Press, 1951.

Muller, Eddie, and Daniel Faris. *That's Sexploitation!!: The Forbidden World of "Adults Only" Cinema*. London: Titan Books, 1997.

Mumford, Lewis. *The City in History: Its Origins, Its Transformations, and Its Prospects*. New York: MJF Books, 1989.

Newell, Adam. *The Art of the B-Movie Poster!* Berkeley, CA: Gingko Press, 2016

Nourmand, Tony, and Graham Marsh. *Film Posters: Exploitation*. Cologne, Germany: Taschen, 2006.

Peary, Danny. *Cult Movies: The Classics, the Sleepers, the Weird, and the Wonderful*. New York: Gramercy Books, 1981.

Pechkoff, Major Zinovi. *The Bugle Sounds: Life in the Foreign Legion*. Uckfield, UK: The Naval & Military Press, 2000.

Puchalski, Steven. *Slimetime: A Guide to Sleazy,*

Mindless Movies. Manchester, UK: Headpress/Critical Vision, 2002.
Raikin, Spas. *Rebel With a Just Cause: A Political Journey Against the Winds of the 20th Century. Vol. 2*. Sofia, Bulgaria: Pensoft Publishers, 2001.
Rausch, Andrew J., and Charles E. Pratt, Jr. *The Cinematic Misadventures of Ed Wood*. Albany, GA: Bear Manor Media, 2015.
Ross, Jonathan. *The Incredibly Strange Film Book*. New York: Simon & Schuster, 1990.
Schaefer, Eric. *"Bold! Daring! Shocking! True!": A History of Exploitation Films, 1919–1959*. Durham, NC: Duke University Press, 2001.
Sconce, Jeffrey. *Sleaze Artists: Cinema at the Margins of Taste, Style, and Politics*. Durham, NC: Duke University Press, 2007.
Singer, James Elliot, Riccardo Morrocchi, and Stefano Piselli. *Bizarre Sinema!: Sexploitation Filmmakers: Wildest, Sexiest, Weirdest, Sleaziest Films: Masters of the Nudie-cutie, Ghoulie, Roughie, and Kinkie*. Florence, Italy: Glittering Images, 1995.
Starr, Kevin. *Golden Dreams: California in an Age of Abundance, 1950–1963*. New York: Oxford University Press, 2011.
Thrower, Stephen. *Nightmare USA: The Untold Story of the Exploitation Independents*. Guildford, UK: FAB Press, 2014.
Turan, Kenneth, and Stephen F. Zito. *Sinema: American Pornographic Films and the People Who Make Them*. New York: Praeger, 1974.
Wagman, Frederick H., and William B. Lockhart. *Technical Report of the Commission on Obscenity and Pornography V. 3*. Washington, D.C.: United States Government Printing Office, 1971.
Warshaw, Matt. *The Encyclopedia of Surfing*. Orlando, FL: Harcourt, 2005.
Weldon, Michael J. *The Psychotronic Encyclopedia of Film*. London, UK: Plexus, 1989.
Welling, David, and Jack Valenti. *Cinema Houston: From Nickelodeon to Megaplex*. Austin: University of Texas Press, 2011.
White, Mike. *Cinema Detours*. Morrisville, NC: Lulu.com, 2013.
Wilson, John. *The Official Razzie Movie Guide: Enjoying the Best of Hollywood's Worst*. New York: Warner Books, 2005.
Wood, Edward D., Jr. *Hollywood Rat Race*. New York: Four Walls Eight Windows, 1998.
_____. *Orgy of the Dead*. San Diego, CA: Greenleaf Classic, 1966.
_____. *A Study in the Motivation of Censorship, Sex & the Movies*. Los Angeles: Gallery Press, 1973.

Newspapers and Periodicals

"Apostolof and Cooper Vows Solemnized." *Los Angeles Times*, March 15, 1971.
"Apostolof Scouting." *The Hollywood Reporter*, November 11, 1956.
Apostolof, Stephen, and Joseph Rome. "Pro and Con. The Question: Will the Televising of Old Films Endanger the Careers of Long-Established Stars." *The Film Daily*, November 13, 1956.
"'Brave' Young Man with Ideas." *Motion Picture Herald*, December 8, 1956.
Crist, Judith. "Bumping the Grinds." *New York Magazine*, March 10, 1969.
"The Curious Craze for Confidential Magazines." *Newsweek*, July 11, 1955.
Denton, Charles. "Dancers Find TV Show Work Nightmare of Labor." *The Cincinnati Enquirer*, October 12, 1958.
"Estabrook Tale to Be Filmed." *Los Angeles Times*, November 15, 1956.
Faust, Michael. "Shock Cinema Talks with Sexploitation Auteur A.C. Stephen a.k.a. Stephen Apostolof." *Shock Cinema*, 1999.
"'Freedom' to Assist Hungarian Refugees." *Variety*, December 14, 1956.
"Friday Night at the Movies." *Los Angeles Herald Examiner*, August 25, 1980.
"Gerald Priestland in San Francisco." *British Broadcasting Corporation*. December 19, 1969.
"Graduate's Career." *Newhall Signal and Saugus Enterprise*, December 3, 1976.
Hackett, Walt. "Bulgarian Refugee Apostolof, 28, Making Big Stir as New Director." *Lansing State Journal*, January 6, 1957.
Henenlotter, Frank, Johnny Legend, Peter Clark, and Mark Isted. "Stephen C. Apostolof: Bulgarian Nudie Director." *Psychotronic Video*, 1990.
Ingilizova, Yordanka. "Burgas Man Conquers Hollywood with Erotica and Horror." *Chernomorski Far* (Burgas), July 10, 2007.
Johnson, Erskine. "New Film Comedy Will Be Lampoon on 'Spellbound.'" *The San Bernardino County Sun*, May 15, 1951.
"Journey to Freedom." *Motion Picture Exhibitor*, July 10, 1957.
King, Jeron Criswell. "Criswell Predicts (An Accurate Glimpse of the Future)." *The Bridgeport Post*, September 5, 1965.
King, Jeron Criswell. "Criswell Predicts (An Accurate Glimpse of the Future)." *The Bridgeport Post*, May 26, 1974.
"L.A. Producer Plans 14 Films Yearly Here." *Toronto Daily Star*, September 27, 1958.
Lake, Howard. "Are you Ready.... For Eddie?" *Sheer Filth #9*, 1990, 26–27.
"Los Angeles." *BoxOffice*, October 2, 1972, W-2.
Miller, Ken, and Greg Lamb. "Orgy of the Dead Director Speaks." *Imaginator* (USA), 1990, issue 6.
"Movieland Events." *Los Angeles Times*, December 25, 1956.
"Movies Said Traffic Hazard." *The Amarillo Globe-Times*, February 26, 1970.
"An Open Letter to Michael Todd." *Daily Variety*, August 22, 1956.
"Radford Man Found Guilty In Film Case." *The Progress-Index* (Petersburg, Virginia), July 3, 1966.
Ray, Fred Olen. "Edward D. Wood Jr. Interview." *Cult Movies #11*, 1993.
"Rode on Back of Wild Lion, Lives to Tell It." *Rochester Democrat and Chronicle*, March 30, 1928.

"Russians Don't Have Anything Against Miss Monroe." *The Bakersfield Californian*, August 28, 1956.

Scanlon, Paul. "Attack of the Killer Turkeys." *Rolling Stone*, December 9, 1982.

Schiff, Laura. "Orgy of the Dead—Ed Wood's Post-'Plan 9' Legacy: Bonding Spirits and Strippers—in Color!" *Femme Fatales*, June 1998.

"Sex in Movies." *The Raleigh Register* (Beckley, West Virginia), October 28, 1969.

"Skin Flicks on Trial Drawing Crowd to Memphis Courtroom." *Kingsport News*, October 10, 1975.

Slotnik, Daniel E. "Eve Brent, Played Jane in Tarzan Movies, Dies at 81." *The New York Times*, September 7, 2011.

Stephen C. Apostolof. Interview by Mike Vraney and James Elliot Singer. May 1998.

Torre, Marie. "Out of the Air." *The Evening Review* (East Liverpool, Ohio), September 30, 1958.

"Video Units, Cable Make for Blue Movie Boom." *Vidette-Messenger of Porter County* (Valparaiso, Indiana), March 8, 1982.

"Wood Primeval." *The Village Voice*, July 30, 1985.

Woodward, Richard B. "Their 15 Minutes." *The New York Times*, October 3, 1993.

Young, Raymond. "Movieguide: Review-O-Rama (Orgy of the Dead)." *Magick Theatre*, 1987.

Zanuck, Darryl F. "20th-Fox Production Chief Cites Studio's Own Impressive Roster of 'New Faces.'" *Variety*, January 3, 1951.

Archives and Special Collections

District Court of Burgas, Bulgaria.
The Margaret Herrick Library. Beverly Hills, CA.
Stephen C. Apostolof papers. Las Vegas, NV.

Source Notes

The authors conducted numerous interviews for this book, largely between 2005 and 2019, as identified in the text. Several persons declined or did not reply to interview requests and others are quoted anonymously at their request. Because a complete listing of articles utilized in the research for this book would require excessive space, only those quoted in the text are listed.

Index

Numbers in **bold italics** *indicate pages with illustrations*

Abbott, Bud (aka William Alexander Abbott) *see* Abbott and Costello
Abbott and Costello 122
Abbott and Costello Meet Frankenstein (1948 film) 75
Abdo, George 161
Abeles, Harold A. 68, 117, 163–164, 244; death 268–270
Abercrombie, Juanita "Jabie" 204, 213, 290
Absinthe (1914 film) 47
Ackerman, Forrest J ix, 96, 98, 100, 246
Adams, Wanda 182
Adamson, Al 107
Adil, Fikret 17
The Adult Film Producers Association 152–153
Adventures of Don Juan (1948 film) 49
The Adventures of Lucky Pierre (1961 film) 96
The Adventures of Ozzie and Harriet (1952–1966 TV series) 103
An Affair to Remember (1957 film) 52
Agar, John 191, 238, 266
Ahlberg, Mac 154
The Airline Hostesses (unrealized film project) 195, 291
Alexander, Scott ix, 261
Alland, William 3
Allen, Mort 243
Allison, Paula 120
Allsbrook, Margo ix
Allyson, June 52
Alone (1921 book) 30
Alonzo, Anthony 249
Altankov, Dr. Nikola x
An American in Paris (1951 film) 59
Anderson, Michael 61
Anderson, Paul Thomas 4
Andrew, Ben 291
Andrews, John 76, 89, 289, 295*ch*8*n*8
The Ann Sothern Show (1958–1961 TV series) 52
Anti-Bolshevik Bloc of Nations *31*, 32

Anton, Leslie 60
Apostolof, Christopher David (son) ix, 8, 16, 38, 58, 61, 63, 117, 129, 160, ***162***, ***163***, 164, ***165***, 171, 188, 226, 228, 237, 243–244, 249, 257–261, 264–271, ***272***, 275, 277, 287–288
Apostolof, Dana (daughter-in-law) x, 271
Apostolof, Maria Patricia (daughter) ix, 70–71, 160, 286; conception and birth 33–35; return to Apostolof family 65–66, ***67***, ***71***
Apostolof, Paula Christine "Polly" (daughter, aka Polly Cross) ix, 32, 34, ***44***, 45, 53, 63, ***67***, 70, ***71***, 78, 118, 122, 184, 235, 250, 265, 270, 272, 274–275, 286
Apostolof, Shelley (third wife, aka Barbara Rachelle Cooper and S.B. Cooper) ix, 8–9, 65, 68–69, ***163***, 164–165, 168, 170, 188, 192, ***194***, 225–226, 264–266, 268–269, 271, 275, 285, 287, 290–291; contributions to Apostolof's films 173, ***175***, 232; early life 159; impact of earthquake on 259–260; marriage to Apostolof 160, ***161***; opinion of Ed Wood 237
Apostolof, Stephen Christov (aka Stefko Christov Apostolov, A.C. Stephen) ix, ***128***, ***129***, ***130***, ***131***, ***134***, ***137***, ***138***, ***139***, ***142***, ***146***, ***156***, ***157***, ***162***, ***163***, ***164***, ***165***, ***171***, ***174***, ***190***, ***192***, ***193***, ***194***, ***206***, ***227***, ***230***, ***247***, ***248***, ***256***, ***257***, ***258***, ***269***, ***272***; American citizenship 69, 250; appearance 3, 9–10, 105, 195, 229, 231, 243, 255; beliefs 8, 29, 46, 61–63, 67, 224–225; birth 9; Burgas and 9–16; cameo appearances 53, ***54***, 148, 173, 217, 289, 290, 291; Canada and 30, ***31***, 32, ***33***; career at ABC 44; career at Bank of America 63, 65, ***66***, 136, 286; career at Republic Pictures 55–57, ***58***, ***59***, 60–61; career at 20th Century-Fox ***41***–42; death 2, 274–277; departure from Bulgaria 16; education 2, 11,

28, 63, 161; filmmaking style 1, 4–5, 143, 147–148, 154, 156, 158, 177–178, 183–188, 196–198, 201, 203, 205, 207, 209, 215–217, 219, 221–222, 226, 229–230, 232–235; friendship with Boris Kutchukov 13–14, 16, 21–23, 28, 39–41; friendship with Herbert F. Niccolls 41–42; golf and 2, 103–104; health problems 265, 272, 274–275; impact of Northridge earthquake on 259–260; imprisonment 15, 17; influence of Russ Meyer on 72–73, 102, 279; Istanbul and 17, ***18***, ***19***; Japan and 250, ***251***, 252–253; love of movies 12, 31, 268; marriage to Joan 32–35, 63–66, 68–69; marriage to Pat ***105***, 117–118; marriage to Shelley 8, 159, ***161***, 162, 260; musical talent and taste 10, 13, 21, 15–16, 18, 26–27, 39–40, 66, 157, 217, 220, 244; ownership of SCA Mini Art Theater 169, ***170***, ***171***, 172; Paris and 21, ***22***, 23, ***24***, 25, ***26***, 27, 28, 29; personality 4, ***10***–11, 269–270; political activity 14–15, 26–27, 31; relationship with Ed Wood 73–75, 78–79, 81, ***84***, ***87***, 90–91, 96–100, 111–112, 162–163, 172–173, 178, 182, 191–192, 195, 205–207, 215, 231–232, 236–239, 242–243, 245–247, 255, 260–264, 266–268; relationship with father 8, 16; relationship with Harvey Shain 120–122, 128–130, 149, 183, 193, 228; relationship with Marsha Jordan 126, 130, 133–135, 155–156, 193, 205; relationship with Rene Bond 178, 180–181, 193; relationship with Rudolph Grey 4, 101, 150, 191, 238, 242–245, 248–249, 251, 255, 263, 265, 267, 269, 272, 287; return to Bulgaria 256–259; skiing and 70, 173–174, 209, 231; superstitions 8, 82; TV watching habits 268; use of A.C. Stephen pseudonym 2, 118, 144, 201–202, 236, 243–244, 248, 255, 264, 291, 299*n*48

307

Index

Apostolof, Stephen Christie "Steve" (son) ix, 32–33, 35, 40, 44, 63, **67**, 68–70, **71**, 84, 118, 122, **146**, 149, 152, 159–161, 169, 209, 224, 226, 231, 243, 248, 288
Apostolof, Susan Joanne "Susie" (daughter, aka Susan Schmideler) ix, 32–33, 63–65, **67**, 70, **71**, 78, 122, 158, 184, 265–266, 268, 286
Apostolov, Christo Nikolov (father) 8–9, **13**, 16
Apostolov, Stefan (nephew) ix, 17
Apostolova, Dessie (grandniece) ix
Apostolova, Elenka St. (paternal grandmother) 9
Apostolova, Kina (sister-in-law) ix, 16
Apostolova, Lila (sister) 9, 269, 285
Apostolov, Stavri (brother) ix, 9, 16, 160, 256, **257**, **258**, 275, 285, 288
Apostolova, Vesa (sister) 9, 12, 15, 285
Arabian Nights (book) 166
Ardolino, Emile 249
Armstrong, Louis 26
Arnold, Maria 204, 290
Around the World in 80 Days (1956 film) 61
Arp, Jean (aka Hans Peter Wilhelm Arp) 21
Asher, William 215
Asimov, Isaac 98
Asmalimescit 74 (1933 book) 17
The Astro-Zombies (1968 film) 84
At a Theater or Drive-In Near You: The History, Culture and Politics of the American Exploitation Film (1995 book) 5
Aumont, Charles 52
Aumont, Geneviève (aka Geneviv Aumont) 49–50, 52, 289
Auster, Paul 2
Autry, Gene 55
Avildsen, John G. 216

Bacall, Lauren 39
Bachelor's Dream (1967 film) 123, **124**, **125**, 287, 288, 289
Baker, George D. 47
Baker, Rick 261
Baldwin, Ben **100**
Ballerina (aka *Dream Ballerina*, 1950 film) 28
Balsam, Jerome "Jerry" 123, 269, 288
Balshofer, Fred J. 49
Bancroft, Anne 104
Bandera, Stepan 31
Barbi, Vincent 118, 143, 150, 152, 235
Bardot, Brigitte 52
Barlow, R.J. 167
Barrington, Pat (aka Pat Barringer and Patricia Annette Bray) 75–76, 87, **88**, **89**–90, 92, **93**, 94, 231, 262, 285, 288, 289, 296n40

Bartley, Nancy x, 42
Barton, Charles 75
Barty, Billy 77–78
The Basketballers (unrealized film project) 195, 291
Bates, William 75–76, 78, 90, **93**, 289, 296n59
Bauer, Mary 146, 290
Baxter, Les 92
Bay, Michael 229
Baykov, Boris x
Beach Blanket Bango (1975 film) 205
The Beach Boys (band) 221
The Beach Bunnies (film) 215–217, **218**, 219–222, **223**, 228, 232, 234, 243, 287, 291
The Beach Girls (1982 film) 215
Beach Party (film franchise) 173
Beach Party (1963 film) 215
Bealey, John (aka Nemo Nomus) 108, **109**, 120 136, 290, 296n59
Beatty, Warren 154, 245
Bechet, Sidney 26
Bed of Fire (1964 film) 114
Béjart, Maurice 23
Below the Belt (1971 film) 187
Benazeraf, Jose 72
Bennett, Clete 136, **138**, **139**
The Benny Hill Show (1955–1991 TV show) 268
Benveniste, Michael 180
Bergman, Ingmar 3
Bergman, Richard 234
Bernhard, Sandra 267
Bertolucci, Bernardo 173
Besbas, Peter E. 49
Bidle, Abner 125, 289
The Big Bird Cage (1972 film) 203
Big Bosoms and Square Jaws: The Biography of Russ Meyer, King of the Sex Film (2005 book) v
The Big Chill (1983 film) 187
The Big Doll House (1971 film) 203
Big Jim McLain (1952 film) 46
The Big Snatch (aka *The Big Catch*, 1971 film) 143
Bigelow, Kathryn 249
Biller, Anna x
Black, Karen 267
Black, Milton 93
Blackburn, Bob x
The Blair Witch Project (1999 film) 268
Blake, Peter 103
Blevins, Joe 3
Blier, Bernard 24
Bloom, Bernard "Bernie" 172, 195
Blue Steel (1990 film) 249
Bogdanovich, Peter 107, 217
Bond, Rene 4, 177, **178**, 180–181, 183, 187–189, 191, **192**, 193, 195, 197, 200, 204–205, 207, 210, 213, 215, 226, 228, 246, 286, 288, 290
Bonfils, Robert 98, 100
Bonjour Tristesse (aka *Hello, Sadness*, 1954 book) 58
Bonnie and Clyde (1967 film) 154
Boogie Nights (1997 film) 4

The Book of Illusions (2002 book) 2
Borden, Stanley 123
Borgia, Lucrezia 125
Borgnine, Ernest 164
Boris III (Bulgarian king) 15, 27
Borzage, Frank 60
The Bostweeds (band) 102
Bosworth, Hobart 83
Bougie, Robin x
Boulanger, Nadia 92
A Boy and His Dog (1975 film) 196
The Boy Who Shot the Sheriff (2013 book) 42
Boyd, Whit 141
Bradbury, Ray 98
Bradbury, Robert N. 55
Brandon, Cory 217, 219, 290, 291
Brandy 111, 289
Brannik **11**
Break the Bank (1985–1986 TV game show) 181
Brenner, Joseph 123
Brenner, Paul 202
Brenner, Wendell John ("Baron Von Brenner") 191
Brenon, Herbert 47
Brent, Eve (aka Jean Ann Lewis and Jean Ann Ewers) ix, 50, **51**, 52, 288–289
Brent, Kevin S. 290
Bretherton, Howard 203
Bride of the Monster (1955 film) 74, 98, 106, **125**, 236, 245, 262
Bride's Delight (1971 film) 168
Bronkowski, Raleigh x
Bronson, Harold 247
Brooks, Conrad 245, 261, 267
Brooks, Mel 260
Brower, Sky x
Brown, Bailey 168
Brown Derby (restaurant) 74, 193, 195, 239, 255
Browning, Tod 98
Bryan, James 205
Buckalew, Bethel 180, 205
The Bugle Sounds: Life in the Foreign Legion (1927 book) 19
Bulgarian-American Cultural Educational Society (aka the Bulgarian Club) 40, 270, 286
Bulgarian National Front **31**, 32
Bullock, Robert 218, 220, 291
Bunny and Clod (1970 film) 154
Bursley, Major Gilbert E. 18–19
Burton, Richard 19
Burton, Tim 2, 47, 125, 242, 255, 260–262, 267
Buxton, Darrell ix
Byington, R.G.F. 127

Cady, Daniel B. 193
Cage, Nicolas 136
Caldwell, Jack 166
Cambridge, Phil 242
Cameo Room (nightclub) 220
Campus Confidential (1968 film) 102
Candy, John 245
Canfield, Edwin Lee "Butch" x

Capra, Frank 70
Capri 127, *128*, 289
Capucine 235
Caramico, Robert H. (aka R.C. Ruben and Robert Ruben) 79, 83, *84*, 86–87, 90, 106, 122, 137, *138*, *142*, 150, 155, 183, 188, 191, 196, 250, 285, 288–291
Carducci, Mark Patrick 255
Carey, Sandy 176–177, 188, 290
Carné, Marcel 24
Carnon, Angela (aka Priscilla Lee, Gloria Jane Medford, Linda Harris and Angela Field) 183–184, 197, 201, 290
Caron, Leslie 59
The Carpetbaggers (1961 novel) 229
Carradine, John 266
Carrillo, Leopold "Leo" 216, 221
Carson, Johnny 80–81, 86, 286
Carter, Carl R. 167–168
Carter, Jimmy 4
Carter, Victor 93–94
Casey, Taggart (aka J.T. Casey) 137, 290
Cassavetes, John 143
Cassidy, Rick 217, 220, 228, 290–291
The Casual Company (1948 play) 261
Cates, Gilbert 183
Cavanaugh, Wendy (aka Wendy Cavanough) *217*, 218, 291
Chandler, Otis 224
Chandler, Raymond 102
Chandu the Magician (1932–1950 radio drama series) 98
Chaney, Lon 236
Chaney, Lon, Jr. 61
Chaplin, Charles Spencer "Charlie" 105
The Chapman Report (1962 film) 112
Charisse, Cyd 59
Charlie's Angels (1976–1981 TV series) 221
The Chasin-Shooter Group (band) 234–235, 291
Chazelle, Damien 191
Chernoff, Sam 152
Chevalier, Maurice 24
Chez Pomme (Parisian cabaret) 24
Chiller Theatre (1961–1982 TV show) 236
CHN International 82
Cimarron (1931 film) 60
Ciro's (nightclub) 39, *48*
The Cisco Kid (1950–1956 TV series) 216
Citizen Kane (1941 film) 3, 275
Clark, Randall 5
Clarke, Edward H. 126
The Class Reunion (1972 film) 173, 187–189, *190*, 191–192, 197, 200, 202–203, 209, 216–217, 232, 236, 287, 290
Clayton, Helena 108, *109*, 120
Cochrane, Lillian Rose "Tallie" 204–205, *206*, 215, 285, 288, 290

The Cocktail Hostesses (1972 film) 192, 193, 195, *196*, 197–201, *202*, 203, 209, 216, 219, 221, 243, 287, 290
Cocoanut Grove (nightclub) 39
Coe, Peter 237
Coen, Ethan 229
Coen, Joel 229
College Confidential (1960 film) 126
College Girls (1968 film) 102, 126–127, *128*, *129*, *130*, *131*, *132*, 133, 137, 150, 187–189, 191, 254, 287–290
College Girls: Bluestockings, Sex Kittens, and Co-eds, Then and Now (2006 book) 126
Collins, Jack 183
Collom, Chester "Chet" ix, 201, *202*, *208*
Color of Night (1994 film) 107
Comb, Starline (aka Starlyn Simone) 177, 188, 191, 200, 290, 291
Comingore, Dorothy 3
Communist Party of the United States of America 46
Conan Doyle, Arthur 231
Confessions of a Bad Girl (1965 film) 114
Connell, W. Merle 125
Connolly, Mike 39, 52
Cooper, Andrea 289
Cooper, Dr. David (father-in-law) 159–160
Cooper, Gary 19
Cooper, George 105, 289
Corman, Roger 79
Corpse Grinders (1971 film) 84
Correll, Rich 173
Costello, Budd 108, 139, 143, 149, 155, *162*; falling out with Apostolof 209
Costello, Lou (aka Louis Francis Cristillo) *see* Abbott and Costello
Country Cuzzins (1970 film) 180
Country Doc (1976 film) 205
Covert, Con 189, 204–205, 217, 219, 290, 291
Craig, Rob 184, 186, 213
Crazy Circle (claimed film project) 61, 291
Cresse, Bob 152, 169
Criss Cross (1949 film) 104
Crist, Judith 114–115
Criswell (aka Jeron Charles Criswell King and The Amazing Criswell) 1, 75, *76*, 80–81, 85, *86*, *87*, 90, 92, 100, 170–172, 191, 193, *194*, 228, 237–238, 245–246, 251, 253, 266, 275, 285–287, 289
Criswell Predicts (1953–1961 TV series) 80–81
Croce, Bal 254–255
The Crooked Circle (1957 film) 61
Crosby, Bing 22
Cross, April (granddaughter) 272
Cross, Chelsea (granddaughter) *256*

Crowe, Mark 111, 289
Crown International Pictures 215–216
Cukor, George 60, 112
Cushman, Al 53
Cushman, William A. 127
Cyr, Ray 136, *142*, 290
Cyril, Archimandrite x

D Generation (band) 247
Dad Made Dirty Movies (2011 film) 2
Dallas (1978–1991 TV series) 79, 229
Damian, Archimandrite x
Damiano, Gerard 5, 114, 167, 187, 225, 287
Damon, Dick 207
D'Andre, Desiree 120
Darby, Ron 177, 188, 290, 291
Darnell, Linda 12
Davis, Bill *84*, 92
Davis, Donald A. (aka Don Davis) v, 91–92, 120, 122, 133, 152, 155, 166, 172, 193, 285, 287, 289; legal problems 167–168
Death of a Transvestite (1967 book) 112, *113*, 238
De Beau, Rene *91*, 289
DeCenzie, Peter A. 72–73
Deep Throat (1972 film) 5, 114, 167–168, 172–173, 187, 225, 287
The Defilers (1965 film) 167
DeFino, Dean J. 102
De Laurentiis, Dino 62–63
Deliver Us from Evil: The Story of Vietnam's Flight to Freedom (1956 book) 54
Dell, Perry 205
Del Valle, David x
De Mering, David 238
DeMille, Cecil B. 74
The Demon (1918 film) 47
Denning, Diana 120
Denny, Martin 92
De Palma, Brian 107, 136
Depp, Johnny 2, 262, 264
DePriest, Ed x, 172
Dertano, Robert C. 46–47, 50, *84*, 86, *87*, 91, 289, 295ch6n7
Descent, Jacques ix, 183
Desmond, Mark (aka Alex Collebrusco, Alberto DaVinci, Mark Del Monde and Mark Da Vinci) 83, *84*, 118, 145, 155, *171*, 177, 289–290
Devil Girls (1967 novel) 203
The Devil in Miss Jones (1973 film) 225
Diamonds (1975 film) 226
Dichner, Arik 226
The Dicktator (1974 film) 205
Digard, Uschi 187
Dimitrov, Svilen x
Dimopoulos, Dinos 166
Dinev, Dino ix, 257–258
DiRosa, Michael ix, 120, 136, *137*, 139, 290
Dirty Dancing (1987 film) 249

Index

The Dirty Mind of Young Sally (1973 film) 205
Dishliev, Yanko 27
Divine (aka Harris Glenn Milstead) 149
The Divorcee (1930 film) 155
The Divorcee (1969 film) 133, *134*, 150, 153–155, *156*, *157*, *158*, *159*, 160, 170, 184, 218, 275, 287, 290
Do It in the Dirt (1979 film) 231
Dobrev, Nadejda (aka Nadejda Klein) ix, 82, 289
Dochev, Ivan *31*, 32
Dolemite (1975–1999 film series) 228
The Doll Squad (1973 film) 232
Donner, Richard 252
Dooley, Thomas Anthony III 54
Doshna, Alan ix, 262–263
Dostoevsky, Fyodor Mikhailovich 19
Douglas, Gordon 46
Douglas, Norman 30
Downey, Deborah 146, 290
Doyle, Clyde 167
Dracula (1931 film) 98
Drop-Out Wife (1972 film) 5, 181, 182–185, *186*, 187, 193, 195–197, 201–202, 209, 216–217, 232, 243, 287, 290
Dubois, Albert 114
Duggan, Andrew 112
Dunaway, Faye 154
Du Plenty, Tomata (aka David Xavier Harrigan) 81
Dupuis, Claudine 55
Duval, Hedi 59

Earl Carroll's Vanities (musical) 83
Earth Girls Are Easy (1988 film) 249
Ebert, Roger 264
Ed Wood (1994 film) 2, 5, 47, *125*, 242, 255, 260, 267, 288; Apostolof's displeasure with 261–262
Ed Wood: Look Back in Angora (1994 film) 255
Ed Wood, Mad Genius: A Critical Study of the Films (2009 book) 184, 213
Eddy, Pam 232, 291
Edmonds, Don 203, 229
Edwards, Blake 235
Eisenhower, Dwight D. 103
Ekberg, Anita 39
Elliott, Tim v
Éluard, Paul 58
Enev, Father Antim 160
Engibarov, Mesrob 258
The Equals 97
Erikson, Erik 264
The Erotic World of A.C. Stephen (1999 VHS series) 248, 264
Esper, Dwain 47
Estabrook, Howard 60

F Troop (1965–1967 TV series) 77
Fain, Johnny (aka John Aquaboy) *218*, 220, 222, 291
Fairbanks, Douglas 105
Falcon Crest (1981–1990 TV series) 79
Famous Monsters of Filmland 98, 246
Fantasy Island (1977–1984 TV show) 218
Farago, Joe 181
Farnon, Dennis 234
Fasano, John M. 255
Faster, Pussycat! Kill! Kill! (1965 film) 102, 237
Father Knows Best (1954–1960 TV series) 103
Faust, Michael ix
Fawcett, Farrah 221
Feazell, Jim 183
Fellini, Federico 3
Fernandel (aka Fernand Joseph Désiré Contandin) 24
Ferrer, Mel 63
Fielding, Henry 145, 150
Fields, Norman 183–184, 195, 197, 290
Fields, W.C. 206
Filov, Bogdan 11
Finney, Albert 150
Finney, Edward 46–47
The Firebird Conspiracy (1984 film) 249
Five Stations to Hell (claimed film project) 61, 291
Flames of Araby (orchestra) 161
Flaming Creatures (1963 film) 250
Fleishman, Stanley 153, 224
Fleming, Victor 60, 192
Flesh Gordon (1974 film) 180
Flying Saucers Over Hollywood: The "Plan 9" Companion (1992 film) 255, 263
Flynn, Errol 49, 74, 149, 206
Flynn, Leisa Reinecke ix
F.O.G. Distributors 96
Fogarty, Brenda ix, *217*, 219, 291
Fonda, Henry 63
Foos, Richard *247*
Ford, John 55
Forsyth, Ed 133
Fournier, Nicolas 25
The Fox (1967 film) 154
Fox, Scotty 218
Franco, Jesus "Jess" 203
Frankenweenie (1984 film) 261
Free Love Confidential (1968 film) 102
The French Peep Show (1949 film) 72–73
Frey, Douglas (aka Douglas Fray) 184, 195, 198, 204–205, *206*, 290
Friedman, David F. v, 4, 76, 97, 133, 143, 152, 166–167, 169, 193, 203, 222, 224, 268, *269*
Fröbe, Gert 87
From Out of the Darkness (unrealized film project) 59–60, 286, 291
Frost, Lee v, 136, 167, 183, 203
Fugitive Girls (aka *Five Loose Women*, 1976 film) 201–203, *204*, 205, *206*, 207, *208*, 209–211, *212*, 213, *214*, 215, 217, 219, 222, 228, 232, 236, 243, 247, 256, 285, 287, 290
Fuller, Dolores 263

Gabin, Jean 24
Gable, Clark 74
Galindo, Steve x, 5
Gallardo, Jun 249
Gardner, Erle Stanley 60
Garis, Roger 61
Garner, James 149
Gassman, Vittorio 63
Gebhardt, Fred O. (aka Friedrich Oliver Gebhardt) 96
General Hospital (1963 TV series) 243
Genital Hospital (1987 film) 218
Gentell, Gee 127, *131*, 188
Geoffries, Christopher (aka Fred Geoffries) 177, 183–184, 188, 195, 198, 290
Georgiev, Kimon 12
Geyer, Harry 193
Gidget (1959 film) 215–216, 218
Gidget, the Little Girl with Big Ideas (1957 book) 215
Gilbert, Lewis 226
Gildersleeve, Linda *217*, *218*, 220–221, 228, 234, 291
Giles, Jane ix
Girl in Gold Boots (1968 film) 84
The Girl with the Hungry Eyes (1968 film) 87
Glaser, Bunny 120, 289
Glazer, Philip "Phil" 215
Glen or Glenda (1953 film) 47, 98, 207, 242, 245, 254, 288
Goddard, John 60
Godiva, Countess of Mercia 144–145
God's Own Junkyard (1964 book) 103
Golan, Menahem 226
Golden, Dan ix
The Golden Child (1986 film) 174
The Golden Turkey Awards (1980 book) 98, 245, 253–254, 287
Goldfinger (1964 film) 87, *89*
Goldman, Edmund 236
Goldman, Michael 256
Gone with the Wind (1939 film) 82
Gonzalez, Conchita 289
Goodsell, Greg ix, 80, 166, 178, 237, 246, 260–261
Görgün, Ege x
The Graduate (1967 film) 104
Graham, Barbara Higgins (ex-sister-in-law) ix, 32, 35, 42
Gramling, Madeleine (mother-in-law) 159–160
Grant, Cary 39
Grauman's Chinese Theatre 39
Grease (1978 film) 216
Green, Elena 289
Green, Jade 111
Greenleaf Classics (publisher) 98, *99*, 100, 101, 153

Greetings (1968 film) 136
Grey, Rudolph (aka Lawrence Bianca) ix, 2, 75, 81, 101, 150, 191, 195, 236, 238–239, 242–243, 245, 248–249, 251, 255, 261–263, 265–267, 269, 272, 287
Groseclose, Alan D. 167
Groueff, Stéphane 25–27, 50, 58, 288
Grozev, Prof. Alexander ix
Guest, Christopher 260
Gugalov, Ivan 41
Gun Girls (1957 film) 295ch6n7
Guthu, Harold "Hal" 82, 180, 183, 288

Haas, Charles F. 52
Hackett, Walt v, 56
Haller, Ray 39
Hamilton, George 164
Hamilton, Guy 87, 226
Hamlet (play) 264
Hand, Fletcher 112
Hardy, Françoise 97
Hardy, Larry 248
Harris, Lynn 136, 195, 198, 290
Harrison, John ix, 178–179, 181
Harrison, Stafford B. 28, 59–60, 289
Hart, Lorali (aka Texas Starr) 83, 289
Hart to Hart (1979–1984 TV series) 229
Haunted George (aka Steve Pallow) 248
The Haunted World of Edward D. Wood, Jr. (1995 film) 262–263
The Head Mistress (1968 film) 133
Hébuterne, Jeanne 59
Hedren, Tippi 267
Hell Chicks (1968 novel) 203
Heller, Gordon 102
Hellman, Monte 107
Helter Skelter (1976 film) 218
Henenlotter, Frank ix
Hepburn, Audrey 63
Higgins, Joan Mary (first wife) 32–33, *34*, 35, 38, 42, 44–45, 48, 58, 65, 74, 285–286, 288; death 269; dissolution of marriage 68–70; pregnancy and 63–64
Hill, George Roy 226
Hill, Jack 203
The History of Tom Jones, a Foundling (1749 novel) 145, 150
Hitchcock, Alfred 53, 137
Hitler, Adolf 191
Hoberman, James 250
Hoffman, Dustin 104
Hold Your Man (1933 film) 203
Holden, William 74
Hollywood Rat Race (1998 book) 246
Hong, James 205
Hooker, Hugh 112, *113*, 289
Hope, Bob 22
Hopper, Hedda 39
Hot Connections (1973 film) 205
Hot Dog... The Movie (1984 film) 173

Hot Ice (1978 film) 4, 5, *121*, 205, 218, 225–226, *227*, *229*, *230*, *233*, 234–237, 243, 285, 287, 291
The Hot Rock (1972 film) 226
Hot Skin and Cold Cash (1965 film) 167
House Un-American Activities Committee (HUAC) 46, 60
Howard, Moose 127, 289
Hroussanov, Matei 26
Huffman, Robert G. x
The Human Tornado (1976 film) 228
Humberstone, H. Bruce 52
Hunebelle, André 72
Hunter (1984–1991 TV show) 218
Hutton, Brian G. 226
Hyde, Buddy 238

I, a Woman (1965 film) 154
I Am Curious (Yellow) (1967 film) 154
"I Am Woman" (1971 song) 197
I Love a Mystery (1939–1944 radio drama series) 98
I Love Lucy (1951–1957 TV show) *62*, 219
I Was a Communist for the F.B.I. (1951 film) 46
I Woke Up Early the Day I Died (1998 film) 266–267
Iliopulos, Aris x, 266–267
Ilsa, Harem Keeper of the Oil Sheiks (1976 film) 229
Ilsa, She-Wolf of the SS (1975 film) 203, 205
The Immoral Artist (unrealized film project) 73, 279–283, 286, 291
The Immoral Mr. Teas (1959 film) 72–73, 125, 279
Inauguration of the Pleasure Dome (1954 film) 250
The Incredibly Strange Creatures Who Stopped Living and Became Mixed-Up Zombies!!? (1964 film) 254
The Incredibly Strange Film Show (1988–1989 TV series) 254
Indiana Jones and the Temple of Doom (1984 film) 174
Ingilizova, Yordanka ix
Interior, Lux (aka Erick Lee Purkhiser) 24
Isted, Marc 254
It Came from Hollywood (1982 film) 245
It's a Wonderful Life (1946 film) 70
It Takes One to Know One (1967 book) 172
Ives, Arnold x

Jackson, Sheri (aka Colleen Murphy) 136, 290
Jail Bait (1954 film) 106
James Bond (1962 film series) 89, 187, 226, 234–235
Javer, Greg x
Jeanne (unrealized film project) 58–59, 286

Jeans, James 289
Jeikoff, Dr. Matthew 66–67, 243, 286–287
Jekyll and Hide (aka *The Adult Version of Jekyll & Hide*, 1972 film) 187
Jensen, L.S. 289
Jines, Mickey 39, 289
The Jitters (1988 film) 255
JFK (1991 film) 50
Johnsen, Sande N. 112
Johnson, Clark 229
Johnson, Hugh 120, 154
Johnson, Lyndon B. 4, 165
Johnson, Nunnally 104
Johnson, Terri 168, *176*, 183–184, 188, 195, 197, 290
Johnson, Tor 4, 52, *53*, 61, 81, 236, 246, 287, 289
Jones, Buck 98
Jones, Donald M. 107, 111, 289
Jones, L.Q. 196
Jones, Stephanie 289
Jones, Thomas Craig "T.C." 296n59
Jones, William Russell 167
Jordan, Marsha (aka Carolyn Marcel Jordan) 1, 3–4, 126–127, *128*, 130, *131*, 132–133, *134*, 135–6, *142*, 145, *147*, 150, 152–153, 155–156, *157*, *158*, 166, 168, 170, *171*, 173, 175, 177, *178*, 180, 183, 187–188, 193, 205, 221, 246, 285, 288–290; early years 133; popularity 133–134
Journey to Freedom (1957 film) 4, 17, 25, 28, 41–42, 46, *49*, 50, *51*, 52, *53*, *54*, 55, 56, *57*, 58–61, 63, 66, 73, 81, 86, 193, 226, 285–286, 289; distribution 53–56; financing 44–45

Kane, Joseph 61
Kanter, Richard 143
Kanters, Robert 232, 250
Karagyozov, Petar 28
Karaszewski, Larry ix, 261
The Karate Kid (1984 film) 216
Kasdan, Lawrence 187
Katsarov, Dimitar K. 14
Kaye, Milton 289
Kazan, Elia 112
Keatan, Harry A. 46, *47*, 48, 286
Keaton, Buster 46
Keaton, Diane 245
Keighley, William 203
Kelley, Patti (aka Patti Clifton) 228, *229*
Kelley, Tom (aka Tom Kelley Sr.) *94*
Kelly, Gene 31, 59
Kelly, Janice 111, 289
Kelly's Heroes (1970 film) 226
Kemp, Earl ix, *99*, 100–101
Kendal, Bob 147, 290
Kennedy, John F. 50
Kent, Gary ix, 106–107, *108*, 111, 289
Kerelov, Dimitar Yordanov 14

Index

Keremidchieva, Zornitsa ix
Kerr, Deborah 52
Killer in Drag (1963 book) 112, 172
The Killing of a Chinese Bookie (1976 film) 143
King, Mackenzie 29
"King Conga" (1971 song) 234
Kinsey, Dr. Alfred 103–104, 110, 112, 114
Kirov, Sava 25
Kitt, Eartha 267
Kleiser, Randal 216
Knowles, Elizabeth 146, 290
Kohner, Frederick 215
Koldamov, Dr. Michael 11–12, 258
Kopetzky, Sam "The Man" 123, 155
Koprinkov, Georgi 15
Kraike, Michael 104, 193
Kramer (aka Stephen Michael Bonner) 92
Kubrick, Stanley 213
Kutchukov, Boris ix, 13, 16, 20, 21, 22, 23, **24**, 25, 27, 28, 39, 40, 59, 257, 285, 286, 288
Kutchukov, Ginette ix, 23, 25, 27, 28, 39, 40, 41, 59
Kutchukova, Vania ix

La La Land (2016 film) 191
Ladies They Talk About (1933 film) 203
Lady Godiva and Tom Jones (claimed book) 144
Lady Godiva Rides (1969 film) 4, 121, **125**, 144, **145**, **146**, **147**, **148**, **149**, 150, **151**, 152–153, 156, 218, 236, 287, 288, 290
Lake, Howard 255
Lamour, Dorothy 52
Landau, Martin 261
Lane, Morgan 49
Lange, Ted 234
Lanier, Margie 204, 205, 290
Lapin Agile (Parisian cabaret) 23, 24
Lardner, Ring, Jr. 46
Lassie (1954–1973 TV series) 79
The Last Condom (1990 film) 218
The Last Mile to El Diablo (claimed film) 28, 51, 291
The Last Picture Show (1971 film) 217
Last Tango in Paris (1972 film) 173
Launder, Frank 203
Lawrence, Harry 111, 289
Leachman, Cloris 217
Leary, Timothy 182
Leavold, Andrew ix–x
Lee, Damian 173
Lee, Randy 127, **128**, 188, 289
Legend, Johnny (aka Martin Margulies) ix, 246, **247**, 253, 254, 262, 287, 288
Lemmon, Jack 52
Leo, Malcolm 245
Leonard, Robert Z. 155
Levin, Henry 215
Lewis, Herschell Gordon 96, 104, 248, 254
Lidman, Geoffrey 117

Lindroth, Lloyd 266
The Lion's Jaws (1930 film) **48**, 49
Lisanti, Tom 126
"Little Boxes" (1963 song) 103
Little Shop of Horrors (1982 musical) 246
Lobanov-Rostovsky, Prince Dmitry 25, 294*ch*3*n*10
Lom, Herbert 203
Looney Tunes (1930–1969 animated film series) 219
Loose Shoes (1978 film) 177
Lorber, Dora 289
The Lost World (1912 novel) 231
Love, Eva 289
The Love Boat (1977–1987 TV series) 234, 235
Love Camp 7 (1969 film) 136, 203
Love Feast (1969 film) 196, 206
Lovelace, Linda (aka Linda Susan Boreman) 173
Lucas, Tim x
Ludwig, Edward 46
Lugosi, Bela 75, 98, 238, 261, 295*ch*8*n*8
The Lustful Turk (1968 film) 96
Lutze, Ric 4, 177, 180, 181, 183, 188, 191, 195, 200, 228, 234, 285, 290, 291
Lynn, Diana 52

Mabe, Byron 96, 133, 143
Macbeth (1948 film) 55
Mahon, Barry 114, 123, 167
Mail Order Confidential (1968 film) 102
Malibu Beach (1978 film) 215
Mamoulian, Rouben 12
Man from the Moon (unrealized film project) 61, 286, 291
The Man from U.N.C.L.E. (1964–1968 TV series) 107
The Man in the Gray Flannel Suit (1956 film) 104
The Man Who Wasn't There (2001 film) 229
The Man with the Glass Eye (unrealized film project) 291
The Man with the Golden Gun (1974 film) 226
Maniac (1934 film) 47
Manolov, Orlin x
Manov, Prof. Bozhidar x
Mantis in Lace (1967 film) 87
Marco, Paul 238, 245, 261, 263
Marcus, Stanley 97
Marino, Jacqueline 168
The Mark of Zorro (1919 book) 8
The Mark of Zorro (1940 film) 12, 105
Markle, Peter 173
Markov, Georgi 258
Marsha: The Erotic Housewife (1970 film) 133, 168
Martin, Dan 143
M*A*S*H (1972–1983 TV series) 268
Match Game (1973–1982 TV game show) 181

Maxwell, Robert **84**, 106, 289
Mayhew, Edward 193
Mazziotti, Tony 181
McArt, Don ix
McCambridge, Mercedes 203
McCarey, Leo 52
McCloskey, Mike 177
McCulley, Johnston 8
McCurdy, Richard ix, 234, 291
McDonald, Meri 146
McDonough, Jimmy v, ix
McKay, Jeff x
McLeod, Victor 290
McQueen, Steve 164, 230
Medved, Harry 98, 245, 254
Medved, Michael 98, 254
Melrose Place (1992–1999 TV series) 70
Mendoza-Nava, Jaime (aka Igor O'Gigagusky and J. Mendozoff) 91, 92, 110, 150, 177, 183, 196, 198, 201, 285, 286, 288, 289, 290
Metzger, Radley 72
Meyer, Nicholas 191
Meyer, Russ v, 72, 73, 76, 87, 102, 125, 154, 166, 237, 279
Meyerson, Sumner 202
Miami Vice (1984–1990 TV Series) 259
The Mickey Mouse Club (1955–1959 TV series) 91
Mikels, Ted V. ix, **84**, 107, 133, 169, 232
Mikhailof, Mikhail "Mike" ix, 70, **164**, 174, 228, 257
Milan, Willy 249
Miller, Glenn 13
Miller, Henry 153
Miller, Ira 177
Miller, John "Yani" ix, 271, 272, 274
Miller, Marvin 193
Milligan, Andy 123
Mishkin, William 123
Mocambo (nightclub) 39
Modigliani, Amedeo 58, 59
Moede, Titus (aka Titus Moody) **130**
Mollov, Krum 14, 15, 258, 259
Monlaur, Yvonne 55
Monroe, Marilyn 61, **78**, **94**, 120
Monson, Carl 177
Monster from the Grave (unrealized film project) 61, 286
Moore, Rudy Ray 228
Mora, Tony (aka Louigi Rogatoni and Luigi Rogatoni) 122, 290
Morita, Akio 224
Morris, Leslie x
Motel Confidential (1967 film) 83, 102, 118, **119**, 120–123, 124, 126, 127, 136, 137, 144, 150, 189, 275, 287, 288, 289
Mother Goose à Go-Go (1966 film) 94
Motion Picture Association of America (MPAA) 112, 154
Mumford, Lewis 103
Muraviev, Konstantin 27

The Murders in the Rue Morgue (1867 book) 96
Murphy, Audie 56
Murphy, Stefanie 289
My Bare Lady (1989 film) 218
My Big Fat Greek Wedding (2002 film) 268
"My Heart Belongs to Daddy" (1938 song) 181
My Odyssey (2003 book) 26
Myers, James E. 146, *147*, 150, 155, *157*, 288, 290
Myrick, Daniel 268

Nagel, Donald Francis "Don" 104, 106, 107, 117, 289
National Legion of Decency 112
Necromania (1971 film) 172, 180
Neill, Ve 261
Nelson, Lloyd (aka Lloyd Bilson) 155, 290
Never Steal Anything Wet (1967 film) 215
Newell, Janet 204, 205, 290
Newsom, Ted ix, 213, 232, 255
Niccolls, Herbert F. (aka Herbert Franklin Niccolls, Jr., and Bruce Mitchell) *41*, 42, *43*, 46, 47, 60, 127, *193*, 285, 287, 289
Nicholas, Guy ix, 205, 215, 228, *230*, *233*, 260, 285, 286, 288, 290, 291
Nichols, Mike 104, 114
Niece, Pat 120
Night of the Ghouls (1959 film) 98, 254, 295*ch*8*n*9
Nightmare of Ecstasy: The Life and Art of Edward D. Wood, Jr. (1992 book) 2–3, 195, 238, 242, 261, 262
Nikolaev, Nikolay P. 28
Nikolov, Dimitar 9
99 Women (1969 film) 122
Niven, David 235
Nixon, Richard M. 4, 165, 166, 172
No Way to Treat a Lady (1968 film) 114
Noonan, Tommy 112
Nordin, Barbara 120, 289
North, Douglas x
North by Northwest (1959 film) 137
Not Tonight Henry (1960 film) 125
Novak, Harry H. v, 87, 102, 166, 180, 187
Nude Jango (1968 film) 133
Nuetzel, Charles 100

O'Brien, Coleen *85*, 120, 289
O'Connell, Mitch ix, *274*
Office Love-In, White Collar Style (1968 film) 135–136, *137*, *138*, 139, *140*, *141*, *142*, 143, 196, 197, 219, 287, 288, 290
The Office Party (1968 film) 141
O'Hara, Sean 127, 289
O'Hara, Tootsie *149*
Ojena, Louis (aka Lou Ojena and Louis Ojarof) 76, *87*, 89, *110*, 111, 150–152, 289

Okuhira, Kenji 256
Olmos, Edward James 259
One Into Three (year unknown, film) 168
The Only House in Town (1970 film) 196
Orbit Films 193, 202
Orgy of the Dead (1965 film) 4, 39, 75–78, *79*, 80–83, *84*, *85*, *86*, 87, *88*, 88–92, *93*, 94, *95*, 96–101, 103, 104, 106, 108, 110, 111, 114, 118, 120, 122, 123, 125, 133, 135, 144, 150, 153, 155, 167, 172, 177, *194*, 202, 205, 215, 222, 226, 231, 239, 243, 245–248, 250–251, *252*, 253–256, 261–262, 263, 264, *273*, *274*, 275, *276*, 279, 285, 286, 287, 288, 289, 291, 295*ch*8*n*8, 296*n*40
Orgy of the Dead (1966 book) 98, *99*, 100–101, 153, 239, 274
Orgy of the Dead (2015 reprint) 1*00*
Orgy of the Dead (soundtrack) 92
Orgy of the Dead, Part II: The New Generation (unrealized film project) 248, 251–253, 266, 270, 287, 291
Orlon, Eve 204, 205, 290
Oswald, Lee Harvey 50
Otis, Dimitrios x
The Outboard Boys (book series) 61

Paar, Jack 80
Pachard, Henri 183
Paligorcheva, Violeta Todorova 9, 10, 15
Pandit, Korla 92, 262
Panev, Dimitry 26
Panitza, Dimitar 27
Paola, Timothy 118
Papazov, George 21, 23, 24
Paprikov, Ivan 32
Paris After Midnight (1951 film) 50
Parisian Passions (1966 book) 96, 296*n*61
Parke, Henry C. x
Parker, Teresa *121*, 228, *230*, 232
Parrish, Larry 168
Parsons, Louella 39
Parvanova, Elena (maternal grandmother) *10*
Pastan, Linda 181
Patino, John 120, 122
Patino, Sharon 120
Patrick, H.Z. 290
Paulsen, Duane 186, 195, 290
Pearl Harbor (2001 film) 229
Pechkoff, Major Zinovi 19
Peck, Gregory 103
Pee-wee's Big Adventure (1985 film) 261
Pellatt, Sir Henry Mill 35
Penchev, Nikolay x
Pendulum Publications 172, 195, 242
Penn, Arthur 154
Pepe, Joe 204
Peraino, Anthony "Big Tony" 225

Peril, Lynn 126
Perl, Ruby 289
Perry, Pete (aka Peter Perry, Jr.) v
Perry Mason (1957–1966 TV series) 60
Peterson, Cassandra (aka Elvira, Mistress of the Dark) 251
Petit, Roland 23, 59
Petroff, Boris 172
Petrucci, Lisa ix
Peyev, Lt. Yordan 25
Phark, Felicia 136, *138*
Phelps, Corry 205
Phelps, Dennis x
Philipe, Gérard 24
Pickford, Mary 83, 105
Pierce, Charles B. 196
The Pink Panther (1963 film) 235
Pink Pussy: Where Sin Lives (1964 film) 114
Plan 9 from Outer Space (1957 film) 47, 74, 80, 81, 98, 236, 238, 245, 246, 254, 261
Planet of Dinosaurs (1977 film) 231
Plante, Robert x
Please Don't Eat My Mother! (1973 film) 177, 187
The Plot to Destroy the Earth (unrealized film project) 73, 286, 291
Pomme, Madame (aka Eugénie-Jeanne de Montfaucon) 24
Poor Cecily (1974 film) 183
Poore, Robert A. 154
Popyanev, Christo (maternal grandfather) *10*
Popyanev, Socrates (uncle) 10
Popyaneva, Haida (aunt) 9
Popyaneva, Maria (aunt) 10
Popyaneva, Polyxena (mother) 9, *10*, 12, 45, 285
Port of Shadows (1938 film) 24
Powell, Dick 52
Power, Tyrone 12
Preminger, Otto 58
Price, Carlton 289
Price, Larry 193
Price, Vincent 251
Priestland, Gerald 128
Proctor, Marland 155, 218, 219, 290, 291
The Producers (1967 film) 260
Psychotronic Video 76
Puchalski, Steven ix
Purcell, Jerry 97, 193
Pussycat (adult theatre chain) 92, 114, *125*, 152, 169, 224, 225
Puzon, Conrado "Boy" ix, 249, 269
Pyro, Howie (aka Howard Kusten) x, 247–248

Queen of Blood (1966 book) 100
The Quiet Man (1952 film) 55
Quincy M.E. (1976–1983 TV show) 218

Racket Girls (1951 film) 50
Ragina's Secrets (1969 film) 112

314 Index

Raging Bull (1980 film) 143
Raikin, Prof. Spas T. ix, 11, 49–50, 53
Ralston, Rudy 55, 56
Ralston, Vera 56
The Ramrodder (1969 film) 133
The Rape (1965 film) 166, 167
The Rape of the Vampire (1968 film) 97
Rare Earth (band) 207
Rascle, Lt. Col. Christian ix
Rat Mort (Parisian cabaret) 60
Rat Pfink a Boo Boo (1966 film) 254
Rathbone, Basil 12
Rausch, Andrew J. ix
Ray, Aldo 238, 266
Rayburn, Gene 181
Reagan, Ronald 39, 181, 245
The Red Danube (1949 film) 46
Red Garter (band) **157**
The Red Menace (1949 film) 56
Reddy, Helen 197
Redman, Joyce 150
Reems, Harry 167, 168, 173
Reifsnider, Lyle B. 49
The Ren & Stimpy Show (1991–1995 TV series) 234
Renay, Liza 155, 290
Report of the Commission on Obscenity and Pornography (1970) 165, 166
Reynolds, Malvina 103
Ricci, Christina 267
Richardson, Tony 149
Ripley's Believe It or Not! 83
Ritchie, Michael 174
Ritter, John 267
Road to … (1940–1962 film series) 22
Roberts, Mariwin **217**, 228, 286, 288, 291
Robertson, Joseph (aka Joe Robertson) 172, 196, 206
Rocamora, Wynn 52
"Rock Around the Clock" (1952 song) 150
The Rockford Files (1974–1980 TV show) 218
The Rocky Horror Picture Show (1975 film) 245
Rodan, Michelle 127
Rogers, Roy 55
Rollin, Jean 97
Romanoff's (restaurant) 39
Romero, Cesar 251
Romero, Vittorio 249
Roquemore, Cliff 228
Rosano, Dianna 127, 290
Rosen, Phil 191
Rosenthal, Robert J. 215
Ross, Jonathan 254
Rotsler, William 87, 167, 296*n*40
Roussos, Demis 97
Rowland, William 104
Rubin, Joe x
Rudl, Patricia Jeanne "Pat" (second wife) **105**, 117, 118, 285, 286, 287
Ruggles, Wesley 60

Rush, Richard 107
Rydell, Mark 154

Sack, Alfred N. "Papa Sack" 97, 114, 123
Sagan, Françoise 58
St. George Bulgarian Eastern Orthodox church 2, 66–67, **68**, 160, 243, 270, 286
Sam & Dave (band) 97
RMS *Samaria* 29, **30**, 31
Samples, Candy 183, 290
Sánchez, Eduardo 268
Santean, Antonio 114
Sarno, Joe 81
Saturday Night Sleazies (1990–1991 VHS compilation) 264, 288
Savage Fugitives (unrealized film project) 248, 249, 291
Schaefer, Eric 143, 224
Schiff, Laura ix
Schlimgen, Michael x
Schlock! The Secret History of American Movies (2001 film) 102
Schneider, Gary 204, 205, 290
Schopenhauer, Arthur 255
Schorr, Arny ix, 254, 255, 266
Scorsese, Martin 143
Scott, Casey ix
Scott, Jacques (aka Jacques Francis Scott-Quekett) 4, 49, **51**, 52, **53**, 60, 289
Scott, Randolph 149
Scott, Ron 141
Segal, George 183
Seider, Didi 289
Sellers, Peter 235
Selznick, David O. 62
Semerdzhiev, Prof. Stanislav x
Sennett, Mack 161
7 Rue Pigalle (aka *69 Rue Pigalle*, unrealized 1960s film project) 96, 291, 296*n*59
7 Rue Pigalle (unrealized 1950s film project) 55, 60, 286, 291
Seven Seas (nightclub) 39, **40**
The Sex Cycle (1967 film) 81
Sex Kittens Go to College (1960 film) 126
Sex in Education: Or, a Fair Chance for the Girls (1875 book) 126
Sex Life of a Cop (1959 book) 153
The Sex Pistols (band) 247
Sexual Behavior in the Human Female (1953 book) 103
Sexual Behavior in the Human Male (1948 book) 103
Sexus (1965 film) 72
Shack, Alan ix
Shain, Harvey (aka Forman Shane and Forman Shain) ix, 4, 117, 120, **121**, 122, 126, 127, 128, **129**, 130, **131**, 135, 136, 145, 148, 149, 150, 155, 174, **176**, 183, 186, 188, 189, 193, 195, 198, 199, 204, 205, 211, 217, 220, 222, 228, 231, 232, 234, 235, 246, 262, 268, 270, 285, 289, 290, 291
Shannon, Mark 120

Sharapanov, Radoslav x
Sharman, Jim 245
Shea, James K. 231
Shearer, Norma 155
Sherman, Vincent 49
Shishmanov, Christo 25
Shivachev, Kiril 14, 15
Shnee, Hidie 111, 289
Sholem, Lee 215
A Shot in the Dark (1964 film) 235
Sidney, George 31, 46
Silliphant, Allan 154
Silver, Fawn (aka Fawn Silverton and Fanya Carter) 4, **76**, 79, 89, 92–93, **94**, 285, 289
Simeon II (Bulgarian king) 15, 67, **68**
Simon, Michel 24
Simon & Simon (1981–1989 TV series) 229
Sinatra, Frank 1, 39
Sinatra, Frank, Jr. 231
Sinema: American Pornographic Films and the People Who Make Them (1974 book) 133
Singer, James Elliot 42, 143, 237
The Sinister Urge (1960 film) 172
Siodmak, Robert 104
69 Rue Pigalle (1966 book) 96
Sjöman, Vilgot 154
Ski Party (1965 film) 173
Ski Patrol (1990 film) 173
Ski School (1991 film) 173
Sleazemania! (1985 VHS compilation) 254, 288
Smith, Jean-Claude 235
Smythe, Jack 114
The Snow Bunnies (1972 film) 61, 172–173, **174**, **175**, **176**, 177, **178**, **179**, 187, 196, 197, 198, 201, 202, 209, 216, 222, 226, 232, 236, 243, 287, 290
So Young, So Bad (1950 film) 203
Solt, Andrew 245
Sonney, Dan 169
Sons of the Keystone Kops (band) 290
The Sopranos (1999–2007 TV series) 40
Spelvin, Georgina x
Spencer, Fred 228, 291
Spielberg, Steven 174, 220
Spisarevski, Dimitar 27, 294*ch*3*n*13
SpongeBob SquarePants (1999 TV series) 234
Springsteen, R.G. 56
The Spy Who Loved Me (1977 film) 226
Standish, Miles 32
Star Trek (1966–1969 TV series) 252
Star Trek II: The Wrath of Khan (1982 film) 191
Star Wars (1977 film series) 252
Starnes, Dene 289
State of Fear (unrealized film project) 248, 249, 266, 270, 288, 291
Steckler, Ray Dennis 107, 254
Stefanov, Stefan 14, 15

Stein, Neil B. 289
Stephen, A.C. *see* Apostolof, Stephen C.
Stevenson, Robert 46
The Stewardesses (1969 film) 154
Stewart, James 39
Stewart, Rex 26
The Sting (1973 film) 226
The Sting-Rays (band) 254
Stone, Allen 173, 290
Storey, Bill 160
Stoyanov, Bisser R. x
A Study in the Motivation of Censorship, Sex & The Movies (1973 book) 144
Sturman, Reuben 153
Suburban Pagans (1968 film) 167
Suburban Roulette (1968 film) 104
Suburbia Confidential (1966 film) 4, 103–107, **108**, 109, **110**, 111–112, **113**, 114, **115**, **116**, **117**, 118, 120, 123, 126, 150, 189, 193, 243, 287, 289
Suburbia Confidential (1967 book) 111–112
Superman: The Movie (1978 film) 252
Surin, Vladimir 61–62
S.W.A.T. (2003 film) 229
Swedish Erotica (1973 film series) 172
Sweet Sweetback's Baadasssss Song (1971 film) 143
Swicegood, T.L.P. 177
Switchblade Sisters (1975 film) 203

Take It Out in Trade (1970 film) 196
Tanev, Toncho 32
Tangier (unrealized film project) 291
Tankova, Asst. Prof. Vasilka x
Tarantino, Quentin **125**, 202, **274**
Tarkovsky, Andrei 3
Tarzan and the Trappers (1958 film) 52
Tarzan's Fight for Life (1958 film) 52
Tashkov, Slavi 29, 31
The Teachers (unrealized film project) 195, 291
Temple, Julien 249
Tentindo, Charles 217
Terrorist Girl (unrealized film project) 248, 291
Tew, Alan 234
Thar She Blows! (aka *Thar She Goes!*, 1968 film) 143
Thayer, Michael "Max" (aka Mike Thayer) ix, 229, **230**, 231–232, 291
Thelman, Hugh 136, 290
Thompson, Brett R. 262
Thompson, William C. 47–49, 73, 74, 238, 286, 289
Thorne, Dyanne 229
The Three Musketeers (1948 film) 31
3 Nuts in Search of a Bolt (1964 film) 112

Tobalina, Carlos 155, 169
Todd, Michael 61–63
Todorov, Jordan 5
Tolstoy, Leo 62
Tom Jones (1963 film) 150
The Tonight Show (1954 TV show) 80–81, 86, 286
Tornatore, Joe 231
Tosi, Giuliano x
Toussieng, Yolanda 261
The Town That Dreaded Sundown (1976 film) 196
Townsend, Bud 215
Trader Hornee (1970 film) 143
Tranner, Todd ix, 236
Trocadero (nightclub) 39
Tropic of Cancer (1934 book) 153
Trumbo, Dalton 46
Tucker, Forrest 77–78
Turan, Kenneth 133
Turner, Lana 31
2069 A.D. (1969 film) 155
The Twilight Girls (1957 film) 72
The Twisted Sex (1966 film) 112
The Two Ronnies (1971–1987 TV series) 234
Two Thousand Women (1944 film) 203

The Undertaker and His Pals (1966 film) 177
Utrillo, Maurice 24

Valentino, Rudolph 191
Vampira (aka Maila Nurmi) 81, 228, 261, 263, **274**
Van Peebles, Melvin 143
Van der Veer, Greg 209
Vardalos, Nia 268
Vartan, Sylvie 97
Vassilev, Dimo 14, 15
Vazrazhdane 25–27
Verdy, Violette 28
Vicious, Sid (aka Simon John Ritchie) 247
Video Vixens! (1974 film) 183
Vidor, King 63
Vincent (1982 film) 261
The Violent Years (1956 film) 203, 211, 254, 288
Vixen! (1968 film) 154
Vixens! (1974 film) 183
Voice of America (broadcaster) 50, 55
Von Brenner, Baron (aka Wendell John Brenner) 191
Vorhaus, Bernard 203
Voyage to the Bottom of the Sea (1964–1968 TV series) 112
Vraney, Mike x, 42, 143, 197, 237, 248, 272, 288

W Is War (1983 film) 249
Waiting for Guffman (1996 film) 260
Walker, Clint 149
Wallace, Irving 112
Wallace, Mike 182
Walsh, Raoul 60

War and Peace (1869 book) 62
War and Peace (1956 film) 63
Ward, David ix, **193**, 195, 237, 238, 262, 285, 288
Warfield, Chris 193
Warhol, Andy 115
Warren Commission Report 50
Watch the Birdie... Die! (1968 film) 183
Waters, John 254
Wayne, John (aka Marion Morrison) 55, 56
Weiner, Al 193, 202
Weisel, Flora 189, 290
Weldon, Michael J. ix, 76
Welles, Orson 3, 55, 73, 275
Wendkos, Paul 216
West, Ashley x
West Side Story (1957 musical) 246
Westward Ho (1935 film) 55
Wheeler (1975 film) 183
Where the Boys Are (1960 film) 215
Whisky a Go Go (nightclub) 82
White, Mike x
White Collar: The American Middle Classes (1951 book) 141
Who's Afraid of Virginia Woolf? (1966 film) 114, **117**
Wielie, Robert 155, 290
The Wild Scene (1970 film) 104
Williams, Kathy 136, 139, **141**, **142**, 290
Williams, Lolita 107, **108**, 111, 289
Wilson, Chelly 123
Wilson, Robert Charleton 106, 125, 289
Wilson, Tom 136
Wise, Damon ix, 254
Wishman, Doris 76, 123, 248, 254
Witten, Lee 180
The Wizard of Oz (1939 film) 192
The Woman on Pier 13 (1949 film) 46
A Woman Under the Influence (1974 film) 143
Wood, Edward Davis, Jr. (aka Emil Moreau and Dick Trent) ix, 1–5, 47, 72–83, **84**, 85–86, **87**, 88–92, **99**, 106, **113**, 123, **125**, 144, 150, 162–163, 167, 170, 173, 175, 178, 180, 182–184, 186–188, 191–192, **193**, **194**, 195–196, 200, 202–211, **212**, 213–215, 219, 221, 226, 228, 231–233, 242–243, **247**, 251, **252**, 274–275, 285–291; background 97–98; cross dressing 74–75, 77–78, 101; cult fame 242, 245–247, **253**, 254–255, 260–264, 266–269; drinking 86–87, 90, 98, 163, 172, 209, 232; final years and death 236–239; first meeting with Apostolof 73–75; writing career and style 77, 82, 96, 98–101, 111–113, 172, 203
Wood, Jennie "Na Pua" 39
Wood, Kathy (aka Kathleen O'Hara Everett Wood) 238, 239, 261, 268
Wood, Natalie 112, 183

Wood, Sam 203
Wood, Shirley 289
Wyer, Carol E. 270

Yates, Herbert J. 55, 56, 60, 61
Yates, Peter 226, 230
Yordanov, Dimitri (aka Bobo) 14, *24*, 285, 288
You Can't Run Away from It (1956 film) 52
Young, Donna 204, 205, 290

Young, Raymond ix, 245
The Young Marrieds (1972 film) 172
The Young Rajah (1922 film) 191
A Youth in Babylon: Confessions of a Trash-Film King (1990 book) 97

Zacherley, John (aka John Zacherle) 236
Zane, Billy 267
Zanuck, Darryl F. 50

Zeman, Jackie 243, 287
Ziehm, Howard 180
Ziggy (1971 cartoon series) 136
Zimanich, Joseph 289
Zimbalist, Efrem, Jr. 112
Zink, James ix, 48
Zito, Stephen F. 133
Zorro (1957–1959 TV series) 91
Zugsmith, Albert 126
Zwick, Joel 268